Praise for this book

'*Reimagining Growth* excavates and restores the rich traditions of Prebisch, Keynes, Minsky, Schumpeter and Veblen and applies them to problems of economic development in the rubble left by the Washington Consensus. These subtle papers find unity in commitment to robust institutions, anchored in democratic legitimacy and in respect for the diversity of needs, conditions, and policies arising around the world. In giving this commitment new theoretical form, *Reimagining Growth* goes far toward emancipating development economics from the straitjackets of neoclassical thought.'
James K. Galbraith, University of Texas at Austin

'This book is essential reading for those who care about the future of economic development. For the past quarter-century, development policy was put at the service of orthodox economic theory. The results have been poor: inequality has increased in a large number of countries, the rate of growth has been frustrating in most of the developing world and macroeconomic crises have been frequent. Now development theory must be put at the service of equity and development. *Reimagining Growth* takes up this challenge, addressing such major issues as national and intra-national power relations, social inequality and discrimination, innovation, and financial fragility. Some of the chapters introduce the reader to new ways of understanding democracy from below, while inviting the reader to find new arenas and ways of creating it. This book moves us closer to a new, broader conceptual basis for economic development.'
Jose Antonio Ocampo, Under-Secretary-General of the United Nations for Economic and Social Affairs

'*Reimagining Growth* is a collection of interesting and provocative pieces in that they renew development schemas, models and theories. Historical experience, political conflicts and other development perspectives are part of the analyses presented. This book's new visions, interpretations and language allow us to better understand development.'
Dr Joao Sayad, Vice President for Finance and Administration, Inter-American Development Bank

Contributors to this book: Ana Maria Bianchi, Leonardo Burlamaqui, Ha-Joon Chang, Silvana De Paula, Nelson Giordano Delgado, Gary A. Dymski, Peter Evans, Geoffrey M. Hodgson, Jan A. Kregel, Erik S. Reinert, Jorge O. Romano, Michael Storper and John Wilkinson

Reimagining Growth

Towards a Renewal of Development Theory

Edited by
SILVANA DE PAULA and **GARY A. DYMSKI**

Zed Books

LONDON AND NEW YORK

Reimagining Growth:
Towards a Renewal of Development Theory
was first published in 2005 by
Zed Books Ltd, 7 Cynthia Street, London N1 9JF, UK and
Room 400, 175 Fifth Avenue, New York, NY 10010, USA.

www.zedbooks.co.uk

Editorial Copyright © Silvana De Paula and Gary A. Dymski, 2005
Individual Chapters © Individual Authors, 2005

The right of Silvana De Paula and Gary A. Dymski to be identified as the editors
of this work has been asserted by them in accordance with
the Copyright, Designs and Patents Act, 1988

Cover designed by Andrew Corbett
Set in 10/12 pt Photina by Long House, Cumbria, UK
Printed and bound in Malta by Gutenberg Ltd

Distributed in the USA exclusively by Palgrave Macmillan, a division of
St Martin's Press, LLC, 175 Fifth Avenue, New York, NY 10010.

A catalogue record for this book
is available from the British Library

US Cataloging-in-Publication Data
is available from the Library of Congress

ISBN   Hb 1 84277 584 7
       Pb 1 84277 585 5

Contents

■

Part ii ▪ Rethinking the Role of Institutions
and Macrostructures in Development   83

■

∎

∎

Figures

Abbreviations

ABONG	Associação Brasileira de Organizações Não Governamentais (Brazilian Association of Non-Governmental Organizations)
AFL-CIO	American Federation of Labor and Congress of Industrial Organizations
ATTAC	Ação pela Tributação das Transações Financeiras em Apoio aos Cidadãos (Action for the Taxation of Financial Transactions in Support of Citizens)
CADTM	Committee for Third World Debt Cancellation
CBJP	Comissão Brasileira Justiça e Paz (Brazilian Commission for Justice and Peace of the CNBB)
CD	certificate of deposit
CEPAL	Economic Commission on Latin America and the Caribbean
Cives	Associação Brasileira de Empresários pela Cidadania (Brazilian Association of Employers for Citizenship)
CLS	core labour standards
CMT	cut-make-trim
CNBB	Comissão Nacional dos Bispos do Brasil (National Conference of Bishops of Brazil)
COSATU	Congress of South African Trade Unions
CREDOC	Centre de Recherche pour l'Etude et l'observation des Conditions de vie
CRIC	Centre for Research on Innovation and Competition
CUT	Central Única dos Trabalhadores
DIP	diffused innovation process
DIY	do-it-yourself
DOMUS	Domestic Consumers and Utility Services project
EPB	Economic Planning Board (South Korea)

EU	European Union
FKI	Federation of Korean Industries
FTAA	Free Trade Area of the Americas
GATT	General Agreement on Tariffs and Trade
HPAEs	highly performing Asian economies
IBASE	Instituto Brasileiro de Análises Social and Econômicas (Brazilian Institute of Social and Economic Analyses)
IC	International Council (WSF)
IDL	Industrial Development Law (South Korea)
ILO	International Labour Organization
IMF	International Monetary Fund
IPO	initial public offering
KOTRA	Korean Trade–Investment Promotion Agency
LETS	Local Exchange and Trading Systems
LTV	lifetime value
MAUSS	Mouvement Anti-Utilitariste dans les Sciences Sociales
MOFE	Ministry of Finance and Economy (Korea)
MOTIE	Ministry of International Trade, Industry, and Energy (Korea)
MPB	Ministry of Planning and Budgeting (Korea)
MST	Movement dos Trabalhadores Rurais Sem Terra (Movement of Landless Rural Workers)
NGO	non-governmental organization
NIE	New Institutionalist Economics
OAS	Organization of American States
OECD	Organization for Economic Cooperation and Development
QI	Quality Index
RBSES	Brazilian Network for the Social and Solidarity Economy
R&D	research and development
SME	small to medium enterprise
TPA	third-party access
TRIPS	Trade-related Intellectual Property Rights
UNCTAD	United Nations Conference on Trade and Development
US	United States
WSF	World Social Forum
WTO	World Trade Organization

Acknowledgements

This volume would not exist without the entrepreneurial vision and energy of Ana Celia Castro and the support of Manuel Montes. Ana was the driving force in the creation of the 2001–02 lecture series that led to the chapters assembled here. BNDES, the Banco Nacional de Desenvolvimento Econômico e Social (the National Bank for Economic and Social Development), and FINEP, Financiadora de Estudos e Projetos (Financial Office for Studies and Projects), provided key support for the lecture series. The Universidade Federal do Rio de Janeiro (UFRJ, the Federal University of Rio de Janeiro) and the Curso de Pós-Graduação em Desenvolvimento, Agricultura e Sociedade (CPDA, the Graduate Programme in Development, Agriculture, and Society) of the Universidad Federal Rural do Rio de Janeiro (UFRRJ, the Federal Rural University of Rio de Janeiro) supplied encouragement, staff support, and classroom and meeting facilities. Manuel Montes of the Ford Foundation, in turn, played a critical role in helping us envision this book and in providing the material conditions that allowed us to bring the book into being.

During the lengthy editorial process, Gary received financial and staff support from the University of California, Riverside and the University of California Office of the President; Silvana received financial and staff support from CPDA/UFRRJ. The University of São Paulo and the Federal University of Rio de Janeiro both extended visiting-scholar invitations to Gary in 2003, providing the space needed to finish editorial work in Brazil.

Cristina Araújo of CPDA deserves special thanks for her logistical support, Eoin O'Neill for translating two chapters from Portuguese to English, and Olivia Lee of the UC Center Sacramento staff for her copy-editing and bibliographical assistance. We also want to acknowledge the cooperation and commitment of the authors and co-authors gathered together here – our colleagues in reimagining development theory.

The editorial staff at Zed Books, Robert, Anna, and Rosemary, provided inspired leadership. Mike and Kate Kirkwood did marvellous copyediting work.

The co-editors dedicate this volume to their children – Tiago, Caio, Jamaal, Andre, and Naima – all of them citizens of a country that does not yet exist. It is our fondest hope that this volume can play some small part in showing how another world – or at least, the beginnings of a conception of another world – can be possible.

i

Framing the
Problem

Introduction

SILVANA DE PAULA
AND
GARY A. DYMSKI

■

Putting Theory in the Service of Development

This volume explores the roles of social and communal relations and institutional structures in determining the pace, depth, and persistence of development. The past several years have seen numerous reflections on the idea of development itself; most famously, Paul Krugman (1995) suggested that this notion could be salvaged by strengthening its links with neoclassical economic theory. This volume also argues for salvaging the idea of development and renewing its conceptual vibrancy. However, the essays collected here suggest that this should not involve closer linking of development with neoclassical economic theory. These essays suggest that theoretical models can best help us imagine new possibilities if they are institutionally specific, historically informed, and able to incorporate diverse social and psychological processes. Since neoclassical theory places a high value on abstraction from institutional and historical details and on conceptual 'thinness' (using models that deviate as little as possible from the assumptions required for Walrasian general equilibrium), this will mean reimagining development using a non-neoclassical framework.

It is our conviction that these shifts in theoretical orientation are needed if economic and social theorists are to respond to the challenge posed by the many social activists and organizations that have come together in Porto Allegre's and Mumbai's 2001–2003 World Social Forums – that is, to level social practices and to democratize them. This democratic imperative encompasses society, cross-border exchanges, and theory itself. Democratizing theory means, at a minimum, developing approaches to conceptual thinking about growth and development that are 'open' – that can respond interactively and inclusively to the concerns and perspectives of multiple interests, social constituencies, and perspectives.

So the essays in this volume participate in the beginnings of a conceptual reimagining of how development operates in the context of historical processes and of multiple dimensions of social and economic inequality, through social institutions that reflect intersecting social and economic dynamics.[1] This introductory essay frames this work by first discussing the methodologies and approaches that have dominated recent work on economic growth and development; it then discusses the themes explored in the chapters that follow.

Is the notion of development relevant any more?

The first waves of literature on development conceptualized it as a distinct field of investigation. Inequality and power emerged as central themes. This field was historically informed and open to contributions not only from economics, but also from other social sciences and the humanities. With the outbreak of widespread crises in the 1980s and early 1990s, including the 'Lost Decade' in Latin America, the momentum of this wave of development thinking was largely broken. The desperate calculus of loan default came to the fore.

These crises led to a double bifurcation in thinking about development. One bifurcation occurred between 'economics' and other social sciences; another, within economics. Social scientists, especially those in the fields of sociology, history and anthropology, questioned the underlying idea of development: it had implicitly been conceptualized as a linear process synonymous with economic growth; thus, it rested implicitly on a simplistic perspective of progress. These critics showed that the discussion of development could not be restricted to the economic sphere *per se*, that is, it could not be oblivious to the urgent questions of poverty, neither to ethnic and gender inequalities.

The thinking of most economists concerned with these issues did not reflect an awareness of this deep criticism (an exception was Sen, whose ideas are discussed below). Instead, a rift in thinking among economists emerged over what model of markets should be used to understand the challenges of development. Some preferred models with asymmetric information, which allow for strategic interactions in markets and which emphasize the importance of unevenly distributed information and resources. The principal–agent models used to rationalize why nations might default, which focus on relationships between agents who control and agents who lack resources, then became the undercurrent of the next wave of development economics.[2] Neoliberal economists had a simpler prescription: dismantle any societal or national institutions that interfere with market flows, and let market forces work.[3] In sum, both 'pro'- and 'anti'-free market views were articulated via technical models that write social and institutional dynamics out of the equation(s).

Recent historical and theoretical events suggest that this technical turn has run its course.[4] Global neoliberalism with free market flows has led to market crashes in East Asia and in the United States. In the past several years, the notion of economic development – improvements in the standard of living for lower-income nations, and for lower-income households in other nations – has become increasingly jeopardized. Apart from the historically singular case of China, success stories are increasingly hard to find. Income and wealth levels in many formerly successful nations, including Argentina, Indonesia, and Mexico, have slid backwards; income growth for lower-income nations around the globe has stalled. In ever-expanding areas of the world, simply maintaining order has taken precedence over even the 'modest' aim of achieving growth.

This retreat is not surprising, given the crisis of foreign-aid programmes and of developmental policy for nations that are, or once were, lower-income.[5] The East Asian financial crisis, combined with the fifteen-year-long stagnation of Japan, put a bitter end to the notion that externally oriented growth coordinated by strong state intervention represented a formula for growth. In the late 1990s, the rapid US growth rate and bubbling global equity markets encouraged International Monetary Fund (IMF) and World Bank experts, following in the footsteps of the Chicago Boys of the 1980s, to insist on neoliberal policy reforms in exchange for foreign exchange and loan rollovers. But now that the slowdown has reached the US and Europe, these institutions have had to admit that their technical 'get the numbers right' policies have failed. Instead, the World Bank and the IMF have increasingly turned to other explanations – inadequate social capital and inadequate supervision of local banking systems, to cite two – to account for their client countries' continued woes.

The possibility of development seems to have all but vanished in the haze cast by these brooding events.[6] And of course, adding to the gloom of recent times have been the shadows cast by global actions against terrorism, by the spread of state violence and war, by the contraction of safety nets, and by the increasingly desperate search of households throughout the world for safety, for security, and for freedom from want and freedom from the fear of want.

Many questions about the future of human society are posed by these unfolding events. One is, what changes are needed, if any, in the economic policies of lower-income nations interested in improving the welfare of their populations? Given the recurrent crises of these nations, this leads directly to the question of what changes are needed, if any, in the economic policy recommendations of the World Bank and IMF? And lying behind this question is the deeper problem of whether any rethinking regarding the process or goals of economic development is needed. What should be done about development theory?

In turn, many answers have been proposed. Some suggest implicitly that the notion of development *per se* – that is, the idea that the governments, residents, and businesses of lower-income nations have tools available to improve their living standards – is misguided. In one view, the heart of the crisis of lower-income nations' development involves the problem of modern-day empire.[7] In another view, globalization itself has created the 'end of geography' and thus a situation in which national development strategies *per se* are implausible.[8]

The perspectives of Stiglitz and Sen

In the past several years, two recent winners of the Nobel Prize in Economics have registered their criticisms of the prevailing wisdom on appropriate policies for developing economies.[9] Joseph Stiglitz (winner of the 2001 Nobel Prize) recently published a book which lays the blame for the global crisis of development and of the global economy more broadly at the feet of the IMF and the rigid structural adjustment programmes imposed by the IMF in response to foreign-exchange and growth crises throughout the developing world.[10] Amartya Sen (winner of the 1998 Nobel Prize) in *Development as Freedom* argues for a broadening of the objectives of development policy: instead of a narrow-minded focus on *per capita* income growth, he calls for attention to the reduction of inequality, and especially for policies that enhance human capability. Sen's notion of 'capability' extends well beyond equalizing (or increasing) income levels; he calls for equalization in the levels of human services such as healthcare and education, as a means of equalizing the levels of human functionings. In this way, he suggests, we can regard 'development as [the attainment of personal] freedom'. [11]

In effect, these two theorists attack development theory and policy from two different ends: Stiglitz at the level of macroeconomic policy implementation, and Sen at the level of the microfoundations underlying development policies. Stiglitz attacks IMF policies for their indebtedness to Chicago-style free-market ideology. He writes:

> Behind the free market ideology there is a model, often attributed to Adam Smith, which argues that market forces – the profit motive – drive the economy to efficient outcomes *as if by an invisible hand.* One of the great achievements of modern economics is to show the sense in which, and the conditions under which, Smith's conclusion is correct. It turns out that these conditions are highly restrictive. Indeed, more recent advances in economic theory – ironically occurring precisely during the period of the most relentless pursuit of the Washington Consensus policies – have shown that whenever information is imperfect and markets incomplete, which is to say always, *and especially in developing countries*, then the invisible hand works most imperfectly. Significantly, there are desirable government interventions which, in principle, can improve upon the efficiency of the market. These restrictions on the conditions under which markets result in efficiency are important – many of the key activities of government can be understood as responses to the resulting market failures. (Stiglitz 2002: 73–4)

By using models that ignore or write off these possible gains from government interventions, then, IMF policies have undermined the institutional frameworks that have provided the basis for growth in Asia and Latin America.[12] Sen's critique is more indirect, if no less impassioned. His argument that policies must be attuned not to *per capita* national-income growth *per se*, but instead to the broad-based achievement of human capabilities, challenges the development policies of both the IMF and the World Bank, as well as many market-oriented economists' conventional wisdom. He is calling, in effect, for a softer path. He spoke of this in an interview published in late 1999:[13]

Q: [D]o you think development has in fact changed? Is it more sensitive, softer, than it used to be?
A: If you look at the early, classical writings in development you find that it was always assumed that economic development was a benign process, in the interest of the people. The view that you have to ignore any kind of social sympathies for the underdog, and that you can't have a democracy, didn't become the dominant thought until the beginning of modern development economics, which is really in the 1940s. That lasted until quite recently. I think it's fair to say that development these days is not quite as harsh as it used to be.

Q: Why did that change come about?
A: Well, I think maybe because the previous view was mostly mistaken. There was a tension in it. The market economy succeeds not because some people's interests are suppressed and other people are kept out of the market, but because people gain individual advantage from it. So, I don't really see that the proponents of the harsh model got the general idea at all right. They had some dreadful slogans like, 'You have to break some eggs to make an omelette'. It's a totally misleading analogy – a pretty costly one aesthetically, and also it's quite mistaken in terms of understanding the nature of man. So, I think the change came about because it was overdue.

Here, Sen attacks the intellectual basis of neoliberal IMF policies by arguing that these policies are inconsistent with individual agents' efforts to improve their lives, and by arguing for the use of market forces. This is an interesting and confusing line of attack, since it is inconsistent with the argument required to establish the basis for using 'human capabilities' rather than income as a guide to development policy.

These interventions by two such distinguished economists are remarkable and insufficient, at the same time. Remarkable, because these pillars of the economics establishment make such explicit critiques of the discipline to which they have devoted their careers. But also insufficient. In effect, both theorists claim that doing economics the right way – their way – will lead to more humane and more stable outcomes in the developing world. Their opponents are charged with incompetence in applying the tools of economic theory. But is this an appropriate response? Is the sort of economic theory taught in the institutions at which Stiglitz and Sen work (Stanford, Columbia, and Harvard, among others), fundamentally sound as a guide to policy, if applied the 'right way'?

The essays in our volume challenge this view, explicitly or implicitly. Let us consider first what economic theory is for Stiglitz and Sen. It is a set of mathematical tools for understanding market-based interactions; and at the core of this toolkit is the model of Walrasian general equilibrium. The Walrasian model shows that when no frictions in price-setting exist, when all agents have perfect information and well-behaved preferences, and when no agent has market power, then maximally efficient decentralized exchange is feasible as a mathematical and – by suggestion – a real-world possibility. No government intervention or development or anti-poverty policy could improve on this outcome. The Walrasian model constitutes the modern-day proof of the Smithian vision referred to by Stiglitz in the quote above.

The challenges issued by Sen and Stiglitz involve a reorientation in the way we understand this ideal vision of efficient market transactions. Stiglitz's well-known model of asymmetric information in credit and labour markets deviates from that ideal by introducing the idea that agents that control key assets (wealth that can be lent, firms that can hire workers) have less than perfect information about the competence and intentions of their prospective workers or borrowers. This has many implications in economic theory: among them, the result that markets will often reach equilibrium without clearing, that is, when some prospective workers are still unemployed, and some borrowers still have not obtained credit. Then the 'textbook' notion of leaving everything to the market is insufficient; and government policies, by affecting how many workers are hired or which prospective borrowers receive credit, can have beneficial effects.

Sen, in turn, essentially calls for a shift in the reference point used to assess outcomes in market processes that allocate scarce resources. The conventional measure of efficiency is the Pareto optimality principle, which asks whether it is possible to reallocate resources in such a way that at least one market participant is better-off (in terms of income and goods) and no market participant is worse off. Sen suggests a different criterion, which asks whether altering a given allocation could result in a higher overall level of human capability attainment. The redistribution of income and wealth is all but ruled out by the Pareto criterion; Sen's criterion raises the possibility of reducing some agents' welfare (wealth levels) so that others may achieve (say) minimal levels of functioning.

What have these arguments yielded? First of all, both are elegant interventions into the abstract algebra of formal models, with arguments and conclusions that draw on economic theory. They represent pleas for loosening the assumptions under which economic theory is done. This plea is important within the frame of economics. There is no doubt that economic theory considered on its own terms provides rich terrain for compelling and interesting models of human interaction. In recent years, technical models in economic theory have pushed to limits that force the recognition of social and institutional factors: the 'new' or 'endogenous' growth theory builds on the empirical fact that national growth rates diverge due to factors other than purely technical variables;[14] and complexity-theoretic models of trade and urban growth, incorporating increasing returns and/or path dependence, highlight the importance of social forces and relations in cross-border and neighbourhood dynamics.[15]

But this doesn't mean that such elegant and intriguing work will alter policy outcomes. Sen's work has caused the World Bank, for example, to begin using multi-dimensional measures of human welfare (including such factors as infant mortality rates, literacy rates, etcetera) in reporting on the 'State of the World'. Stiglitz, during his tenure as chief economist at the World Bank, sponsored numerous research projects on the functioning of credit and labour markets, on anti-poverty policies, and so on. Does this constitute what Kapur called a 'paradigm shift' in development economics – that is, the substitution of human-centred criteria for income-based criteria in assessing policy success? And has it led to global recognition of the legitimacy of systematic government interventions in credit and labour markets?[16]

Regrettably, no and no. The question that economists concerned with such issues must ask is, why? Is it that enough time has not passed for these good ideas and insights at the margin of economic modelling to work their way into core ideas about economic policy making? Is it that the global economy has not experienced a crisis deep enough to force adjustments in market-oriented economists' insights? The shared perspective of the authors gathered here is that the problem lies somewhere deeper, in the core conceptual commitments embedded in the neoclassical model of economic behaviour. This model, as a starting point for analysis of market dynamics, has its uses; but as a starting point for a complex, historically embedded, multi-level, institutionally dependent problem like the analysis of economic development, it is woefully lacking. Even two such well-meaning experts as Stiglitz and Sen develop only partial analyses, in large part because they retain a commitment to the neoclassical framework – and that framework, in turn, embeds the Walrasian general equilibrium as its basic reference point. Most economists with US university doctorates are trained to be sceptical of analyses that deviate too far from the Walrasian.[17]

The hypothesis of the authors of this volume is that these two theorists' efforts are partial because of their intellectual pre-commitment to neoclassical theory. Stiglitz and Sen have been singularly successful in drawing unorthodox results from economic modelling approaches that normally reach orthodox conclusions. But moving from 'getting the prices right' and 'autonomous market outcomes are the best assurance of social justice' to activist policies and other justice criteria will require more than the tweaking of some well-chosen parameters.

Moving from the neoliberal world order to a human and open world order will require the support of energized, empowered, and organized activists world-wide. And the concerns of these masses of people and many organizations are not with abstract assumption sets, but with lived historical experiences. Those whose passion for justice is strong enough to bring them to social action, in a world that discourages social action, have little interest in the niceties of the parameters of neo-Walrasian models.

Joseph Stiglitz and many other economists may be able to explain how the success of the 'Asian economic model' had something to do with the ability of East Asian governments to channel credit to targeted firms and sectors, and to defend this assertion on the basis of a model of asymmetric information in the credit market. But should they – or we – stop there, with the conclusion that the 'Asian economic model' as embodied in the policies of South Korea, Indonesia, and Taiwan, among others, represented an ideal of economic development policies? Should these states' capacity to control credit and other factors of production be restored to mid-1980s levels, as a means of achieving higher levels of human development? Was the 'Asian model' an avatar of understanding, wisdom, or justice for those who lived in these nations? No, it was not. This line of argument collapses because a 'thick' historical situation is being supported on the basis of an overly 'thin' economic model. The many-faceted Asian models succeeded on the basis of many varieties of state-controlled economies for reasons that are historically specific and geopolitically rooted. There is not a formula that can be drawn out, a simple corrective that will re-initiate equitable, capability-expanding growth in any developing country.

This extended reflection on two of the most thoughtful and eloquent economists of our day illustrates how hard it is to look squarely at the entirety of the crisis of development. Their critiques of neoliberal policies fit uncomfortably with equilibrium-based economic theory, even while being rooted in this theory. The point is not that theory is useless, or misleading, or irrelevant. To the contrary. Theoretical models – in the very broadest sense of shared understandings – are utterly crucial as guides for social action. But action cannot be appropriately informed by theory that remains the exclusive domain of theorists. Those engaging in theory formation should be open to practitioners' interventions and suggestions, as now occurs in some fields of scientific inquiry. Theory cannot be 'thin' if the social problems we confront are 'thick'. Theory cannot be 'closed' if the activists and organizations seeking to empower women, to end discrimination and injustice, to reduce poverty and attack health maladies, require spaces for interconnections and interaction that are 'open'.

From technical models to social theory, from thin models to thick ones
How then should social and institutional forces be reincorporated into development theory, in an open way? The approach taken by the authors writing here might be termed critical institutional analysis. They belong to

different matrices of economic and social thought, including the Keynesian, Schumpeterian, and communitarian approaches. What these essays share is that they all reimagine growth and development as an inherently thick process, encompassing multiple social processes that can be illuminated differently by insights from different disciplinary fields. These essays uniformly appreciate social linkages as inherently complex, and social processes as historically specific. They share a commitment to a *critical* approach in that the terms used to convey core meanings must be continually scrutinized and re-evaluated.

The core of this reimagining involves understanding the role of institutions in social analysis. In rational-agent models, institutions are invariably seen as game-theoretic resolutions of prisoners' dilemma and other cooperation puzzles; that is, they always enhance welfare for participants in social decisions. In the richer institutionalist analysis developed here – building on the older development literature – institutions are seen in a more complex way. It is certainly possible that atomistic, goal-seeking agents might create institutions that serve their interests; but, in creating institutions, these agents are not bound by decision rules specifying that institutions can be created only if all agents are left at least as well off. Further, any set of agents at any point in time may confront a set of pre-given institutions that may involve the assertion of social power. Finally, the preferences of agents cannot be understood independently of this richer social milieu.

Fundamentally, taking institutions seriously in development theory means understanding them as components of social and community scenarios that have assumed a broad importance in contemporary life. That is, institutional structures cannot be understood as inconvenient constraints pulling agents away from optimal outcomes they could otherwise achieve. These structures – and societal and local relations more broadly – shape agents' opportunity sets and preferences. No one, including elites with access to cross-border goods and destinations, is outside these circular processes of individual will/ social force. This is well understood by novelists and cultural theorists, and by those engaged in community action. It is a key step in transforming global and local dynamics in ways that better reflect the needs of the poor.

In sum, meso- and micro-analytical insights – about the interactions of institutions, individuals, and communities in the midst of historically specific contexts – have to be reincorporated into development theory, so that conceptual bridges can be built from lived individual experience to aggregate social dynamics.

■

A Tour through the Contributions

The remainder of this introduction tours through the essays in our book, drawing out the underlying thematic connections among the chapters regarding how to reimagine growth. It will be helpful to keep several questions in mind as we proceed. First, is neoclassical theory an adequate basis for building a framework for this reimagination? If not, what does it leave out? Second, whose interests are left out of the conventional framework? That is, on what basis is it adequate to develop a critique of the neoclassical model? For example, are all residents of the developing world disenfranchised by a neoclassical approach, so that all can unite (as in Prebisch's model) in attacking the imperial powers? Or are there other, deeper divides? In considering this question, we come to a third. If deeper divides in society are fundamental – and left out of neoclassical theory – then how can they be brought into theory? Fourth, is it necessary to think in an interdisciplinary way to do this reimagining?

Framing the problem

The essay that opens the book, by Ana Maria Bianchi, confronts the problem of what is required to rethink the problem of development by re-examining the intellectual roots of post-war development theory in Latin America. Bianchi's article engages in a rhetorical analysis of three documents prepared a little over 50 years ago, presented by Raúl Prebisch to the first general assemblies of the Economic Commission on Latin America and the Caribbean (CEPAL). These documents were decisive in creating the 'Latin American School' of economics that informed the region's development policies in the period just after the Second World War. This article analyzes these documents' rhetorical structure, including Prebisch's ideas about planned development and his criticisms of conventional (neoclassical) theories of international commerce. Of course, Prebisch gives very firm answers to the questions posed above. He regarded neoclassical theory as an inadequate vehicle for developmental thinking, pointing to its severe methodological flaws and conceptual limitations. Instead, Prebisch developed his own bold ideas about the structure of the development problem for Latin America.

His core insight was the notion of centre and periphery in the world economy – for, in his analysis, the conventional analysis left out the interests of the periphery. This led him to emphasize planned development and investment 'push' as elements of a growth agenda. This led directly to the founding of CEPAL and what Bianchi characterizes as 'a powerful ideological canon'. The creation of CEPAL, then, was also an exercise in institution building that played a decisive role in the academic and professional formation of new generations throughout Latin America, as Prebisch wished. The documents that Bianchi reviews gave his readers a sense of identification with the continent, and thus constructed a 'strong feeling of solidarity' among Latin American development theorists and practitioners. In Bianchi's view, Prebisch's approach was an explicit rhetorical strategy, and one which was received with great enthusiasm within Latin America. It provided theoretical support for the import substitution process, which constituted the main economic strategy of Latin American countries in the decades following the Second World War.

But while Prebisch's ideas were enthusiastically, if not unanimously, accepted in Latin America, foreign theorists and policy makers regarded the Cepalino discourse as naïve and mistaken. In the Cold War period, then, opinion makers in the market-oriented camp dismissed his views. A rift consequently arose between Latin American intellectual discourse about economic development and the views of neoclassical theorists. And since the latter (neoclassical) perspective underlies the policy prescriptions of the IMF and World Bank, this rift was perceived in the hallways of power in Washington DC as a contrast between a fanciful wrong-headedness and a hard-headed orthodoxy.

This volume does not trace out further the trajectory of Latin American discourse on economic development (a history in which Henrique Cardoso, President of Brazil from 1994 to 2002, plays a central role). It is important to note, however, that development strategies in many Asian nations closely resembled the Cepalino discourse in crucial ways. Specifically, the problem of poverty was attacked through a strong commitment to a national development strategy, orchestrated by explicit state planning, and by public oversight over (and in some cases public decision making about) credit and labour markets. So many East Asian nations, like those in Latin America pursuing import-substituting industrialization strategies, orchestrated and pursued development policies that varied significantly from those recommended under the neoclassical approach of the IMF and World Bank.[18] The key contrast between most Asian and Latin American nations' development approaches was perhaps that the former generally (though not exclusively) pursued export-oriented growth strategies, whereas the latter pursued import-substituting industrialization.

The essays in this book refer to, but do not systematically review, subsequent experience in these developing areas. Both experienced and, in different periods, encouraged sizeable inflows of external capital. In both cases, these inflows both enhanced the pace of business and consumption activity and created more financial fragility – preparing the way for the Latin American debt crisis of 1982 and for the East Asian financial crisis of 1997. Given these parallels in developmental strategy, there is some irony, in the wake of the Latin American crisis, in policy makers from that region being invited to examine the East Asian model as an example of how to 'do it'. The fact was, however, that both regions had pursued development strategies with greater or lesser degrees of success in large part by selectively ignoring large portions of the neoclassical orthodoxy – that is, by explicitly creating institutions for orchestrating investment strategies and channelling resources, by selectively interfering with relative prices for key product areas, and so on. The subsequent crises of nations in these regions would lead orthodox economists to say 'I told you so'. But the fact is that nations that have attempted to follow orthodox policies in a fervent manner – such as Jamaica after the mid-1980s and Argentina in the 1990s – have hardly escaped from the pattern of cyclical crisis and chronic stagnation. To the contrary.

This sequence of events suggests, at the very least, that there is no 'one best way' to achieve development. No one model should be privileged, nor should any one approach to economic theory. This is the entry point of Reinert's contribution to this volume. Reinert asserts that because neo-classical models of economics are capable only of producing harmonious results, the suffering caused by their undiluted application has appeared to be the result of shocks or unwarranted disturbances to market processes. Commitment to these models makes it nearly impossible to see how they could set off dynamic problems causing disharmony and stagnation. Further, this perspective is unable to appreciate the importance of many key contemporary developments, such as the institutional breakdown now occurring in many lower-income nations.

Reinert asserts that this exposes a basic global problem: the lack of diversity of economic ideas. The alternative is what he terms the Other Canon. The reader should note that Chapters 3 to 6 were originally written as contributions to an 'Other Canon' conference held in Oslo in 2000, thanks to the sponsorship of the Norwegian Shipbuilding Federation.[19] This conference explored the possibility of a distinct 'Other Canon' approach to economic theory that would incorporate key elements of several traditions, including those of Keynes, Schumpeter, institutionalism, and Marx.

Reinert's essay, then, not only investigates the core elements of a theory of growth, but does so by putting forward a forceful contrast between neoclassical and Other Canon approaches to economic theory. In Reinert's view, a key flaw in the neoclassical approach is what the 'equality assumption' – the notion that all people fundamentally behave and process information in the same way. This assumption leaves out the importance of human skills and human knowledge in the creation of wealth; and also the idea of the qualitative diversity of economic activities. Further, because it assumes economic exchange is equivalent to barter, neoclassical theory regards harmony as a natural outcome of unimpeded market activity. By contrast, the Other Canon views 'any approximation to harmony to be the result of conscious economic policy', as 'the natural tendency of the market is *away from harmony*' (p. 59).

Reinert builds on Schumpeter's notion that economic growth stems from disequilibria induced by entrepreneurial invention. Indeed, because of its pre-commitment to equilibrium, mainstream theory contains no theory of growth. Conceptualizing growth means allowing for invention and human knowledge, and the way in which these interact with economic societies characterized by diversity in the broadest sense – 'of agents, of opportunities, of knowledge, and of activities' (p. 69).

In Reinert's view, orthodox theory's conceptual precommitments lead to a misunderstanding of the basis of wealth creation, and to a tendency to confuse growth with the spread of trade fuelled by low wages. It is useful to regard productive activities as falling somewhere between two poles: low-quality and high-quality goods. The former involve repetition and low learning curves; the latter involve great opportunities for increasing-returns effects, for learning, and for gains from innovation. Low-quality activities have low entry barriers and substantial competition, whereas high-quality activities have high barriers to entry and provide opportunities for exports.

Reinert, then, issues a theoretical challenge. This means reconstructing economics as a science of practice, and learning to observe again. To filter good insights (like X-efficiency or endogenous growth theory) through the 'wrong' paradigm will not suffice. For neoclassical economic theory mistakenly regards it as natural and inevitable that the few nations that have specialized in 'inventions and new knowledge' are increasingly in conflict with 'the rest which base their "comparative advantage" in international trade on ignorance and low wages' (p. 61). Needless to say, a challenge this broad and encompassing goes well beyond the concerns of this volume; at the same time, by articulating the need for this rethinking as a *cri de coeur*, Reinert captures the sense of urgency shared by this volume's editors and authors alike.

Rethinking the role of institutions and macrostructures in development
The next sections of this volume consider three dimensions that require rethinking if development is to be renewed. These dimensions are, respectively, the institutions and macrostructures that shape economic agents' choices; microstructural aspects of human behaviour — consumption behaviour and local development processes; and participatory processes. The first dimension (Part II) involves a conceptualization of the factors that govern how agents (and nations, implicitly) move, and within which communities and individual choices arise. The second dimension (Part III) considers the dynamics and constraints that originate with individual choice processes and with agents' organization into distinct spatial communities. Then, given these largely market-determined factors, the third dimension (Part IV) explores the impact of non-market human interactions and exchanges, exploring first the role of communal associations and ties in economic outcomes, and second the potential impact of cross-border linkages on institution creation (and hence on unfolding historical dynamics).

Part II begins with Hodgson's re-examination of the role of institutions in economic growth. Hodgson's central point is that the constraints that institutions place on markets are crucial in maintaining (or blocking) growth. This contrasts with the received view that economies work best when markets function under minimal constraints. Hodgson defines institutions as 'durable systems of established and embedded social rules that structure social interactions' (p. 86). These social rules are intrinsic to economic behaviour, not external to it. In effect, institutions embody social constraints on behaviour within the commercial sphere; and of course, they are also enabling. There are several implications for economic development: a viable institutional framework is clearly a prerequisite for economic development; and institutional rules are established by practice, not by decree. The tension between constraining and enabling rules is especially critical, as these rules, when functioning well, both provide information and reduce uncertainty.

Hodgson goes on to discuss the need to consider, both in theory and in policy formation, the macro determinants of micro conditions. He does this via the notion of 'reconstitutive downward causation'. This concept suggests that a complete (macro) model cannot be built up from microfoundations based on individuals' behaviour; such an approach would miss the shared milieu and shared codes that govern agent interactions. Hodgson notes that institutions do not develop autonomously from the bottom 'up', so governments should not regard 'non-intervention' in market institutions as optimal in any sense.

Ha-Joon Chang and Peter Evans also reflect on the institutional underpinnings of development. They write: 'Everyone recognizes that institutions are fundamental to economic change ... [but] we are still a long way from a satisfying theory of institutions and their economic effects.' These authors criticize the 'false parsimony' of neoclassical economics and conventional 'institutionalist' explanations, which overemphasize functionalism or instrumentalism. They call for a shift from a 'thin' to a 'thick' view of institutions, especially as a means of reinterpreting globalization and its consequences. This shift will permit institutions to be understood in all their complexity. As Hodgson notes, institutions are enabling as well as constraining; and their effects are interlinked structurally in ways that generate follow-on shifts. Change is cumulative, involving both flows and counter-flows; it is also multi-causal. Small changes and shifts in institutional arrangements can thus lead to profound – and surprising – reversals. In these reversals, the role of culture in a very broad sense is crucial – including the specific impact of ideology and political conflict and struggle in shaping events. Culture shapes the ideas and expectations of agents regarding what changes are feasible and permissible.

These authors then explore two case examples of this view of the linkages between institutions and economic growth, those of South Korea and the World Trade Organization (WTO). The Korean developmental state shows how 'enabling' institution creation can work when put into practice. Korea's growth dynamic is explained as involving a contradictory process of institutional creation, political response, and adaptation. The Korean crisis of 1997–8 is presented as an example of how a relatively small shift in 'initial conditions' can lead to the dismantling of sizeable institutions, with tremendous consequences for future growth. The authors explore this shift, and find that it resulted from several factors; among these, a key factor is cultural – that is, the emergence of a large US-educated economic elite. Another lesson of the Korean developmental state is the central role of class conflicts and geopolitical factors in change. Change is not efficiency-driven; but instead it emanates from a thick set of factors, inextricably interwoven with political and ideological factors and with class interest.

The WTO case illustrates the problem of global institution building, which involves additional considerations – that is, what is involved in imagining and thinking through global institutions? The authors describe the 'Polanyi problem', the idea that unconstrained markets create unparalleled opportunities but also generate feedback effects as elites and other classes react. In general, action at the global level can generate complex multi-layered reactions, with consequences that are difficult to predict or control. The authors use as an example the effort to establish a global governance structure for labour standards.

The essay by Leonardo Burlamaqui and Jan Kregel then offers an analytical approach to the sort of rich institutional framework that Chang and Evans advocate. Burlamaqui and Kregel explore the role of finance in economic growth by re-examining the ideas of Schumpeter and Minsky, both of whom emphasize the centrality of non-equilibrium and instability in economic processes. In Schumpeter's framework, finance plays the role of the handmaiden of creative destruction; financial firms' lending permits industry to generate technological advances. Minsky's vision of finance in the economic process, by contrast, focuses on how financing leads to overlending and extensive financial fragility, ultimately throwing the economy into crisis.

These theorists' insights suggest that the policy problem of designing financing structures that best facilitate growth in countries with lower *per capita* income levels is no simple matter. There is no single financial model that facilitates growth and minimizes risks at every point in any nation's development process. Instead, developing nations should be permitted to mould national financial structures which best facilitate growth in light of their inherited economic and social structures and their historical trajectories. However, Burlamaqui and Kregel go on to emphasize that global banking competition puts an increasing premium on understanding price movements in financial markets, more than on detailed knowledge of borrower firms' capacity. Thus, the kind of banking relations that Schumpeter viewed as crucial in supporting growth are threatened by current global trends.

This raises the question of whether a particular type of banking system is a prerequisite to growth based on the financing of competitive innovation. The authors contrast the historical experience of Germany and the US. Despite large apparent differences, these authors find little difference between the two forms of bank regulation. This suggests that much policy discussion, contrasting the stability of segregated and mixed-bank regulatory structures, has been misplaced. From the point of view of Schumpeterian 'creative destruction' or Minskyan 'endogenous financial fragility', a certain amount of evolutionary instability is necessary to allow the competitive innovation that makes the system viable. Perfectly safe and stable banks who never back losers would most likely stifle, not ignite, economic development. This implies that the major objective of bank regulatory policy, contrary to current IMF wisdom, cannot be the elimination of change and instability – for such a policy would encourage economic stagnation, not growth. Rather, policy should be directed towards ensuring financing of innovative capital projects. There is no permanent structural fix. However, this review of German and US experience suggests that indigenous financial systems should be developed and defended in much the same way as nations have acted to develop and protect industrial 'competitive' advantage.

Rethinking the microstructure of development: individuals and communities in global and local spaces

The two essays in Part III both emphasize, in different ways, that individual and community behaviour can only be understood as involving interactions between individual agent/community action and broader structures of constraint and possibility. John Wilkinson engages in a critical re-examination of that bastion of individual choice, consumption. His first point is that the individual consumer should be understood, in fact, as an assemblage of larger social categories: 'consumers, both individually and collectively, are much more active in product creation and subsequent use than studies which focus on the consumer as purchaser would suggest' (p. 193). In recent years, consumption has increasingly been framed as a phenomenon of culture (who do I want to be?) – not a manifestation of social forces (keeping up with the Joneses). Wilkinson shows how the emphasis on the former approach assumes the relative primacy of consumption over production, and the assertion of consumption choice over and against oligopolistic market control.

Wilkinson goes on to examine two authors, Bauman and Rochefort, who retain a material basis even in exploring cultural resonances of consumerism. Bauman regards the emergence of consumption as a dual response to processes of economic globalization that have utterly transformed the role of the individual in production and in society. As institutions and economic security have eroded, in Bauman's view, consumers increasingly adopt consumerism as a means of establishing their identities and their continuity in a world that promises less and less of both. There is thus a desperation, a search for pleasure that is a kind of self-abnegation. By contrast, Rochefort suggests that globalization has transformed people into consumer entrepreneurs, that is, entrepreneurs engaged in consumer production. There is a reciprocal process between such consumer entrepreneurs and the product worlds that supply them. There is some hope that those engaged in such processes of personal transformation will regain autonomy – an 'autonomy of the new consumer-producer [is] premised on interdependence and connectedness' (p. 176).

Wilkinson develops a critique of these two authors' positions by exploring whether 'consumer involvement and organisation, at present still in their infancy ... can ... be seen to comprise a necessary and strategic component of any shift to a more virtuous phase in the organisation of consumer society' (p. 173). He argues that this question can be satisfactorily addressed only if theoretical generalizations about consumers are replaced by careful specifications of consumption practices. These should bring the consumer into focus as an active participant in consumption practices. Wilkinson suggests that such an understanding can 'pinpoint better the differential leverage that the new consumer is able to exert at different stages in the conception, regulation, production and distribution of products and services' (p. 173).

So there is no need to settle for the Bauman/Rochefort polarity between consumers who are being duped and enchained and consumers who are entering into ever-greater degrees of satisfaction. Wilkinson instead proposes that consumption under globalization be understood as involving 'stages'. Consumers initially engaged in some resistance to globalization at the point of sale; next, they have been increasingly active in shaping post-purchase activities to reflect individual idiosyncracies and cultural preferences. Finally, the 'consumer citizen' is becoming an important force in defining and regulating markets and market opportunities. Indeed, Wilkinson envisions consumption as a possible political arena in which consumers might organize for organic food, for food safety and security, and against genetically modified products.

The essay by Gary Dymski develops a spatial Keynesian approach to the problems of poverty and social discrimination. This approach shows that the spatial distribution of households and businesses is a key factor in shaping the character and extent of poverty in any society. Poverty involves not simply the circumstances of households who are poor, but structural characteristics of the bordered spaces within which most lower-income people live. These structural characteristics are deeply impacted by spatially specific social and economic dynamics. These dynamics involve economic clustering combined with social separation, and create distinct areas with very uneven cross-border patterns of goods and financial flows. These cross-border patterns tend to systematically encourage accumulation in some spaces and decumulation in others. Some areas become locations for the long-term cultivation of asset growth, while others become sites for finding prey to exploit for short-term returns. Similarly, the impact of social discrimination depends not just on the depth and pattern of personal animus, but on the degree to which those who are targets of this discrimination are segregated into distinct spatial communities, and on whether these communities are sites of production and wealth building.

This spatial wealth/income perspective shows first that the disadvantages associated with social discrimination invariably have a spatial and community dimension. Further, when mobility between spatial communities is constrained (by social custom or by wealth variations), social discrimination and poverty cannot be attacked meaningfully at the individual level. Policies aimed at reducing poverty and social discrimination must be informed by the spatial configuration of economic and social resources. Third, any attack on social discrimination should not focus solely on the personal level, but instead should encompass the structural inequality that personal discrimination invariably creates. In addition, this analysis shows the relevance of core elements of the Keynesian approach for understanding and intervening in situations of poverty and discrimination. Finally, this chapter makes the point that anti-poverty policies are inherently development policies, and development policies cannot avoid being anti-poverty policies. In particular, the larger the percentage of a nation's population experiencing poverty and social discrimination, the more policies for reducing poverty and social discrimination will overlap with overall national economic policies. In sum, this chapter argues that an attack on poverty, inequality, and social discrimination must be a component of any sustainable development strategy.

■

Rethinking the Participatory Process: Local and Global Connections

Part IV examines the power of participation – at both the local and the global levels. Michael Storper examines the links between the 'anonymous' forces of market, state, and bureaucracy, on the one hand (*gesellschaft*), and the localized contexts of community and neighbourhood (*gemeinschaft*), on the other. Economists aren't sure what to make of the latter: do they build social capital and reduce transactions costs and moral hazard, promoting the social good; or do they lead to nepotism and institutional rigidity?

Storper argues that, on the face of it, this stand-off is unresolvable. The societal and the local must be in a mutually supportive relationship for development to proceed. This relationship underlies some other currents of thought about how development should or can be pursued (state-led, market-led, and so on). 'In place of this pitched debate between partisans of society or community as key to development, we shall argue that both societal and communitarian bonds between economic agents shape long-term economic development, and that it is the specific nature of their interrelations that matters' (p. 199).

His argument quickly touches upon Hodgson's theme: 'successful economies are characterized by generalized confidence in the economic process and especially in the transactional relationships upon which it depends; effective and acceptable distributional trade-offs between groups; and means for successful ... conflict resolution' (p. 216). Storper lists the key elements in economies with successful development as (1) generalized confidence in economic processes/allocative mechanisms, embodied in incentives and coordination; (2) effective and acceptable distributional trade-offs, so that immiserization is avoided in the process of growth; and (3) ongoing conflict resolution and problem solving, especially important when sacrifices must be made.

Storper notes that social scientists are confused about how these positive features are to be achieved – through societal mechanisms, or through communitarianism. Initially, sociologists such as Durkheim and Weber regarded community as atavistic and anti-modern, an obstacle to development. However, new thinking suggests the value of community. The communal level involves 'bonding' and 'bridging' processes, in Putnam's terminology. The former is relatively easy when there are homogeneous sub-communities involved in economic development; the latter is the true challenge, as this involves figuring out ways to share gains to share losses. Economics also has trouble with the society/community distinction. Neoclassical theory is broadly antipathetic to the notion of social ties within the economy; however, newer work on networks and imperfect information increasingly appreciates the role of distinctive social arrangements in resolving informational and/or coordination problems. Storper then turns to work on economic development *per se*, and finds that authors in this area increasingly understand the centrality of community resources and processes in economic outcomes.

Nelson Delgado and Jorge Romano then evaluate the role of participation in a global setting by summarizing the themes and debates at the recent World Social Forum meetings in Porto Allegre, Brazil. This essay describes the World Social Forum as a process that should be understood in the context of the field of 'new' social movements. The authors first describe the characteristics of the Forum meetings since 2001, summarizing the principle of these meetings, their administrative organization, and the trajectory of the activities that have taken place. The authors also present a systematic analysis of the evolution of the structure and the content of the thematic areas discussed (that is, the conferences and panels) during the three Forums held to date. They go on to conduct a comparative analysis of the 2002 and 2003 conferences and panels on the World Trade Organization and international trade, external debt, and the solidarity economy; this analysis highlights the complexity and the multiplicity of subjects analyzed and proposals discussed.

The authors are especially interested in understanding the uses and consequences of the World Social Forum meetings. What results have come from these meetings, and what should be expected? Delgado and Romano argue that these meetings should be considered first of all as a space for translating the diversity of struggles and social movements against neoliberal globalization, and as a space for building dialogues between distinct actors with diverse visions, characteristics and purposes, without the necessity for the imposition of a single language. The authors assert that this effort at translating diverse views so as to create the possibility of global sharing among activists and analysts is not exclusively an intellectual exercise, as its explicit objective is mobilization and social action. This process *per se*, then, is the key outcome of the World Social Forum meetings, and as such is far more important than any consensual list of action items that might be drawn up by any subgroup of participants.

■

Conclusion

It is high time to admit that the notion of 'one best way' to development – that being the market-driven model favoured by neoclassical orthodoxy – is a path to global stagnation, not prosperity. The orthodox model is mistaken in part because it leads to a fallacy of composition – that is, all nations in the world save one cannot engage in export-oriented growth aimed at the remaining nation's current account without generating deep structural contradictions in global payments systems and currency values. But the orthodox model is also mistaken at the level of individual nations. The rhetoric of market-driven growth – that is, that growth will naturally occur once all barriers to wage and price level adjustments have been removed, all taxes on capital have been eased, and all government regulations have been eradicated (so that the conditions for a Walrasian equilibrium have been created) – is a chimera.

Development requires institution building by committed national and regional leaders who have the means to experiment. This is nothing new in any historical sense: as Ha-Joon Chang has argued, the United States and other high-income nations generally succeeded in development through policies that involved substantial government intervention, the creation of significant public (or quasi-public) institutions, and so on.[20] What is needed is to recognize explicitly the incompatibility between the institutional pre-requisites for development and the policy prescriptions of neoclassical orthodoxy. Policy analysts must learn not to equate seriousness of develop-mental purpose with commitment to neoclassical economics. Just as a diverse array of approaches to development have been (and should be) tried, so too should diverse economic approaches be encouraged; for an openness to experimentation in all realms (rather than the use of one standard approach to close and reduce options) is the best way to achieve innovation and growth.

The essays in this book go some way toward identifying some of the dimensions of social reality that are treated too simply (or that are ignored) in neoclassical theory. The macrostructural, institutional, microstructural, and participatory layers considered here are all crucial in social outcomes, as are the specific roster of social concerns – the developmental state, global governance, community, the World Social Forum, and so on. All this adds up, as mentioned earlier, to a 'thick' theoretical perspective and to a 'thick' set of substantive concerns.

The 'open' approach to theory suggested here implies that no one conceptual level or set of substantive concerns can be privileged as most essential. Indeed, others could be added; in particular, the issues of gender inequality and oppression, national minorities, and various forms of social exclusion have received only passing mention in these essays. There is much more to be added to this already 'thick' mix. Given that each analytical and substantive dimension is important, the challenge for theory is then to develop a syntax for model construction and analysis that does not require privileging one or another layer or issue as more fundamental.

The openness that is sought may indeed be a matter of analytical attitude and not one of formal model construction or of social discourse. After all, the structures of formal (mathematical or symbolic) models typically force theorists to make arbitrary choices about variable exclusion and directions of causation. This will not change. What can change, however, is the notion that any one way to imagine these models' closure can be taken as the best approach. Model reconfiguration and reparameterization must become as important as model building. In social discourses that do not rely on formal models, analytical priority can still be signalled through the writer's choice of which social dimensions to privilege. Unconscious or conscious decisions that privilege some social segments at the expense of others have to be challenged and reconsidered, themselves made topics for debate.

Those of us who want both change and democracy and diversity must recognize, then, that theory – self-awareness in the definition and use of conceptual ideas – is as crucial for us as for those who are committed to market liberalization. But whereas theory leads, in the case of neoclassical theory, to broad agreement on a small number of factors that really matter, theory in the democracy/diversity perspective will necessarily be rough-edged, thick, indeterminate. There will be no one final perspective, no one definitive model – but many contending models, each emphasizing (or selectively eliminating) different elements of the same problems. The challenge will arise as much in translating results as in creating them. And it will be necessary to put a high premium on tolerance and open-mindedness in these discourses of the diverse and the disenfranchised.

Prebisch imagined growth as a framework outside of neoclassical economics, whose organizing ideas of centre and periphery could provide all of Latin America with a sense of belonging and commonality, as well as a common economic agenda – import-substituting industrialization. We too, some fifty years later, are reimagining growth as a framework outside the neoclassical economic framework. Prebisch's core ideas have been further refined into the analysis of a divide – South versus North – that cuts across the globe, dividing one set of 'developing' nations from those in 'developed' nations. We do not reject these binary oppositions – core/periphery or North/South; to the contrary, we find them useful as organizing ideas. But instead of relying on one or two organizing ideas, we recognize the need for many – for a thick theoretical approach – because of the diversity of circum-stances and of the many divides that arise within the nations of the South. Indeed, these divides equally affect the nations of the North, and make development theory equally applicable to the 'advanced' nations as well. And because mobilizing people means finding bridges across the social and economic divides that separate us, reimagining growth also requires a democratization of theory. This democratization must take the form of a broadening of the concepts and constituencies included in the conception of growth itself. We welcome all readers of this text to join its authors in this ongoing process.

Bibliography

Benabou, R. (1993) 'Workings of a city: Location, education, and production', *Quarterly Journal of Economics*, Vol. 108, No. 3, August.

Chang, H.-J. (2002) *Kicking Away the Ladder*, London: Anthem Books.

Durlauf, S. N. (1994) 'Spillovers, stratification, and inequality', *European Economic Review*, Vol. 38, Nos 3–4, April.

Easterly, W. (2001) *The Elusive Quest for Growth: Economists' Adventures and Misadventures in the Tropics*, Cambridge, MA: MIT Press.

Easterly, W. and R. Levine (2001) 'It's not factor accumulation: Stylized facts and growth models', *World Bank Economic Review*, Vol. 15, No. 2, August.

Eaton, J. (1993) 'Sovereign debt: A primer', *World Bank Economic Review*, Vol. 7, No. 2, May.

Eaton, J., Gersovitz, M. and J. Stiglitz (1986) 'The pure theory of country risk', *European Economic Review*, Vol. 30, No. 3, June.

Friedman, B. (2002) 'Globalization: Stiglitz's case', *New York Review of Books*, Vol. 49, No. 13, August.

Fujita, M., Krugman, P. and A. J. Venables (1999) *The Spatial Economy: Cities, Regions and International Trade*, Cambridge, MA: MIT Press.

Guitian, M. (1998) 'The challenge of managing global capital flows', *Finance and Development*, Vol. 35, No. 2, June.

Hardt, M. and A. Negri (2000) *Empire*, Cambridge, MA: Harvard University Press.

Kapur, A. (1999a) 'Atlantic Unbound interview with Amartya Sen', *The Atlantic Online*, web-published, http://www.theatlantic.com/unbound/interviews/ba991215.htm,December

—— (1999b) 'A third way for the Third World', *Atlantic Monthly*, Vol. 284, No. 6, December.

Krugman, P. (1995) *Development, Geography, and Economic Theory*, Cambridge, MA: MIT Press.

Kuhn, T. (1971) *The Structure of Scientific Revolutions*, Princeton: Princeton University Press.

Lucas, R. E. (1990) 'Why doesn't capital flow from rich to poor countries', *American Economic Review*, Vol. 80, No. 2, May.

—— (2001) 'Externalities and cities', *Journal of Economic Dynamics*, Vol. 4, No. 2, April.

Martin, R. (1994) 'Stateless monies, global financial integration and national economic autonomy: The end of geography?', in Corbridge, S., Martin, R. and N. Thrift (eds) *Money, Space and Power*, London: Blackwell Publishers.

O'Brien, R. (1992) *Global Financial Integration: The End of Geography*, London: Pinter Publishers.

Romer, P. M. (1990) 'Capital, labor, and productivity', in Baily, M. N. and C. Winston (1990) *Brookings Papers on Economic Activity, Microeconomics 1990*, Washington: Brookings Institution Press.

—— (1993) 'Idea gaps and object gaps in economic development', *Journal of Monetary Economics*, Vol. 32, No. 3, December.

Sen, A. (1992) *Inequality Reexamined*, Cambridge, MA: Harvard University Press.
—— (1999) *Development as Freedom*, New York: Alfred Knopf
Stiglitz, J. (2002) *Globalization and its Discontents*, New York: W. W. Norton.
—— (2003) 'How to reform the global financial system', *Harvard Relations Council International Review*, Vol. 25, No. 1, Spring.

Notes

1 An apology of sorts is in order. This is a book of social theory written at a time when nothing less than action seems an adequate response to unfolding global events. Even at such a time, however, theory – that is, self-aware analysis aimed at exposing conceptual connections – is crucial, as it can lead to deeper insights and better pragmatic ideas. A commitment to theoretical engagement is a prerequisite to understanding contemporary policy debates.

2 See, for example, Eaton, Gersovitz and Stiglitz (1986) and Eaton (1993).

3 A clear statement of this perspective, written in the midst of the East Asian crisis, is Guitian (1998).

4 Krugman (1995) suggests that the blame for the dissolution of development economics rests with its practitioners' unwillingness or inability to put in place a thorough-going set of rigorous, formal models – the result being that development thinking has become vague and/or undisciplined. Implicitly, our argument here disagrees with Krugman. Development economics, in our view, is not in trouble because its practitioners don't use models with sufficient rigour; instead, we suggest, the very idea of development economics is threatened by the wave of real-world policy failures in recent years, across the market-constraining/market-friendly spectrum.

5 This crisis is paralleled by the demise of serious efforts to ensure minimal living standards in higher-income nations – notably, the retreat of the welfare state in Europe, and the attack on what welfare benefits remain in the US.

6 Benjamin Friedman (2002), reviewing Joseph Stiglitz's *Globalization and its Discontents*, notes the remarkable shift from the optimism of the development theorists of the immediate post-war period to the atmosphere surrounding discussions of development today.

7 See Hardt and Negri (2000).

8 See O'Brien, (1992). For a critique of this perspective, see Martin (1994).

9 There have been numerous reassessments of development policy over the past several decades, apart from those by Stiglitz and Sen. One especially interesting work is Easterly (2001).

10 See Stiglitz (2002).

11 Sen's work and personal involvement was fundamentally important in constructing the Human Development Index (HDI, or, in Portuguese, the Índice de Desenvolvimento Humano); see Sen, A. (1999). A recent book by Sen focusing more narrowly on his views about inequality in the context of social choice theory is *Inequality Reexamined*.

12 Stiglitz's critique of the global financial system goes beyond criticism of IMF conditionality. In 'How to Reform the Global Financial System', Stiglitz argues that reform also requires reforms in the international reserve-currency system, a global bankruptcy procedure for sovereign debtors, and a neutral mechanism (that is, one not administered by the IMF) for handling such sovereign debt problems.

13 Kapur (1999a).

14 Useful guides to endogenous growth theory and its implications for comparative analyses of developed and developing economies are Romer (1990, 1993) and Easterly and Levine (2001).

15 See, for example, Benabou (1993) and Durlauf (1994).

16 Akash Kapur (1999b). Note that Kapur's definition of paradigm shift stops short of the sort of methodological revolution envisioned by Kuhn (1971).

17 For an example of this, note the 'gloves off' critique of Stiglitz's book in Benjamin Friedman (2002) – a rather surprising performance for an economist often identified (as is Stiglitz) as a Keynesian.

18 This is not to suggest that Asian development was completely autonomous. To the contrary, the trajectory of development in Japan, South Korea, the Philippines, and other nations was deeply affected by US intervention, often in the context of post-war reconstruction (as in Japan) or of extended periods of military occupation.

19 This is the first volume to encompass work explicitly exploring the Other Canon as an approach to economic theory. Obviously, Reinert's views concerning Marx, Schumpeter, and other theorists are his own; and the reader should not assume that all the contributors to this volume would agree with his characterization of what an 'Other Canon' might contain. More discussion and debate of this concept are clearly warranted. The Oslo Conference essays have been substantially rewritten here so that they pertain more directly to the narrower theme of this volume. Those interested in the Oslo Conference essays should contact Erik Reinert, these papers' authors, or the Other Canon website (www.othercanon.org).

20 The essay by Chang and Evans in this volume refers to this argument; for the full analysis, see Chang (2002).

2

The Planned Development of Latin America: A Rhetorical Analysis of Three Documents from the 1950s

ANA MARIA BIANCHI

Just over half a century has elapsed since the foundation of the Economic Commission on Latin America and the Caribbean, commonly referred to in Latin America (and in this essay) as CEPAL. This anniversary provides an opportunity to reflect on the current of economic thought associated with this institution, whose ideas are often designated as the 'CEPAL School', the 'Prebisch–Singer thesis', or the 'structuralist current'. This chapter focuses on three documents presented by Raúl Prebisch to the first general assemblies of the organization held, respectively, in 1949 in Havana, in 1950 in Montevideo, and in 1951 in Mexico City.

This chapter focuses on Cepalino economic thought from a rhetorical point of view – that is, as a discourse aimed at persuading one or more audiences.[1] The analysis will be made from two principal angles. One angle is the internal dynamics of Prebisch's idea at the beginning of his time with CEPAL. As Perelman and Tyteca's seminal treatise on rhetoric (1969) recommends, in the analysis of argumentative discourses the author should be seen as someone who actively advocates a point of view, for which he aims to conquer the sympathy of his public.

A second angle of observation here is the contradictory repercussions of these ideas in Latin America and elsewhere. In Latin America, although it was not unanimously accepted, Prebisch's discourse was received with great enthusiasm. His role was decisive in providing the theoretical support for the import substitution process, which constituted the main economic strategy of Latin American countries in the decades following the Second World War. Elsewhere, to the contrary, Prebisch's theses received an adverse reception. The Cepalino discourse was considered naïve and mistaken by foreign readers, some of whom even described him as a heretic. Apart from any technical and conceptual errors he may have made, what weighed against him was his heterodox character. The criticism of orthodox economics formulated by Prebisch and others on the CEPAL team sharpened a resistance to the organization itself which was fed by the Cold War climate of the period.

An important bibliographic reference for this investigation is Celso Furtado's account in *A fantasia organizada* [The organised fantasy] (Furtado 1985). An eyewitness to history, Furtado entered the technical corps of CEPAL before Prebisch and has been an artisan of the transformations undergone by Latin America ever since. Furtado worked closely with 'Don Raúl' during the entire period in which the documents analyzed here were produced. His collaboration was indispensable for collecting, organizing, and interpreting statistical data, and for the theoretical discussion on which political recommendations were based.

Note that this chapter is not concerned with the economic history of Latin America, nor with the situation of the continental economies in the second half of the twentieth century. Focusing primarily on the history of ideas, it extends analyses presented in Bianchi and Salviano Jr (1999) and in Bianchi (2002).

It is hard to untangle the history of thought and economic history proper. This chapter begins with the supposition that the knowledge on which any discourse is based is socially constructed. To study it adequately, the researcher needs to move beyond the notion that ideas evolve from their own internal logic. Of course the social context is incapable, by itself alone, of accounting for the intellectual brilliance and originality of the thought of Prebisch and his team. However, the social and political environment of Latin America opened the way for Cepalino thought, favouring a discourse whose nature was defined by a quite peculiar combination of theoretical reflection and recommendations for economic policy.

The next sections examine, in order: the historical circumstances of the creation of CEPAL and the basic content of the documents analyzed; the principal theoretical influences on Prebisch's work; the thesis of the deterioration in terms of trade, based on the centre–periphery metaphor; the thesis of the necessarily planned character of economic development; the use of empirical evidence; the heterodox character of the documents; finally, the repercussion of Cepalino thought in Latin America and in the rest of the world.

■

Raúl Prebisch and Cepalino Discourse

Before entering into the analysis of the selected documents, it is useful to remember the historical circumstances that led to the foundation of CEPAL. In 1947 the United Nations created its first regional economic commissions, the first related to Europe, the second to Asia and the Far East. These institutions had the mission of accumulating data about the economic tendencies and problems of the regions in their areas of jurisdiction, with the purpose of proposing solutions to these problems.

The movement to create a UN Commission on Latin America, however, faced strong opposition, especially on the part of the United States government, whose representative abstained in the final vote on the project (Hodara 1987: 385). Critics of a Latin American commission argued that priority should be given to the reconstruction of continents directly affected by the war. They also argued that this organization was redundant, given the existence of the Washington-based Organization of American States (OAS). Both Pollock (1987) and Street (1987) comment that the Cold War climate then being experienced by the world created barriers to organizations not clearly aligned with the United States. US interests were better served by the OAS, since the US belonged to the OAS and thus had greater control over its actions in the geopolitical field. The 'docility' of the OAS, about which Furtado speaks (1985: 108), was not guaranteed in the design of CEPAL.

This resistance was overcome, and CEPAL was created on a provisional basis in 1948. Based in Santiago do Chile, CEPAL was greeted by Latin American governments as a victory for continental interests (Hodara 1987: 385–6). A year later, more resistance greeted the nomination of Raúl Prebisch to serve as part of CEPAL's technical corps. Estranged from the Peronist government, which he had served for many years as founder and director of the Argentinian Central Bank, Prebisch was then Professor of Economics of the University of Buenos Aires. At CEPAL's first assembly, held in Havana, he appeared in the role of a consultant, presenting a work on 'The economic development of Latin America and its principal problems' (Prebisch 2001). The essay was later baptized by Hirschman (1961) as the *Manifesto*, the name with which it came to be identified in the literature.[2]

As a member of the CEPAL team, Prebisch wrote the introduction of the *Estúdio Económico de América Latina 1949* [Economic Study of Latin America 1949], presented in 1950 at the Montevideo assembly (CEPAL 1949; hereafter referred to in the text as *Estúdio 49*). In the same year, he was raised to the position of CEPAL executive secretary, a function he held until 1963, when he became secretary-general of the United Nations Conference on Trade and Development (UNCTAD), a body he had helped create.

By 1951 CEPAL had survived the test of its first three years; soon after its annual conference in Mexico, it became a definitive part of the UN system. As executive secretary, Prebisch led the preparation of the introductory essay to the *Estúdio Económico de América Latina 1950* [Economic Study of Latin America 1950], 'Problemas teóricos e práticos do crescimento econômico' [Theoretical and practical problems of economic growth] (CEPAL 1952; hereafter referred to in the text as *Estúdio 50*). As highlighted by Furtado (1985: 106), this third document reflected the broad debate instituted by the technical corps of CEPAL at its beginning, and represents, therefore, the most complete exposition of the organization's thought.

This chapter is primarily concerned with the commonalities in these three documents. However, some differences among them should be acknowledged at the outset: while the first two adopt positions, criticize the theory of foreign trade, and outline the principal Cepalino theses, the third essay has a clear programmatic objective. This third essay is distinguished by its open defence of a development programme aimed at the conditions of Latin America and delineating targets and stages.

Furtado (1991) describes CEPAL's initial years as the organization's most creative phase. As is well known, the doctrine adopted by CEPAL elaborated the thesis of the deterioration of the terms of exchange suffered by the countries on the periphery. Traditional exporters of raw materials and primary products to the industrialized countries of the centre, countries on the periphery faced a secular decline in their terms of trade. In the case of Latin America, this situation threatened prospects for economic development, since the asymmetric relationship with the central countries fed a vicious circle of low productivity and a low level of savings. Moreover, technological progress created an imbalance unfavourable to the periphery, since the increase in industrial productivity did not translate into a reduction of prices in international trade. In *Estúdio 50* this characteristic was associated with the low income elasticity of demand in products which the countries on the periphery exported to the central countries, in contrast to the high income elasticity of industrial products bought in the external market, including capital goods essential to industrialization.

■

Principal Theoretical Influences

What were the principal theoretical influences on Prebisch's work during CEPAL's initial years? Love (1996) argues that the diverse theses defended by the Argentinian economist illustrate his theoretical eclecticism, which resulted from his own particular amalgam of different intellectual traditions.

Other biographers and commentators suggest various influences on Prebisch, with three names in particular being highlighted: List, Manoilescu, and Keynes. A pioneer of the German Historical School, List created the concept of 'nascent industry' and preached the need for an initial period of protection for industrial activities, so that the sector could become competitive in the international arena (Love 1996: 105). There are indications that other members of this school influenced the teaching of economics at the University of Buenos Aires. Gondre (1945), in particular, refers to Roscher and von Schmöller.

Prebisch makes an explicit reference to Keynes in the *Manifesto* (p. 72), where he questions the premise of full employment assumed by economic theory. It is known that he admired the English economist, whose teachings he discussed with his students at the University of Buenos Aires; indeed, he wrote a book, published by Fondo de Cultura, entitled *Introducción à Keynes*.[3]

The Romanian economist Manoilescu is also mentioned as an influence, although Prebisch makes no mention of him in the documents analyzed here (Love 1996: 101; Hodara 1987). Manoilescu, author of the *Theory of Protectionism* (1929), called attention to the inherent inequality in patterns of international trade, leaving countries that export primary products at a growing disadvantage *vis-à-vis* exporters of industrial products. During the 1940s, Manoilescu's theory was outlined in articles published in the periodical *Economia*, a regular publication of the University of Chile.

A fourth theoretical influence on Prebisch highlighted by Love (1996) is Kindleberger. Prebisch cited him in the seminar presented in Mexico in 1944. He was initially reticent about Kindleberger's thesis, which argued that the United States suffered from a persistent commercial imbalance with its trade partners due to differences in the elasticities of traded products. Over time, however, Prebisch became convinced of the validity of this thesis.

Finally, the influence of the Chilean-German economist Ernst Wageman cannot be ruled out. Wageman, who took over the direction of a research institute in Nazi Germany at the end of the 1930s, studied the economic cycles of the international movements of capital, and used the terms 'centre' and 'periphery' to describe the fluctuations of these cycles. Hodara (1987) suggests that the theoretical affinity between Prebisch and Manoilescu can be attributed to the intervention of Wageman. Love (1996), though, highlights important differences in the meanings each gives to the terms 'centre' and 'periphery'.

■

The Deterioration of the Terms of Trade Seen through a Metaphor

Perelman and Tyteca's treatise on rhetoric (1969) highlights the importance of metaphors as elements of argumentation, describing them as mechanisms that facilitate the development and extension of thought. The invisible hand, elasticity, equilibrium, utility, the auctioneer, and economic man are just some of the many metaphors that populate economic discourse. Although they help to extend the meaning of a concept and illuminate new areas of investigation, the use of metaphors also has its disadvantages, since, at the same time, they can obscure other areas of investigation (Henderson 1994).

Latin America owes Raúl Prebisch the centre–periphery metaphor, the pillar on which the theoretical reflection of CEPAL was built.[4] According to Dosman (2001), the author used it for the first time in 1921, to refer to the internal situation of Argentina. In 1945 it was adapted for the use that would come to be consecrated: emphasizing the dualism existing in international trade. Launched in the *Manifesto*, this metaphor came to be widely used in Cepalino discourse, and later to influence the theory of dependency.[5]

In the first two documents analyzed, the centre–periphery metaphor is crucial to Prebisch's argumentation. It appears on the first page of the *Manifesto*, with the author situating Latin America on the 'periphery' of the world economy, a location that reserves to it the task of producing food and raw materials for the centre countries. Similarly, the expression 'peripheral countries' is created on the first page of *Estúdio 49*. The argumentation that follows it expands the metaphor, identifying the increase in the distance between the two poles of the world economy. The centre countries appropriate the fruits of their own technological progress, in the form of greater profits for employers and higher salaries for workers.

By adopting a spatial metaphor, Prebisch relocates the responsibility for underdevelopment from the domestic conditions of Latin America to the 'centre' of the international economic system. More precisely, as Furtado (1985) explains, he sees in the international division of labour the source of this unequal model. The replacement of Great Britain by the United States as the world's economic centre of gravity caused additional difficulties for Latin American countries, according to Prebisch. On the one hand, the prices of industrial products did not fall in a similar rhythm to the increase in productivity. On the other, the import coefficient of the United States, historically inferior to that of Great Britain, had been diminishing since 1929, as a result of the adoption of protectionist policies (Prebisch 2001: 60–2).[6]

In the fourth chapter of *Estúdio 49*, Prebisch's central proposition is reinforced: the complexity of the industrialization process has increased substantially during the century, thereby creating a growing income and productivity gap between centre countries and those of the periphery. The economic cycle tends to perpetuate this gap, since in the declining phases the countries that export raw materials incur losses that outweigh their profits in the economic expansion phase. Moreover, given the conditions of the actual process of industrialization, the newly adopted technology imposes high capital coefficients per labour unit, demanding a level of savings incompatible with the *per capita* income of the peripheral countries (CEPAL 1949: 66).

With all of this, and despite referring to a 'dramatic contrast' between centre and periphery, Prebisch's discourse cannot be called anti-imperialist. This 'sin' cannot be attributed to CEPAL, Furtado states (1991: 34), because Prebisch limited himself to verifying the existence of a centre–periphery structure, without focusing on its historical origin, and, principally, without applying the label 'imperialist' to the countries that benefited from it.

An important by-product of the centre–periphery metaphor is the emphasis given to Latin American identity. The very creation of CEPAL expressed the ideal of the integration of the continent, a dream pursued by Simón Bolívar, but never achieved in fact. Furtado (1985: 75) described Prebisch's enthusiasm when he realized, as his assistants produced the statistical tables and charts for *Estúdio 49*, how important it was to see Latin America as a whole. Inspired at the beginning by Argentinian experience, Prebisch's ideas were now confronted by a more encompassing reality, 'whose image began to be sketched in front of us, the discoverers of a new Latin America'. Here, in just a few words, the role carried out by CEPAL in regard to the centralization of ideas and thought is described. It is as if Latin America only now began to exist: coming together under the same banner, the different countries had at last become aware of their geographic proximity, their common colonial heritage, and the similarity of their problems.

It should be added that, like any condensed analogy, Prebisch's metaphor is reductionist, and tends to overlook the internal differences within the two blocs, centre and periphery. While turning the lens to look at the asymmetry of the relations of international trade, Prebisch minimized the presence and the importance of conflicts on the periphery of the system, such as those that arose out of the dispute between industrial employers and the agrarian elite. Also obscured was the possibility of conflict between different regions or countries in Latin America. In addition, the possibility that any particular country could adopt its own trajectory for development is summarily ruled out. As FitzGerald argues, CEPAL 'logically' adopted a regional point of view, according to which the economic growth of isolated countries could not be interpreted as the increase in the welfare of the region as a whole (1998: 49).

Prebisch actually made some specific observations on some countries, such as Argentina, Venezuela, and Cuba, but did not discuss the viability of isolated growth trajectories. In *Estúdio 49* (CEPAL 1949: 9, 84–7), for example, he comments on Venezuela and Cuba, which had registered a significant increase in imports in the period analyzed. He argues, though, that the income obtained was insufficient to meet the import needs determined by industrial development, as well as being subject to large oscillations. In a similar manner, in *Estúdio 50* (CEPAL 1952: 14) the author allows the possibility of a small producer country reducing the price of its products to increase its participation in international trade – a localized solution, he hurriedly clarifies, that cannot resolve the problems of the continent as a whole.

■

Planned Development

The idea of planned development dominates the introductory chapter in *Estúdio 50*, entitled 'Problemas teóricos e práticos do crescimento econômico' [Theoretical and practical problems of economic growth]. The document uses words such as 'programme' and 'programmatic' in referring to the development of Latin America; this development process would necessarily be organized in stages, to guarantee the achievement of targets.[7]

The text presented to the assembly in Mexico City in 1951 has a very different style from that in documents previously produced by CEPAL. The evolution can be seen as follows: *Estúdio 48*, written before Prebisch joined, is an essentially descriptive work, little more than a set of statistical tables; the *Manifesto* is an engaged text, in which Prebisch introduces the centre–periphery metaphor and passionately defends the need to resolve the problems of peripheral countries; *Estúdio 49* is a document written for a specialized audience, which first sets out classical and neoclassical trade theories, and then defends a model of development based on import substitution; in turn, *Estúdio 50* is a *sui generis* work, in which CEPAL defends the need for a deliberate intervention in the economic development process of Latin America.

In contrast to the other documents, in *Estúdio 50* there are no stylistic traits announcing the presence of Prebisch. It is more of a collectively authored text, written by the team under his command. The centre–periphery metaphor is visibly watered down. Instead of grouping countries according to the spatial metaphor, the text prefers to speak of countries 'more' and 'less' developed. At one point, *Estúdio 50* apologizes for using the latter measure, terming it 'schematic'.[8] Another difference is that the theoretical concern characteristic of *Estúdio 49* is no longer present; in effect, discussion in *Estúdio 50* starts where *Estúdio 49* finishes.

The principal thesis of *Estúdio 50* is that development can no longer be the spontaneous process it was in the nineteenth century. To carry it out, a firm and defined policy is needed. The occurrence of two world wars and a serious economic crisis (that of 1929) contributed to the intensification of the process and building the ideas related to development. The time had now arrived to give precision and consistency to these ideas, advocated by economists and government leaders, 'since the principles which can guide practical action can emerge from them, in other words, the deliberate purpose of guiding facts to the fulfilment of the fundamental design of economic development' (CEPAL 1952: 2).

The new approach to development differed from previous approaches in its objective, extent and form. Development had to be concerned with the growth of internal production, aimed at increasing the level of consumption of the masses. This implied extending technological progress, until then restricted to export activities, to all areas of the economy, including the primary sector, where much of the economically active population was concentrated. On the other hand, the adoption of modern technology should be done with care, to guarantee that workers displaced by it could find new jobs (CEPAL 1952: 5). They could be absorbed by the growth of employment in the industrial sector and in activities associated with it (CEPAL 1952: 12).

For the income of the less-developed countries to grow, a selective policy had to be adopted regarding the range of imports. *Estúdio 50* provided a critique of observed consumption patterns in these countries, focusing especially on the consumption of luxury goods. While opening imports to permit inflows of capital goods was crucial, luxury consumption goods accounted for too heavy a share of imports and had to be discouraged.

All this implied an enormous capitalization effort. One of the main questions raised by *Estúdio 50*, revealing its pragmatic character, is the problem of how this capital would be found. A large part of it would come from internal savings; however, internal savings would not be sufficient, imposing the need for complementary foreign investment. If the United States was truly concerned about economic development in Latin America, as its representatives officially stated, it should provide practical proof and lend needed resources to private Latin American employers (CEPAL 1952: 1).

An investment programme was, therefore, necessary to guarantee the efficient use of both internal resources and those coming from loans (CEPAL 1952: 8). The state had to assume an important role in this process, if not as the principal actor, then, at least, as an indispensable coordinator and cooperator. It was up to the state to create the conditions favourable to private investment: the state had to select targets and ensure they were met, either directly as an employer or indirectly through customs or fiscal policies, through price control, or through direct regulation of production (CEPAL 1952: 27). A development programme would be at the same time a forecast, projected onto the economic horizon of the countries adopting it (CEPAL 1952: 9).

The overall idea of Estúdio 50 was thus 'to leave aside the general considerations' and 'to discuss the concrete elements of a development programme' (CEPAL 1952: 26). The fourth and last chapter of the document detailed the successive stages of this programme, including a systematic accounting of results. For certain, 'a certain degree of flexibility' was permitted in executing this programme, which, like any plan, would be subject to continual changes (CEPAL 1952: 41).

■

Empirical Data and Cepalino Discourse

Rhetoric manuals, such as that of Perelman and Tyteca (1969), teach us that the credibility of a discourse is directly associated with the capacity that its author demonstrates in the selection and treatment of the data presented in favour of his hypothesis. The adaptation of the discourse to the audience is more complex when the orator directs it to a universal audience, as in the case of scientists. The universal audience distinguishes itself by an important concern, growing over time, with the measurement of facts (Perelman and Tyteca 1969: 102). To persuade this type of audience, the orator resorts to tables, charts and other information which provide evidence regarding the propositions advocated. Not only are the data chosen to support a discourse important; so too is the interpretation of these data by the author of a written or oral text. The author selects the data that he judges relevant; this choice endows these data with 'presence'. Deliberate suppression of presence is equally noteworthy.

A notable characteristic of CEPAL's discourse, evident from the outset, is the concern with presenting empirical data capable of grounding the propositions. It is important to understand that this is not a routine practice in the texts produced in the middle of the twentieth century on Latin American reality, even those directed at an academic public. The style was essay-based, without any systematic concern with the handling of statistics for the purpose of diagnosing problems and suggesting adequate solutions.

Not by chance, CEPAL's actions promoted a rupture in this discursive model. It was a birthmark, consistent with the philosophy of the UN's regional commissions. Even before the entrance of Prebisch, CEPAL's technical corps was concerned with collecting statistical data about Latin America, to compensate for chronic deficiencies in this area. The data related to foreign trade, production, income, currency, employment, and other economic and social variables. It was not an easy task, not just because so little information was available, but because the available information was dispersed and of low quality. There were no reliable statistical series; many countries did not have minimal systems of national accounting. There were countries whose populations were unknown (Salviano Jr 1993: 87)!

Prebisch was clearly aware of this state of near calamity. During his management of the Argentinian Central Bank, according to Dosman (2001: 91), he became used to the preparation of annual reports on the performance of the economy, whose production required the collection of statistical series organized in a systematic manner. Once in CEPAL, he shared with his team the conviction that the availability of statistical material was crucial to support his conclusions in the doctrinal field and translate them for the directives of economic policy. Hodara (1987: 30), amongst others, praises the revolutionary role of Prebisch in pushing forward data-based research in a region where it was badly needed.

The *Manifesto* contains two tables and five charts, most of which were based on official UN statistics. They covered, roughly speaking, the first half of the twentieth century. The introductory essay to *Estúdio 49* is even richer in this respect: there are in all twelve tables and six charts, the majority in the second chapter, presented as evidence that Latin America was losing its import capacity. *Estúdio 50* mentioned the tendencies described in the previous document, and added two scenarios: the first relates invested capital to the labour absorbed in different stages of the process of introducing technological innovations; the second evaluates the impact of the growth of *per capita* productivity on the increase in the occupation rate. The last two documents also contained an extensive statistical appendix for the different Latin American countries.

None of this empirical work can be compared in a straightforward way with the econometric apparatus of current academic articles: no models, no sophisticated statistical tests, no complicated algebraic formulae.[9] In the body of the text, only tables containing absolute values, price and other indices, percentages, averages, coefficients; the text also contains a smaller number of charts portraying tendencies observed in some simulations. On the one hand, there is nothing comparable to the style until then predominant in Latin America; on the other hand, these empirical sections are not very different from the style of academic publications in the middle of the twentieth century (McCloskey 1985: 4).

Bielchowsky (1998: 29) also recognizes that the richness of the Cepalino method was exactly in this fertile interaction between an original theoretical formulation and the inductive method. This is explicit in the documents analyzed here, especially in *Estúdio 50*. The implementation of the systematic collection of statistics was crucial for the planning of development. As Bielchowsky observes, the preparation of a plan presupposes a minimum of macroeconomic foresight.

In the field of national accounts, the situation was much better than in 1948, when CEPAL was created. Nonetheless, the data about employment were clearly insufficient. *Estúdio 50* complains about the 'lamentable lack of statistics about the composition of the economically active population and its movements' (CEPAL 1952: 39), which made it even more difficult to develop economic activities compatible with the available labour. Latin American governments, who were supposed to perform a strategic role in leading the intended changes, did not have reliable information about the movement of the population in the labour market or its inter-sectorial composition, which obliged them to rely on 'conjectural statistics'. One of the document's main recommendations, therefore, was to conduct periodic research on the labour market.

Another reason for the heavily statistical character of CEPAL documents is that this approach would help win the approval of its audience (Salviano Jr 1993; Bianchi 2002). The potential readership of *Estúdios Económicos* included the regular public of UN publications, readers familiar with economic theory and accustomed to reading texts with tables, charts, and descriptive statistics. Prebisch indicates his awareness of this audience in the final part of the *Manifesto* when he complains about the precariousness of the information available about the Latin American economy. The extended preparatory work of *Estúdio 49* left him more confident, since it responded to the need for analysis supported by a 'careful investigation of the facts' (CEPAL 1949: 84).

At the same time, careful investigation did not mean completely even-handed analysis. As Bianchi and Salviano Jr (1999) point out, Prebisch confers 'presence' on data about foreign trade, growth rates, gold reserves, and other monetary variables, while leaving other data series half-obscured. In particular, country-by-country data highlighting distinctive characteristics of various Latin American countries are presented but not emphasized. The introduction in particular highlights similarities, not differences, among these nations' experience.

Seen through contemporary eyes, the principal statistical omission involved demographic data. CEPAL was not indifferent to the seriousness of the problems resulting from the population growth of Latin America. The question, practically ignored in the *Manifesto*, is prominent in two other documents, which point out the existence of a surplus of labour in the labour market, attributed to two factors: (1) the high rate of population growth (CEPAL 1949: 50; CEPAL 1952: 6); and (2) the technological modernization of agriculture (Prebisch 2001: 80; CEPAL 1949: 50, 68). The latter, in turn, leads to rural exodus and the resulting urbanization, worsening unemployment, (CEPAL 1952: 31). *Estúdio 50* goes on to add that the high rates of demographic growth in Latin America are due to the diffusion of hygienic and sanitary practices that have lessened the mortality rate, especially infant mortality, 'without having been followed by other reactions – much slower, of course – which could bring about the fall in birth rate' (CEPAL 1952: 6). So high fertility rates were accompanied by a fall in mortality, resulting in the intense natural growth of the population. The general scenario also involved an accelerated process of urbanization, creating problems of employment analyzed closely in these CEPAL documents.

Despite making reference to the negative impact of a high population growth on employment and income, the *Estúdios* see this as an immovable barrier: the high rate of demographic growth exists; the question is knowing how to deal with its negative consequences. There is no mention of the possibility of a birth control policy, for example, through explicit governmental policy. It should be mentioned that in the middle of the twentieth century the possibility of promoting a birth control policy in countries with Catholic majorities was nil; the passage from *Estúdio 50* cited above appears to express this in a veiled way. In addition to restrictions of a religious and cultural nature, at the time there were no secure birth control methods: the 'pill' was an invention of the 1960s.

■

The Heterodox Character of Cepalino Discourse

Although the style of the two documents is very different (Bianchi 2002), the *Manifesto* and *Estúdio 49* are equally critical of the conclusions of traditional economic theory regarding international trade in goods and services. Both documents recommend the revision of this theory to account for conditions in the peripheral economies. This critical perspective was evident from the very first page of the *Manifesto*, where Prebisch questioned the theoretical superiority of the doctrine that preached the virtue of the international division of labour, alleging that it involved 'a premise terminally denied by the facts' (Prebisch 2001: 47). The argument reappears in various passages, in which the author states that the mistake of classical theory is to treat features that apply only to the industrialized countries as general characteristics of all nations. Prebisch insists on this basis that this theory does not apply to the periphery of the world economic system (Prebisch 2001: 47–8).

Prebisch is caustic about economic theory, to which he imputes the defect of reflecting the judgemental standards of the countries of the centre. Theory constructed in this way is incapable of supplying adequate solutions for the peripheral countries (Prebisch 2001: 48). Two pages later, he repeats the note of caution regarding 'dogmatic generalizations' and warns that a 'good doctrine' for Latin America has not yet been formulated. Such an 'ample reformulation' of economic theory demands an active educational policy, which would privilege the training of economists 'capable of comprehending the new manifestations of reality, foreseeing problems and collaborating in the search for solutions' (Prebisch 2001: 94). However, it was not the case of constructing a new theory from zero. The effort at revision should not be animated by a spirit of 'exclusive particularism', but should instead be based on a 'solid knowledge of the theories drawn up in the large countries, with their stream of common truths' (Prebisch 2001: 54).

This critical approach is maintained in *Estúdio 49*, although with a less polemical approach. Prebisch begins by making a respectful outline of the arguments in the classical and neoclassical economic theories of inter-national trade, which he brings together under the title 'classical'.[10] This theory, he said, has it merits but is fundamentally static, both as originally conceptualized (referring here to Ricardian theory) and as later modified (Hecksher-Ohlin's and Samuelson's revisions thereof).

Interestingly, the classic articles of Samuelson on the equalization of the prices of factors were published in the June 1948 and June 1949 numbers of the *Economic Journal* – that is, immediately before the publication of *Estúdio 49*. Although Prebisch makes no explicit reference to these – detailed bibliographic references were not part of the writings of that time – he demonstrates his knowledge of their content in describing how marginal productivity of the factors of production tends to equalize within all countries (CEPAL 1949: 69–71). In this passage, the author uses typically neoclassical assertions, such as the complete mobility of factors of production and the equalization of factor prices. These references show his familiarity with economic literature produced abroad.

Prebisch argues that classical theory limits itself to observing that all disturbances generate movement from one situation of equilibrium to another, without attributing proper importance to the time consumed by such transitions. Now, the gap between theoretical thinking and the real economy has a special significance for Latin America, whose development requires 'a serious effort of theoretical revision' (CEPAL 1949: 59–60). The criticism is made again in various parts of the text. The current economic world, Prebisch reiterates, differs profoundly from the abstract world of classical theory. In the international sphere, the free play of market forces is powerless to equalize the income of countries who participate in trade. The complete mobility of factors of production is not a purely economic phenomenon, and depends on overcoming obstacles that cannot always be avoided (CEPAL 1949: 84). In the countries of the centre, where trade unions exercise vigorous pressure on enterprises, increases in productivity invariably lead to increases in wages, impeding the reduction of export prices. This trade union strength is not found on the periphery (nor, indeed, is it today, in virtually any nation).

In closing the introduction to *Estúdio 49*, Prebisch again justifies the intellectual effort of discussing classical (and neoclassical) trade theory. Here his argument moves to the theoretical contribution of this effort for an economist interested in the specificities of peripheral economies. The time devoted to the task of looking back at theoretical advances is not wasted, he asserts, since theory constructed in this way acquires a universal significance; and these general results, when properly applied, can illuminate efforts at theorizing special cases (CEPAL 1949: 84). In the 1940s, the idea that there is something fundamentally different about undeveloped economies was still a novelty (Love 1980). The concept of underdevelopment itself would only emerge a while later, as the fruit of the theoretical reflection carried out by CEPAL.

If *Estúdio 50* did not return to an explicit critique of economic theory, it did not disassociate itself from the theoretical critique that had already been advanced. The preparatory work for the Mexico conference imposed a different agenda on the CEPAL team; their principal concern, as noted, was to plan development. Given the pragmatic nature of this third document, reiterating theoretical criticisms was not a priority. The critiques had been registered; the mission now was concretely to carry out the strategy which reflection had indicated was suited to Latin America.

Regarding this agenda, *Estúdio 50* highlighted the importance of the creation of professionals in Latin America. In particular, it reiterated the need to train economists for the tasks of economic development, based on the teachings of conventional theory or, more precisely, 'on the scientific knowledge in economic material prepared in the large centers' (CEPAL 1952: 43). The task that CEPAL took on was the organization of postgraduate courses that would provide the technical competence necessary for formulating theory appropriate to the diagnosis of Latin American conditions and the solution of Latin American problems.

■

The Committed Character and Enthusiastic Reception of Cepalino Thought

Understanding how economic ideas evolve requires taking into account their social context — the era and social environment in which they emerge. The success or failure of a particular discourse and its dissemination depends centrally on this context. Economic theories are not rejected because they are refuted in empirical tests, or because they are badly written; and while empirical evidence and clear argumentation are crucial components for successful economic theories (Backhouse 1995: 218), these elements are not sufficient. For a document to sway opinion, what is decisive is that its argument be communicated at the opportune moment. For then it deals with current anxieties, and meets a public that responds to its arguments and identifies with its message.

This hypothesis is perhaps most defensible for economic arguments that have been written with the intention of affecting policies and reaching a general public. As such, it is pertinent to the case analyzed here; for the spirit that animated the theses of CEPAL at its inception was aimed at going well beyond merely provoking an intellectual reaction. Prebisch and his team were not just interested in diagnosing the problems of Latin America, collecting statistics about its economy, highlighting the deficiencies of orthodox economic theory, or defending the formation of economists for the continent. All this was important primarily because it opened the way for the practical solution of the problems identified. This is the aspect of Cepalino thought highlighted by various critics and commentators who emphasized its 'committed' nature and the 'militant' personality of Prebisch, compared by Hodara (1987) to an 'armed prophet'.

This mobilizing intention, the fusing together of theoretical reflection and political recommendations, is one of the hallmarks of Cepalino thought. Milberg (1996) calls attention to the fact that writings in international economics frequently draw political implications from theoretical analysis. In the case of the Cepalino writings analyzed here, this recurrent pattern is converted into a clear engagement. Prebisch's professional profile was decisive for this: as Jaguaribe says (1998: 357), he was a man of thought and action, innovative in the theoretical sphere while also fertile in the practical.

What were the concrete repercussions of CEPAL's discourse? The writings of Prebisch and his team were greeted with enthusiasm by their Latin American audience(s), but with with scepticism and opposition by their foreign public(s). To understand these binary reactions, it is opportune to return to the reflections of Sikkink (1988) on Prebisch's contradictory image in Argentina. How, the author asks, can the 'paradox of the multiple public images' of Raúl Prebisch be explained?[11] Sikkink (1988: 92) answers this question by arguing that new ideas never maintain the same significance in all contexts, but instead vary according to the political and ideological contexts into which they are inserted. This response encompasses Prebisch's later Latin American and overseas audiences, who also reacted very differently to the same writings. Ideas make history, but, at the same time, they express the tensions of history itself.

For his Latin American audience – made up primarily of employers, businessmen and political leaders – the proposals of Prebisch and CEPAL happened at exactly the right moment, giving support to economic policies that were already under way. As Bielchowsky (1998: 25) has noted, there was a theoretical vacuum for the justification of the continent's industrialization, which the CEPAL documents could fill. In Brazil, the Cepalino theses were widely accepted by the business elites. In 1950, the Confederação Nacional da Indústria [the Brazilian National Confederation of Industry] invited Prebisch and Furtado to speak to employers, and to visit factories and technological research institutes. This affirmation was crucial because of the weight of Brazil in the continent as a whole.

Burger (1999) registers the moment of extraordinary optimism caused by the creation of CEPAL, shortly after the end of the Second World War. The organization's founding resulted in a process which the author characterizes as corresponding to the creation of 'a powerful ideological canon'. From an institutional perspective, this process was decisive for the academic and professional formation of new generations throughout Latin America, as was the wish of Prebisch. The effort put into the creation of CEPAL and the production of documents with a doctrinaire character gave its readers a sense of identification with the continent, in relation to which a strong feeling of solidarity was constructed.

CEPAL exhibited what Hirschman (1961) defined as a 'cohesive personality', which generated loyalty in its technical team. Moreover, a natural elective affinity emerged between the tastes of the Latin American audience and the Cepalino perspective (Hodara 1987). This reinforced initiatives originating in the concrete interests of social groups willing to roll up their shirtsleeves to confront the practical problems of development. These groups represented the new Latin American middle class, who identified with the process of industrialization, and whose political and economic power was ready to outstrip that of the traditional agrarian elites.

For its Latin American audience, then, CEPAL saw itself as the bearer not just of a new thesis, but of a new 'potential cause', as Dosman (2001: 102) aptly puts its. Prebisch himself admitted, in an interview given later in his career, that the Cepalino ideas 'were in the air', ready to sprout at that moment (Sikkink 1988: 108). The merit of Prebisch and his team lay in demonstrating that these ideas were defensible in theoretical terms and thus could plausibly support successful economic policies. At the end of the 1950s, a 'CEPAL consensus' was formed in Latin America, corresponding to the wide-ranging acceptance of the agenda that CEPAL had defined. It was in this context that the import substitution process, which was already under way in countries such as Brazil, Argentina and Chile, reached a new level, becoming the predominant development strategy on the continent.

However, the adoption of Cepalino policies did not occur without some resistance on the part of lay and academic readers in Latin American society. One of the first opponents was Eugenio Gudin (1952), who sprang quickly to the defence of neoclassical economic theory.[12] He organized a series of seminars in the Fundação Getúlio Vargas in Rio de Janeiro, inviting Jacob Viner as the principal speaker. Added to this effort was the *Revista Brasileira de Economia* (Brazilian Economic Review), published by the same institution: while in 1949 it published Furtado's translation of the *Manifesto*, in the years immediately following (perhaps as compensation for the space that had been given to the Cepalinos) it published articles by Baldwin, Bernstein and Gudin himself; all these rebuttals were critical of the thesis of the deterioration of the terms of trade.

The opposition of names such as Gudin was not sufficient, however, to halt the industrialization movement under way in important Latin American countries, or to inhibit the spread of Cepalino ideas. In this respect, Hirschman's testimony is especially noteworthy, as he was an eyewitness on the continent in the 1950s and 1960s:

The voice of CEPAL is, without a doubt, that which is most heard in debates about Latin American economic problems, and there can be little doubt that their visions are representative of a large part of the new middle class. (Hirschman 1961: 291)

■

Negative Reactions

If Latin America generally gave Cepalino theses a very favourable reception, the same did not occur outside the continent. There the attitudes of readers varied from indifference to open opposition. Certainly, there is no reason to expect theses reflecting Latin American interests to draw a positive reaction from foreign audiences. As Perelman and Tyteca (1969: 76) note, these theses had low persuasive capacity at least in part because they were associated with local aspirations in Latin America. This helped establish a negative predisposition in foreign audiences, who gave a hostile reception to Cepalino writings and critiques of conventional theory; see the discussions of this reception by Dadone and Di Marco (1972), Dosman (2001), Hirschman (1961), Pollock (1978 and 1987) and Street (1987), amongst others. The intercontinental communion of minds needed to permit Cepalino discourses to be more persuasive overseas did not occur.

According to Pollock (1978: 66), the reaction to the Cepalino doctrine – or the Prebisch–Singer thesis, as the author prefers to put it – in the United States varied between two extremes: it was considered naïve by many, and heretical and dangerous by others, so much so that relations between the United States and Latin America became increasingly difficult during the 1950s. These negative repercussions were observed in various circles: universities, business circles, governmental organizations and international organizations. In business circles, which saw the Latin-American consumer goods industry as a potential rival receiving the benefits of protectionist mechanisms, Prebisch was even accused of manipulating his ideas to benefit his personal interests (Pollock 1978: 67).

In the US government and in international organizations, the documents created a climate described by Dosman (2001) as one 'of consternation'. It is not difficult to understand this climate, since the articulation of CEPAL had created a forum in which Latin American governments might jointly pressure the United States to change its foreign policy. In Pollock's picturesque expression (1987: 368), it was as if CEPAL was waving a red cape in front of the American bull. The Cepalino documents were interpreted as a means of pressuring the United States to transfer resources to Latin America, just when the US was busy with European and Asian reconstruction.

Street (1987: 652) also highlights the critical reaction of US government representatives, as well as those of specialists at the International Monetary Fund. According to him, these critics questioned the Cepalino policy conclusions, which suggested that the free operation of market forces was unable to guarantee a fair distribution of the benefits of trade among all its participants.

In the academic world, the dissemination of Cepalino theses led to an organized counter-offensive, including the seminars led by Gudin. Furtado (1985) describes a powerful 'crusade of ideological purification' in reaction to the Cepalino theses. Two English-speaking economists, Dadone and Di Marco (1972: 29), did not spare their criticism in a collection written in homage to Raúl Prebisch. On the one hand, a small circle of economists declared themselves willing to accept Prebisch's ideas, at the cost of modifying them and expanding his argument. On the other hand, the large majority severely criticized Cepalino discourse as a whole, calling attention to numerous theoretical deficiencies and to inadequacies in the treatment of empirical data.[13]

The empirical basis of Prebish's work was the focus of most criticisms from specialist audiences. Many initial critics, including Jacob Viner (1952), argued that the estimates of the terms of exchange in international trade were suspect. For example, Haberler (1950 and 1988) argued that CEPAL had resorted to inadequate empirical measures and ignored the operation of economic cycles. He added that neoclassical theory does not profess that free trade results in the equalization of income between countries – it only says that all countries are better served by having trade than by forgoing it.[14] Baldwin (1952) highlighted the difficulty in finding reliable statistics on foreign trade and working with them accurately, due to the large range of commercial goods, quality improvements, and reduced transport costs. Therefore, the thesis of the deterioration of the terms of trade could not be demonstrated in a conclusive form. Prebisch's empirical evidence drew sustained fire over the course of several years from a list of critics that included Ellsworth (1956), Meier (1958), and Morgan (1959). For example, Morgan (1959) criticized the argument that wage pressure generated by trade unions in industrialized countries was the source of the high prices of goods exported to Latin America.

Prebisch's assertions also faced criticism of a theoretical nature. For example, Flanders (1964) argued that Prebisch, in extolling the virtues of protectionism as a solution to terms of trade problems, was mistakenly applying the theorem of the equalization of factor prices. In his critic's view, Prebisch generalized inappropriately from a model based on two countries, two factors and two goods. He went on to suggest that population growth, neglected by CEPAL, was the real cause of the reduction in Latin America's *per capita* export capacity (Flanders 1964: 14). Even a sympathetic reader such as Baer suggested that while CEPAL's theory 'has some validity', it 'was never fully evaluated' (Baer 1962: 169) and thus 'is not a threat to the classical theory of international trade' (*ibid.*: 180).[15]

If the reaction to the first two documents was adverse, the hostile chorus grew more vociferous with the release of *Estúdio 50*, which advocated planned development, albeit with a democratic character. The thesis was greeted with a hail of criticism due to its geopolitical implications. After all, Latin America was traditionally a foreign-policy ally of the United States. A Cold War climate had overtaken the world after the Korean War began in 1950, feeding belief in a world divided into opposing capitalist and communist blocs. As Pollock (1987: 367–8) has observed, CEPAL's first ten years correspond closely with the Eisenhower government in the United States (1952–60), a period characterized by the prevalence of Cold War ideologies. The idea of a strong government overseeing business was associated with a centralist theoretical imprint, and thus had to be repudiated. As noted by Furtado (1985: 152), the United States needed to adopt a set of policies able to contain the spreading force of the Soviet Union. It was thus especially anxious to impede any possible change in Latin America's alignment.

■

Conclusion

More than half a century has elapsed since the documents analyzed here appeared in public for the first time and set out the principal Cepalino theses. Did the recommended import substitution industrialization policies work? If 'work' means significantly pushing forward *per capita* product over a pro-longed period, the answer has to be positive. After all, Latin America went through a period of continuous growth in industrial product, gross internal product and *per capita* revenue in the three decades following the Second World War (United Nations/CEPAL 1979). Between 1950 and 1980, the gross internal product of the continent grew at an annual rate of 5.5 per cent, better than the world average. Industrial product multiplied by six in the same interval of time, growing at rates much higher than the population growth rate of 2.8 per cent a year. The growth of industrial product per inhabitant averaged 2.6 per cent.

However, if 'working' means solving the economic problems of the region, significantly reducing poverty and lessening the concentration of income, the response is negative. Latin America, in fact, became less poor in the second half of the twentieth century, but its indices of inequality, already com-paratively high in 1950, remained high during the entire 1950–80 period (Hofman 2001). And price inflation, an object of concern to CEPAL in the three documents analyzed here, accelerated at an unprecedented rate towards the end of the century. Latin America also had to contend with growing foreign debt and a swollen, inefficient, and corrupt state sector. The actual integration of the continent, a dream of CEPAL from its very beginning, continues at a snail's pace.

On the other side of the world, a new model of development was tested, beginning in the 1980s, with theoretical foundations and principles very different from those characterizing the import substitution model. The experience of East Asia showed that a developing country's domestic market did not need to absorb the additional product generated by industrialization; on the contrary, it could guide its economy towards the production of export commodities. Analysts such as Krueger (1997) consider that this strategy demonstrates in practice the mistake of believing import substitution to be the only path to development.[16]

In time, the Asian model of externally orientated development lost its impetus. This model, which benefited from the expansion of world trade, is now regarded with reservations even by defenders such as Bruton (1998: 304), who speak of repairs and qualifications. The truth is that there is no magic formula capable of resolving, in theory and practice, the serious problems of imbalance between (and within) the different countries in the contemporary world.

The primary purpose of this essay was not to evaluate the correctness of the Cepalino theses regarding theory or policy. More modestly, I have tried to show how a well-articulated, competent and opportune discourse won the sympathy of Latin American audiences and served as the theoretical backdrop to the ongoing process of development. Fonseca (2000) is right in emphasizing that the great achievement of CEPAL was to systematize, in a manner comprehensible to scientific canons, theses that were already being disseminated in Latin America in a more fragmented manner. In its time, CEPAL collaborated in meeting the challenge put forward by this collection, which is to 'reimagine' growth – what it is, what it means, how to achieve it, and how to convince different audiences of its importance. Prebisch and his team won space for themselves in international economic encyclopaedias; but, more important, they built what may be the last original theory conceived by Latin American economists concerned with the fate of their continent.

Bibliography

Backhouse, R. E. (1995) *Interpreting Macroeconomics*, London and New York: Routledge.

Baer, W. (1962) 'The economics of Prebisch and ECLA', *Economic Development and Cultural Change*, Vol. 10, No. 2, January.

Baldwin, R. E. (1952) 'A modificação secular das relações de troca', *Revista Brasileira de Economia*, Vol. 6, No. 3, September.

Bianchi, A. M. (2002) 'For different audiences, different arguments: economic rhetoric in the beginning of the Latin American School', *Journal of the History of Economic Thought*, Vol. 24, No. 3, September.

Bianchi, A. M. and C. Salviano Jr. (1999) 'Raúl Prebisch and the beginnings of the Latin American School of Economics', *Journal of Economic Methodology*, Vol. 6, No. 3, November.

Bielchowsky, R. (1998) 'Evolución de las ideas de la CEPAL', *Revista de la CEPAL*, extraordinary issue, October.

Bloch, H. and D. Sapsford (1997) 'Some estimates of Prebisch and Singer effects on the terms of trade between primary producers and manufacturers', *World Development*, Vol. 25, No. 11, November.

Bruton, H. (1998) 'A reconsideration of import substitution', *Journal of Economic Literature*, Vol. 36, No. 2, June.

Burger, H. (1999) *An Intellectual History of the ECLA Culture, 1948 to 1964*, Cambridge, MA: Harvard University Press.

Cardoso, F. H. and E. Faletto (1969) *Dependencia y desarrollo en América Latina*, México: Siglo Veintiuno Editores.

CEPAL (Economic Commission on Latin America and the Caribbean) (1949) *Estúdio Económico de Latin America 1949* (*Estúdio 49*), Mexico: United Nations/CEPAL.

——— (1952) 'Problemas theoreticales y practices del crecimiento económico', in *Estúdio Económico de Latin America 1950* (*Estúdio 50*), Mexico: United Nations/ CEPAL.

Cuddington, J. T. (1992) 'Long-run trends in 26 primary commodity prices – A disaggregated look at the Prebisch–Singer hypothesis', *Journal of Development Economics*, Vol. 39, No. 2, October.

Dadone, A. A. and L. E. Di Marco (1972) 'The impact of Prebisch´s ideas on modern economic analysis', in Di Marco, L. E. (ed.) *International Economics and Development: Essays in Honor of Raúl Prebisch*, New York: Academic Press.

Diakosavvas, D. and P. L. Scandizzo (1991) 'Trends in the terms of trade of primary commodities, 1900–1982: The controversy and its origins', *Economic Development and Cultural Change*, Vol. 39, No. 2, January.

Dib, D. S. (2001) 'A Controvérsia do Planejamento na Economia Brasileira: a Retórica Como Instrumento de Formação de Crenças', unpublished Masters dissertation, Faculdade de Economia, Administração e Contabilidade, Universidade de São Paulo, São Paulo, Brazil.

Dosman, E. (2001) 'Los mercados y el Estado em la evolución del 'manifiesto' de Prebisch', *Revista de la CEPAL*, Vol. 75, December.

Dutt, A. K. (1988) 'Inelastic demand for southern goods, international demonstration effects, and uneven development', *Journal of Economic Development*, Vol. 29, No. 1, June.

Ellsworth, P. T. (1956) 'The terms of trade between primary producers and industrial countries', *Interamerican Economic Affairs*, Vol. 10, No. 1, Summer.

Findlay, R. (1980) 'The terms of trade and equilibrium growth in the world economy', *American Economic Review*, Vol. 70, No. 3, June.

FitzGerald, V. (1998) 'La CEPAL y la theory de la industrialización', *Revista de la CEPAL*, extraordinary issue, October.

Flanders, M. J. (1964) 'Prebisch on protectionism: an evaluation', *Economic Journal*, Vol. 74, No. 294, June.

Fonseca, P. D. (2000) 'As origens e as vertentes formadoras do pensamento Cepalino', *Revista Brasileira de Economia*, Vol. 54, No. 3, July/September.

Frank, A. G. (1967) *Capitalism and Underdevelopment in Latin America; Historical Studies of Chile and Brazil*, New York: Monthly Review Press.

Furtado, C. (1985) *A Fantasia Organizada*, Rio de Janeiro: Paz e Terra.

——— (1987) 'Raúl Prebisch, el gran heresiarca', *Comércio Exterior*, Vol. 37, No.

5, May.

—— (1991) *Os Ares Do Mundo*, Rio de Janeiro: Paz e Terra.

Gondre, L. R. *et al.* (1945) *El Pensamiento Económico Latin American*, Mexico: Fondo de Cultura Económica.

Grilli, E. R. and M. C. Yang (1988) 'Primary commodity prices, manufactured goods prices, and the terms of trade of developing countries: What the long run shows', *The World Bank Economic Review*, Vol. 2, No. 1, January.

Gudin, E. (1952) 'O caso das nações subdesenvolvidas', *Revista Brasileira de Economia*, Ano/Year 6, No. 3, September.

Haberler, G. (1950) 'Some problems in the pure theory of international trade', *The Economic Journal*, Vol. 60, No. 238, June.

—— (1988) *International Trade and Economic Development*, San Francisco: International Center for Economic Growth and ICS Press.

Henderson, W. (1994) 'Metaphor and Economics', in Backhouse, R. E. (ed.), *New Directions in Economic Methodology*, London and New York: Routledge.

Hirschman, A. (1961) 'Ideologies of Economic Development in Latin America', in Hirschman, A. (ed.), *Latin American Issues: Essays and Comments*, New York: Twentieth Century Foundation.

Hodara, J. (1987) 'Orígenes de la CEPAL', *Comércio Exterior*, Vol. 37, No. 5, May.

Hofman, A. A. (2001) 'Long run economic development in Latin America in comparative perspective: proximate and ultimate causes', *Macroeconomía del Desarrollo*, Vol. 8, December.

Jaguaribe, H. (1987) 'Raúl Prebisch: la renovación permanente de su pensamiento crítico', *Comércio Exterior*, Vol. 37, No. 5, May.

Kindleberger, C. (1958) 'The terms of trade and economic development', *Review of Economics and Statistics*, Vol. 40, No. 1, Part 2, February.

Krueger, A. (1997) 'Trade policy and economic development: How we learn', *American Economic Review*, Vol. 87, No. 1, March.

Love, J. (1980) 'Raul Prebisch and the origins of the doctrine of unequal exchange', *Latin American Research Review*, Vol. 15, No. 3, 1980.

—— (1996) *Crafting the Third World: Theorizing Underdevelopment in Romania and Brazil*, California: Stanford University Press.

Manoilescu, M. (1929) *Theory of Protectionism*, Paris: M. Giard.

McCloskey, D. (1985) *The Rhetoric of Economics*, Madison: University of Wisconsin Press.

Meier, G. (1958) 'International trade and international inequality', *Oxford Economic Papers*, Vol. 10, No. 3, October.

Milberg, W. (1996) 'The rhetoric of policy relevance in international economics', *Journal of Economic Methodology*, Vol. 3, No. 2, November.

Morgan, T. (1959) 'The long-run terms of trade between agriculture and manufacturing', *Economic Development and Cultural Change*, Vol. 8, No. 1, October.

Perelman, C. and L. Olbrechts-Tyteca (1969) *The New Rhetoric: A Treatise on Argumentation*, Notre Dame: University of Notre Dame Press.

Pinto, A. and J. Knakal (1973) *América Latina y el Cambio en la Economía*

Mundial, Peru: Instituto de Estudios Peruanos.

Pollock, D. (1978) 'La actitud de los Estados Unidos hacia la CEPAL', *Revista de la CEPAL*, 2nd Semester.

—— (1987) 'Raúl Prebisch visto desde Washington: Una percepción cambiante', *Comércio Exterior*, Vol. 37, No. 5, May.

Prebisch, R. (2001) 'Desarollo económico de Latin America y sus principales problemas', *(Manifesto)*.Santiago: CEPAL, E/CN.12/0089, September.

Salviano Jr., C. (1993) 'O discurso cepalino: ensaio de análise retórica', unpublished dissertation, Faculdade de Economia, Administração e Contabilidade, Universidade de São Paulo, São Paulo, Brazil.

Sikkink, K. (1988) 'The influence of Raul Prebisch on economic policy-making in Argentina, 1950–1962', *Revista de la CEPAL*, Vol. 23, No. 2, April.

—— (1997) 'Development ideas in Latin America: Paradigm shift and the economic commission for Latin America', in Cooper, F. and P. Randall Packard (eds), *International Development and the Social Sciences*, Berkeley: University of California Press.

Singer, H. W. (1950) 'The distribution of gains between investing and borrowing countries', *American Economic Review*, Vol. 40, No. 2, May.

Singer, H., Hatti, N. and R. Tandon (eds) (1998) *Export-led versus Balanced Growth in the 1990s*, Delhi: BR Publishing Co.

Street, J. H. (1987) 'Raúl Prebisch, 1901–1986: An appreciation', *Journal of Economic Issues*, Vol. 21, No. 2, June.

Sunkel, O. (1990) 'Reflections on Latin American Development', in Dietz, J. L. and D. D. James (eds) *Progress toward Development in Latin America*, Boulder: Lynne Rienner Publishers, Inc.

United Nations/CEPAL (1979) 'Latin America en el umbral de los años 80', Santiago: CEPAL-Ilpes, November.

Viner, J. (1952) *International Trade and Economic Development*, Glencoe: The Free Press.

Ziesemer, T. (1998) 'A history of economic theorizing on the Prebisch Singer thesis', in Glombowski, J. *et al. History of Continental Economic Thought*, Marburg: Metropolis Verlag.

Notes

1 This chapter was prepared for the International Postgraduate Programme in Institutions, Organizations and Strategies, organized by CPDA/UFRRJ, IE/UFRJ and by UCAM. I would like to thank Ana Célia Castro, programme coordinator, for her support. Gary Dymski and Silvana De Paula read the chapter very carefully and made important comments.

2 This name was interpreted as an allusion to the *Communist Manifesto*, though this was not its creator's intention. The Portuguese translation by Furtado was also published in 1949 in the *Revista Brasileira de Economia*, with summaries in English and French. This translation had a greater impact than the Spanish original, which 'circulated with the slowness characteristic of official documents,' as Furtado puts it (1985: 73).

3 Fonseca (2000) questions the intellectual relationship between the two authors, saying that Prebisch's theoretical reflections should not be confused with the analytical apparatus of the General Theory, as there are differences on many substantive points. However, the influence of one author on another is certainly present, even if the views of Prebisch and Keynes do not coincide.

4 There is no clear idea about the origin of the terms centre and periphery, which Love (1980) attributes to Sombart. Hodara (1987: 389) also mentions the work of S. E. Harris and highlights the influence of Wageman, who referred to the 'economic peripheries' and visited CEPAL in 1949.

5 Also a Latin-American creation, dependency theory emphasized the 'dependent' character and the limited nature of the development opportunities available to the periphery in the world capitalist system. See Frank (1967), Cardoso and Faletto (1969), and Pinto and Knakal (1973).

6 This sort of complaint persists to the present day. Chapter 10 by Delgado and Romano in this volume discusses the recurrence of this issue in recent meetings of the World Social Forum.

7 Hodara (1987: 387) suggests that CEPAL's team may have deliberately avoided using the term 'planning', in order not to giving the text any connotations of 'socialization.' The impact of the Cold War on Cepalino thought is discussed further below.

8 This can be credited to the greater participation of Furtado, who would reveal his preference for the term 'colonial economies', in order to stress the historical dimension, in preparing this document.

9 In this respect, it is interesting to consider this empirical work in the context of McCloskey's comparison of the articles published in the *American Economic Review* during two different periods, 1931–3 and 1981–3 (McCloskey 1985: 3–5).

10 The references here are to Ricardian theory and to Samuelson's revisions of Hecksher-Ohlin, respectively.

11 Sikkink (1988) focuses on the evaluation of Prebisch by different parts of his Argentinian audience. Part of this audience, whom Sikkink identifies as being the spokespersons of the interests of the Argentinian agrarian elite, showed a certain hostility to the author.

12 Gudin showed himself to be particularly hostile to the idea that economic development should be planned, as *Estúdio 50* recommends, citing an alleged incompatibility between planning and democracy. Defending these liberal ideas, he entered into a debate with Roberto Simonsen, defender of planned industrialization. This debate was the core of the so-called 'planning controversy' analyzed by Dib (2001).

13 Dadone and Di Marco (1972: 26) use this example to illustrate the ideological nature of economic doctrines. According to these authors, most readers of Prebisch in developed countries questioned his theses, whereas most readers in underdeveloped countries supported them.

14 Haberler associated the Cepalino view with a 'neo-Marxist' approach propounding the questionable thesis that while poor countries become

progressively more impoverished, rich countries would become even richer (Haberler 1950: 32).

15 Diakosavvas and Scandizzo (1991) argue that research in this area is inevitably subject to ambiguities. Grilli and Yang (1988) present empirical results corroborating the thesis of a secular decline in the prices of goods exported by the Third World, with the exception of oil. For further details, see Block and Sapsford (1998), Cuddington (1992), Dutt (1988), Findlay (1980), Kindleberger (1958), Singer (1950 and 1998) and Ziesemer (1998).

16 For different reasons than Krueger's, Prebisch and CEPAL also came to question this model, regarding it as incapable of solving the serious social problems of Latin America. This scepticism is shared by Sunkel (1990). This change in the conception of CEPAL is described by Sikkink (1997) as 'paradigmatic'.

3

The Other Canon and Uneven Growth: The Activity-specific Elements of Economic Development

ERIK S. REINERT

Henceforth, my dear philosophers, let us be on guard against the old and dangerous myth that postulates 'a pure, will-less, painless and timeless knowing subject'. Let us take care not to get caught in the tentacles of such contradictory concepts as 'pure reason', 'absolute spirituality', and 'knowledge in itself'; these always demand that we should think of an eye that is absolutely unthinkable, an eye which cannot be allowed to be turned in any particular direction, and in which the active and interpreting forces – through which seeing becomes seeing *something* – are supposed to be lacking; these always demand of the eye a contradiction and a nonsense. The only seeing which exists is a *seeing in perspective*, a *seeing with perception*; and the more feelings we allow to get involved about an issue, the more eyes – different eyes – that we mobilize to observe one thing, the more complete will our concept of this thing, our *objectivity*, be. Would not eliminating the will ... be the same as to castrate the intellect?
– Nietzsche (1988: 365)

True enough: economists are interested in growth. The trouble is that, even by their standards, they have been terribly ignorant about it. The depth of that ignorance has long been their best-kept secret.
– 'Explaining the Mystery', *The Economist* (4 January 1992: 17)

■

Introduction: Steeped in a Paradigm Lacking Key Conceptual Tools

This chapter develops an explanation for why growth and development are uneven among the nations of the world. This explanation follows from an approach to economic theory that is known as the Other Canon; and this approach is based on a fundamental critique of standard economic theory. Indeed, the objective of this chapter is twofold: both to propose a different theoretical basis for economic development and to propose an explanation about one aspect of economic development, that is, *uneven* growth. This section reflects on the intertwined trajectories of economic theory and global development; then come two sections that develop a critique of standard theory, followed by an exposition of the Other Canon and an application of Other Canon ideas to the phenomenon of uneven development.[1]

Kuhn's 'insulating paradigm'

After the initial euphoria subsequent to the fall of the Berlin Wall, in many poor countries the suspicion gradually grew through the 1990s that the theoretical foundations of the present world economy are flawed at some very basic level. Contrary to the predictions of economic theory, globalization has been accompanied by a falling standard of living in many countries. The 2002 Johannesburg summit contended that since the Rio summit ten years earlier, 66 poor nations had grown poorer. This chapter argues that the factors causing the process of economic development to be uneven lie outside the framework of today's standard economic theory. To use Lionel Robbins's term, standard economics is a *Harmonielehre* – a system which, due to its core assumptions, only produces harmonious results. The elements that cause unevenness and social disharmony are missing from the toolbox of today's economists.

Thomas Kuhn's celebrated book on the development of science describes very well the situation in which the standard paradigm of economics now finds itself:

> A paradigm can, for that matter, even insulate the community from those socially important problems that are not reducible to the puzzle form, because they cannot be stated in terms of the conceptual and instrumental tools the paradigm supplies. (Kuhn 1970: 37)

Following the fall of the Berlin Wall, standard textbook economics, never before applied anywhere in so undiluted a form, was used to exorcize the Second and Third Worlds of what were seen as 'statist' deviations from market-based textbook practice. Even in nations where the state was virtually non-existent, such as Guatemala where it controlled less than 2 per cent of the economy, the same anti-state medicine was applied. A remarkable feature of this process was that the professionals of the Washington institutions who were in charge of the policies of the 1990s, with very few exceptions, had never been practitioners either of business or of economic policy in the developed world. This was recognized by President Wolfensohn of the World Bank, who belatedly started a massive crash course for all his professionals at business schools. The practice of economic development in the Third World came to deviate fundamentally both from the historical and present practice of the developed world – the poor were treated with a medicine that the now-rich countries had never been near. 'Do as we say, don't do as we do' became the marching order.

The rising poverty of the Second (former communist) and Third Worlds is accompanied by institutional breakdown. In several African countries the state as a civilizing agent has, for all practical purposes, ceased to exist, and there are clear signs of 'Africanization' in many Latin American countries. Economists have a hard time explaining how the notoriously inefficient planned economies in Eastern Europe produced a considerably higher standard of living in most countries than capitalism now does. After more than ten years of 'transition', it is by now reasonably clear that an approximate 50 per cent drop in real wages in the former Soviet Union is of a rather permanent nature. Compared to the normal demographic development in the former Soviet Union and Ukraine, 9.7 million people are 'missing' – victims of poverty, malnutrition, alcohol, violence and suicide.

So consider today's situation: standard economic theory has insulated the world community from the true causes of immense poverty problems. 'Development aid' treats symptoms of poverty as well as the social conscience, but rarely touches on the true causes of poverty. The 'good news factory' of the Washington Consensus generally downplays the bad news, effectively maintaining what Gunnar Myrdal once called 'opportunistic ignorance' in the First World about the extent of this increasing poverty. Pressed for results, the Washington institutions focus on factors that are decidedly more symptoms than true causes of poverty and underdevelopment. Economic development is not subsistence agriculture with a better water supply: it is a deep structural change of productive life. The Millennium Goals for development are to a large extent 'palliative economics' – they ease the pains of poverty, but amount to little in terms of development except a list of good intentions.

The awareness that there is something fundamentally wrong with the prevailing *Weltanschauung* of standard economic theory is growing. Joseph Stiglitz, for example, has written, 'A strong case could be made for the proposition that ideas about economics had led close to half the world's population to untold suffering' (Stiglitz 1994: ix).

One fundamental problem in this global situation is the lack of diversity of economic ideas. The overwhelming intellectual and political fight of the twentieth century was between a communist planned economy and 'the free market'. When 'the free market' won that fight in 1989, standard neoclassical economics descending from David Ricardo became the only game in town. This is a situation similar to that of the Irish potato famine: while an illiterate Peruvian farmer in the Andes could distinguish up to 200 varieties of potato by name, only two varieties of potato were cultivated in Ireland. For centuries the people of the Andes secured survival by blending a large variety of potatoes in every field, but when blight hit the Irish potato varieties no buffer stock of variety protected against famine. The interwar pluralism in economic methodology had given way to a Cold War monoculture of neoclassicism. We are left with one single variety of intellectual potato and face an intellectual famine.[2] Arguably, one aspect of this 'single variety' problem is that the apparently opposite theoretical extremes – communist planned economy and extreme liberalism – are theoretical siblings in some respects.

Neoliberalism and communism: the same theory clothed in different garbs?

In 1955, in the midst of the Cold War, Nicholas Kaldor wrote that 'the Marxian theory is really only a simplified version of Ricardo, clothed in a different garb' (Kaldor 1960: 211). It was not at all obvious to most people at the time that the two political extremes contending in the Cold War could be regarded as having the same basis in economic theory.

Marx's dynamic analysis clearly differs from Ricardo's more mechanical view. Marx's understanding is deeply rooted in the German tradition: there, economists at the time of Adam Smith were already writing books about the importance of production and technology, even while the English economists were emphasizing the importance of barter and trade. However, when it came to identifying the evils of the system he had described so well (and to prescribing solutions), Marx based his analysis on a theory which is and was completely foreign to his own tradition: Ricardo's labour theory of value. As Cambridge economist Herbert Foxwell put it, 'whatever qualifications Ricardo may have made upon it in his own mind, ninety-nine readers out of a hundred took him literally, and the main impression left by his book was that while wealth was almost exclusively due to labour, it was mainly absorbed by rent and other payments to the unproductive classes' (Foxwell, introduction to Menger 1899: xlii). Gone from Ricardo's economic theory are the creative forces of mankind, human wit and will – what Nietzsche called *Geist- und Willens-Kapital*.

The bifurcation of Ricardian economics had already started at the time of Ricardo: the Ricardian socialists and the Ricardian liberalists drew entirely different conclusions from the same master. These two traditions – the theories that fought the Cold War – both left out knowledge building, innovations, entrepreneurship, and various other important factors. Foxwell, founder of great economics libraries at Harvard and in London, wrote that, 'as Jevons has observed, Ricardo gave the whole course of English economics a wrong twist. ... after the appearance of Ricardo's *Principles*, the economists were largely given over to sterile logomachy and academic hair-splitting' (Foxwell, introduction to Menger 1899: xli, lxxii).

Nonetheless, an alternative to Ricardian economics did exist up until the Second World War, a tradition with a longer history than the standard canon: the German historical school and the old institutional school. It is essential to revitalize this almost defunct tradition of economics. Foxwell called it 'the realistic school'; here it is called the Other Canon.

Blind spots: constant and diminishing returns
and the 'equality assumption'

Standardization and equality were main characteristics of the age of Fordist mass production. 'You can have the car in any colour as long as it is black' was Henry Ford's dictum. In the Scandinavian social democracies, children's songs proclaimed that all children were alike; in Mao's China everybody even dressed alike. Neoclassical economics is a product of this age of standardization: in a world of perfect information all human beings are implicitly assumed to have the same information and think alike. The science of economics attributed to human beings a rationality based upon the impossibility of viewing the world without at the same time having a point of view (see quote from Nietzsche, p. 52).

With Adam Smith the role of production as opposed to trade disappeared from economic theory. This is a critical absence, since the roots of the inequality of wealth are found in the realm of production. Adam Smith makes no distinction between *commerce* and *industry*, he assimilates the process of production to that of exchange, and labour time becomes the common measuring rod of both.[3] This was an important first step towards making standard economics into a *Harmonielehre*.

In contrast, the Other Canon is essentially a theory of production, wherein the personal or national standard of living largely depends on what the person or the nation produces. The wealth of a nation in the Other Canon is based on the nation's capacity to produce – or, as it was termed in nineteenth-century American and German economic theory, its 'productive powers'.

Due to the inattention to production in Adam Smith's economic theory, and to the choice of mathematics as a principal language of communication, 'the equality assumption' (Buchanan 1979: 231ff.) became perhaps the most important – and the least discussed – assumption of economics. In a model 'which embodies constant returns to scale of production over all ranges of output, all of which are private, this economy would be without trade. In such a setting, each person becomes a complete microcosm of the whole society' (Buchanan 1979: 236). International trade originates in increasing returns and in the many dimensions of diversity of geography, firms, products, human beings, cultures, and societies, but these factors – the very cause of trade – tend to be assumed away in neoclassical economics. It is paradoxical that the assumption needed to produce a harmonious result from international trade – factor-price equalization – approximates a situation where there will be no trade at all.

The equality assumption derives from the mechanistic origins of standard economics, a heritage that is built into every fibre of equilibrium theory. Producing a theory that explains uneven economic growth requires getting rid of this 'equality assumption'. It will be impossible to eliminate the equality assumption as a norm in economics, thus introducing true diversity, without simultaneously relaxing all the fundamental assumptions of the standard theory.

Yet the standardization and equality of goods and of human beings that underlies modern economic theory is fundamentally at odds with the fact that the theory itself does not allow for mass production and its concurrent increasing returns. Paradoxically, huge increasing returns – which are at the very core of mass production – were evicted from economic theory by Alfred Marshall at the conception of mass production society in the 1890s. This was done to fit the economic world to the type of mathematics chosen as the metaphor for economics. Marshall only did this reluctantly – it contradicted all he had seen in his *Wanderjahre* in industry – paradoxically using a biological metaphor to rid neoclassical economics forever of all biological metaphors. During the nineteenth century the existence of economies of scale in industry and diminishing returns in agriculture had been a major argument for industrialization in all the nations that followed England's path.

Removing the increasing/diminishing returns dichotomy from the toolbox of standard economics helped all economic activities to be seen as qualitatively alike. The first important step in this direction was made by Adam Smith, who rid economics of diversity by forcefully arguing that all economic activities were alike in terms of wealth creation. Smith repeatedly goes out of his way to explain why human knowledge and human skills do *not* produce a higher standard of living than ignorance – either to society or to the individual. If people with more knowledge and more skills have higher incomes – which was also observable in Smith's time – this is to Smith never due to the fact that skills and knowledge produce value. In the same paragraphs, in the same line of reasoning, Smith eliminates from economics both the idea that skills and knowledge are the foundation for wealth and the idea of qualitative diversity of economic activities.[4]

Eliminating diversity, different skill levels, increasing returns, synergies between different economic activities and the resulting path dependency of development were the most important steps in making the static neoclassical theory into a *Harmonielehre.* That the economic theory that achieved a monopoly position in the age of mass production could only function by removing mass production from the theory itself is a major contradiction. The economic theory of the age of mass production was essentially a more elegant version of David Ricardo's corn economy. Neoclassical economics therefore represents a much better description of the economic reality of Third World agriculture and mining than of the fundamentally increasing returns-based activities of the First World.

■

Barter-based Economics as *Harmonielehre* – a System of Automatic Harmony

In *The Empire of Business,* Andrew Carnegie summarized the view of the Manchester School as follows:

Nature has decreed, and wisely so, that all nations of the earth shall be interdependent, each with a mission. To one is given fertile soil, to another rich mines, to a third great forests; to one sunshine and heat, to another temperate zone, and to another colder clime; one nation shall provide this service, another that, and a third shall do something else; all cooperating, each furnishing its natural product, forming one grand harmonious whole.

It is clearly seen that our beloved land, Great Britain, has been assigned the high mission of manufacturing for her sister nations. Our kin beyond the sea shall send us in our ships their cotton from the Mississippi valley; India shall contribute its jute, Russia its hemp and its flax, Australia its finer wools, and we, with our supplies of coal and ironstone for our factories and workshops, our skilled mechanics and artificers, and our vast capital, shall invent and construct the necessary machinery and weave these materials into fine cloth for the nations; all shall be fashioned by us and made fit for the use of men. Our ships which reach us laden with the raw materials shall return to all parts of the earth laden with these our higher products made from the crude. This exchange of raw for finished products under the decrees of nature makes each nation the servant of the other, and proclaims the brotherhood of man. Peace and goodwill shall reign upon the earth, one nation after another must follow our example, and free exchange of commodities shall everywhere prevail. Their ports shall open for the reception of our finished products, as ours are open for their raw materials. (Carnegie 1903: 314)

The nineteenth-century prose above has qualities which makes it more readable than the 1948 paper by Paul Samuelson on factor-price equalization, but the conclusions are the same: if only left undisturbed, the forces of the market will create world harmony (Samuelson 1948). The theoretical foundation of the Washington Consensus and of the present world economic order is essentially the neoclassical Samuelson theory of factor-price equalization; and the barriers to entry in this theory are considerably higher than those suggested in Carnegie's passage. What this policy essentially says is: we specialize in Schumpeterian innovation, and you specialize in supplying raw materials and goods with minimal content of innovation under perfect competition. In the neoclassical model, where knowledge and innovation are excluded, it is possible to argue that this situation will produce economic harmony. In a Schumpeterian model, where the imperfect competition resulting from innovations is what fuels both investments and economic growth, such a model means that one group of nations specialize in being knowledgeable and wealthy while another group of nations specialize in being poor and ignorant.

Carnegie's Manchester School prose makes it clear that this sort of arrangement is at the same time a *Harmonielehre*. In the Other Canon, by contrast, the natural tendency of the market is *away from harmony:* left alone, the market will tend to increase already existing differences in income. Diversity at the level of economic activities and of human beings, along with the cumulative effects which abound in the economy, cause any approximation to harmony to be the result of conscious economic policy. The aim of this chapter is to explain the rationale for this divergent economic vision.

One important German criticism of nineteenth-century English economics was that the latter reduced all phenomena to *qualitätslose Grössen* – units void of any qualities or differentiations. Here lies the root of the equality assumption, which causes economic theory (including trade theory), to 'prove' things that are completely counter-intuitive and counter-factual.

The equality assumption produces an economic science devoid of any taxonomy. This in itself is idiosyncratic. An important scientific goal of many sciences at the time of Adam Smith was precisely to create such taxonomies. In the Other Canon there are no representative firms. Firms are – as in the economics of Edith Penrose – unique. Figure 3.1 (p. 74) represents an attempt to create a dynamic taxonomy of firms' and industries' potential for increasing national wealth.

From a Schumpeterian viewpoint it is interesting expressly to find in the statement above that, in the world division of labour, Great Britain shall have the *monopoly of inventing*, while the other nations shall have the job of essentially harvesting the bounties of nature. This problem still persists in standard economics, which fails to understand why some nations – in today's system – specialize in being poor and uneducated. Today's standard theory hardly has a theory of economic development other than one of adding capital to labour.

Missing the diversity of human production – and the relationship between this diversity and the diversity of growth and welfare – is probably the most serious shortcoming of contemporary economic theory. Neoclassical trade theory essentially proves that if all the stockbrokers of the world could be put into one nation, and all the shoeshine boys into another, stockbrokers and shoeshine boys would suddenly start getting the same real wages. This is, in practice, the postulate on which today's world economic order rests. John Stuart Mill comments on this type of situation:

> It often happens that the universal beliefs of one age of mankind – a belief from which no one *was*, nor without an extraordinary effort of genius and courage *could* at the time be free – becomes to a subsequent age so palpable an absurdity, that the only difficulty then is to imagine how such a thing can ever have appeared credible.... It looks like one of the crude fancies of childhood, instantly corrected by a word from any grown person. (Mill 1929: 3)

We believe that the world is again in the situation described by Mill, wherein the need to reconstruct an alternative theory is urgent. Mill sees the need for courage and genius, but other qualities could also be important. In the fairy tale of the Emperor's New Clothes the naïveté of a young boy substituted for courage, and probably the systematic observations of complexities in the real world coupled with ordinary common sense will substitute for theoretical genius in the traditional sense. What has to be reconstructed is a *science of practice:* a theory based on human observations of facts. This contrasts with today's standard economics where all observations of reality are filtered through a set of arbitrary and – from the point of view of observable reality – totally inappropriate assumptions. As one noted trade theorist put it: 'The nice thing about economics is that it contains no facts, it is just a way of thinking' (Norman 1994).

Reconstructing the alternative theory of facts and practice faces barriers of several kinds. The metaphors of barter-based economics are well entrenched: institutional inertia and also considerable vested interests must be confronted. Consequently, a true *gestalt* shift is required. In an academic world where 'hardness of paradigm' tends to be seen as a sign of quality, theory should be undertaken with a lower level of abstraction. This perspective has also been advanced by Pierre Bourdieu, who wrote:

> [T]he most formidable barrier to the construction of an adequate science of practice no doubt lies in the fact that the solidarity that binds scientists to their science (and to the social privilege which makes it possible and which it justifies and procures) predisposes them to profess the superiority of their knowledge, often won through enormous efforts, against common sense, and even to find in that superiority a justification for their privilege. (Bourdieu 1980: 28)

The economic debate of the twentieth century was overly coloured and distorted by the fight against communism and, during the last 50 years, by the Cold War. There was a time when any idea could be reduced to its position on a one-dimensional axis from political 'left' to 'right'. The Other Canon operates completely independently of this axis. In shorthand, the Other Canon view claims that the ills of communism originated when Marx's excellent analysis of the world production system – which was solidly in the German and Other Canon tradition – was coupled to the mechanical world view of David Ricardo's labour theory of value, an idea completely alien to the German and Other Canon tradition. (If human *Geist* and *Will* are the essential moving force of the economy, how is it at all thinkable to claim that the mechanical executor of a job should get *the whole* value of the produce?)

Common sense tells us that under free trade a nation of stockbrokers will be considerably richer than a nation of shoeshine boys. A theory that insists that these two activities are qualitatively equal in terms of creating wealth will not, of course, do any short-term harm to the nation of stockbrokers. When science is fundamentally wrong – when reason is abused, as in the case of neoclassical economics – the burdens are unevenly distributed. Similarly, when medical science for hundreds of years continued the practice of bloodletting, only the weakest died. In the long term, however, the world is facing the same kind of 'social question' that plagued the European nations in the nineteenth century. This time, however, the conflict will be between nations: between the nations that have specialized as England did – in Carnegie's terms – in inventions and new knowledge, and the rest, which base their 'comparative advantage' in international trade on ignorance and low wages.

This modern version of scholasticism cannot be put right via a piecemeal approach. As long as the standard theory remains the foundation for economics, all observations of the real world will be filtered through inappropriate basic assumptions, and the policy conclusions will therefore continue to be distorted. In this way otherwise healthy insights – like, for example, the New Growth Theory with its attempt to include technology – result in the same *Harmonielehre* as before, because the assumptions of perfect competition and general equilibrium are kept in the model. Attempting a convergence between standard theory and the Other Canon invariably seems to produce theories of the kind that the world is flat except where it is a bit curved and hilly.

The timing is good for an alternative theory: 'Nothing is stronger than an idea whose time has come.' Consider this question of timing from the perspective of the demand factors that influence the production of economic theories. In this perspective, the strength and dominance – but not the origins – of the neoclassical paradigm are to some extent connected to the Cold War. In the war against the communist utopia, the metaphors from equilibrium physics were excellently suited to constructing 'proofs' of the superiority – also in distributive justice – of the capitalist market utopia. Samuelson's 1948 article on factor-price equalization coincides with the Berlin Blockade and its political build-up (Samuelson 1948), and Milton Friedman's 1953 defence of 'unrealistic assumptions' with McCarthyism.[5] In the development of economic theory, the continued use of metaphors from equilibrium physics along the path of least mathematical resistance also happened to produce theories proving the superiority of a market system. However, the main driving forces of this market economy, human wit and will, were not part of the capitalist theory.

The Other Canon takes from Schumpeter the insight that the whole notion of equilibrium is a misleading metaphor in economics:

> It lies in the very foundation of our way of thinking that there is no such thing as a dynamic equilibrium. Economic development is in its very nature a disturbance of the existing static equilibrium, without any tendency whatsoever for the system either to move back to the original point of equilibrium, or to any other point of equilibrium.[6]

■

Models of Growth

Few economists would disagree that economic growth is fundamentally caused by the accumulation of knowledge. However, this assertion creates more questions than it answers: How is the knowledge created? How does knowledge get transformed into an economic good? What kind of institutional and financial scaffolding is required to create and sustain this edifice of increasing knowledge? How does the knowledge structure move and spread? What are the synergetic effects and linkages between various economic activities? Do changes come gradually – *natura non facit saltum*, as Marshall claimed – or in jerks and jolts? And – the central question addressed in this chapter – why is this process of growth so uneven?

Economists have long been aware of their inattention to the links between knowledge and growth. As Edith Penrose, in her *Theory of Growth of the Firm* (1959), observed, 'Economists have, of course, always recognized the dominant role that increasing knowledge plays in economic processes but have, for the most part, found the whole subject too slippery to handle.'[7] No doubt efforts have been made since Penrose made this observation. From his roots in the German tradition, Fritz Machlup (1962) made an impressive pioneering effort to map the production of knowledge in the United States. But neither his efforts, nor those of Robert Solow (1957) to pin down changing knowledge as 'technical change', nor those of Harvey Leibenstein (1978) to introduce an organizational 'X-factor', nor those of Paul Romer (1990) to endogenize technical progress have produced a quantum leap in our understanding of the evolving growth of economic knowledge and welfare – much less why this growth is so unevenly distributed. The observations of reality are filtered through inappropriate assumptions – as in Kuhn's 'insulating paradigm' (p. 53): the problems we face are not reducible to the puzzle form that enables standard theory to handle the issues at hand.

The fundamental problem with standard economics is that it does not contain a theory of growth – neither why economic growth is so uneven, nor why growth occurs at all. The papers of Abramowitz (1956) and Solow (1957) showed that capital, the traditional explanatory variable, could explain only 12.5 per cent of US economic growth. At the time, Abramowitz saw the huge residual as 'a measure of our ignorance about the causes of growth'.

These two papers precipitated an avalanche of literature on 'growth accounting' – accounting for the 'residual'. This growth accounting took place in a framework of the standard canon of economics, in a moving competitive equilibrium. This approach therefore inherited all the built-in weaknesses of standard economics. There was little room for discussing disequilibrium aspects, market imperfections, or the interaction and synergies of the factors of growth. Very little – if any – analysis took into account the obvious fact that different economic activities would contribute very differently to the 'residual' and therefore to economic growth. Clearly, information technology these days contributes more to the 'residual' of the US economy than do that nation's barbershops. The claim made here is that the 'residual' – as well as growth itself – is *activity-specific*, as discussed below.

Neoclassical growth models invariably attempt to explain that the world is round in a framework that retains the fundamental assumption that the world is flat. That equilibrium economics produces economic harmony is almost a truism. By including elements from the Other Canon one by one, these models give an illusion of having produced a more relevant model, but economics continues to be a *Harmonielehre* because these models retain one or more of the fundamental assumptions of perfect information, general equilibrium, and/or that all economic activities are qualitatively alike. This includes the models of Romer (for example, Romer 1990). Today it is obviously possible to model uneven growth: Paul Krugman did so in 1979;[8] and Lucas (1988) also produced an interesting depiction of economics as no longer a *Harmonielehre*. However, these more realistic models do not reach the policy level. Common-sense observations contradicting the very foundations of standard theory are normally treated as if they were intellectual sideshows – oddities that are amusing but hardly threaten the basic paradigm. The exceedingly important observation that 'the law of one price' does not apply to inter-industry wage differentials is but one example in a book by Thaler (1992) listing systemic abnormalities in economics. The paradigm is so deeply rooted in the 'equality assumption' discussed above that common-sense observations, aired and filed away one by one, are not enough to threaten it.

Nearly 40 years after writing the article that started 'growth accounting', Moses Abramowitz returned to the argument. His comment on the progress of economic science since then was devastating:

> the old primitive Residual is really an understatement, a lower-bound measure of our ignorance about the sources of growth.... Perhaps some of you are thinking 'If we are already ignorant of 90 per cent of the sources of *per capita* growth, how much worse can it be? Can it be worse than 100 per cent?' In a sense, it can.... 'It ain't what we don't know that bothers me so much; it's all the things we do know that ain't so.' That is really the nub of the matter. (Abramowitz 1993: 219)

Knowledge and innovations as the engines of growth

As Daastøl and I have argued (1997), a necessary precondition for economic growth – in effect its root cause – is a religious/philosophical *gestalt* switch, a fundamental change of world view. Our contention is that the *attitude to the creation of new knowledge* – which is changed by this *gestalt* switch – is a basic but neglected explanatory variable for economic growth and its absence. This *gestalt* switch took place in the Renaissance.

The changing meaning of the word 'innovation' provides an illustration of this change. Before the Renaissance, innovation was synonymous with heresy: seeking forbidden knowledge outside the scriptures and outside the writings of Aristotle. In the thirteenth century Roger Bacon of Oxford spent ten years in jail for 'suspicious innovations', while 300 years later Francis Bacon could hail the importance of innovations in an essay without any risk. The attitude towards seeking new knowledge had changed from being heresy to being a human's duty to his creator.

Much more could be said about growth and development *per se*; but, as noted above, this chapter attempts to explain *uneven* growth. Standard economic theory faces the problem of introducing change into a framework that is fundamentally static. When change is introduced into this system, any growth automatically tends to become even growth, due to the lack of diversity in the models. Consequently, this chapter follows Schumpeter's view that diversity and disequilibrium should be present from the very beginning.[9]

The starting point of the Other Canon is that what distinguishes the human economy from the economy of animals is that humans not only *harvest*, they *produce*. Human wealth will be based on Man's capacity to produce, or, as it was called in the nineteenth century, his 'productive powers'. Also the wealth of a nation is determined by its 'productive powers', not by a stock of capital. Three main clusters of factors constitute the primary engines of economic change:

Supply factors:

- Human knowledge employed in production.

- Human will and organizational ability (entrepreneurship, leadership, organizational capability/all of these both at the level of the firm and of society).

Demand factors:

- Human needs (actual or potential). These demand factors can be seen as clustered around *generic* human needs – food, shelter, transport – over time climbing in sophistication in a Maslowian hierarchy of needs. This hierarchy will to some extent determine the sequence of technical change (a techno-economic paradigm based on textiles is likely to occur before one based on entertainment).

The 'animal economy' of bartering nature's produce should be excluded here; the difference between human and animal can be seen as consisting in the human ability to produce, not in the ability to barter (as Adam Smith claims). As human knowledge of production extends – and fixed costs and diversity develop in education/training and/or in tools – the division of labour becomes an economic necessity. From this follows the kind of barter that is based on *man-made* comparative advantages, as opposed to *nature-given* comparative advantages. Over time the diversity of the human economy will fan out – adding more and more knowledge into the product to substitute for nature's raw materials – producing an ever-increasing number of products and niches, each subject to increasing returns and high barriers to entry. In this system of increasing complexity, the unique Penrosian firms enjoy innovation rents that are very different from those experienced in the commodity competition of Third World raw materials.

The traditional factors of production in standard economics, land (Nature) and labour – as well as water, wind or gravity – may be factors of *production*, but they are in and of themselves not factors of *change*. Human production is *caused* by the factors added by Man to the produce and forces provided by nature: wit and will.

In this respect, the views of the American economist Erasmus Peshine Smith (1853) on the human economy are of interest. Peshine Smith regarded the harnessing of Nature's energy as the main moving force of the economy; nature's resources, especially her energy resources, have infinite potential. His view, and indeed that of German and American nineteenth-century economics in general, stood in sharp contrast to the pessimistic 'scarcity' economics of British Ricardian orthodoxy. Whereas the theories of Adam Smith had developed into pessimistic Malthusianism, Peshine Smith's theories kept alive the spirit of the Renaissance and of undeveloped human potential, forever pushing ahead the never-ending frontier of knowledge. His views are interesting as the world economy moves from an era of taming the wild forces of nature – from an age of blasting steel furnaces and violent water turbines – to an age more characterized by working *with* nature, wrestling with her to reveal her secrets, as in the human genome project.

Peshine Smith sought to develop economics into a quantitative engineering science: 'to construct a skeleton of political economy upon the basis of purely physical laws'. As opposed to the static 'physics envy' of standard economic theory, Peshine Smith's dynamic physics envy is entirely acceptable because the real agent of change in his system is human wit and will. Peshine Smith believed all economic laws have their counterparts in those of the natural sciences, and proceeded to characterize the reproduction of wealth as a vast energy transfer system within Nature's overall equilibrium, the basic question being the extent to which Man would proceed to exploit Nature's latent wealth. He wrote to Henry Carey, a fellow economist: 'The entire universe then *is* motion, and the only point is how much of the universal and ceaseless motion we shall utilize, and how much we shall permit to be working against us' (Hudson 1969: 104).

The increased wealth produced by increased productivity was to Peshine Smith a product of the forces of nature – harnessed by Man – substituting for manual labour. His 1853 book used the example of a paper box of matches, which once sold for a shilling; he noted that in the present day, as many matches, of superior quality, would be sold for a halfpenny – and further, chemical and mechanical improvements would permit 25 matches to be made by the same expenditure of human labour as one match required in an earlier day. In a box with 25 matches, argued Peshine Smith, 24 may be regarded as the contribution from the harnessing of Nature – a Nature who gives her aid, and asks no recompense – and *one*, as the result of muscular action.

The fundamental factors that have to be added to Nature's forces are human wit (knowledge) and will (entrepreneurship). A perusal of 500 years of European economic policy suggests that the root cause of European economic development was that it was *willed*. Growth resulted from conscious nation building where, for centuries, the presence of manufacturing industry was seen as a mandatory element. This unleashing of technological change in an activity-specific economic policy (the importance of war industry and luxury goods should be especially noted) produced relatively uniform growth patterns.

The traditional factors labour and capital in standard economic theory are secondary factors, in this connection. Without new knowledge, and without new initiatives and entrepreneurship, the traditional factors of capital and labour are sterile as agents of change. The three original factors are strongly influenced by attitudes – what the French call *mentalité*. Conscious changing and moulding of the mentality of the population was a mandatory passage point of all capitalist development. As Frederick the Great of Prussia said: 'The plebes will never give up their humdrum tune, unless you drag them by their noses and ears to their profits' (quoted in Lowe (1988: 21)). The 'backward-bending supply curve of labour' (= 'laziness') was seen as a universal phenomenon in all pre-capitalist societies.

Different fixed costs incurred in learning skills and in new tools simultaneously create diversity and minimum efficient sizes of human societies. For example, the fixed costs created by the blacksmith's fire created a minimum efficient size for human settlements. In order for knowledge to develop and propagate, thus creating inventions and innovations and a demand for these innovations, a diversity of approaches and differences in knowledge and experience are needed. As Arthur Koestler says: 'New knowledge is created by connecting previously unconnected facts.' This is another factor creating minimum efficient sizes of societies. Following Koestler, we can assert that as an economy becomes increasingly diverse, the possibility of connection points for new knowledge – and consequently for serendipity – will grow exponentially.

Historically such knowledge creation often leaps from activities that are seemingly completely unrelated. In seventeenth-century Holland, it is possible to identify a close-knit maritime–scientific–artistic cluster where innovations leap to and from seemingly unrelated sectors centred in Delft. Dutch artists invented oil painting and painting on canvases. The raw materials for these inventions – linseed oil, linen and hemp fibre – were widely used in Dutch shipbuilding and readily available. They would not have been as readily available to the artists of Florence and Sienna. The painting techniques of Jan Vermeer (1632–75) included seeing his subjects through lenses and a *camera obscura*.[10] The navy and the merchant marine created a demand for lenses for binoculars, but lenses were also in demand among natural scientists and the producers of early microscopes at the time. Antonie van Leeuwenhoek (1632–1723), who lived a couple of hundred metres away from the painter Vermeer, was famous for his microscope lenses and his research correspondence. Upon Vermeer's death, Leeuwenhoek was appointed to deal with his estate. The Huygens family, who later improved on the microscope, used another lens grinder in Delft, Johan van Wyck. Vermeer, a painter who also experimented in the natural sciences, is linked to the microscope builders *cum* natural scientists.[11] The Delft lens grinders thus formed the core of an extremely dynamic and path-breaking cluster, including such diverse activities as the Navy (binoculars), painters like Vermeer, the natural scientists, and the microscope builders. The philosopher (and lens grinder) Spinoza, born in Amsterdam in the same year as Vermeer and van Leeuwenhoek, added to and expresses the productive vitality of the Dutch knowledge system of the time. Such synergetic cumulative causations and the path dependency they create are no doubt at the core of knowledge creation and the process of economic growth. They are, however, impossible to reproduce in any meaningful way by quantitative methods.

Geography and climate – historically the first factors discussed in nineteenth-century development economics – are also responsible for diversity. What economic historians have started to call 'the commodity lottery' – according to which the providence of nature has supplied each nation arbitrarily with a given raw material – is clearly also an important factor. Many examples, from early history on – such as Venice and the Dutch Republic – point to a lack of resources being an advantage for development, because it forces nations into increasing return activities and the virtuous circles they create.

If necessity is the mother of invention, geography and climate may provide essential stimuli. But the growth of early civilizations in the fertile alluvial plains of the Middle East, rather than among the Eskimos, suggests the limits to this theory. The abundance of domesticable plants and mammals, rather than their scarcity, gave rise to civilization.

Inventions, innovations and 'good' and 'bad' capitalists

Thorstein Veblen's model of economic growth is representative of an Other Canon understanding of development. To Veblen, 'idle curiosity' – an essentially non-economic instinct, research in its original form – was the basis for economic progress.[12] This roughly corresponds to, or leads to, what Schumpeter later would call 'invention'. This intellectual invention would have to be combined with workmanship and capital to be converted into an economic innovation. This process required a sense of one's obligations to society and history, what Veblen refers to as the 'parental bent'. This trinity – idle curiosity, the parental bent and workmanship – forms the core of Veblen's theory of economic development.

When an invention has been successfully created, the world of capitalism splits in two for Veblen. His analysis here is a logical extension of the separation of the 'world of goods and services' (*Güterwelt*), on the one hand, and the 'world of money' on the other hand, which is essential to the German economics from which Veblen received much inspiration. On one side is the industrial capitalist, who bases his profitability on *production*, and therefore increases the size of the real economy, providing welfare. On the other side, there is the financial capitalist who bases his profitability on *vendability*, not production. While finance clearly is necessary, capitalism degenerates when financial capitalism gets into the driver's seat of the capitalist system.

In our interpretation 'idle curiosity' will be converted into potentially profitable investment opportunities only under certain conditions. This requires both entrepreneurship and 'organizational capabilities' on the part of society – creating the institutions that are needed to sustain both the constant flow of innovations and the precarious balance between the financial and real sectors of the economy. Standard economic theory tends not to distinguish between the real and the monetary aspects of the economy. Veblen's theory has many similarities with Schumpeter's (1912, 1934, 1939), but with added emphasis on the possible ruinous imbalances between production and finance (see Hilferding 1919), a theme treated excellently in our own time by Carlota Perez (Perez 2002).

■

Production-based Economics:
How Economic Activities Differ, and Why it Matters

Paul Romer's theories exemplify the limitations of standard economic theory: new factors are added, but because the fundamental equality assumptions are maintained, the overall theoretical framework continues to produce 'economic harmony'. In the Other Canon, diversity is the main factor in explaining why the natural tendency of the market is to enlarge already existing differences in income, and why the main countervailing forces are based on political intervention.

The equality assumption is – in a sense – the 'mother of all assumptions' in economics. If increasing returns are introduced, a *Harmonielehre* still exists so long as all economic activity is subject to the same degree of increasing returns. If imperfect competition is introduced, but again exists to the same degree for all economic activities, then too a *Harmonielehre* is retained. Only a theory that allows for diversity at the outset can produce a theory of uneven economic growth (other than that the poor are lazy).

One important aspect of *Methodenstreite* is what is allowed to count as facts. Diversity is a key factor on which our economic order rests. This was recognized long ago by William Robertson, who wrote in his 1777 volume *The History of America*, 'In every inquiry concerning the operations of men when united together in society, the first object of attention should be their mode of subsistence. Accordingly as that varies, their laws and policies must be different.'[13] David Landes, an acute modern-day analyst of economic dynamics, expressed much the same view in his 1998 volume, *The Wealth and Poverty of Nations*:

As history has shown, some countries will do much better than others. The primary reason is that comparative advantage is not the same for all, and that some activities are more lucrative and productive than others. They require and yield greater gains in knowledge and know-how, within and without. (Landes 1998: 522)

However, diversity has not been allowed into the standard canon. So doing would force theory to a lower level of abstraction. Intuitively it seems useless to look for differences of results (in income levels, for example) in today's standard theoretical construction where everything is alike: the conclusion (economic harmony) is already built into the assumptions. Differences in income are caused by diversity (almost a truism) – diversity of agents, of opportunities, of knowledge, and of activities.

Diversity can emerge and play a key theoretical role in less abstract theories than those used in standard economic theory. For example, Charles Babbage took a look into Adam Smith's pin factory and found that the wages differed from 4½ pence to 6 shillings a day, or by a factor of almost 1 to 15 (Babbage 1835: 186). These differences were based on skill level, the person 'twisting and cutting heads' of the pins receiving the highest wage. If the low-skilled person in this factory is placed in one nation, and the high-skilled person in another (and if labour mobility between nations is excluded), these considerable wage differentials will not decrease, they will increase. Today industrial value chains have to a large extent been broken up, and the operations in Babbage's factory that require low skills or cannot be mechanized are now contracted out to the poor countries in the Second and Third Worlds. The First World is left with the best-paid jobs, the 'twisting and cutting heads' in Babbage's example. This is a division of labour that further opens the breach between rich and poor countries.[14]

The present world economic order is based on a world view that essentially does not allow for diversity. By allowing neither for diversity nor for synergies between economic activities, the standard economic paradigm blocks our fundamental understanding of uneven economic growth, and consequently also blocks the remedies against poverty.

In their ability, at any point in time, to absorb new knowledge
At any point in time, technical change and human learning are focused in certain business areas. No one doubts that the possibilities for technical change today are larger in the Internet business than in sheep farming. This is one crucial area in which standard economic theory lacks the necessary conceptual tools – this activity-specific aspect of economic growth cannot be reduced to Kuhn's 'puzzle form' in the ruling paradigm. For this reason, the windows of opportunity for incorporating research and development, and for other methods of advancing productivity, vary enormously from one type of business to another.

One implication of this situation is that national states sometimes must be deeply involved in encouraging technical change in the economy. Indeed, the history of economic policy supports this idea. Consider the case of Henry VII, who came to power as King of England in 1485. Henry was obsessed with England's 'slack trade'. He revitalized it by going into a key area for technical change at that time – textile manufacturing. In his youth, Henry had seen that textile manufacturing was generating vitality and wealth on the Continent.

The different qualities of economic activities are also at the root of the concepts of 'good' and 'bad' trade which dominated English and Continental trade policy for centuries. These concepts are based on the idea that economic activities differ as potential carriers of economic growth. At any point in time different economic activities can profitably absorb very different quantities of human knowledge and capital. That is, they present different windows of opportunity. You cannot upgrade the level of skill and salary of a person picking lettuce to that of a computer engineer by educating the lettuce picker, because the absorption capacity of human skills for the two professions are different. The absorption capacity for capital and skill of lettuce picking will only change at the point in time when lettuce picking is mechanized. Upgrading the economic situation of the lettuce picker can only take place by his changing his job. That this fact applies to a nation as well as to an individual was the core argument of US economist Daniel Raymond in 1820.[15] Raymond laid the foundation for 'the American System of Manufactures', and follows *real-ökonomisch* mercantilism and the Other Canon tradition by defining national wealth as the capacity to produce, rather than stocks of commodities or precious metals. He also heavily influenced Friedrich List. In fact, whole passages from List resemble Raymond's arguments step by step.[16]

As long as there is a demand for goods produced with both high and low skills, economic growth – left to the market – will be very uneven and strongly history-dependent. A small, even accidental difference may cause a nation to specialize in low-skilled activities, bereft of technical change and increasing returns – a point made by the mercantilist Joshua Gee and in our era by Brian Arthur (1994). The recognition that vicious and virtuous economic circles originate in this way was suggested by Antonio Serra (1613) nearly four centuries ago; this same insight also underlay German and American nineteenth-century opposition to English classical theory. Only by producing a theory of economic barter that leaves out production can neoclassical trade theory (specifically, the theory of factor-price equalization) prove that the wage earners in a nation making a living picking lettuce will be as rich as the wage earners in a nation of computer engineers. If production were introduced, the theory would be valid only if one introduced the counter-factual assumption that all economic activities have the same capacity to profitably absorb skills and capital – that is, that a barber shop can profitably be made as capital-intensive as a nuclear power plant, and that picking lettuce can profitably be made as skill-intensive as developing new Internet applications.

A fundamental difference between barter-based neoclassical economics and the production-based Other Canon is therefore that in production-based economics the process of economic development is *activity-specific*: it can only take place in certain economic activities at any given point in time. In the nineteenth century there was a general understanding in Continental Europe and in the US that England had achieved her wealth by going into skill- and scale-intensive manufacturing. By exporting a barter-centred economic theory that excluded these factors, England was attempting to 'draw up the ladder' behind her so as to achieve a world monopoly in manufacturing.[17] 'Of course it would be in the interest of the English if we actually believed their stories', Daniel Raymond said, but 'we are not that gullible' (Raymond 1820: 88). There was a tacit understanding outside England that an economic theory at a high level of abstraction (such as English theory) was damaging to the national wealth of the laggard countries.

The Other Canon, by conceptualizing the world as inhabited by diverse economic activities, suggests optimizing paths both for individuals and for societies. In any country, a mediocre lawyer has a much higher income than the most efficient restaurant dishwasher. For a person washing dishes, studying to become a lawyer is an optimizing path that will yield more future income than doing nothing (the *laissez-faire* option). Yet the theory of comparative advantage suggests that doing nothing – washing dishes and staying poor – is the appropriate course of action.

A similar situation faces poor nations. Today the world's most efficient producers of baseballs, in Haiti and Honduras, make 20 US cents an hour. Baseball production has not yet been mechanized, and their production consequently absorbs very little formal skill. The world's most efficient producers of golf balls, at a high-tech plant in New Bedford, Massachusetts, have an hourly wage which is 30 times higher than the world's most efficient baseball producers. Instead of exchanging 30 hours of labour producing baseballs for export for 1 hour of US labour in imported golf balls, Haiti could optimize national welfare by producing golf balls less efficiently than the US. Even if the United States managed to stay ten times as efficient as Haiti in producing golf balls, Haitians would be three times as rich (at today's prices) in golf-ball terms under autarky than under specialization and free trade. Under autarky in sports balls, Haiti could improve its position compared to free trade. How would Haiti get the capital? Presumably the same way our law student will: taking up a loan and paying it back from his future 'industry rent'.

Daniel Raymond – along with Alexander Hamilton a spiritual father of North American protection of industry – compared the situation of individuals to that of nations (Raymond 1820). According to Raymond a nation could upgrade its skill level and wage level in the same way that an individual could do. The core of Raymond's argument was one of optimization: the increased prices paid in the US for industrial products under protection would be more than compensated by the increase in wages, since industrial workers everywhere had wages so much higher than those for farm labour. This requires a trade-off between two economic aspects of being a human being, between *man-the-consumer* and *man-the-producer*. Man-the-consumer will have to live with a higher price level until the higher wage level in manufacturing will have caught up and exceeded the higher prices for manufactured goods in the laggard nation.

In the case of the nineteenth-century US economy, the trade-off between man-the-consumer and man-the-producer led to the conclusion that free trade was then a suboptimal option. Both the Second (former communist) World and the Third World present many cases of Schumpeterian under-development, with similar optimizing paths to be explored. Exploiting these requires more 'theoretical nerve' from economists, and a conscious move into factual investigation to complement the purely theoretical investigations that dominate today.

In the mode of spreading the benefits from new knowledge and technical change

As indicated above, it is necessary to take into consideration that in a market economy every individual plays two roles: man-the-consumer and man-the-producer. In its barter-based tradition, standard economics almost exclusively focuses on man-the-consumer, whereas the Other Canon tends to emphasize man-the-producer.

The fruits of new knowledge and new technology may spread in the economy in two different ways, reflecting two different regimes of appro-priation: in the *classical mode*, through reduction in prices to the consumer; in the *collusive mode*, through higher wages to the producer, in a shared rent-seeking between capital, labour and government.

In the classical mode, technological change and new knowledge will spread in the economy in terms of reduced prices. This is the 'manna from heaven' way in which Adam Smith and David Ricardo assume this to happen, and no doubt – particularly with dramatic technical change – this is an important mechanism. In commodity competition, this is the main way that the benefits from technological change spread.

The word 'collusion' does not imply any conspiracy. The whole idea of Schumpeterian growth indicates a large degree of the collusive spread of technical change. The entrepreneur will constantly see his profits eroded by imitators, and must continuously innovate to keep his profits up. In industries that might be labelled 'high-quality activities', this profit-enhancing innovation can involve increasing the skill levels of workers. Note that this will increase workers' value in the labour market – this is precisely the US nineteenth-century 'high-wage strategy' argument. Under Schumpeterian competition, a high degree of collusive spread is normal; so the individual rent-seeking of the Schumpeterian entrepreneur is converted into collective rent-seeking on behalf of society. Under these conditions what's good for General Motors really is what's good for the country.

So in avoiding ruinous price competition, the dynamic process of Schumpeterian rent-seeking produces an ever-increasing diversity of products;

competition is based on product differentiation and different quality levels. Development and the impact of innovation will – over time – fan out to encompass more and more of the economy.

In any system with differing degrees of increasing and diminishing returns, and with a mixture of collusive and classical means of distributing gains from technical progress, some nations will be better off under autarky than under free trade – at least until they have secured a competitive base in increasing-return/collusive spread activities. This is the basic reason why Werner Sombart and most other German historical economists were critical of free trade between nations at different levels of development.[18] The American system of industrial protection, initiated in the 1820s, made the United States, in a period of less than 100 years, the world's economic powerhouse. In so doing, it illustrates what restrictions on free trade – that is, diversity in economic policies – can achieve. So the Haitian example is far from a far-fetched theoretical argument.

In how they differ over time: the combined dynamics of imperfect competition, learning and life cycles

The challenge in economic theory is to find a level of abstraction at which useful generalizations can be made without assuming economic activities to be either all equal or all different. To a businessman, his firm is unique. The opportunity seen by an entrepreneur is a unique vision, if only in the geographical location of his business. At this level of abstraction we are faced with billions of economic agents who are all unique. At the other extreme – in neoclassical theory – all economic activities are equal. Case studies of firms, industries, and nations are useful building blocks for theories, but a theory on a higher level of abstraction is needed.

The theory of unequal development suggested here has a strong element of what Kaldor calls a 'degree of monopoly' theory of distribution.[19] Ours is a dynamic, skill- and innovation-based variety of such a theory. The Quality Index below (p. 74) plots the effect on wage levels and standards of living created by different technological regimes.

What are the characteristics of growth-inducing – 'good' – economic activities in such a system? Identifying these characteristics must be seen as a task comparable to measuring intelligence via an IQ test — quantifying the unquantifiable. Economic theory has defined two extremes of a continuum reasonably well: perfect competition and, at least statically, monopoly. Under perfect competition, factor-price equalization is achieved – all are equally rich. Under monopoly, high rents are transferred to the monopoly holder from the rest of the world. A core problem in economic theory is that the profession has little meaningful to say about varying degrees of imperfect competition, the conditions under which virtually all economic activities produce and trade. The situation is similar to being able to measure two extremes, black and white, without having any way of measuring the various intermediary shades of grey. This is particularly bothersome in economics, where no

**innovations
new technologies**

Dynamic imperfect competition
(high-quality activity)

Characteristics of high-quality activities
• new knowledge with high market value
• steep learning curves
• high growth in output
• rapid technological programme
• high R&D content
• necessitates and generates learning by doing
• imperfect information
• investments come in large chunks/are divisible (drugs)
• imperfect but dynamic, competition
ᵃ high wage level
• possibilities for important economies of scale and
  scope
• high industry concentration
• high stakes: high barriers to entry and exit
• branded product
• produce linkages and synergies
• standard neoclassical assumptions irrelevant

Shoes (1850–1900)

Golf balls

Automotive paint

Characteristics of low-quality activities
• old knowledge with low market value
• flat learning curves
• low growth in output
• little technological progress
• low R&D content
• little personal or institutional learning required
• perfect competition
• low wage level
• little or no economies of scale/risk of diminishing
  returns
• fragmented industry
• low stakes: low barriers to entry and exit
• commodity
• produce few linkages and synergies
• neoclassical assumptions are reasonable proxy

House paint
Shoes (1999)

Baseballs

Perfect competition
(low-quality activity)

Figure 3.1 The Quality Index of Economic Activities

activities over any length of time belong to either of the two well-defined categories. In their degrees of perfect or imperfect competition, economic activities are scattered over the spectrum from almost white – where the assumptions of neoclassical theory are reasonably valid – to almost black, where the same assumptions are highly unrealistic. Game theory seems to be in a similar situation, in that only games involving the extreme cases of two players and an infinite number of players are well defined.

Differences in wage levels, both nationally and between nations, seem to result from varying degrees of imperfect competition, due to both static and dynamic factors. The factors at work have long been identified both by businessmen and in industrial economics, and they are correlated. Figure 3.1 presents a Quality Index (QI) of economic activities as an attempt to create an area from light to dark grey where the 'quality' of economic activities at any time can be roughly plotted on a scale from white (perfect competition) to black (monopoly). The latter is only a temporary state, as new technologies fall towards a lower score as they mature. The upper part of the Quality Index corresponds to Schumpeter's metaphor of the upper strata of a market economy – these strata are like hotels that are always full of people, but people who are forever changing.

Activities with a high QI score are *growth-inducing*, activities with a low score are *growth-inhibiting*. It is important to note that traditional industrial categories do not fit easily into this scheme; indeed, one product or product group may have different market segments varying from 'high-quality' to 'low-quality'.

The factors listed in the Quality Index are correlated, but clearly not perfectly. The two lists of factors creating high-quality and low-quality activities exhibit a negative relationship: in the extreme, the characteristics of the two groups are mutually exclusive. Each of the characteristics in one group is, in this form, incompatible with *all* characteristics in the other. The 'quality' of an economic activity for a nation, its ability to pay high wages and potential for high profits, can be read off on this scale. Since barriers to entry also carry with them high risks and high barriers to exit, there is no direct relationship between the quality of an activity and its profit level, only its *potential* profit level. A high-quality activity can be ruined in shake-out periods by huge losses across the industry. These losses are caused by high barriers to exit. However, this normally does not drastically affect wage levels.

The classical spread of the effects of technological change represents the gravity in this system. Commodities, pure process innovations, and Nathan Rosenberg's (1972) example of innovation in shipping containers all score reasonably close to perfect competition at the bottom of the Quality Index (a *classical* spread, that is, of the fruits of technological change). Patent drugs fall lower – they provide an example of innovations due to technological change whose benefits spread collusively and have a high impact on wealth creation in the country of production. Patents are of course established for this very reason – they bolster profits and thus encourage investment in research. Even when technological progress no longer takes place in an economic activity, static scale effects may give the activity in question a high-value score (= dark grey). The gravity in the system – the speed with which economic activities fall from temporary monopolies to perfect competition – is also determined by the intensity of competition.

It is my contention that the powerful vortices in economic life – the vicious and virtuous circles conceived, but essentially not described, by economists like List and Myrdal – originate at the bottom and at the top of the Quality Index respectively. Increasing versus diminishing returns and varying degrees of technological windows of opportunity lie at the very core of these vortices, one dragging nations into poverty, the other propelling nations to new heights of welfare. South Korea, poorer than Tanzania in 1950, was propelled to economic growth on the basis of increasing returns and new technologies specific to very few economic activities, while Tanzania stayed poor, locked into diminishing-return activities. The different economic conditions today in Silicon Valley and in sub-Saharan Africa cannot be understood without reference to the fit of these two areas' economic activities on the Quality Index of economic activities.[20]

For centuries in Europe, a key economic policy for each nation state involved capturing the economic activities that at the time had the potential for technical change and increasing returns – that is, that had a high score on the Quality Index. In practice mechanization was used as the proxy for these two factors: every nation promoted economic activities that were in the process of being mechanized.

Historically, several factors have pushed the productive system in this direction:

- Firms' needs to innovate continuously to stay profitable;

- The need for production for war;

- The need for production for luxuries;

- The need to create a tax base;[21]

- Pushing the never-ending frontier of knowledge as a goal in and of itself (Veblen's 'idle curiosity').

There are important synergies and linkages among these factors, which all combine in powerful processes of cumulative causation when import sectors produce under increasing returns. At the same time, there is a close connection between power and economic specialization. As the eminent historian Frederic Lane observed regarding the Republic of Venice, military and political power is itself produced and utilized under considerably increasing returns.[22]

■

Conclusions

In my view, the present world economic order is built on two of the worst vices of economics. One is the Ricardian vice – working with a theory constructed on a set of totally arbitrary assumptions, none of them (except the notion of diminishing returns) having any empirical foundations. The second is the Krugmanian vice – the practice that more realistic models, although they may attract attention in the playpen of academic journals, do not carry through into economic policy. These two academic vices interlock in an extraordinary way, forming the theoretical foundation and practical policies that are carried out in the Second and Third Worlds today – with the effect of frustrating and blocking development, not augmenting it.

These two vices must be overcome. Arguably, all successful catching-up policies in the past 500 years – in England, Germany, and the United States, in smaller states of Europe, and elsewhere – have been based on the Other Canon: on an approach to economic theory and policy that contrasts starkly with standard economics. It is increasingly acknowledged that, for the large number of smaller developing nations, policies based on standard economic theory produce retrogression rather than development. Still, the same medicines continue to be applied. The relative success of the two most populous nations on the planet, China and India, is used as an argument in favour of globalization. What tends to be left out, however, is that for more than 50 years China and India have not followed Washington Consensus type policies; rather, they have followed different – more or less successful – varieties of Other Canon strategies, emphasizing the role of manufacturing.

Students of the history of economic thought will recognize the similarity between the approach developed here and that of the German Historical School and US institutionalism, both of which grew out of the excesses of the mechanical world view of the 1840s. In the terminology suggested by Nietzsche's passage placed at the beginning of this chapter, understanding economic growth requires 'seeing with perception' – in other words, 'seeing in context'. A full understanding of unequal economic growth requires understanding this phenomenon in ways suggested by the Other Canon approach to economic theory:

- Diversity, rather than equality, is the salient feature both of nature and of society. Theory ought to be built from diversity upwards towards higher levels of abstraction, rather than assuming equality as a fundamental proposition.

- The economy must be understood fundamentally as a system of learning, wherein the moving focus of technological changes creates widely different windows of opportunity for growth.

- Increasing returns is a key factor in understanding both economic growth and its absence.

- The system must be understood dynamically, rather than through statics or comparative statics.

- Contrary to Alfred Marshall's dictum that *natura non facit saltum*, human production systems are characterized by 'productivity explosions', as in the case of information technology in the 1990s (Perez 2002).

- Synergies or linkages between economic activities are a core feature of economic systems.

- Understanding should be based on qualitative *verstehen* rather than on *begreifen*, which is a mechanical understanding; and the historian's approach (many explanatory variables) is preferable to that of the standard economist (few variables) (Drechsler 2004).

- Understandings should be developed at different levels of abstraction, with frequent communications between the specific and the general. This means a full integration of macro, meso, and micro levels – of the theory of the firm with the theory of economic development.

- Finally, the understanding of development should be regarded as an interdisciplinary exercise; the sort of nutrition that is provided by contact with other disciplinary approaches is part of the nutrition that feeds the Other Canon of economics.

Bibliography

Abramowitz, M. (1956) 'Resource and output trends in the United States since 1870', *American Economic Review, Papers and Proceedings of the Sixty-eighth Annual Meeting of the American Economic Association*, Vol. 46, No. 2, May.

—— (1993)'The search for the sources of growth: areas of ignorance, old and new', *The Journal of Economic History*, Vol. 53, No. 2, June.

Arthur, W. B. (1994) *Increasing Returns and Path Dependence in the Economy*, Ann Arbor: University of Michigan Press.

Babbage, C. (1835) *On the Economy of Machinery and Manufactures*, London: Charles Knight.

Biernacki, R. (1995) *Fabrication of Labor*, Berkeley: University of California Press.

Bourdieu, P. (1980) *The Logic of Practice*, Cambridge: Polity Press.

Buchanan, J. (1979) *What Should Economists Do?* Indianapolis: Liberty Fund.

Carnegie, A. (1903) *The Empire of Business*, London: Harper.

Chang, H.-J. (2002) *Kicking Away the Ladder: Development Strategy in Historical Perspective*, London: Anthem.

Deardorff, A. and R. Stern (1994) *The Stolper-Samuelson Theorem: A Golden Jubilee*, Ann Arbor: University of Michigan Press.

Drechsler, W. (2004) 'Natural versus social sciences: on understanding in economics', in Reinert E. (ed.), *Globalization, Economic Development and Inequality: An Alternative Perspective*, Cheltenham: Elgar.

Friedman, M. (1953) *Essays in Positive Economics*, Chicago: University of Chicago Press, 1953.

Hilferding, R. (1919) *Das Finanzkapital. Eine Studie über die jüngste Entwicklung des Kapitalismus*, Vienna: Brand and Co.

Hudson, M. (1969) *E. Peshine Smith: A Study in Protectionist Growth Theory and American Sectionalism*, Ann Arbor: University Microfilm.

Huerta, R. D. (2003) *Giants of Delft. Johannes Vermeer and the Natural Philosophers: The Parallel Search for Knowledge during the Age of Discovery*, Lewisburg, PA: Bucknell University Press.

Kaldor, N. (1960) *Essays on Value and Distribution*, Glencoe, Illinois: Free Press.

Krugman, P. (1996) *The Self-Organizing Economy*, Cambridge: Blackwell Publishers.

Kuhn, T. S. (1970) *The Structure of Scientific Revolutions*, second edition, Chicago: University of Chicago Press.

Landes, D. (1998) *The Wealth and Poverty of Nations: Why Some Are So Rich and Some So Poor*, New York: W. W. Norton.

Lane, F. C. (1979) *Profits from Power: Readings in Protection Rent and Violence-Controlling Enterprises*, Albany NY: State University of New York Press.

Leamer, E. (ed.) (2001) *International Economics*, New York: Worth.

Leibenstein, H. (1978) *General X-Efficiency Theory and Economic Development*, New York: Oxford University Press.

List, F. (1841) *Das Nationale System der Politischen Ökonomie*, Stuttgart and Tübingen: Cotta, 1841.

Lowe, A. (1988) *Has Freedom a Future?* New York: Praeger.

Lucas, R. Jr. (1988) 'On the mechanics of economic development', *Journal of Monetary Economics*, Vol. 22, No. 1, July.

Machlup, F. (1962) *The Production and Distribution of Knowledge in the United States*, Princeton: Princeton University Press.

Menger, A. (1899) *The Right to the Whole Produce of Labour*, with an introduction and bibliography by H. S. Foxwell, London: Macmillan.

Mill, J. S. (1929) *Principles of Political Economy*, London: Longmans, Green.

Morgan, M. S. and M. Rutherford (eds) (1998) 'From interwar pluralism to postwar neoclassicism', In *History of Political Economy*, Supplement, Vol. 30, Durham: Duke University Press.

Neill, C. P. (1897) *Daniel Raymond, an Early Chapter in the History of Economic Theory in the United States*, Baltimore: the Johns Hopkins Press.

Nietzsche, F. (1988) 'Zur Genealogie der Moral', in *Sämtliche Werke*, Vol. 5, Munich: de Gruyter.

Norman, V. (1994) Interview in daily *Dagens Næringsliv*, Oslo, 31 December 1994, p. 21.

Penrose, E. (1959) *The Theory of Growth of the Firm*, New York: Wiley.

Perez, C. (2002) *Technological Revolutions and Financial Capital: The Dynamics of Bubbles and Golden Ages*, Cheltenham: Elgar.

Raymond, D. (1820) *Thoughts on Political Economy*, Baltimore: Fielding Lucas.

Reinert, E. (1996) 'The role of technology in the creation of rich and poor nations: underdevelopment in a Schumpeterian system', in Aldcroft, D. H. and R. Catterall (eds), *Rich Nations – Poor Nations: The Long Run Perspective*, Aldershot: Edward Elgar.

—— (1999) 'The role of the state in economic growth', *Journal of Economic Studies*, Vol. 26, Nos 4–5, November.

—— (2003) 'Increasing poverty in a globalized world: Marshall Plans and Morgenthau Plans as mechanisms of polarization of world incomes', in Chang, H.-J. (ed.), *Rethinking Economic Development*, London: Anthem.

—— (2004) 'Globalization in the periphery as a Morgenthau Plan: the under-development of Mongolia in the 1990s', in Reinert E. (ed.), *Globalization, Economic Development and Inequality: An Alternative Perspective*, Cheltenham: Elgar.

Reinert, E. and A. Daastøl (1997) 'Exploring the genesis of economic innova-tions: the religious gestalt-switch and the duty to invent as preconditions for economic growth', *European Journal of Law and Economics*, Vol. 4, Nos 2–3, May.

Robertson, W. (1832) *The History of America*, New York: Harper.

Romer, P. (1990) 'Are nonconvexities important for understanding growth?', *American Economic Review Papers and Proceedings*, Vol. 80, No. 2, May.

Rosenberg, N. (1972) *Technology and American Economic Growth*, New York: Harper and Row.

Samuelson, P. (1948) 'International trade and the equalization of factor prices', *Economic Journal*, Vol. 58, June.

Saussois, J.-M. (1998) 'Knowledge production, mediation and use in learning economies and societies', draft report, Centre for Educational Research and Innovation, OECD–CERI, Stanford University, September.

Schumpeter, J. (1912) *Theorie der wirtschaftlichen Entwicklung*, Leipzig: Duncker and Humblot.

—— (1934) *The Theory of Economic Development*, translated by R. Opie, Cambridge: Harvard University Press.

—— (1939) *Business Cycles*, New York: McGraw Hill.

Serra, A. (1613) *Breve trattato delle cause che possono far abbondare li regni d'oro e argento dove non sono miniere, con applicazione al Regno di Napoli*, Naples: Lazzaro Scorriggio.

Smith, E. P. (1853) *A Manual of Political Economy*, New York: G. P. Putnam.

Solow, R. (1957) 'Technical change and the aggregate production function', *Review of Economics and Statistics*, Vol. 39, No. 3, August.

Sombart, W. (1928) *Der Moderne Kapitalismus*, 6 vols., Munich and Leipzig, Duncker and Humblot.

Steadman, P. (2001) *Vermeer's Camera*, Oxford: Oxford University Press.

Stiglitz, J. (1994) *Whither Socialism?* Cambridge: MIT Press.

Thaler, R. H. (1992) *The Winner's Curse: Paradoxes and Anomalies of Economic Life*, New York: Free Press.

Veblen, T. (1899) *Theory of the Leisure Class*, New York: Macmillan.

—— (1914) *The Instinct of Workmanship*, New York: Macmillan.

—— (1919) *The Vested Interests and the State of the Industrial Arts*, New York: B. W. Huebsch.

Notes

1 Preliminary versions of this chapter and of chapters 5 and 6 were originally presented at an August 2000 meeting of members of 'The Other Canon' group in Oslo, Norway. The authors of these chapters acknowledge the support they received from the Norwegian Shipowners' Association. The term 'The Other Canon' refers both to an approach to economic theory and to a scholarly working group. Further information is available at the website http://www.othercanon.org.
2 This loss of pluralism of methods is discussed in Morgan and Rutherford (1998).
3 For an excellent discussion of this point, see Biernacki (1995: 253).
4 This is extensively discussed in section 9 of Reinert (1999).
5 The references are to Samuelson's 1948 extension of his 1941 article with Stolper, 'International Trade and the Equalization of Factor Prices', reprinted in Leamer (2001: 19–32), and to Friedman (1953).
6 Schumpeter (1912: 489). In English, this book has been published as Schumpeter (1934).
7 Penrose is quoted in Saussois (1998). The same paper, which was a contribution to a 1998 OECD study of knowledge and growth, includes this apt 1956 quote from Kenneth Boulding: 'The economists have badly neglected the impact of information and knowledge structure on economic behaviour and processes. There are good reasons, or perhaps one should say excuses, for this neglect. With deft analytical fingers, the economist abstracts from the untidy complexities of social life a neat work on commodities. It is the behaviour of commodities, not the behaviour of men, which is the prime focus of interest in economic studies.'
8 Paul Krugman's 1979 paper 'Increasing returns, monopolistic competition, and international trade' is reprinted in Leamer (2001: 255–65); see also Krugman (1996).
9 For example, Schumpeter wrote, 'What dominates the picture of capitalistic life and is more than anything else responsible for our impression of a prevalence of decreasing cost, causing disequilibria, cut-throat competition and so on, is innovation, the intrusion into the system of new production functions which incessantly shift existing cost curves' (Schumpeter 1939: 66).
10 See Steadman (2001).
11 See Huerta (2003).
12 Veblen's ideas about economic growth appear in several of his works; see especially Veblen (1899), Veblen (1914) and Veblen (1919).
13 This volume was privately published in Dublin in 1777. It was published in the US as Robertson (1832).
14 These mechanisms are discussed in Reinert (1996).

15 Raymond (1820). Raymond's work appeared in four editions from 1820 to 1840.
16 See Neill (1897).
17 Ha-Joon Chang's recent volume (2002) picks up this argument from Friedrich List (1841) and provides historical examples of this same theme.
18 Sombart's key work is Sombart (1928). The key volumes have been translated from the German and published in French, Spanish, and Italian.
19 This concept was originally explored in Kaldor's 1956 essay 'Alternative theories of distribution', reprinted in Kaldor (1960).
20 The cumulative effects of learning, life cycles and increasing and diminishing returns are discussed in greater detail in Erik Reinert (2003) and (2004).
21 The treasurers in the early small European states soon found out that the short-term subsidies to manufacturing in the long term increased public revenues. In short: the people who produced with machinery were able to pay more taxes than those who worked only with their hands.
22 See Lane (1979).

Rethinking the Role of Institutions and Macrostructures in Development

4

Institutions and Economic Development: Constraining, Enabling, and Reconstituting

GEOFFREY M. HODGSON

Real-world institutions are often inefficient, and sometimes unjust or corrupt.[1] For those that cherish individual liberty, institutions are often seen as unwarranted constraints. Many economists have approached matters of policy with similar sentiments, believing that markets always work best when there is a minimum of regulation or restriction. However, matters are in truth much more complicated, and there is evidence that the performance of economies and markets typically depends on institutional structures or restraints. The purpose of this chapter is to help to understand the role of institutions in economic life. In particular, the potentially positive and enabling aspect of institutions has to be placed alongside their function as constraints. In addition, the ways in which institutions may not merely restrict us, but also mould our very wants and desires, have also to be considered.

The next section defines institutions and distinguishes them from organizations. This is followed by a discussion of the enabling role of institutions and the ways in which they can facilitate decisions and actions. The chapter goes on to review the possibility of 'reconstitutive downward causation' from institutions to individuals, and concludes by summarizing some implications of these ideas for economic development.

■

What Are Institutions?

Nobel Laureate Douglass North (1990: 3) described institutions as 'the rules of the game in society or ... the humanly devised constraints that shape human interaction.' Essentially I follow this conception here, but it requires some elaboration and clarification. Institutions are systems of rules. But the concept of a rule and its effects needs to be considered. We are not concerned with decreed or written rules that are largely ignored and have little effect. Inhabitants of developed as well as underdeveloped countries ignore some legal rules. We are concerned not with rules that lack social impact, but with rule systems that are effective in that they 'shape human interaction'.

Partly for this reason, I modify North's definition: *Institutions are durable systems of established and embedded social rules that structure social interactions.* In short, institutions are social rule systems. The term 'rule' is broadly understood as an injunction or disposition, that in circumstances X do Y. Hence it includes norms of behaviour and social conventions, as well as legal or formal rules. By their nature, institutions must involve some shared conceptions. Language, money, law, systems of weights and measures, traffic conventions, table manners, firms (and all other organizations) are institutions.

Most rules are potentially codifiable. The members of the relevant community or society share tacit or explicit knowledge of these rules. If a rule is not codified, then it is more difficult to identify explicitly any breaches of this rule. As John Searle (1995) argues, the mental representations of an institution or its rules are partly constitutive of that institution, since an institution can only exist if people have specifically related beliefs and mental attitudes. Hence an institution is a special type of social structure that involves codifiable rules of interpretation and behaviour. Some of these rules concern commonly accepted tokens or meanings, as is obviously the case with money or language. However, as Max Weber (1978: 105) pointed out in 1907, rules are often followed 'without any subjective formulation in thought of the "rule"'. Nevertheless, the rules can in principle be codified, so that breaches of these rules can be more readily detected.

What is the difference between an organization and an institution? North (1994: 361) wrote: 'If institutions are the rules of the game, organizations and their entrepreneurs are the players.' Some people have interpreted North as saying that organizations are not themselves institutions. But North does not actually say this. He simply asserts his primary interest in economic systems rather than the internal functioning of individual organizations. Furthermore, in correspondence with the present author, North has made it clear that he believes that organizations are also institutions. North accepts that organizations themselves have internal players and systems of rules, and hence by implication organizations are a special type of institution.[2]

We may define an organization as a special type of institution involving (1) criteria to establish its boundaries and to distinguish its members from its non-members; (2) a principle of sovereignty concerning who is in charge; and (3) a chain of command delineating responsibilities within the organization. Organizations are here defined as a type of structure with the capacity for goal-directed behaviour, irrespective of whether goals are actually declared. In this sense, an organization has the capacity to be a 'collective actor' (Knight 1992: 3).

North also makes another important distinction between formal and informal 'constraints'. His examples of 'formal constraints' are 'rules, laws, constitutions' and of 'informal constraints' are 'norms of behaviour, conventions, self-imposed codes of conduct' (1994: 360). This suggests that rules are a special kind of formal constraint. Again contrary to some interpreters, North does not make a distinction between formal or informal institutions. Typically he applies the qualifier 'informal' to 'constraints', rather than rules or institutions. This raises problems concerning the meaning of 'constraint' and its difference from a rule, as well as the meaning of the distinction between the 'formal' and the 'informal'.

Social rules are themselves often constraining, hence any distinction between rule and constraint is not particularly useful. Institutions are systems of embedded rules, from which constraints may follow. North identifies 'formal rules' with legal rules 'enforced by courts'. In contrast: 'Informal norms are enforced usually by your peers or other who impose costs on you if you do not live up to them.'[3] These 'norms' also have a rule-like character: *if* one does not follow a norm, *then* sanctions will be imposed. Hence I propose to deploy the terms 'rule' and 'institution' more broadly than North, to cover both legal and non-legal systems of rules.

All legal institutions depend on inexplicit and informal rules, as well as on codified laws. As Émile Durkheim observed in 1893: 'in a contract not everything is contractual' (Durkheim 1984: 158). Whenever a contract exists there are rules and norms that are not necessarily codified in law. The parties to the agreement are forced to rely on institutional rules and standard patterns of behaviour, which for reasons of practicality and complexity cannot be fully established as explicit laws. Legal systems are invariable incomplete, and give scope for custom and culture to do their work (Hodgson 2001).

Some non-legal institutions may evolve largely spontaneously, that is without overall human plan or design, and can have enormous social effects. Language is a prime example; it was caused but not designed. With the possible exception of Esperanto, no one planned or designed a living language. Language is ridden with rules that have to be observed for communicators to convey their intended meaning. In any given culture, there are many other informal rules of human interaction. Many of these, including the rules of language, are essentially coordination equilibria that are reproduced simply because it is convenient for agents to conform to them.

Coordination rules typically provide incentives for everyone to conform to the convention. For this reason, coordination equilibrium can be highly stable and self-policing. For example, Willard van Orman Quine (1960) made the point that language has an error-correcting regime. Individuals have an incentive to make their words clear. As an essential condition of communication, the coding itself (the signifier) must be unmistakable, even if the meaning (the signified) remains partly ambiguous. In communication we have strong incentives and inclinations to use words and sounds in a way that conforms as closely as possible to the perceived norm. Although languages do change through time, there are incentives to conform to, and thus reinforce, the linguistic norms in the given region or context. Norms of language and pronunciation are thus largely self-policing.

In contrast, other systems of rules do not correct themselves spontaneously and require constant intervention by or support from other institutions. The institution of property is an important case in point. Contrary to the view that property rights can emerge and be sustained generally without the intervention of the state, Itai Sened (1997) shows that with large numbers of players in relatively complex environments, it is more difficult for individuals to establish mutual and reciprocal arrangements that enforce property rights and ensure contract compliance. In a world of incomplete and imperfect information, high transaction costs, asymmetrically powerful relations and agents with limited insight, powerful institutions are necessary to enforce rights. These institutions result from complex bargaining processes. Sened uses an n-person Prisoners' Dilemma to show that the introduction of a government, enforcing rights, can often improve on a suboptimal outcome.

To summarize the points made so far in this section, institutions have been defined broadly as social systems of embedded rules. Organizations are a special subset of institutions, which have additional characteristics of membership and sovereignty. Within institutions, a distinction can be made between formal (or legally specified) and informal (or legally unspecified) rules. All institutions, including legal institutions, involve informal rules. Some institutions are made up entirely of informal rules. A further distinction must be made between, on the one hand, those institutions that evolve spontaneously and, on the other hand, those that result from design or require exogenous intervention or enforcement.

All these points are relevant for problems of economic development. It is important not simply to recognize the importance of institutions and rules, but also to understand the ways in which appropriate rules are established and followed. The above discussion suggests that rules are never fully established simply by proclamation or decree. Even when legal rules are essential, such as in the protection of property rights and the enforcement of contracts, the rules have also to be sanctioned in the sentiments and day-to-day practices of the people. On the other hand, appropriate customs and informal rules have to be protected by, and be consistent with, statute law. Severe ethnic rivalries, and networks of nepotism or corruption, are often barriers to the establishment and operation of universal and impartial legal rules. Part of the problem of economic development is to establish a fair and effective state administration, and an efficient system of property rights that are sustained in both informal culture and formal legal rules (De Soto 2000).

Countless case studies of economic underdevelopment attest to the difficulty of establishing social rules unless they have an effective presence in both formal and informal spheres. Tradition and statute – the informal and the formal – sustain and depend upon each other. Likewise, developed economies have prospered precisely because they have overcome these problems to a significant degree; of course a tension between legal formalities and actual practice always remains, however, especially as law and economic relations become more complex. Further considerations that are relevant to the establishment of social rule systems are raised below.

■

The Necessity of Institutions and the Nature of Markets

I argue here that, contrary to prevailing libertarian ideology, institutions are necessary to enable human action and, in particular, some institutional rigidities are necessary to make markets work.

The necessity of institutions is most obvious in the case of language. Without the rules of language – which are often idiosyncratic and arcane – communication would be impossible. The English language, for example, entails a maze of perplexing rules and spellings. Yet the very rigidity and 'ceremonial' reproduction of many of these rules helps maintain the integrity and usefulness of the language, alongside its fluidity and capacity to evolve in other respects.

We are born into a world of chaotic confusion. We are confronted by a mass of sense data that is difficult to understand. Driven initially by our instincts, we focus on specific stimuli and begin to observe regularities of behaviour.[4] We then begin to rely upon them for our own interaction with the world. Our initial socialization relies on the learning of not only the rules of language but also a myriad of other social rules relevant to our particular culture. These rules concern matters of social interaction, rights, hygiene, property, and so on. Much of this learning is implicit or tacit, in that we absorb rules without full consideration of their codified form (Reber 1993). Acquisition of these rules is essential for our social interaction with others and often for our survival. Accordingly, rules enable social behaviour as well as constraining it.

The combination of enabling and constraining features is found among more complex institutions as well. Consider markets. A market is an institution through which multiple buyers and multiple sellers exchange a substantial number of commodities of a particular type. Exchanges themselves take place in a framework of law and contract enforceability. All markets involve rules of involvement, price declaration, negotiation and so on. Hence, contrary to much of mainstream economics, and as John Hobson put it long ago: 'A market, however crudely formed, is a social institution' (1902: 144).

North has rightly remarked: 'It is a peculiar fact that the literature on economics and economic history contains so little discussion of the central institution that underlies neoclassical economics – the market' (1977: 710). A striking feature of much economic thought is that it cannot conceive of the market in institutional terms. It presumes, like the classic liberalism of the nineteenth century, that the market is the 'natural' order; it is the ether within which the preferences and purposes of free-floating individuals are expressed. The notion of the market as an institution, organized to structure and, inevitably to some extent, constrain economic activity is overlooked. In much economic theory the 'constraints' relate exclusively to market 'imperfections' or extra-market institutions. The idea of the market as an organized and enabling entity, more than the aggregation of mere individual exchanges, and which may actually mould the tastes and preferences of actors, is missing.

On the contrary, it is often assumed that markets would work better if rules and restrictions were generally removed. A problem in this position is that it does not recognize the necessity and inevitability of rules within markets themselves. Another line of criticism is to consider the limits of free competition and the degree to which constraints upon it could be removed.

For example, George B. Richardson (1959, 1960) argues that if neoclassical 'perfect competition' did actually exist it could not actually function for long. The problem would be that no individual agent would be aware of the investment intentions of others. The incentive to invest depends in part on the knowledge of a limited competitive supply from other firms. 'Perfect competition' does not provide this. Precisely because of its 'perfection' it places no limit on the number of firms that can be expected to compete. Consequently the investment process will be impaired.

Richardson argues that in the real world investors obtain information in a number of ways about the prospective activities of those to whom they are interrelated. There is explicit collusion or agreement, implicit collusion resulting possibly from cultural habits and accepted routines, and there are so-called 'frictions', 'imperfections', and 'restraints'. All these, although they appear to stand in the way of 'free competition', are actually in some measure necessary to make the market system function at all.

Jan Kregel (1980) also developed this idea that constraints and restrictions provide information and actually help the market to function. He regards so-called market 'imperfections' such as 'wage contracts, debt contracts, supply agreements, administered prices, trading agreements' as 'uncertainty-reducing institutions' (p. 46). Kregel's argument is reminiscent of that of John Maynard Keynes (1936) in Chapter 17 of *The General Theory*, where it is suggested that the partial rigidity of the money wage is necessary for the working of the economy.

Andrew Schotter (1981, 1985) provided a related argument. He uses a game-theoretic framework to show that institutions and routines are, far from being market 'imperfections', actually necessary to supply vital information, particularly about the future stratagems of other agents. 'Perfect competition' does not signal this information other than through the restrictive mechanism of the price system. 'Imperfect' markets enable much more information to be transmitted, and in ways other than through price: 'economies contain an information network far richer than that described by the price system. This network is made up of a whole complex of institutions, rules of thumb, customs and beliefs that help to transfer a great deal of information about the anticipated actions of agents in the economy' (Schotter 1981: 118).

As a result, the necessity of institutions extends beyond the working of human society and the socialization of individuals; the rules and constraints inherent in institutions can also play a functional role in markets. The idea of the market as the unconstrained epitome of liberty is misconceived. Any attempt to remove all restraints and regulations from a market system would be dysfunctional.

Again this has relevance for problems of economic development and transition, illustrated most graphically in the post-1989 economic trans-formation in the former Eastern bloc. A common assumption was that the market order would rapidly germinate and grow in the primordial soil of human relations, once the old state bureaucracies were swept away. As the influential Western adviser Jeffrey Sachs (1993: xxi) contended: 'markets spring up as soon as central planning bureaucrats vacate the field'. In fact, markets did not spring up spontaneously. The requisite commercial rules, norms and institutions were lacking (Kozul-Wright and Rayment 1997; Grabher and Stark 1997). As Nobel laureate Ronald Coase (1992: 718) rightly observed: 'The ex-communist countries are advised to move to a market economy ... but without the appropriate institutions, no market of any significance is possible.'

Similar remarks apply to underdeveloped economies. There too we should not expect markets to spring up automatically, even if individual trade is relatively unconstrained, without the formal and informal arrangements that are necessary to sustain market institutions. A developed market economy requires an appropriate and developed civil society, working through effective institutions including the legal system.

■

Reconstitutive Downward Causation

Part of the task of understanding institutions is to appreciate how and why rules are followed, and how and why they bear upon individual behaviour. In part, the answers to these questions depend upon human psychology. Rules are embedded partly because people choose to follow them repeatedly. In addition, pragmatist philosophers (in the tradition of William James and John Dewey) and 'old' institutional economists (in the tradition of Thorstein Veblen, John Commons and Wesley Mitchell) argue that institutions work only because the rules involved are embedded in shared habits of thought and behaviour.

The American institutional economist Thorstein Veblen (1919) saw insti-tutions as depending upon ingrained 'habits of thought' common to a group of people. The mechanism of habit, as William James (1892: 143) proclaimed, is 'the enormous fly-wheel of society, its most precious conservative agent'. Once relevant habits are acquired among a group of people, then the related rules will be followed and reinforced. From this perspective, institutions are emergent social structures, based on commonly held habits of thought: institutions are conditioned by and dependent upon individuals and their habits, but they are not reducible to them. Habits are the constitutive material of institutions, providing them with enhanced durability, power and normative authority. Habits also provide a mechanism that explains how individuals become moulded by institutional circumstances – by adopting accordant habits – and the durability of habits and rules once they are formed (Hodgson 2002, 2003, 2004; Hodgson and Knudsen 2004).

Habits themselves are formed through repetition of action or thought. They are influenced by prior activity and have durable, self-sustaining qualities. Through their habits, individuals carry the marks of their own unique history. Habits are the basis of both reflective and non-reflective behaviour. For the human agent, habits are themselves means of higher deliberation and conscious resolve.

However, habit does not mean behaviour. It is a *propensity* to behave in particular ways in a particular class of situations. Crucially, we may have habits that lie unused for a long time. A habit may exist even if it is not manifest in behaviour. Habits are submerged repertoires of potential behaviour; they can be triggered by an appropriate stimulus or context.

The dependence of institutions upon habits partly roots institutions in the dispositions of individuals. Institutions are structures that face individuals, as well as stemming from individuals themselves. Accordingly, institutions are simultaneously both objective structures 'out there', and subjective springs of human agency 'in the human head'. Actor and structure, although distinct, are connected in a circle of mutual interaction and interdependence. However, the relationship is not symmetrical; structures and institutions typically precede individuals (Archer, 1995; Hodgson, 2004). We are all born into a world of pre-existing institutions, bestowed by history.

Institutions are the kind of structures that matter most in the social realm. They matter most because of their capacity to form and mould the capacities and behaviours of agents in fundamental ways. Instead of merely enabling individual action, the hidden and most penetrating feature of institutions is their capacity to mould and change individual dispositions and aspirations. Hence in all human societies a process of 'downward causation' is associated with institutions. It is not confined to the conscious designs of the advertisers or propagandists. It emanates more widely from the ordinary routine of everyday life.

The idea of 'upward causation' is already widely accepted in the social and natural sciences. Elements at a lower ontological level affect those at a higher one. For example, influenza epidemics reduce economic productivity and voting can change governments. Upward causation can be reconstitutive, because lower-level changes may alter fundamentally a higher-level structure.

However, reductionists are obliged to deny the possibility of reconstitutive downward causation that is being proposed here. With reconstitutive downward causation it is impossible to take the parts as given and then explain the whole. Furthermore, for reasons examined below, the notion of reconstitutive downward causation does not fall foul of past critiques of 'holism' or methodological collectivism.

The term 'downward causation' originates in psychology in the work of the Nobel psycho-biologist Roger Sperry (1964, 1969). In its literature, the notion of 'downward causation' has weak and strong forms. In a relatively weaker case, Donald Campbell (1974) sees it in terms of evolutionary laws acting on populations. He argues that all processes at the lower levels of an ontological hierarchy are restrained by and act in conformity to the laws of the higher levels. In other words, if there are systemic properties and tendencies then individual components of the system act in conformity with them. For example, a population of individual organisms is constrained by processes of natural selection.

The concept of downward causation does not rely on new or mysterious types of cause or causality. As Sperry (1991: 230) rightly insists: 'the higher-level phenomena in exerting downward control do *not disrupt* or *intervene* in the causal relations of the downward-level component activity'. This could usefully be termed Sperry's Rule. It ensures that emergence, although it is associated with emergent causal powers at a higher level, does not generate multiple types or forms of causality at any single level. Any emergent causes at higher levels exist by virtue of lower-level causal processes.

Adherence to Sperry's Rule excludes any version of methodological collectivism or holism where an attempt is made to explain individual dispositions or behaviour entirely in terms of institutions or other system-level characteristics. Instead, Sperry's Rule obliges us to explain particular human behaviour in terms of causal processes operating at the individual level, such as individual aspirations, dispositions or constraints. Higher-level factors enter in the more general explanation of the system-wide processes giving rise to those aspirations, dispositions or constraints.

A stronger notion of downward causation, which I describe as 'reconstitutive downward causation', involves both individuals and populations not only restrained, but also changed, as a result of causal powers associated with higher levels. But how does this happen? We have to consider how the dispositions, thoughts and actions of human actors are changed. People do not develop new preferences, wants or purposes because mysterious 'social forces' control them. The argument here is that the pragmatist and institutionalist concept of habit provides part of a plausible and reconstitutive mechanism.

From the pragmatist and institutionalist perspective, habits are foundational to all thought and behaviour. As argued elsewhere, all deliberations, including rational optimization, themselves rely on habits and rules (Hodgson 1997). Even rational optimization must involve rules. In turn, as suggested above, rules have to become ingrained in habits in order to be deployed by agents. Hence rationality always depends on prior habits and rules as props (Hodgson 1988). This primary reliance on habits and rules limits the explanatory scope of rational optimization. Hence rational optimization can never supply the complete explanation of human behaviour and institutions for which some theorists seem to be striving. At the centre of a more adequate explanation of human agency would be the reconstitutive processes through which habits are formed and changed.

Our habits help to make up our preferences and dispositions. When new habits are acquired or existing habits change, then our preferences alter. Dewey (1922: 40) thus wrote of 'the cumulative effect of insensible modifications worked by a particular habit in the body of preferences'. Alternatively, we could presume, following Gary Becker and Kevin Murphy (1988) and others, that habitual modifications are consistent with some unchanging 'meta-preference' function. However, those that place behaviour within a meta-preference function neglect the argument that these preferences too must be grounded on learned habits and dispositions. Otherwise, as suggested above, we have no plausible story of their origin.

Generally, institutional changes and constraints can cause changes in habits of thought and behaviour. Institutions constrain our behaviour and develop our habits in specific ways. What does happen is that the framing, shifting and constraining capacities of social institutions give rise to new perceptions and dispositions within individuals. Upon new habits of thought and behaviour, new preferences and intentions emerge. Alfred Marshall (1949: 76) observed 'the development of new activities giving rise to new wants'. But we need to know how this happens. Veblen (1899: 190, emphasis added) was more specific about the psychological mechanisms involved: 'The situation of today shapes the institutions of tomorrow through a selective, coercive process, *by acting upon men's habitual view of things.*'

An implication for economic development is that attention should be given to institutions and institutional features that are conducive to norms and values that serve social integration, personal development, and human needs more generally. The choice of institutions becomes a doubly important policy decision, not only because they provide incentive structures for individual behaviour, but also because institutions can mould individual mentalities and preferences.

■

Conclusions

We started by considering the definition of an institution, seeing it essentially as a system of established and embedded social rules. Some institutions emerge spontaneously and are often self-policing. Language and some traffic rules come into this category. By contrast, other institutions require exogenous agencies of enforcement. Examples in complex societies include property rights and contract law. A further distinction within institutions is between formal (or legally specified) and informal (or legally unspecified) rules. Some but not all institutions involve formal rules. All institutions involve some informal rules. Some institutions are made up entirely of informal rules. Institutions of a specific type are known as organizations. These are institutions with criteria of membership and rules of sovereignty.

Institutions are the stuff of socio-economic life. This is because systems of rules are necessary for human interaction and cooperation. The idea of freedom as freedom of rules is an unattainable utopia. Institutions do not merely constrain behaviour; they can typically enable activity in a number of ways. In particular, markets are systems of rules and thus also enable and constrain behaviour. For several reasons touched on above, rules and constraints are necessary to make markets work. Hence the ideal of an entirely 'free' and minimally constrained market overlooks the institutional character of markets and proposes yet another unattainable utopia.

The third section explored the ways in which institutions can affect and alter individual dispositions, purposes or preferences by forming or acting upon ingrained habits. This brief excursion into the psychology of habit points to a means of explaining the durability of socio-economic institutions and the ways in which rules become embedded in the dispositions of individuals.

Some implications for economic development can be noted. First, the identification of the informal aspects of institutions and the basis of institutional durability in individual habituations suggests that institution building is much more than a matter of governmental decree. Furthermore, the process involves changes in individual mentalities as well as the organization of social relations or structures. Typically, institution building takes a long time.

Second, the spontaneous and self-organizing mechanisms within institutions should be recognized. These mechanisms often belittle attempts at institutional design or decree, especially where the system is so complex or opaque that legislators are unable to gather together all the necessary information. However, several important institutions cannot develop through spontaneity alone. Accordingly there is a role for institutional design or legislation.

A policy of economic development must necessarily involve institution building. Taken together, the observations in the previous two paragraphs suggest that institution building must involve a judicious combination of careful legislation with simultaneous efforts to encourage the development of habits and other informal cultural features that are consistent with policy goals. Legislation cannot go faster than the development of human habits and informal social norms. But, at the same time, a policy of non-intervention, in the name of individual freedom or social self-organization, is misguided. There is no good theoretical argument to suggest that appropriate economic institutions will always evolve by themselves.

Bibliography

Archer, M. S. (1995) *Realist Social Theory: The Morphogenetic Approach*, Cambridge: Cambridge University Press.

Becker, G. S. and K. M. Murphy (1988) 'A theory of rational addiction', *Journal of Political Economy*, Vol. 96, No. 4, August.

Campbell, D. T. (1974) '"Downward causation" in hierarchically organized biological systems', in Ayala, F. J. and T. Dobzhansky (eds), *Studies in the Philosophy of Biology*, London, Berkeley and Los Angeles: Macmillan and University of California Press.

Coase, R. H. (1992) 'The institutional structure of production', *American Economic Review*, Vol. 82, No. 4, September.

De Soto, H. (2000) *The Mystery of Capital: Why Capitalism Triumphs in the West and Fails Everywhere Else*, New York: Basic Books.

Degler, C. N. (1991) *In Search of Human Nature: The Decline and Revival of Darwinism in American Social Thought*, Oxford and New York: Oxford University Press.

Dewey, J. (1922) *Human Nature and Conduct: An Introduction to Social Psychology*, New York: Holt.

Durkheim, É. (1984) *The Division of Labour in Society*, translated from the French edition of 1893 by W. D. Halls with an introduction by L. Coser, London: Macmillan.

Grabher, G. and D. Stark (eds) (1997) *Restructuring Networks in Post-Socialism: Legacies, Linkages and Localities*, Oxford: Oxford University Press.

Hobson, J. A. (1902) *The Social Problem: Life and Work*, London: James Nisbet.

Hodgson, G. M. (1988) *Economics and Institutions: A Manifesto for a Modern Institutional Economics*, Cambridge and Philadelphia: Polity Press and University of Pennsylvania Press.

—— (1997) 'The ubiquity of habits and rules', *Cambridge Journal of Economics*, Vol. 21, No. 6, November.

—— (2001) *How Economics Forgot History: The Problem of Historical Specificity in Social Science*, London and New York: Routledge.

—— (2002) 'Reconstitutive downward causation: social structure and the development of individual agency', in Fullbrook, E. (ed.), *Intersubjectivity in Economics: Agents and Structures*, London and New York: Routledge.

—— (2003) 'The hidden persuaders: institutions and individuals in economic theory', *Cambridge Journal of Economics*, Vol. 27, No. 2, March.

—— (2004) *The Evolution of Institutional Economics: Agency, Structure and Darwinism in American Institutionalism*, London and New York: Routledge.

Hodgson, G. M. and K. Thorbjørn (2004) 'The complex evolution of a simple traffic convention: the functions and implications of habit', *Journal of Economic Behavior and Organization*, Vol. 54, No. 1, May.

James, W. (1892) *Psychology: Briefer Course*, New York and London: Holt and Macmillan.

Keynes, J. M. (1936) *The General Theory of Employment, Interest and Money*, London: Macmillan.

Knight, J. (1992) *Institutions and Social Conflict*, Cambridge: Cambridge University Press.

Kozul-Wright, R. and P. Rayment (1997) 'The institutional hiatus in economics in transition and its policy consequences', *Cambridge Journal of Economics*, Vol. 21, No. 5, September.

Kregel, J. A. (1980) 'Markets and institutions as features of a capitalistic production system', *Journal of Post Keynesian Economics*, Vol. 3, No. 1, Fall.

Marshall, A. (1949) *The Principles of Economics*, London: Macmillan.

North, D. C. (1977) 'Markets and other allocation systems in history: the challenge of Karl Polanyi', *Journal of European Economic History*, Vol. 6, No. 3, Winter.

—— (1990) *Institutions, Institutional Change and Economic Performance*, Cambridge: Cambridge University Press.

—— (1994) 'Economic performance through time', *American Economic Review*, Vol. 84, No. 3, June.

Plotkin, H. C. (1994) *Darwin Machines and the Nature of Knowledge: Concerning Adaptations, Instinct and the Evolution of Intelligence*, Harmondsworth: Penguin.

Quine, W. V. (1960) *Word and Object*, Cambridge, MA: Harvard University Press.

Reber, Arthur S. (1993) *Implicit Learning and Tacit Knowledge: An Essay on the Cognitive Unconscious*, Oxford and New York: Oxford University Press.

Richardson, G. B. (1959) 'Equilibrium, expectations and information', *Economic Journal*, Vol. 69, No. 274, June.

—— (1960) *Information and Investment*, Oxford: Oxford University Press.

Sachs, J. D. (1993) *Poland's Jump to a Market Economy*, Cambridge, MA: Harvard University Press.

Schotter, A. R. (1981) *The Economic Theory of Social Institutions*, Cambridge: Cambridge University Press.

—— (1985) *Free Market Economics: A Critical Appraisal*, New York: St. Martin's Press.

Searle, J. R. (1995) *The Construction of Social Reality*, London: Allen Lane.

Sened, I. (1997) *The Political Institution of Private Property*, Cambridge: Cambridge University Press.

Sperry, R. W. (1964) *Problems Outstanding in the Evolution of Brain Function*, New York: American Museum of Natural History.

—— (1969) 'A modified concept of consciousness', *Psychological Review*, Vol. 76, No. 6, November.

—— (1991) 'In defense of mentalism and emergent interaction', *Journal of Mind and Behavior*, Vol. 12, No. 2, Spring.

Veblen, T. B. (1899) *The Theory of the Leisure Class: An Economic Study in the Evolution of Institutions*, New York: Macmillan.

—— (1919) *The Place of Science in Modern Civilization and Other Essays*, New York: Huebsch.

Weber, M. (1978) *Max Weber: Selections in Translation*, Cambridge: Cambridge University Press.

Notes

1 I thank Ana Celia Castro, Silvana De Paula, Gary Dymski, Anthony Kasozi and Alex Lascaux for helpful comments on an earlier draft of this essay.

2 More specifically, in a letter to North of 19 September 2002 I asked if he would agree to 'a definition of organization that accepted that organizations themselves had internal players and systems of rules, and hence organizations were a special type of institution.' In his reply of 7 October 2002, North expressed 'complete agreement' with this idea.

3 Letter to G. M. Hodgson dated 7 October 2002.

4 The concept of instinct was central to Veblen's institutionalism. It dropped out of favour in psychology in the 1920s, but has slowly made a comeback since the 1960s (Degler 1991; Plotkin 1994; Hodgson 2004).

5

The Role of Institutions in Economic Change

HA-JOON CHANG
AND
PETER EVANS

■

Introduction

Institutions are systematic patterns of shared expectations, taken-for-granted assumptions, accepted norms and routines of interaction that have robust effects on shaping the motivations and behaviour of sets of interconnected social actors. In modern societies, they are usually embodied in authoritatively coordinated organizations with formal rules and the capacity to impose coercive sanctions, such as the government or firms.[1] Everyone recognizes that institutions are fundamental to economic change. Nonetheless, despite a resurgence of institutionalist thinking inside and outside of economics over the course of the past 25 years, we are still a long way from a satisfying theory of institutions and their economic effects.

This chapter is a modest attempt at pushing forward our thinking about institutions and economic change. Discontent with existing approaches to institutions is one motivation for this effort. The dominant economics canon, bent on conceptualizing economic change in ways that facilitate more elegant mathematical representation, has allowed itself to fall into a false parsimony that cripples its ability to understand major shifts in economic structures. Even conventional institutionalist explanations tend to reduce institutions to functionalist consequences of efficiency considerations or instrumental reflections of interests. Our aim is to move beyond this 'thin' view of institutions toward a 'thick' view, one which recognizes both the key role of culture and ideas and the constitutive role of institutions in shaping the ways that groups and individuals define their preferences.

Another conviction guiding this chapter is that a better understanding of major changes in the global political economy is essential for practical as well as theoretical reasons. The current global economy leaves too much to be desired. Despite the paeans of the dominant canon to the new efficiency of global markets, growth rates have still not recovered to match those of the pre-globalization period before 1973. More disturbingly, the growth that is occurring is of a highly inegalitarian sort that divides societies and provides a small minority of the world's citizens with large gains at the expense of social, cultural and ecological assets that are irreplaceable from the point of view of the vast majority. Equally disturbing is the increased volatility of new global markets, especially financial ones.

Concern over the negative outcomes associated with current patterns of globalization and the intellectual endeavour of replacing thin approaches to institutions with thicker ones are two sides of the same coin. Intellectually inadequate approaches to institutions lead to bad policy and welfare-damaging outcomes on the ground. People are hurt because social scientists and policy makers misunderstand institutions. Only a broadly conceived institutional analysis can provide a basis for theorizing a serious restructuring of globalization. To shy away from the effort to construct such an analysis would seem irresponsible, regardless of how difficult it may be to produce even a modest and preliminary version.

We set out our general conceptual framework in the next section. We argue that an institutional approach must do two things: first, develop a more adequate vision of how institutions shape economic behaviour and outcomes; second, create a more systematic and general understanding of how institutions themselves are formed and change over time. To construct such a vision we must get beyond the traditional view of 'institutions as constraints', focusing attention instead on institutions as devices that *enable* the achievement of goals requiring supra-individual coordination and, even more important, are *constitutive* of the interests and world views of economic actors. Our goal is to move beyond the 'thin' economistic models that dominate the current discourse on institutions. Neither a functionalist view – in which what is must be efficient since otherwise it would not exist – nor an instrumentalist view – in which institutions are created and changed to reflect the exogenously defined interests of the powerful – is adequate. Instead, we argue for a more culturalist (or perhaps Gramscian) perspective in which institutional change depends on a combination of interest-based and cultural/ideological projects (in which world view may shape interests as well as *vice versa*). Simply put, changing institutions requires changing the world views that inevitably underlie institutional frames.

Obviously, our simultaneous emphasis on the constitutive role of institutions and on a culturalist perspective on institutional formation suggests a perspective in which institutions and economic actors are mutually constitutive. This in turn leads to the danger of imagining a self-reinforcing homeostasis: if institutions shaped world views and world views shaped institutions in some simple way, stasis would result. To avoid this, it is necessary to understand how the process of constructing and maintaining institutions generates tensions and contradictions that force change, and further, how exogenous shocks may set off or redirect such processes. Lacking systematic theoretical leverage on this problem, we rely on our two case studies to give us some purchase.

The remaining sections of the chapter present two strategic case studies; these illustrate our theoretical perspective and, at the same time, generate substantive propositions about the causes and consequences of institutional change with applications beyond these cases. The first case study focuses on the national context – specifically, the Korean developmental state. The developmental state provides a classic example of how institutions make a difference in economic change, as it is among the institutions that have most dramatically reshaped the relative national trajectories of economic growth in the late twentieth century. Our attention centres not on the well-documented emergence of this state, but on its *fall*. Why should such an obviously effective institution be subject to political attack? And why should such an attack succeed so well in undermining this institution?

Next we present a case study of the World Trade Organization (WTO) in the context of the global political economy. This permits us to focus on how existing organizations of global governance shape the way rules are made and enforced. Our interest in creating more ideal configurations of global rules then leads us to ask: what kind of institution building is required to make the projected rules work, and what is the likelihood that such institutions can be constructed?

The two case studies complement each other and demonstrate the relevance of an institutional approach to the contemporary global political economy. Substantively, the question of what kind of division of labour does and should exist between nation states and international organizations in governing the global economy is hotly contested. The dominant canon has a simple answer: uniform rules, objectively enforced, are the key to global efficiency; distinctive strategies, such as those created by developmental states, will and should be punished by the market. Without buying this hypothesis we also assume that understanding the global context is essential to understanding the evolution of the developmental state. Conversely, the WTO is, after all, a membership organization whose members are states; its functioning is fundamentally shaped by old ideas of national sovereignty. Theoretically, the developmental state and the WTO provide opportunities for examining very different processes of institutional change: in the case of the developmental state, how established institutions are undermined and transformed; in the case of the WTO, how new institutions are invented.

Having analyzed the possibilities (and failures) of economic governance in the contemporary political economy, our chapter concludes by returning to more general issues. On the substantive level, we examine the implications of the institutional trajectories we have described for the functioning of the contemporary political economy, and especially for the possibility of more equitable global growth. On a theoretical level, we set out more general hypotheses about the role of institutions and processes of institutional change. We close with some thoughts on the prospects for building a real institutionalist alternative to the currently dominant canon.

■

Conceptualizing the Causes and Consequences of Institutional Change

In this section, we set out our general conceptual framework for understanding the nature and the changes of institutions, which will inform our discussions in the following sections. We begin by underlining the limitations of conceptualizing institutions as *constraints*, and go on to argue that they must also be seen not only as *enabling* but also as *constitutive* of the preferences and world views of their constituents. We then go on to critique theories of institutional change that see only efficiency considerations or the realization of interests as driving institutional change; we argue for a more culturalist position.

Three views on institutions

Mainstream economists do not usually think about institutions; when they do, they see them as constraints on free markets that create inefficient rigidities. The limits of this view are increasingly well known and we do not dwell on them here. What is surprising is that the rhetoric of 'institutions as constraints' is also used by many institutional economists who lean toward the mainstream – the so-called New Institutional Economists (Douglass North, Oliver Williamson, and others). For example, according to North, 'institutions consist of a set of *constraints* on behaviour in the form of rules and regulations; a set of procedures to detect deviations forms the rules and regulations; and, finally, a set of moral, ethical behavioural norms which define the contours that *constrain* the way in which the rules and regulations are specified and enforcement is carried out' (North 1984: 8; italics added).

Of course, the New Institutionalist Economics (henceforth NIE) would not be seen as breaking new ground if it regarded these constraints as simply creating inefficiencies, as in mainstream economic theory. Many NIE theorists are in fact saying that institutions are there only because they improve efficiency, even if so doing they commit functionalist errors. However, by employing the rhetoric of 'constraints', they still maintain the myth that the unconstrained market is the natural order, while institutions are man-made substitutes that should be (and will be) deployed only when that natural order breaks down.

If we want to move away from the view of the institution as something unnatural, we need to employ a different rhetoric, namely, seeing institutions as enabling devices rather than constraints. For example, it is only because traffic rules make individuals drive in a certain way that we can drive faster. To take another example, firms can engage in innovation more aggressively because there are intellectual property rights, which remove the fear that other agents will copy our ideas and usurp the gains that should accrue to us. And so on.

This is, of course, *not* to say that institutions do not impose constraints. Just about all enabling institutions involve constraints on some types of behaviour by some people. In many cases that involve a collective action problem, these constraints are general constraints that apply to everyone. In these cases, we are putting constraints on everyone's behaviour so that we can collectively do more things, although even in such cases the distribution of constraints and the benefits from them may differ across different groups. However, in other cases, enabling some people means constraining others. For example, affirmative action enables certain disadvantaged groups to have greater freedom to choose an occupation by constraining the behaviours of the potential employers in choosing their employees.

So shifting our rhetoric to the enabling dimension of institutions from the constraining dimension does not mean that we are negating the constraining nature of institutions. However, this is an important shift of perspective because we are then in effect negating the view implicit in the 'institutions as constraints' rhetoric that the unconstrained market (if such a thing is possible at all) is the 'natural' order (or what we call the 'market primacy assumption' – see Chang 1997, 2000a, and 2000b).[2]

However, there is a third and critically important view of institutions, which gets relatively little attention among economists.[3] This view sees institutions not just as enabling or constraining, but also as constitutive.[4] This is because all institutions have a symbolic dimension and therefore inculcate certain values, or world views, into the people who live under them. In other words, as we continue to behave under a certain set of institutions, we begin to internalize the values embodied in those inst-itutions, and as a result to change our selves.[5] This could not happen if human beings took a totally instrumental attitude towards institutions and rule abiding; if they did, they would only keep the rules that are beneficial to themselves (after due calculation of the changing opportunities for gain and loss as rules are maintained or discarded, etcetera). In such a situation, value-laden statements and actions could only be regarded as cynical and manipulative marketing ploys advancing agents' own interests. And indeed this is what is often implicitly assumed in the mainstream economic litera-ture on institutions, where institutions are seen as products of rational choice by selfish individuals interested only in material gain. However, if we follow this line of reasoning, we cannot really explain why institutions exist at all.

To begin with, if everyone is a selfish rational individual with an instru-mental attitude towards rule keeping, then there will be inordinate amounts of cheating and shirking around. If this is the case, no institution will be sustainable, because then the cost of monitoring the possible deviations and punishing them will be truly prohibitive. Moreover, in this situation, it is questionable whether any monitoring and sanctioning mechanism against rule breaking can exist at all. This is because the monitoring/sanctioning mechanism itself is a public good (in the sense that people who have not devoted their efforts to monitoring and sanctioning deviants can also benefit from the improved behavioural standards as a result of such activities), and therefore no selfish individual will find it rational to spend his/her time and resources in maintaining the monitoring and punishment mechanism.[6]

Therefore, unless we accept that people believe (in varying degrees across individuals, needless to say) in the values which lie behind the institutions concerned and that they usually act in accordance with these values without constant monitoring and sanctioning, we cannot explain the existence of any institution.

Needless to say, all the above should *not* be interpreted as meaning that people's motivations are more or less determined by the institutional structure. If we are not to lapse into an unwarranted structural determinism, we need to accept that individuals also influence the way institutions are formed and run, as NIE models typically do. However, our approach differs from that of the NIE in that it postulates a two-way causation between individual motivation and social institutions, rather than a one-way causation from individuals to institutions, although we believe that in the final analysis institutions are at least temporally prior to individuals (Hodgson 2000).

The three views of institutions that we have outlined above are not necessarily mutually exclusive, of course. There is no inconsistency in saying that institutions are constraining, enabling, and constitutive all at the same time. And indeed, unless we recognize all three aspects our analysis of institutions will not be complete, as we try to show below.

Formation and change of institutions

Whether one sees institutions as constraining, enabling or constitutive, the question of how they change is crucial. The strong element of legacy, inertia, and path dependence in the determination of institutional forms must be acknowledged at the start. Even new institutions are built out of the raw material of existing institutions – the developmental state out of old bureaucratic traditions, the WTO out of the General Agreement on Tariffs and Trade (GATT), and so on. Formalistic models that don't take institutional inheritance seriously and fail to recognize that new institutions are likely to be first and foremost adaptations of prior institutions will miss the mark. Nonetheless, institutions do change and we need better theories of how and why they change. If we want to understand how and why particular institutions decay, or what conditions create opportunities for renovating or reinventing institutions, we must begin from a general perspective on how institutions are created and change.

We can broadly divide the different approaches to the origins of and changes in institutions into two groups, namely, the efficiency-driven approach and the interest-based approach, with sub-approaches in each group, each with very different theoretical and policy implications.

Efficiency-driven approaches

In the most simplistic version of the efficiency-driven view of institutional change, institutions are seen as emerging when the market mechanism fails to allow all the potential efficiency-enhancing transactions to be realized. In this version, the rational wealth-maximizing agents will not fail to seize upon the opportunities for efficiency enhancement, if setting up a new institution – say, a firm – is going to increase the gains from trade. In this Panglossian vision, therefore, all institutions that exist are efficient (examples will include authors like the early Douglass North, Harold Demsetz, Armen Alchian, and the property rights school of Frubotn and Pejovich, and Yoram Barzel). And if any institution that is ostensibly capable of enhancing efficiency in a given context does not exist, it is only because the transaction costs involved in constructing such institution are larger than the benefits the institution delivers, in which case it is not really worth having.

It is clear that in this simple form, this view is untenable for both theoretical and empirical reasons. Theoretically, when bounded rationality[7] is one of the important reasons for institutions, it stretches credulity to argue that individuals who are not even capable of doing the standard optimization exercise involving only resource costs are capable of engaging in a meta-optimization exercise involving both resource costs and decision-making costs (or transaction costs). Empirically, we simply observe too many examples of inefficient institutions, whose persistence does not really serve anyone's interest.

As a result, some of those who hold this vision acknowledge that, at a given point in time, there may exist inefficient institutions, but they argue that these institutions will be selected against in an evolutionary process in the long run (Alchian 1950 is the classic example of this view).[8] However, even this more sophisticated evolutionary version has an obvious limit. The problem is that institutions are, by definition, not very malleable (a perfectly malleable institution would be as good as no institution), and therefore that typically 'the rate of change in the environment will exceed the rate of adjustment to it' (March and Olsen 1989: 168). If this is the case, there cannot be any presumption that institutional evolution is moving in an optimal direction (see Chang 1995 for further discussion).

In a more sophisticated version of the efficiency-driven approach to institutions, it is admitted that not all institutional changes are of the efficiency-enhancing kind and therefore that many of them will not be optimal even in the longer run (so the simplistic evolutionary argument is rejected). The reason for this, according to those who take this approach (such as Brian Arthur, Paul David, and Joel Mokyr), is that the evolution of institutions involves path dependency.

In this view, certain institutions (say, technological regimes) may be chosen over others, not because of their inherent efficiency but because of certain irreversible 'events' in history. The best example in this regard is probably that of 'network externality', which gives the first-movers a selection advantage through the frequency-dependent definition of evolutionary fitness (for example, the competition between different computer-operating systems). For another example, if certain irreversible investments have been made in certain physical, intellectual, and relational 'specific assets' (for this concept see Williamson 1985) assuming the presence of particular institutions, the relative efficiency of the existing institutions vis-à-vis alternative institutions will have been enhanced, as the holders of these assets will have vested interests in preserving the existing institutions (see Chang and Rowthorn 1995 for an elaboration of this point).

This perspective has allowed us a better understanding of the process of institutional change. However, at least in its present form, it remains very economistic in that the process of institutional change is driven basically by technological factors, while individuals are seen as operating on the basis of purely economic, rational calculations (even though it is admitted that rational calculations by individuals do not necessarily amount to a socially optimal outcome). The essential problem with this approach is that there is no room for human agency in the sense that what people believe (instead of what they 'should' believe, given the technological imperatives) does not make a difference to the process of institutional change.[9]

The most sophisticated version of the efficiency-driven approach extends the argument to the cultural dimension in the sense that the world views possessed by human agents matter. Proponents of this view start from the assumption that human agents have bounded rationality (a concept to which Williamson and other more purist efficiency-driven theorists give lip service but do not really adopt in practice) and argue that institutions make the complex world more intelligible to them by restricting their behavioural options and also by confining their scarce attention to a truncated set of possibilities.

Bounded rationality, according to this vision, makes it inevitable that we operate with a mental model of the world (or value system, ideology, world view, or whatever we may choose to call it) that may not necessarily be a good, not to say perfect, model of the real world. Given the actors' adherence to a certain world view, they may prefer a certain institution because it happens to fit that world view (or set of moral values), even when it is not necessarily efficiency-enhancing from an 'objective' point of view. In this way, the optimality conclusion is negated, albeit not in the economistic (or technology-driven) way that the second version of the efficiency-driven approach disposes of it.

Some of those who espouse the culturalist version of the efficiency-driven approach go one step further and argue that what world view people hold is not independent of the institutions under which they have been operating – or that there is 'endogenous preference formation' (see for example, Hodgson

1988; Bowles and Gintis 2000). The argument is that institutions embody certain moral values, and that by operating under certain institutions for a period of time, it is likely that people begin to internalize those values (this is what we called the 'constitutive' role of institutions).

Note that even with these subjective elements (such as moral values and world views) thrown in, the approach is ultimately driven by efficiency – it is only that the definition of efficiency now takes on a subjective dimension. And in this sense, we can still call this a version of the efficiency-driven approach, however different it may appear from simpler versions of efficiency-driven institutionalist theory that we discussed earlier.

Interest-based approaches

The most simplistic of the interest-based approaches to the origins of institutions and institutional change is neoclassical political economy, as pioneered by Anthony Downs, James Buchanan, Gordon Tullock, George Stigler, Ann Krueger, Jagdish Bhagwati, Mancur Olson, and Douglass North. The same view is found in some cruder versions of Marxian political economy (those who see the state as the executive committee of the bourgeoisie) (for some critical reviews of this literature see chapters 1–2 in Chang 1994; Stretton and Orchard 1994).

In this view, institutions are but instruments for advancing the sectional interests of groups that are politically organized enough to initiate changes in institutions in a way that suits their interests – the so-called rent-seeking theory of Buchanan, Tullock, and Krueger being a good example, and Buchanan *et al.* 1980 the representative work. Advancement of global interests, as far as it happens, is treated as an unintended consequence.

In this approach, it is believed that interests are not socially structured but exogenously given at the individual level. So interest groups have no internal constraints to their agenda setting and decision making, which is patently not the case in reality (see March and Olsen 1989).

Also, the proponents of this view believe that institutions can be quickly changed, given the political power base to support the change. In this respect, this view is similar to the most simplistic version of the efficiency-driven view of institutional change, because in both views institutions are seen as malleable to the degree that there is a good reason to change them (be it some global 'efficiency' or some dominant 'interest'). In this respect, many of the criticisms that we lodged against the simplistic efficiency-driven view apply here too.

The more sophisticated version of the interest-based view of institutions agrees with the first view that institutions change not on the basis of some global efficiency but according to sectional interests and are therefore fundamentally 'biased' towards certain groups. However, in this version, interests are not exogenously given but 'structured' by existing political and social institutions. Hence the name we give to it, namely, 'structured-interest-based' version.

In his famous discussion of the emergence of the capitalist factory system, 'What Do Bosses Do?', Stephen Marglin (1974) argued that existing (capitalist) property relations determined the way in which capitalist-style firm organization was chosen over worker-managed firms, despite the latter's efficiency advantages (but see Williamson 1985 for a critique from an efficiency point of view). Robert Brenner, in his famous discussion of the revival of feudalism in Eastern Europe, argued that the same exogenous shock of rising grain prices led to the demise of feudalism in Western Europe whereas it led to its strengthening in Eastern Europe because of the differences in their existing institutions (Brenner 1976; see Aston and Philpin 1985 for the subsequent debate). Sam Bowles and Herb Gintis, in a series of recent articles, have emphasized that the contested nature of exchange relationships in credit and labour markets makes the market outcomes dependent on the existing power relationships (for example, Bowles and Gintis 1993 and 1996).

The structured-interest-based view also differs from the Neoclassical Political Economy view in that it does not see institutions as extremely malleable, as the latter view does. This is because the proponents of this view see interests as structured by existing institutions, which means that changing the balance of power between existing interests (which is necessary for an institutional change) is not going to be instantaneous or straightforward but will have to involve changes in deeper institutional structure.

The most sophisticated version of the interest-based view on institutional change may be called the 'culture-based structured-interest' view. Those who hold this view argue that there cannot be such a thing as 'objective interests, which can be understood independently of the actors' understandings' (Friedland and Alford 1991: 244). Therefore, while they agree with others who hold an interest-based approach that institutional changes are driven by interests, they argue that institutional changes are 'simultaneously material and symbolic transformations of the world', which involve 'not only shifts in the structure of power and interests, but in the definition of power and interests' (Friedland and Alford 1991: 246).

While the proponents of this view agree with those who believe in the most sophisticated version of the efficiency-driven view that people internalize the values embodied in institutions, they also point out that 'rules and symbols ... sometimes ... are resources manipulated by individuals, groups, and organizations' (Friedland and Alford 1991: 254).

For example, Friedland and Alford (1991: 257) argue that the success of the American capitalists in the early twentieth century in persuading the society to accept the (fictitious) legal status of a juridical person for a corporation was crucial in allowing them to institute limited liability, which then enabled large-scale mobilization of capital through the stock market. They also argue that the success of workers in advanced capitalist economies in making the wider society accept the extension of the notion of citizenship rights of due process and even participation to employment relations in private firms allowed them to institute grievance procedures.

Thus the proponents of this view see the project of institutional changes not simply as a material project but also as a cultural project in the sense that changes in institutions require (or at least are helped by) changes in the world view of the agents involved. And once we allow the possibility of 'cultural manipulation', the role of human agency becomes a lot more important than in any other version of the theories of institutional change that we have talked about, as it is necessarily the human agents who actively interpret the world (albeit under the influences of existing institutions) and develop discourses that justify the particular world view that they hold. Indeed, we should not forget, to paraphrase Marx, that it is human beings who make history, although they may not do so in contexts of their own choosing.

In this case, context is actually a complex nesting of contexts, especially in a globalized world. The world views of individual agents are nested composites of the immediate culture of communities and organizations, national ideologies and, as we will see in the discussion of the developmental state, an increasingly pervasive global culture. Having admitted the cultural construction of interests, political economy should also have a theory of culture, which obviously is a tall order. Nonetheless, introducing even a primitive theoretical consideration of ideology and world view into the discussion of institutional change allows for qualitative improvement over simple efficiency and interest-based theories.

■

The (Rise and) Decline of the Korean Developmental State

Why the developmental state?

In the post-Second World War period, a small set of countries in East Asia stand almost alone in having significantly improved their position in the world hierarchy of nations. During the post-war period, *per capita* income growth rates in Japan, Korea, and Taiwan have been in the region of 5–6 per cent annually. By contrast, the *per capita* income growth rate in the major now-advanced capitalist countries during the Industrial Revolution (1820–70) was about 1 per cent.[10]

This unprecedented growth involved a fundamental transformation of East Asian economies from poor exporters of primary products to sophisticated producers of high value-added manufactured goods; even in Japan, silk and silk-related raw materials were the biggest export item until the 1950s. Flying in the face of Western advice that they should stick with those products that reflected their 'natural comparative advantage', these countries constructed new bases of comparative advantage. Starting from economic levels comparable to the more prosperous countries of Africa in the 1950s (even Japan's *per capita* income during the 1950s was lower than that of South Africa), they had moved to European income levels by the mid-1990s. Further, all this was accomplished in countries whose Confucian cultures had been derided in the West and whose elites had seemed hopelessly corrupt and ill-suited to anything beyond agrarian exploitation or tax farming.

Conventional growth models that depend on individual entrepreneurs responding to market signals did not predict and could not explain the kind of transformation that occurred in East Asia. Only dramatic institutional innovation can explain it; and to the chagrin of neoclassical theories, there is a consensus that the state played a critical role in this unprecedented process of economic and social transformation. It is for this reason that these states were dubbed 'developmental states'.

Without recapitulating the voluminous writing on the developmental state,[11] it is worth underlining some of this literature's basic postulates. At the root of these changes was a revitalization of centuries-old bureaucratic traditions and their redirection, for a variety of ideological and geopolitical reasons, toward the accumulation of industrial capital. This permitted relationships with local private sector elites, combining support, protection, and discipline, that fostered the willingness of these elites to invest in risky industrial ventures. The transformation of the state fostered a transformation of the capitalist class into a singularly effective variant of the classic industrial bourgeoisie.

All of this makes the subsequent decline of the developmental state a fascinating puzzle from the point of view of institutional analysis. With the recent economic crises in the region, conventional theorists were quick to try to wipe out the troubling 'developmental state anomaly' by claiming that the crisis demonstrated that the developmental state had been a charade all along. Unfortunately for their quest for parsimony, this interpretation does not stand up to even minimal scrutiny. First of all, whether or not the recent crisis is due to the failure of the developmental state, the economic and social progress achieved by the developmental states over the last half century or so in the region cannot be erased from history. Second, the recent crises in the region are the result of the decline, rather than the persistence, of the developmental state (see below and also Wade 1998; Singh 1999; Chang 2000b). Third, the developmental state is a threatened institution not primarily because it was economically ineffectual, or even because its potential economic efficacy has been undercut by globalization. The problems of the developmental state lie first of all in domestic politics and in the domestic political consequences of economic success.

While this analysis applies in varying degrees to the full range of East Asian developmental states, the Korean case stands out as the most interesting. When it was in its ascendancy, it was the most dramatic, if not necessarily the most effective, specimen of this species; and its subsequent decline was the earliest and most comprehensive. The transformative projects envisaged and implemented by the developmental states of Japan and Taiwan during the post-war period were not as comprehensive and forceful as that of Korea. In the case of Japan, its longer history of industrialization not only required less state involvement in the transformative project, but also necessitated a more consensus-oriented approach in the state's dealings with the private sector. In the case of Taiwan, the Kuomintang's position as an 'occupation authority', as well as its allegiance to the semi-socialist ideals of Sun Yat-sen's Three Peoples' Principle, implied that the transformative project could not be as ambitious or as well-integrated with the activities of the private sector as that of Korea.

Equally dramatic as its success, however, was the decline of Korea's developmental state, although, as we point out later, its institutional and ideological legacies still remain considerable and some of them may even be revived in the future, depending on the economic and the political evolution of the country. While the other East Asian developmental states also went through changes that saw declines in their dominance and legitimacy over time, these do not rival what has happened in Korea. The Japanese developmental state has been under considerable criticism since the late 1980s and particularly recently with the continuing recession, but its loss of political legitimacy has not reached anywhere near the Korean level. In the case of Taiwan, the dominance of the developmental state continues, albeit in a somewhat muted form, as exemplified by its near-imperviousness to the world-wide trends of privatization and capital market opening.

How then did the mightiest, if not necessarily the most shrewd and agile, developmental state fall so spectacularly? And what are the lessons that we can draw from this experience for the theories of institutional change? To answer these questions, we need to discuss the rise of the developmental state in Korea in the first place.

The rise of the Korean developmental state

The Korean developmental state emerged from a most unpromising environment. While the legacies of the proto-developmental state that existed under Japanese colonial rule were important (Kohli 1994), the enormity of the destruction of the colonial institutional fabric after 1945 (the end of Japanese rule) cannot be underestimated. For one thing, the end of Japanese colonialism in 1945 unleashed political turmoil, which wreaked havoc on the institutional structure the Japanese left behind. The American occupation of what eventually became South Korea until 1948 increased the nation's institutional turmoil, as many American-style institutions were grafted onto this Japanese institutional structure. Needless to say, the Korean War (1950–3) exacerbated social and institutional dislocation even further.

The regime of Syng Mahn Rhee that ruled South Korea from its birth in 1948 until 1960 was fundamentally anti-developmentalist. Its only stab at developmentalism was the establishment of the Ministry of Reconstruction in 1955. This ministry, however, acted primarily as a means of liaison with aid donors; it did not even formulate a development plan until 1959, and this plan was never implemented. The bureaucracy was nominally organized along meritocratic lines; but between 1949 and 1961, only 336 passed the High Civil Service Examination, far fewer than the 8,263 who got government jobs through 'special appointments' (Cheng *et al.* 1998: 105). The quality of the bureaucracy was such that, until the late 1960s, Korean bureaucrats were being sent to Pakistan and the Philippines, among other places, for extra training.

As is well known, things began to change after the coup by General Park Chung Hee in 1961. It should be noted that, as some authors emphasize (Chibber 1999), the Park regime did not begin with a clear blueprint for a new developmental state, and engaged in a series of institutional experiments in its early days. However, it had a fundamentally developmentalist outlook and implemented some critical institutional changes from the beginning, laying the foundation for the fully fledged developmental state that we saw later. The more important of these changes included: the establishment of a super-ministry, the Economic Planning Board (EPB), with both planning and budgetary authority, and the start of five-year plans; the nationalization of the banks (after the privatization of many banks by the Rhee regime in the late 1950s with prodding from American aid officials); civil service reform; the establishment and/or encouragement of various business sector 'peak organizations'; and the establishment of public and semi-public agencies to help business, such as the state trading agency, KOTRA.

What is often ignored is that these institutional changes also resulted in a critical ideological or world view change. The institutional changes made by the Park regime in the early days embodied a nationalistic, pro-industry (not pro-finance), pro-producer (not pro-consumer) outlook, which emphasized capital accumulation, innovation, and structural transformation – namely the ideas associated with developmentalism. This outlook contrasts with Anglo-American market liberalism with its emphasis on consumer welfare, price competition, and allocative efficiency – all emulated, if poorly, by the Rhee regime.

These institutional changes formed the basis for a cascade of changes in the behaviour of the private sector, which in turn produced an extra-ordinary transformation of the Korean economy. From a backward exporter of tungsten and ginseng, Korea became first an exporter of labour-intensive manufactured goods (textiles, shoes, wigs) and then a world power in capital- and technology-intensive exports. In steel, an industry in which Western advisers were uniformly convinced that it had no comparative advantage, it was able to make profits while selling at half the US list price (Amsden 1989: 317). In semi-conductors, an even more improbable area for investment, the Korean output surpassed that of the major industrial powers of Europe (Evans 1995). All of this, of course, makes explaining the subsequent decline of the developmental state a particularly crucial task for any institutional theory of economic change.

The decline of the developmental state

In a sense, the Korean developmental state was challenged from the beginning – in the 1960s, by the conservative, pro-democratic alliance led by

Yoon Bo Sun, and in the 1970s by the pro-democracy, centre-left opposition forces led by Kim Dae Jung (President, 1998–2003) and (to a lesser extent) Kim Young Sam (President, 1993–8), since the 1970s. However, the fundamental challenge came from the neoliberal forces, which began to crystallize from the late 1970s onward in an alliance among the 'liberal' faction of the bureaucracy, the majority of the intellectual community, and the increasingly powerful business conglomerates (the *chaebols*).

Neoliberal forces made a critical breakthrough after the assassination of General Park in 1979 by his intelligence service chief. Initially, the political vacuum left by the death of Park seemed to open a space for the pro-democracy centre-left forces led by the two Kims. However, these were soon crushed by the two-stage military coup (1979–80) staged by the 'new military', led by General Chun Doo Hwan, and culminating in the Kwangju massacre (May 1980).

General Chun was by no means a neoliberal, but he allied himself with neoliberal bureaucrats and implemented a series of institutional changes signalling the start of a neoliberal offensive against the developmental state. He adopted the anti-inflationary rhetoric of neoliberalism in a bid to deal with the inflationary pressures created by the second oil shock and the subsequent world recession exacerbated by the monetarist macroeconomic policies of major industrialized countries. He privatized a number of banks and partially liberalized the financial market in 1983. He also introduced the 1986 Industrial Development Law (IDL), which shifted the country's industrial policy in a functional (as opposed to a selective) direction.

By no means, however, did changes under Chun's rule make the subsequent demise of the developmental state inevitable. While its force was somewhat diminished, developmentalism still remained the overarching ideology of the regime, and proved formidably effective in certain areas, such as information technology industries (Evans 1995). Many of the formal institutional changes in a neoliberal direction made under Chun, such as financial liberalization (Amsden and Euh 1990) and the IDL (Chang 1993), were limited in scope. Their effectiveness was curtailed in part by the inertia built into more-slowly-changing informal institutions such as bureaucratic convention and business practices.

Massive pro-democracy protests in the summer of 1987 triggered a more fundamental shift. Huge public actions protested Chun's attempt to use the rigged electoral college system to hand the presidency over to General Roh Tae Woo, his chosen successor and erstwhile collaborator. These protests succeeded in forcing the military to capitulate to public demands for a democratic presidential electoral system (Roh did manage to win the subsequent election held in late 1987).

The consequent political discrediting of military rule led to a rapid weakening of the legitimacy of developmentalism, because it was seen (in our view mistakenly) as the former's Siamese twin. What was decisive in this process was the increasing conversion of the intellectual elite, especially the bureaucratic elite, to neoliberalism. An increasing number of elite bureau-crats and academics earned advanced degrees in the US at the height of its neoliberal revolution; the return of this cohort to Korea meant more and more people inside and outside the government who were convinced of the virtues of the free market, and who regarded developmentalism as a backward and mistaken ideology.[12] In this ideological battle, the neoliberals were critically helped by the ideological dominance of Anglo-American academia and media at the world level. Neoliberalism thus established itself as the dominant ideology among Korean elite circles, including the elite bureaucracy, in the late 1980s and early 1990s.

Many of the bureaucrats, however, still had an instinctive attachment to developmentalism. This is readily seen in the intellectually confused policy documents of the time, in which neoliberal pronouncements on overall policy direction make an uneasy fit with developmentalist policies in particular areas. However, the conversion of many bureaucrats to neoliberalism was wholehearted and even dogmatic. For example, by the early 1990s one frequently encountered bureaucrats from the EPB, which somewhat para-doxically had become the home of neoliberalism in the Korean state at the time, calling for a radical retreat of the state and especially for the abolition of their own ministry on the ground that planning, if it ever was desirable, was no longer feasible due to the increasing complexity of the economy.[13]

Moreover, after the late 1980s the *chaebols* increasingly viewed the Korean state as more of a liability than an asset in their competitive struggle in the world market. The many spectacular successes they had had in export markets, such as memory chips and automobiles, which were previously regarded as the exclusive domains of more advanced economies, convinced them that they could now stand on their own. Their confidence was corroborated by the approval they started gaining in the international capital market. By the mid-1990s, the leading *chaebols* were considered creditworthy enough to float bonds in advanced-country capital markets. Their rapidly growing foreign ventures also started to weaken their identification with the nationalistic outlook of developmentalism.[14]

By the mid-1990s, the *chaebols* had become staggeringly aggressive in calling for the withdrawal of the state from economic management. 'Owners' and the top managers of leading *chaebols* made public pronouncements against state intervention at every conceivable opportunity. The *chaebols* also set up a small but extremely well-funded research institute called Korea Centre for Free Enterprise, which churned out numerous documents with a neoliberal flavour, translated classical works in the neoliberal tradition (such as Hayek and Buchanan), and invited well-known American neoliberal thinkers to give high-profile talks in Korea.

The height of this offensive was the ultra-neoliberal policy report prepared by the Federation of Korean Industries (FKI), the club of the *chaebols*, in the spring of 1997. This report called for a radical retrenchment of the state and, among other things, the abolition of all government ministries except Defence and Foreign Affairs and the consequent reduction of government bureaucracy by 90 per cent. The public uproar following this document's pre-publication leak forced its official withdrawal, and showed that the Korean public was not yet ready for this kind of ultra-neoliberalism. But the mere fact that this report could be prepared as a public document by the FKI shows how aggressive the *chaebols* had become in their offensive against the developmental state.

It was not simply the *haute bourgeoisie* who wanted to dismantle the developmental state. The professional classes also started to revolt against the nationalistic and anti-consumer biases of developmentalism. These people previously had been happy to comply with the 'buy Korean' policy and the consequent restriction on luxury consumption, but they now wanted to exercise their newly-acquired purchasing power on domestic and foreign luxury consumption goods without guilt about being unpatriotic or anti-social. As a result, they now wanted further trade liberalization and the lifting of restrictions on luxury consumption goods and luxury housing. They were also beginning to feel frustrated by the protective regulations concerning agriculture, urban planning, and small-scale retailing, which put restraints on their ability to engage in consumerism – a frustration that found its most vivid expression in fascination with the 'quality of life' (cheap food, spacious housing, large cars, and huge shopping malls).

A further push towards neoliberalism was provided from the late 1980s onward by the insistence of the US and other advanced countries that what was now regarded as a developed country should abandon the 'unfair' protections provided to its industrial and financial enterprises and thus give these nations' firms better access to an increasingly attractive market. When the Kim Young Sam government decided in 1993 to join the Organization for Economic Cooperation and Development (OECD), opening up markets became more imperative, as this was a condition of membership.[15]

The resulting changes leading to the dismantling of the Korean developmental state and (in our view) subsequently to the current crisis, have been documented elsewhere (see Chang 1998; Chang *et al.* 1998; and Chang and Yoo 2000, for further details). The dismantling of industrial policy, the hallmark of the developmental state, had its tentative beginning in the late 1980s, and was completed by the mid-1990s. Financial liberalization, including capital account liberalization, gained momentum after 1991, but accelerated in 1993, when Korea signed a bilateral agreement with the US for financial market liberalization and opening. Most symbolically, the five-year plan was terminated in 1993; and in that same year, the EPB was abolished (a wish some of its own members had expressed for some time) and merged with the Ministry of Finance to form the Ministry of Finance and Economy in 1994. Although certain residues of developmentalism could still be found in places (such as supports for R&D in certain high-technology industries), the dismantling of the developmental state was effectively finished by the middle of Kim Young Sam's presidency (that is, by about 1995).

As is well known, the subsequent financial crisis contributed to a further decline of the developmental state. At the ideological level, the discrediting of the developmental state model has become even stronger. Neoliberal forces inside and outside the country have managed to blame the current crisis on the developmental state, despite the fact that it was already effectively, if not completely, dismantled before the crisis – various models identifying industrial policy, cronyism, and the so-called 'logic of too big to fail' as the main cause of the crisis are examples of such efforts (see Chang 2000c for some detailed criticisms).[16] As a result, subsequently many additional institutional changes were made by the Kim Dae Jung government, sometimes willingly and sometimes under IMF pressure, that further destroyed the foundations of the developmental state.

The additional liberalizations of financial markets, of international trade, and of foreign direct investments that were implemented in the early days of the current crisis under IMF pressure are well known by now. Less well-known is the rewriting of the central bank constitution to give it both independence and a single-minded focus on inflation control, both features that are contrary to the pro-industry (and anti-finance) outlook of developmentalism (for further details, see Chang and Yoo 2000). Even less well-known, however, are the changes in the organization of the government.

After the crisis, the head of the Ministry of Finance and Economy (MOFE) was demoted from the position of a deputy prime minister to a simple minister. Control over the government budget, which had given the MOFE such clout in earlier days, was transferred in May 1999 to a new small ministry, the Ministry for Planning and Budgeting (MPB); this new ministry was also given the (perhaps largely symbolic) role of overseeing 'government reform'. The Ministry of International Trade, Industry, and Energy (MOTIE) saw its crucial trade-related functions transferred to the Foreign Ministry, as a result becoming the much weaker and demoralized Ministry of Commerce, Industry, and Energy (MOCIE).

These changes in government organization symbolize a fundamental shift in the role of the state in the economy. The reassignment of the EPB's former functions to the MOFE and the MPB, along with the demotion of the MOFE minister, implies that whatever remains of the government's planning function no longer requires concerted efforts and serious inter-ministerial coordination. The new central bank constitution eliminates the pro-industry bias in macroeconomic management. The transfer of trade functions to the Foreign Ministry means that trade policy is now seen as a part of diplomacy and not an integral part of industrial policy.

Another important post-crisis development is the weakening of the elite bureaucracy itself.[17] As many people attributed the recent crisis to the *dirigiste* model of development, the elite bureaucracy as its protagonist naturally came under severe criticism. The criticism did not simply involve criticisms of particular policies. Now the very legitimacy of the institution of bureaucracy itself was being undermined, with the help of the neoliberal 'government failure' rhetoric. At the same time, the Kim Dae Jung government has been keen to weaken the elite bureaucracy, which it sees as representing the corrupt and inefficient *ancien régime*, and imbue a more entrepreneurial and service-oriented ethos into the bureaucracy by vastly expanding, and indeed setting up a quota for, mid-career 'special appointments' through a competitive recruitment process open to those who are not career bureaucrats – in other words, it has started the process of destroying the Weberian bureaucracy that was so critical in its development and moving to a more American model of bureaucracy.

All these changes have led to an unprecedented demoralization in the elite bureaucracy; when combined with aggressive head-hunting by the private sector, this has led to an unprecedented haemorrhaging of personnel from the elite bureaucracy. For example, since the crisis, dozens of high-flying young bureaucrats between their mid-thirties and mid-forties in the elite ministries, especially the MOFE, have moved to *chaebol* firms – something such people would have never have done before the crisis.[18]

Despite these *gestalt* shifts and formal institutional changes in the wake of the recent crisis, paradoxically the imperatives of crisis management have reactivated some of the developmentalist policy devices that were laid to rest during the mid-1990s. For example, the Kim Dae Jung government implemented various programmes of state-mediated industrial and corporate restructuring, a staple of the Korean developmental state – such as the so-called 'Big Deal' programme of 'voluntary' business swaps and mergers among the leading *chaebols*, on the one hand, and the state-led restructuring of Daewoo and other bankrupt *chaebols*, on the other hand. For another example, the MOCIE in late 1999 introduced a programme of promoting 'star firms' in the parts and materials industries and stepped up export promotion measures. Further, in autumn 2000, the Kim Dae Jung government restored the post of the Minister of Finance and Economy to its former status at the deputy prime ministerial level. However long-lasting or effective such revivals of developmentalist policies may be, these trends show how some patterns can recur even in times of the most radical institutional overhaul.[19]

Theoretical implications

This analysis of the rise and decline of the Korean developmental state supplies us with some interesting insights into the process of institutional change. It shows that institutional change is a highly complex process, involving multi-directional and often subtle interactions between 'objective' economic forces, ideas, interests, and existing institutions themselves, unlikely to be captured by a simple application of efficiency- or interest-based models.

Simple efficiency-driven explanations of institutional change (as discussed earlier in this chapter) perform poorly when applied to this case. For example, many people argue that the demise of the Korean developmental state was inevitable, because, with economic development, the economy has become too complex to coordinate centrally. Even if we accept the argument that economic development necessarily makes centralized coordination more difficult by making the task of coordination more complex, which in itself is a highly contentious proposition,[20] the argument still does not explain why such a demise happened in Korea at the time when it happened. If it is the stage of development at which a particular country is that determines the functionality of a given state form (for example, the developmental state), why did the Korean developmental state go into a decline when the country was at a stage of development similar to Japan's in the 1960s or the 1970s, when the latter's developmental state was in its prime?

If we are to understand the exact timing and the manner of the demise of the Korean developmental state (and more generally the timing and the exact form of any institutional change), we also need to look at the ideological battles and the changes in interest group politics (and their interaction with each other) that surrounded the process. For example, the fact that many government bureaucrats in Korea turned against state interventionism – so much so that by the early 1990s some EPB bureaucrats were calling for the abolition of their own ministry – flies directly in the face of what we call the 'simple interest-centred view of institutional change', such as the one found in Neoclassical Political Economy, which, *à la* Niskanen, predicts that bureaucrats have interests in expanding their bureaux. Unless we understand the influence of neoliberal ideology, which denies the legitimacy of state intervention in general and particularly of planning, on these bureaucrats, we will never be able to understand why they campaigned for the reduction of their own power and influence.

Having emphasized the importance of ideas in the process of institutional change, we do not wish to give the impression that ideas should be treated as a uniquely independent force that things like interests and institutions are not. While ideas are not simply marketing ploys by interest groups, it is difficult for an idea to be sustained in the long run without some appeal to important interest groups. The offensive by the *chaebols* and the revolt by the upper-middle classes, both of whom had been great beneficiaries of the success of the developmental state, against Korean developmentalism in the 1990s – discussed above – are very good illustrations of this point.

To take another example, while our discussion shows how powerfully ideas can shape the course of institutional change, it is wrong to envisage a one-way relationship between the two. As we argued above, institutions affect the ways in which people who operate under them perceive the world (the constitutive role of institutions). And therefore it is not possible to see them as objects of manipulation by agents with exogenously formed preferences, because the way in which such preferences are formed is itself affected by the nature of existing institutions. In the Korean case, for example, we may say that the historical association between the developmental state and military dictatorship made many people who may not otherwise have been inclined to do so object to developmentalism.

Another point that emerges from our discussion is the need to think more seriously about the importance of human choices in determining institutional changes – not the empty neoclassical choices, which are more or less pre-determined by 'objective' conditions and fixed preferences, but hard-to-predict choices involving a complex process of balancing ideology and interests. For example, some people who put emphasis on path dependency in institutional changes (or follow the 'sophisticated version of efficiency-driven explanation of institutional change') argue that Park's choice of a Japanese-style develop-mentalism was an obvious one, given the institutional legacies of Japanese colonialism (see, for example, Kohli 1994). However, when Park came to power, the American model would have been the *more* obvious choice. At the time, many of Korea's formal institutions had already been implanted by the US Occupation Authority, and the tendency towards the American model was further strengthened by what the Rhee regime did (establishment of a quasi-independent central bank, privatization of banks, American-style spoils system in the bureaucracy). Also, given the country's near-total economic and political dependence on the US at the time, a Korean leader would have benefited most by emulating the American model (regardless of the possibility of success of this approach, given local conditions). Given all these factors, it required a certain amount of initiative on the part of Park and his key aides to move away from the easy choice of embracing the American model.

The decline of the developmental state involved the same kind of complex choices. The Kim Young Sam government did not have to go to the extent it actually did in dismantling the developmental state. The easier choice would have been to do what its predecessor, the Roh government, did – namely, to let it wither away slowly. We have argued that there was no compelling economic need for Korea to dismantle its developmental state when it did. Moreover, although there were strong domestic and foreign interest group pressures for a weakening of the developmental state, there was no necessity to formally end the five-year plan, which by the late 1980s had already lost many of its teeth anyway, or to join the OECD, a course of action for which no interest group was actively asking. In other words, the Kim government's dismantling of the developmental state needs to be seen as containing an important element of active choice by its key policy makers on the basis of their ideology, rather than simply reflecting interest group pressures or 'objective' economic conditions.

Finally, the rise and especially the decline of the Korean developmental state demonstrate the way in which the 'nesting' of world views shapes processes of institutional change. Kim Dae Jung government's identification of both *chaebols* and the state bureaucracy with anti-democratic militarism represents an ideological view generated by Korean experience and political debates. The convictions of American-trained economists that the develop-mental state could not possibly work, on the other hand, represent the impact of a global world view on Korean institutional change. The increasing importance of global institutions and world views in shaping the evolution of national institutions like the developmental state is one of the reasons that it makes sense at this point to turn our attention to institutional change at the global level.

■

Institution Building at the Global Level: The World Trade Organization (WTO) as an Illustrative Case

States have been the central public actors in the definition of economic policy for hundreds of years, but their powers are now challenged by the construction of global institutions. While modern states have always had to share power with private transnational actors, during the past 50 years a set of public organizations has been established that can be considered the embryonic embodiment of global governance institutions. It is not completely fanciful to suggest that they might eventually come to play a role at the global level analogous to the role that states have played within their national territories over the past 400 years.

This contemporary period of intensive institution building is particularly intriguing from the viewpoint of an institutional approach to economic change. For despite the extensive literature on international organizations, we know surprisingly little about how key contemporary global governance institutions function as organizations, how their own structuring facilitates or impedes the possibility of realizing different visions of the global economy, or how modifying their structures might affect the future evolution of the global system. Looking at the formation of these new institutions thus provides an opportunity to develop and test theoretical ideas about how institution building works.

Global institution building also has implications for institutions at other levels, including the developmental state. Global institutions both embody and reshape global norms and world views, which in turn are incorporated into the world views of actors at the national level. Global institutions are also a constraining and enabling context for institutions at the national level, making it harder to maintain some institutions and easier for others to emerge. At the same time, the relationship between global institutions and nation states is anything but one-way. Global governance institutions depend fundamentally on the capacities of nation states to execute their goals, even while they may enhance the capacities of nation states in certain areas by providing political clout and technical assistance. Looking at global institutions is a powerful reminder that institutional change is a multi-level process.

In this section, we will focus on one global governance institution, the newest addition to the Bretton Woods family. While the WTO is a unique institution, it illustrates some archetypical features of global governance institutions. Examining it will permit us to underline the point that institutional questions are not superseded by the shift toward a political economy organized on a global instead of a national level, and to the contrary gain a new salience as economic actors attempt to re-scale the organization of production and exchange.

The WTO (like other global governance institutions) exists because the more sophisticated, internationalist currents in the corporate and political leadership of the US and other developed countries realized that a global market requires a complex set of institutional underpinnings. As the 'realist' theory of international relations (see Waltz 1979) correctly underlined, an international system of independent sovereign states (commonly referred to as a 'Westphalian' system) has strong elements of anarchy at the global level. Anarchy does not lend itself to stable market relationships, to say nothing of long-term investments. Reducing the level of anarchy to get the stability and predictability necessary for a global economy to operate is the whole point of global governance institutions.

Institutionalization involves a trade-off wherein the strong accept certain constraints to get more reliable consent from weaker players (and from one another), enabling them to do more. It is by no means an uncontested trade-off. Opting for the benefits of institutionalization instead flies in the face of a world view, constructed over the course of hundreds of years, in which sovereignty is politically sacred. Even developing countries – India, for example – are fiercely defensive when they see international norms infringing on their sovereignty. The point is that, as Steven Weber (1999) has pointed out, global governance institutions, as organizations, attract little political loyalty. The supposedly anachronistic institution of the nation state looks charismatic when compared to these institutions.

Within the US political class, the 'bilateral *realpolitik*' version of global governance, in which economic and political threats against less powerful nations replace invocations of international norms, is a very attractive alternative to the compromises involved in trying to institutionalize govern-ance norms at the international level. In short, while prerogatives of sovereignty have unquestionably been eroded, political world views built on the foundation of sovereignty continue to be very powerful and to make the construction of global governance institutions into a very uncertain task.

Support for global governance institutions requires a sophisticated sense of the long-term dangers of normlessness and a corresponding appreciation of the returns on institution building. Sophisticated internationalists like George Soros and Robert Rubin have at least implicitly realized that the current global economy is haunted anew by the 'Polanyi problem'. Looking at the rise of national markets, Polanyi (1957) argued that the socially unsustain-able character of 'self-regulating' markets generated a natural 'protective' reaction on the part of a variety of social groups, including a portion of the elite. Unfortunately, in Polanyi's analysis this protective reaction was overwhelmed by its own inability to prevail at the international level. Inter-national markets, particularly financial and currency markets, could not be successfully regulated. First the collapses of the gold standard and then degeneration into the barbarism of Fascism were the result.

In the post-Second World War period, the Polanyi problem of reconciling free markets with stable social and political life was taken up again through the construction of a set of international norms and institutions, including the Bretton Woods institutions at the global level, complemented by an understanding of the importance of continued regulation (especially of capital flows) at the national level (Hveem 1999). This made possible what John Ruggie (1982) called 'embedded liberalism' – international openness combined with social protection and regulated through an interconnected set of powerful nation states. Embedded liberalism helped produce the generation of prosperity in the core industrial countries that is sometimes called the 'Golden Age' of capitalism (on the rise and the fall of the Golden Age, see the essays in Marglin and Schor 1990).

Gradually, however, the evolution of transborder economic relations undermined this new set of institutions. Embedded liberalism had never been successfully extended to the Third World, and had no good way of dealing with increased Third World participation in world-wide manufacturing production. In addition, its international institutions depended heavily on the foundation of the nation state, whose power was undercut by the increasing speed and magnitude of international transactions. Once again, inability to regulate markets at the international level created social dislocations that seemed beyond the ability of normal domestic politics to resolve. The re-scaling of the global economy brought the Polanyi problem back to life (see Block 1999 for further discussion).

As globalization erodes the institutional foundations of embedded liberalism and the Polanyi problem rears its ugly head once again, it becomes necessary to construct new institutional structures at the global level. Failure to do so would threaten profits as well as the well-being of ordinary citizens, but success can by no means be taken for granted. The difficulty of the task creates new risks of descent into barbarism. Global governance institutions like the WTO represent a strategy for transcending the Polanyi problem.

There are, of course, other strategies. The goal of the US Treasury and the international financial community is to provide an institutional foundation for the universalistic enforcement of narrowly defined market norms. The political base for this form of transcendence is very powerful but equally narrow. Embedded liberalism went well beyond this conception and it is not at all clear that the narrower view is politically viable.

Another quite different view of building global governance institutions is the vision that was adumbrated in the formation of the United Nations, and is epitomized in efforts to enforce universal norms around issues like human rights and environmental sustainability (see Keck and Sikkink 1998; Evans 2000). This vision of globalization aims at the universalistic enforcement, not of a narrow set of market norms, but of a broad set of democratically formulated socio-political norms. For holders of this view, global institutions that only enforce narrow market norms, even if they do so universally, may easily be judged worse than no global institutions at all. This was probably the position of the majority of the protesters in Seattle in December 1999. An alliance between supporters of this view and nationalist adherents to the bilateral *realpolitik* view could be politically potent.

Such an alliance would also draw the support of a fourth group – believers in a romantic version of a decentralized political economy, organized not around sovereign states but at the local level. John Zerzan, intellectual leader of the 'black block' anarchist faction that drew major headlines in Chicago, represents this view,[21] but its adherents are spread widely across the left–right spectrum. Any kind of global governance is an anathema to this group. For them, the Polanyian collapse is part of the solution.

All of this is to say that building global governance institutions is a delicate business. Interests remain important, but world views are even more so. Definitions of what is efficient for whom are slippery. Individuals whose apparent interests would seem to be identical may have diametrically opposed positions, and alliances among people who define their interests in completely different ways are equally likely. All of this can be illustrated by looking at the brief and tumultuous life of the WTO.

Four features of the WTO as an organization should be underlined. First, and most obvious, is its centrality to global economic governance. Second is the surprisingly democratic character of its formal decision-making procedures. Third are the tensions and contradictions between formal and informal realities, both in terms of its governance role and in terms of its decision-making procedures. Finally, and perhaps most important, the political vulnerability of the WTO (and global governance institutions more generally) needs to be underlined.

The formally democratic character of the WTO (in contrast to the IMF, for example) is, at first, surprising. Formally, each of the WTO's 135 member states has an equal vote. Since there is no equivalent to the Security Council, this makes the WTO in theory even more democratic (in the Westphalian sense of one nation, one vote) than the United Nations. Its governing General Council allows representatives of all major countries (with the notable exceptions of China and Russia, although the former is expected to join soon) to participate in relative equality (at least formally) and the WTO ministerial conferences have been accompanied by extensive public debate.

On the other hand, if we turn from theory to practice, the WTO is a classic oligarchy. The precedent, established in the GATT, that all decisions are made by consensus allows the US and other major nations to set the agenda. Nonetheless, informal oligarchy remains in tension with formal democracy and this tension creates some interesting potential for change.

Despite the dominance of the informal rules in practice, the formal rules still provide a basis for political threat. The United States and the advanced industrial countries would be in a difficult political position if a large block of developing countries were to say, 'It is not possible to achieve consensus. Therefore, this issue must be taken to a vote.' However, recent experience – in particular the recent struggle over electing a WTO Director-General and the collapse of the Seattle Millennium Round – demonstrates that, on the one hand, it will not be easy for the US and the EU to simply ignore developing countries when they decide collectively to fight for something, but on the other the impact of such political threats on outcomes is not clear.

The contrast between formal and informal realities also applies to the WTO's power and centrality to the global trading system, but in a different way. As the organizational embodiment of the GATT, the WTO is the central forum for regulating international trade (see Krueger 1998). As Ruggie (1998) has nicely underlined, regulating international trade has come to include passing judgement on trade-related domestic policies, which can mean anything from environmental regulations to tax laws. This creates the impression that the power of the WTO might even extend inside domestic boundaries. Furthermore, unlike organizations like the ILO, the WTO has the ability to legitimate sanctions if its rulings are not followed. It is, therefore, a legitimate reflection of the general perception of the importance of the WTO when a former member of the WTO secretariat (Blackhurst 1997: 533) writes of its 'emerging role as the pre-eminent international economic organization'.

In formal terms, the WTO does not appear to be a very powerful organization.[22] But the WTO is seen as powerful because it is viewed as embodying the interests of the world's major economic powers. The WTO exists because powerful national players wanted to focus the politics of international trade disputes on an international organization whose decisions are likely to be considered legitimate, precisely because it is formally democratic and because those who make individual decisions are bureaucrats not beholden to any particular country. The WTO's informal power then lies in the fact that it is the concrete representation of the informal consensus and solidarity that make the international trading system work.

Yet at the same time, the formal aspects of the WTO regime remain a potentially important source of support from smaller countries looking for relief from the world of bilateral *realpolitik*, in which they are relentless bullied by the great powers (most obviously the United States). The dispute settlement mechanism, which interprets rather than formulates policies, is more formal and transparent. While informal oligarchy is still not irrelevant, Costa Rica may occasionally prevail in a case against the US, which is not likely to happen in a world of bilateral *realpolitik*. The dispute settlement mechanism is, in fact, a good example of how universally enforced norms help bring weaker parties on board, even if they have little effective say in the formulation of the rules themselves, and even if the general content of the rules does not reflect their interests. Apparently transparent and objective governance features, like the dispute settlement mechanism, are fundamental to the ability of organizations like the WTO to claim international legitimacy, but they are obviously no help *vis-à-vis* US politicians interested in avoiding any limitations on the hegemon's sovereignty.

Curiously, organizations like the WTO may be more vulnerable to attack from the hegemon that pushed for their creation than from the poor nations that are excluded from the informal oligarchy that shapes their policy. The unusual ideological character of the United States makes it peculiarly unsuited to play the institution-building role that one might expect the global hegemon to play (see Evans 1997). There is a powerful current of elite ideology within the United States that is both profoundly distrustful of any kind of public governance institutions and deeply apprehensive of anything that might reduce the absolute sovereignty of the United States itself. This segment of the conservative political elite is completely supportive of free markets but has little appreciation of the institutional infrastructure necessary to make such markets work, particularly at the global level. Distrust of government in any form combined with deep-seated xenophobia turns any institution of global governance into the enemy. Hostility from traditional conservatives (principally in the United States) who will be hypersensitive to any WTO actions considered to infringe on US sovereignty is almost inevitable.

At the same time, an increasingly active civil society has begun to take a serious and vociferous interest in the politics of globalization. These groups are either interested in governance in the sense of universalistic enforcement of a broad set of democratically formulated socio-political norms that would reconstruct the market rather than simply expand it, or they are hoping to re-establish some political and economy autonomy at the local level. The success of global governance in the Soros/Rubin sense of universalistic enforcement of narrow market norms would be a defeat for both groups. Unless organizations like the WTO can convince the first group that it can somehow serve as an instrument in promoting the broader set of socio-political norms, something at least along the lines of embedded liberalism, frustrated civic groups have every reason to try to get their national governments to withdraw support from the organization. A progressive-conservative alliance of political groups whose only point of agreement is that the WTO should be dismantled is far from fanciful, especially in the United States.

The political vulnerability of the WTO is compounded by the lurking power of the global democratic majority, which is to say the developing countries. In the Uruguay Round, the developing countries were willing to accept promises in return for their concessions on issues like trade-related intellectual property rights (TRIPS), finances, and services. In Seattle, perhaps emboldened by the willingness of the demonstrators outside the meetings to challenge the *status quo*, they drew the line.

For developing countries, universal enforcement of narrow market norms (as in the case of the dispute settlement mechanism) may represent a marginal improvement over the bilateral bullying of a *realpolitik* world, but as long as the mandate is narrowly defined and the content of these narrow rules is determined by an oligarchy of rich countries with advice from private firms, global governance is only a marginal improvement over Westphalian anarchy for them.

Developing countries want, and need, a set of rules that not only resuscitates the social protections of embedded liberalism, but expands embedded liberalism beyond the OECD countries. They also need rules that don't simply reinforce the privileges of the firms and countries that currently control global markets, but provide some support for efforts to 'catch up'. If global governance is to gain their reliable political support, it must go beyond narrow market norms. Are the sophisticated internationalists who have the most to gain from a stable institutionalized global system willing to use the WTO and other similar institutions to reconstruct global markets in a way that responds to such demands? Or will they risk their efforts at global institution building (and in the longer run increase the possibility of Polanyian collapse) to preserve the current definition of the legitimate global market?

If institution building were simply a question of efficiency and interests, the outlook would seem hopeful. Transnational capitalist elites are much better off if global governance organizations enforce some broader norms, while providing stability and predictability, than they are if global governance founders for lack of political allies. Even in the short run, having to abandon an organization like the WTO would be a major shock to investor confidence in the predictability of global political economy, something that sophisticated internationalists must avoid at all costs. The bargain is not all that dissimilar from the one that produced the welfare state and embedded liberalism, except that it must be constructed at the global level.

Unfortunately, the process of institution building is more complicated and less predictable. If we could count on global elites making rational choices, the world would be a more pleasant place than it is. If experience is any guide, elites are unlikely to accept rational compromises unless they are under political pressure sufficiently intense to jar them out of 'business as usual'. Opportunities for more progressive trajectories of institution building at the global level depend not just on the responsiveness of elites but on the formation of complex alliances among groups with disparate interests as well as common ones.

The complexities of building such alliances are well illustrated by the 'core labour standards' issue. Core labour standards (CLS) at their most basic are epitomized by the recent ILO version, which the US finally agreed to sign up to and is a good example of a minimalist version, but everyone recognizes (some with hope, some with fear) that this is the thin end of a wedge and that ultimately CLS could come to mean things like protecting the right to organize, which is why the concept is politically interesting.

The argument for inclusion of CLS in the WTO's mandate is simple and logical. The absence of CLS in a particular country can be considered a trade-related basis for unfair competition just as the absence of intellectual property rights is considered a basis of unfair competition. Like the privilege of not having to pay royalties to Bill Gates, not having to pay the wages that labour could demand if it were free to exercise its collective rights constitutes a subsidy to local producers.

The politics are more complicated. At the national level, advanced industrial countries with social democratic regimes (especially the Nordic countries) have predictably been strong proponents of making the enforcement of CLS part of the WTO's mandate. On the other side, the main opponents of including labour standards in the WTO's mandate are developing countries. Their opposition stems from two different sources.

First there is always the sovereignty issue. Third World leaders see CLS as giving the WTO one more excuse to intrude on their internal affairs. Second, they see limitations on local firms' ability to exploit labour as threatening their comparative advantage. Desperate to increase their exports to developed country markets, Third World governments are terrified that the labour standards issue might be used against their exporters. And, of course, many developing country leaders may see normative changes at the global level that might increase the bargaining power of local labour as a bad thing for their local business allies.

The US labour movement, which is a central political constituency from the point of view of the current US administration, sees institutionalizing global labour standards comparable to those that operate in the US, especially in the more economically competitive regions of the Third World, as a bedrock issue (see Palley *et al.* 1999).[23] For the administration's corporate constituency, on the other hand, the issue is less salient. While they are beneficiaries of the absence of labour standards in developing countries, major US transnationals are also aware that the diffusion of CLS would be at most of minor detriment to their global profit rates. For US labour, then, trying to get a US administration to support core labour standards beyond its boundaries certainly has more prospect of being a winner than trying to prevent capital from investing abroad or trying to impose general restrictions on the entry of foreign consumer goods into the US.

To make progress on this issue, however, international allies are essential. US labour must have significant allies within at least the most important developing countries. Again, logically it would make sense for Third World labour to support CLS, even if national political leaders did not. Being able to threaten both employers and national politicians with international sanctions if local labour rights were not respected could be a powerful new bargaining tool. Yet there are no visible examples so far of public political support for trade-enforceable international labour standards by major Third World trade union movements.[24]

The reasons for the lukewarm response of Third World trade union movements are not hard to understand. For decades the international position of US labour has combined opposition to the most militant Third World labour movements on grounds that they might be communists with unabashed protectionism. Not surprisingly, then, Third World labour sees the support of US trade unionists for CLS as motivated less by international labour solidarity than by the desire of privileged Northern workers to deny Southern producers access to Northern markets and thereby avoid sharing the returns from global productivity increases with their brothers and sisters in the South – in short, protectionism (see Amsden 2000: 14).

For US labour, then, trying to use the WTO to improve global enforcement of labour rights means completely renovating its relationships with Third World labour movements, building concrete ties and demonstrating solidarity. Old attitudes in which Third World workers are dangerous because they are 'willing to work for too little' have to be replaced by a new vision in which Third World labour is a key political ally that must be supported.

In short, the core labour standards case provides a very clear illustration of how institution-building efforts can play a constitutive role, pushing groups to redefine their interests in interesting and unexpected ways. The argument can now be recapitulated briefly. An international organization is created by governments acting as agents of the more sophisticated elements of transnational capital, to provide a more politically efficient and effective institutional means of allowing a more stable, less costly expansion of international openness and increasing the transparency and predictability (while consequently reducing the volatility) of the global economy, thereby responding to the threat of the 'Polanyi problem'.

Once these aims are embodied in a concrete organization, the organization inevitably becomes the focus not only of the aspirations of those that like the existing mode of globalization and are hoping (through the creation of the organization) to strengthen it, but also of those who are hostile to globalization. Thus, on the one hand, we have powerful conservatives interested in recovering an idealized Westphalian past, in which sovereign power was the vehicle of global aspirations rather than being compromised by them, and, on the other hand, we have a host of less privileged social actors substantively threatened by the inegalitarian consequences of globalization and therefore hostile to the idea of strengthening the institutional infrastructure of globalization (as long as globalization is defined as 'governed free markets'). This inevitable but unintended (and apparently unforeseen) consequence leaves the organization (and its original project) politically vulnerable.

The existence and potential power of the organization also change the incentives and potential strategies open to groups harmed and threatened by the existing mode of globalization – in this case developed country labour and particularly US labour. This adds the strategy of imposing a different set of global norms to their traditional (and hitherto relatively ineffectual) strategies of trying to resist globalization through national level strategies aimed at insulation from the global economy.

The one-nation/one-vote definition of democracy that was (naturally and indeed almost inevitably) incorporated into the internal governance of the WTO forces any group that wants to try imposing a different set of global norms to find allies within a range of developing countries and do whatever is possible to strengthen the local political position of these allies. Thus, one of the unintended consequences of the creation of the WTO was to create an additional incentive for the US labour movement to redefine its interests in a more internationalist direction and to engage in concrete efforts to strengthen both its ties to Third World labour movements and the local political clout of these movements. The important role of labour in the demonstrations in Seattle (largely ignored by the media) underlies the WTO's role in helping to shift labour's attention from domestic to global politics.

Regardless of how the core labour standards issue ends up playing out, the case of the WTO serves to illustrate the necessity of taking an institutional perspective to understand economic change at the global level. It reinforces our initial argument that institutional change cannot be explained by functional/efficiency or instrumental/interest logics but must also take into account the independent impact of world views and ideologies. Likewise, it validates our contention that institutions must be seen as constitutive of the world views as well as being shaped by them.

■

Conclusion: Towards an Institutionalist Approach to Economic Change

When our analysis of the developmental state and the WTO are combined, we have two very different instances of institutional transformation with quite different lessons. Both of them are too central to the evolution of the current global political economy to be ignored by the dominant canon. Yet, in both cases, explanation via the dominant canon's analytical apparatus requires embarrassing contortions – if, indeed, it can be achieved at all. In short, we have confronted the existing canon with anomalies that it can neither ignore nor dispose of easily.

At the same time, exploration of these cases has proved fruitful in terms of refining and reconstructing the conceptual sketch of institutional dynamics with which we started. Both cases illustrated our basic premise that an adequate theorization must see institutions as both *constructed* (or reconstructed) in response to changes in interests and ideology (or world view), on the one hand, and *constitutive* of interests and ideology, on the other hand. But they did more than this. While the cases were not chosen to illustrate the variant ways in which ideas, interests and institutions might interact, they ended up serving this function.

In the case of the developmental state, the process whereby social groups that previously formed integral parts of its political foundations came to view their interests as lying in its dismantling provides a nice rebuttal of simplistic theories of interests and institutions. This is most obvious in the case of the bureaucrats who behaved completely irrationally from a Buchanan/Kreuger/Niskanen viewpoint on bureaucratic behaviour by calling for their own disempowerment. Their new 'free market' attitudes cannot be explained without heavy reliance on a shift in world view, rooted in turn in new patterns of professional training. The sequence, then, is one in which world view rather than position in the economic structure shapes interest definitions.

In the case of local entrepreneurs (the *chaebols*), the logic is more mixed. On the one hand, their objective economic position did shift. Their investments and markets became increasingly international and so their adoption of an internationally prevalent anti-statist ideology makes some sense in economistic terms. At the same time, however, it is important to recognize (as became apparent in the aftermath of the Asian crises) that their ability to sustain their own growth independently of the developmental state was, to a significant degree, fictitious. So the shift in their interests was also inseparable from a shift in world view. The irony here, of course, is that the shift in both world view and interests was made possible by the success of the developmental state as an instrument of economic transformation. Thus, prior institutional change can be considered to underlie changes in interests and ideas.

The case of the political leadership is also complex. On the one hand, the new generation of political leadership had an ambivalent relation to the developmental state from the beginning, not because of its aggressive pursuit of economic transformation but because of its authoritarian and repressive face. At the same time, they saw the developmental state as guilty of unduly concentrating economic power in the hands of a few *chaebols*. Despite these ambivalences, it is clear that their abandonment of the pro-producer, nationalist elements of the economic policy of the developmental state must be explained to a large extent in terms of their adherence to a global free-market world view. This adherence might, of course, represent an interest-based conformity founded on fear that nationalist policies would bring punishment by international financial markets, but the extent of the over-conformity suggests an irreducible element of ideological conversion.

In sum, the developmental state's loss of political support best fits a model in which a change of world views, more specifically the adoption of the globally dominant world view on the part of the local elite, was more important than shifts in their 'objective' economic interests in generating institutional change with negative consequences for economic performance (contributing, that is, to the creation of the Asian crisis) and, therefore, negative consequences for the 'objective interests' of the key actors who formulated and implemented the decline of the developmental state.

The WTO case is not inconsistent with the developmental state case but it emphasizes a different sequence. Again, world view plays a dominant role in generating institutional change (in this case, the sophisticated internationalist Soros/Rubin world view that recognizes the necessity of creating institutions to govern global markets). Likewise, in the event that the current project of global institution building collapses, conservative ideologies that exalt the privileges of sovereignty and the short-term advantages of bilateral bullying are likely to play a major role.

The main part of the story, however, leads from the creation of an institutional context to the subsequent redefinition of interests and world view, with the added twist that the institutional effects are fully decoupled from the intentions of the institution's creators. Concretely, the creation of the WTO provides a stimulus for the redefinition of labour's interests and world view in an internationalist direction. This change in world view and interest definition on the part of a significant set of social actors is, in turn, projected to shift the way that the WTO functions as an institution in the future, and thereby the way in which legitimate global markets are defined.

Our analysis also strongly reinforces Block's (1999) admonition that it is a grave mistake to think of the global political economy as a 'natural' system in which each element is logically and organically connected to the others, so that tinkering with any part of it will disrupt the functioning of the whole. We have tried, as Block (1999: 10) suggests, to 'reconceptualize international capitalism as a constructed system'. We have shown how the rise and demise of the developmental state reflected a complex process of individual agency, changing world views and shifting political alliances, not some 'inexorable economic logic' of the global system as a whole. The WTO demonstrates even more clearly the extent to which the global political economy is a system under construction, with the economic logic of the resulting system dependent on the outcome of the process of institution building.

The juxtaposition of the two cases also illustrates the benefits of thicker institutional analysis. Obviously, the emergence of the WTO and the decline of the developmental state take place in the same global arena. Thin institutional analysis often sees their interrelation in simple 'zero sum' terms – as a competition over a fixed amount of total sovereignty in which increasing global governance is locked in struggle with the national economic strategies of Third World governments. Our analysis suggests a very different picture. The complicated political dynamics of the decline of the developmental state had little to do with governments being forced by the WTO or other global governance organizations to give up nationalist political strategies. Conversely, among the myriad threats to the institutionalization of the WTO, the nationalist economic policies of Third World governments hardly feature. The implications of our analysis for the interrelation of the two cases reinforce the basic point: thin institutional approaches lead to misleading conclusions regarding institutional dynamics.

The overall point is clear. Our analysis illustrates the reasons for our discontent with the dominant canon. The false parsimony of its non-institutional view offers little or no analytical leverage on the dynamics of either case. Its basic assumptions prevent it from doing so. 'Preferences' (both in the sense of interests and world views) must remain exogenous and unchanging. A story in which interests and world views are variables shaped by institutional context but also playing a role in causing institutional change is impossible. False parsimony has robbed the canon of its ability to deal with these key cases. Unfortunately, however, when it comes to explaining economic change, it will take more than an intellectually plausible overall framework combined with superior ability to explain particular cases, even very important cases, to displace the institutionally anaemic, dominant approach.

In addition to the 'QWERTY' sort of 'path dependency' advantages that the dominant canon has, simply on the basis of longevity and network effects, the nature of the coupling between theory and practice gives the particular kind of false parsimony that the dominant canon has developed tremendous advantages. Powerful social actors care much too intensely about getting clear answers delivered with full conviction to tolerate the kind of complexity that an adequate institutional explanation involves. Theories must generate simple rules that enable decision makers to take prompt action. They must also generate confidence among the decision makers and ideological hegemony *vis-à-vis* the rest of society.

Elegant, parsimonious theories whose basic premises are at one with the existing, taken-for-granted assumptions of powerful social actors (and to a lesser extent of society at large), and which can also claim broad applicability, provide powerful ideological support as well as clear bases for action. Such theories may be incomplete, or wrong, but until the decision-making rules they generate are clearly connected to obviously disastrous outcomes, those rules will prevail. The prevalence of the rules in turn reinforces the legitimacy of the theory, since knowledge of the theory enables prediction of a broad set of important decisions (based precisely on the theory), and makes the theory's predictions to some extent self-fulfilling.

Of course, two additional conditions are also crucial to making rules hegemonic. First, the decisions they produce should not imply sacrifice or discomfort to the decision makers themselves or their most politically powerful constituents. Second, the theories on which they are based should work reasonably well in simple contexts (short-term microeconomic decision making in firms, say) that are salient and valued by decision makers. As long as these two conditions are met, the contexts in which the theories are applied are likely to be extended indefinitely, despite obvious inconsistencies or illogicality and even though their application may lead to immediately deleterious outcomes for the less powerful and raise the risk of crisis and disaster for the decision makers themselves in the long run.

The contemporary economic canon enjoys all the necessary conditions for sustaining false parsimony, and under current conditions it is unlikely to be unseated by a complex and 'mushy' institutionalist alternative. Even if an institutionalist alternative could unequivocally demonstrate its scientific superiority, the practical and ideological costs of changing decision rules would militate against jettisoning the established canon. And, an institutional alternative is still a long way from such unequivocal demonstrations.

To improve its chances, a more institutionally oriented alternative canon must do two things. First, it must continue to demonstrate that events that are anomalous for the existing canon become comprehensible and predictable once a more institutionalist view is applied. Given the ambiguities inherent in most social and political outcomes, this is not an easy task, but it is still essential. Second, while eschewing false parsimony, an institutionalist approach must still work in the direction of showing that its explanations are not simply *ad hoc* stories concocted after the fact but are consistent with each other and with some body of general propositions. This is even harder.

Despite the difficulties involved, the prospects for the rise of an alternative, institutionalist view are not as bleak as this discussion makes them appear. First, conquest is not the only form of success. Just as religious dogmas transform themselves by assimilating oppositional positions without admitting that the previous orthodoxy was ever in error, intellectual canons can be transformed substantially without ever appearing to capitulate. Positions that might have seemed blasphemous thirty years ago – the important role of increasing returns, for example – are already accepted by the more innovative practitioners of the conventional canon. Such changes create useful building blocks for the construction of an alternative canon.

At the same time, the aim is certainly not to reinvent the wheel. Manufacturers trying to calculate the costs of making widgets in a given organizational and institutional context need the kinds of tools that standard microeconomics has developed. We also need to take advantage of the immense amount of work that has been put into techniques of calculating national incomes, estimating changes in the money supply, and so on. It would be foolish not to take advantage of all the work that has been done on these issues under the aegis of the conventional paradigm. Such tools become misleading because they are used without the acknowledgement of their institutional assumptions. The problem with conventional economics is that it would prefer to ignore the fact that changes in the institutional context are both possible and can dramatically change the implications of the numbers it interprets.

As North and others have pointed out, it is precisely the taken-for-granted character of institutions that makes them invaluable to individuals and societies that don't have the time or ability to optimize. It would be foolish to suggest that consideration of the full range of institutional alternatives should be a part of all day-to-day decision making. Nonetheless, ongoing preoccupation with the question 'How might existing institutions be organized differently and what would happen if they were?' is not just healthy but essential. The current hegemony of the dominant canon cuts off that question and that is what makes it dangerous.

Both an accurate assessment of the possibility that an institutional perspective might gain more sway and a strategy for achieving such an end must obviously depend on political as well as intellectual factors. The ascendance of an alternative canon is unlikely to happen in isolation from the mobilization of social actors who see their interests harmed by the policies generated by the dominant canon. Thus anyone interested in the intellectual project of developing an alternative canon must be equally interested in the political project of empowering those most prejudiced by the logic of the existing canon.

There is, of course, an uglier scenario for the creation of a political base for new ideas – a traumatic economic crisis. A sufficiently profound practical crisis would rob the existing canon of its ideological charisma, but it would wreak havoc in the lives of everyone (not just the privileged). Those who would like to unseat the existing canon should hope that this kind of occasion for their success never arrives, which is not to say that aversion to a traumatic crisis should diminish enthusiasm for working toward the construction of an alternative canon. First of all, infusing existing policy debates with some alternative perspectives is probably the best way to diminish the possibility of such a crisis. Second, if a crisis cannot be avoided, the worst of all possible worlds would be to have the existing canon stumble and fall into crisis with no better alternative waiting in the wings to replace it. Anyone who really believes that the false parsimony of the existing canon has crippled its ability to understand and predict economic change had better be working furiously to construct an alternative view, not because they wish for crisis but because they are terrified of what crisis would mean in the absence of a sound intellectual basis for formulating alternative strategies.

Bibliography

Akyuz, Y. (ed.) (1999) *East Asian Development: New Perspectives*, London: F. Cass.

Alchian, A. (1950) 'Uncertainty, evolution, and economic theory', *Journal of Political Economy*, Vol. 58, No. 3, June.

Amsden, A. (1989) *Asia's Next Giant: South Korea and Late Industrialization*, New York: Oxford University Press.

—— (1991) 'The specter of Anglo-Saxonization is haunting South Korea', in Cho, L. and Y. Kim (eds), *Korea's Political Economy – An Institutionalist Perspective*, Boulder: Westview Press.

—— (2000) 'Ending isolationism', *Dissent*, Vol. 27, No. 2, Spring.

Amsden, A. and Y. Euh (1990) 'Republic of Korea's financial reform: what are the lessons?', Discussion Paper No. 30, United Nations Conference on Trade and Development (UNCTAD), Geneva.

Armstrong, P., Glyn, A. and J. Harrison (1991) *Capitalism Since 1945*, Oxford: Blackwell.

Arrow, K. J. (1974) *The Limits of Organization*, New York: Norton.

Aston, T. and C. Philpin (eds) (1985) *The Brenner Debate – Agrarian Class Structure and Economic Development in Pre-Industrial Europe*, Cambridge: Cambridge University Press.

Barnett, M. and M. Finnemore (1999) 'The politics, power and pathologies of international organizations', *International Organization*, Vol. 53, No. 4, Autumn.

Blackhurst, R. (1997) 'The WTO and the global economy', *World Economy*, Vol. 20, No. 3, August.

Block, F. (1999) 'Deconstructing capitalism as a system', paper presented at the symposium on 'Approaches to Varieties of Capitalism', University of Manchester, March.

Bowles, S. and H. Gintis (1993) 'The revenge of *homo economicus*: contested exchange and the revival of political economy', *Journal of Economic Perspectives*, Vol. 7, No. 1, Winter.

—— (1996) 'Efficient redistribution: New rules for markets, states, and communities', *Politics and Society*, Vol. 24, No. 4, June.

—— (2000) 'Walrasian economics in retrospect', *Quarterly Journal of Economics*, Vol. 115, No. 4, November.

Brenner, R. (1976) 'Agrarian class structure and economic development in pre-industrial Europe', *Past and Present*, Vol. 70, February.

Buchanan, J., Tollison, R. and G. Tullock (eds) (1980) *Towards a Theory of the Rent-Seeking Society*, College Station, TX: Texas A & M University Press.

Chang, H.-J. (1993) 'The political economy of industrial policy in Korea', *Cambridge Journal of Economics*, Vol. 17, No. 2, March.

—— (1994) *The Political Economy of Industrial Policy*, London and Basingstoke: Macmillan.

—— (1995) 'Explaining "flexible rigidities" in East Asia', in T. Killick (ed.), *The Flexible Economy*, London: Routledge.

—— (1997) 'Markets, madness, and many middle ways – some reflections on the institutional diversity of capitalism', in Arestis, P., Palma, G. and M. Sawyer (eds), *Essays in Honour of Geoff Harcourt, Volume 2: Markets, Unemployment, and Economic Policy*, London: Routledge.

—— (1998) 'Korea: the misunderstood crisis', *World Development*, Vol. 26, No. 8, August.

—— (1999) 'Industrial policy and East Asia: the miracle, the crisis, and the future', paper presented at the World Bank workshop on 'Rethinking the East Asian Miracle', San Francisco, February.

—— (2000a) 'An institutionalist perspective on the role of the state – towards an institutionalist political economy', in Burlamaqui, L., Castro, A. B. and H.-J. Chang (eds), *Institutions and the Role of the State*, Aldershot: Edward Elgar.

—— (2000b) 'The hazard of moral hazard – untangling the Asian crisis', *World Development*, Vol. 28, No. 4, April.

—— (2002) 'Breaking the mould – an institutionalist political economy alternative to the neo-liberal theory of the market and the state', *Cambridge Journal of Economics*, Vol. 26, No. 5, September.

Chang, H.-J., Park, H.-J. and C. G. Yoo (1998) 'Interpreting the Korean crisis: financial liberalisation, industrial policy, and corporate governance', *Cambridge Journal of Economics*, Vol. 22, No. 6, November.

Chang, H.-J. and R. Rowthorn (1995) 'Role of the state in economic change – entrepreneurship and conflict management', in Chang, H.-J. and R. Rowthorn (eds), *The Role of the State in Economic Change*, Oxford: Oxford University Press.

Chang, H.-J. and C.-G. Yoo (2000) 'The triumph of the rentiers?', *Challenge*, January.

Cheng, T., Haggard, S. and D. Kang (1998) 'Institutions and growth in Korea and Taiwan: the bureaucracy', *Journal of Development Studies*, Vol. 34, No. 6, August.

Chibber, V. (1999) 'Building a developmental state: the Korean case reconsidered', *Politics and Society*, Vol. 27, No. 3, September.

Douglas, M. (1986) *How Institutions Think*, London: Routledge and Kegan Paul.

Evans, P. (1995) *Embedded Autonomy: States and Industrial Transformation*, Princeton, NJ: Princeton University Press.

—— (1997) 'The eclipse of the state? Reflections on stateness in an era of globalization', *World Politics*, Vol. 50, No. 1, October.

—— (2000) 'Fighting marginalization with transnational networks: counter-hegemonic globalization', *Contemporary Sociology*, Vol. 29, No. 1, January.

Evans, P. and J. Rauch (1999) 'Bureaucracy and growth: a cross-national analysis of the effects of "Weberian" state structures on economic growth', *American Sociological Review*, Vol. 64, No. 5, October.

Finnemore, M. (1996) 'Norms, culture, and world politics: insights from sociology's institutionalism', *International Organization*, Vol. 50, No. 2, Spring.

Fligstein, N. (1996) 'Markets as politics: a political-cultural approach to market institutions', *American Sociological Review*, Vol. 61, No. 4, August.

Friedland, R. and R. Alford (1991) 'Bringing society back in: symbols, practices, and institutional contradictions', in Powell, W. and P. DiMaggio (eds), *The New Institutionalism in Organizational Analysis*, Chicago: University of Chicago Press.

Granovetter, M. (1985) 'Economic action and social structure: the problem of embeddedness', *American Journal of Sociology*, Vol. 91, No. 3, November.

Haworth, N. and S. Hughes (1997) 'Trade and international labor standards: issues and debates over social clause', *Journal of Industrial Relations*, Vol. 39, No. 2, June.

Hodgson, G. M. (1988) *Economics and Institutions: A Manifesto for a Modern Institutional Economics*, Cambridge and Philadelphia: Polity Press and University of Pennsylvania Press.

—— (1993) *Economics and Evolution*, Cambridge: Polity Press.

—— (2000) 'Structures and institutions: reflections on institutionalism, structuration theory and critical realism', mimeo, Business School, University of Hertfordshire.

Hveem, H. (1999) 'A new Bretton Woods for development?', *Journal of International Relations and Development*, Vol. 2, No. 4, December.

Johnson, C. (1982) *MITI and the Japanese Miracle*, Stanford, CA: Stanford University Press.

Keck, M. and K. Sikkink (1998) *Activists Beyond Borders: Advocacy Networks in International Politics*, Ithaca, NY: Cornell University Press.

Kohli, A. (1994) 'Where do high growth political economies come from? – The Japanese lineage of Korea's "developmental state"', *World Development*, Vol. 22, No. 9, September.

Kregel, J. and L. Burlamaqui (2000) 'Finance, competition, instability, and development: the financial scaffolding of the real economy', paper presented to meetings of the Other Canon Group, Venice, January and August.

Krueger, A. (1998) *The WTO as an International Organization*, Chicago, IL: University of Chicago Press.

March, J. and J. Olsen (1989) *Rediscovering Institutions – The Organizational Basis of Politics*, New York: The Free Press.

Marglin, S. (1974) 'What do bosses do? – The origins and functions of hierarchy in capitalist production, part I', *Review of Radical Political Economy*, Vol. 6, No. 2, June.

Marglin, S. and J. Schor (eds) (1990) *The Golden Age of Capitalism*, Oxford: Oxford University Press.

North, D. (1984) 'Transaction costs, institutions, and economic history', *Journal of Institutional and Theoretical Economics*, Vol. 140, No. 1, March.

Palley, T. I., Drake, E. and T. Lee (1999) 'The case for core labor standards in the international economy: theory, evidence, and a blueprint for implementation', report submitted to the International Financial Advisory Commission of the Department of the Treasury, Washington, DC: AFL–CIO.

Polanyi, K. (1957) *The Great Transformation*, Boston: Beacon Press.

Rauch, J. and P. Evans (2000) 'Bureaucratic structures and bureaucratic performance in less developed countries', *Journal of Public Economics*, Vol. 75, No. 1, January.

Ruggie, J. (1982) 'International regimes, transactions and change: embedded liberalism in the postwar economic order', *International Organization*, Vol. 36, No. 2, Spring.

—— (1998) *Constructing the World Polity: Essays on International Insitutionalization*, New York: Routledge.

Schotter, A. (1985) *Free Market Economics: A Critical Appraisal*, New York: St. Martin's Press.

Simon, H. (1983) *Reason in Human Affairs*, Oxford: Blackwell.

Singh, A. (1999) '"Asian capitalism" and the financial crisis', in Michie, J. and J. Grieve Smith (eds), *Global Instability: The Political Economy of World Economic Governance*, London: Routledge.

Stretton, H. and L. Orchard (1994) *Public Goods, Public Enterprise and Public Choice*, Basingstoke: Macmillan.

Wade, R. (1990) *Governing the Market: Economic Theory and the Role of Government in East Asian Industrialization*, Princeton, NJ: Princeton University Press.

—— (1998) 'The Asian debt and development crisis of 1997– Causes and consequences', *World Development*, Vol. 26, No. 8, August.

Wall Street Journal, 6 December 1999, A17.

Waltz, K. (1979) *Theory of International Politics*, Reading, MA: Addison-Wesley.

Weber, S. (1999) 'Ethics, actors, and global economic architecture – what is the role of international organizations?', discussion paper, Carnegie Council Workshop, June.

Williamson, O. (1985) *The Economic Institutions of Capitalism: Firms, Markets, Relational Contracting*, New York: The Free Press.

Woo-Cumings, M. (ed.) (1999) *The Developmental State*, Ithaca, NY: Cornell University Press.

World Bank (1993) 'The East Asian miracle: economic growth and public policy', in *A World Bank Policy Research Report*, New York: Oxford University Press.

—— (1997) *World Development Report: The State in a Changing World*, New York: Oxford University Press.

Notes

1 It should be emphasized that the market is also an institution supported by a range of formal and informal rules concerning its boundaries, its participants, and the terms of their participation. See Chang (2000b).

2 Attributing institutional primacy to the market does *not* necessarily imply endorsing a minimalist view of the state; the question here is *not* where the 'correct' boundary between the state and the market should lie. Many economists start their analyses (at least implicitly) from the market supremacy assumption but are keenly aware of the failings of the market and willingly endorse a relatively wide range of interventions, as well as other 'institutional' solutions (for example, Arrow (1974); Schotter (1985).

3 This view is most explicitly adopted by non-economists such as Granovetter (1985); Douglas (1986); March and Olsen (1989); Friedland and Alford (1991); Fligstein (1996); Finnemore (1996); and Barnett and Finnemore (1999). Economists who adopt this view, although using somewhat different language, include Simon (1983); Hodgson (1988 and 2000); Bowles and Gintis (2000); and Chang (2000b).

4 Hodgson's essay in this volume denotes this as 'reconstitutive downward causation'.

5 Of course, the 'original' selves are themselves products of the existing institutional structure.

6 In the words of Mary Douglas (1986: 27), '[c]ollective sanctions are a form of collective action'.

7 The term is Herbert Simon's. Simon (1983) is the best exposition of this view.

8 For a comprehensive discussion of evolutionary approaches in economics, see Hodgson (1993).

9 Chang and Rowthorn (1995) attempt to combine this approach with what we call the 'culture-based structured-interest approach'.

10 This figure equals the arithmetic average of *per capita* output growth rate figures for the US, Canada, Japan, the UK, France, West Germany, and Italy. The same figure for the subsequent periods was 1.4 per cent in 1870–1913 and 1.2 per cent in 1913–50. The figure was 'only' 3.8 per cent even during the 'Golden Age of Capitalism' (roughly 1945–73). See Table 8.1 in Armstrong *et al.* (1991: 117). If sustained over time, small gaps in growth rates have huge consequences. If a country's *per capita* income is growing at 1 per cent per annum (this is the case of Argentina during the postwar period), *per capita* income will double in 70 years – not the 12–15 years that it took Korea or Taiwan to do it. A country with *per capita* income growth of 0.3 per cent per annum – the case of Bangladesh until the 1980s – would require 230 years to double its *per capita* income.

11 The concept originated with Johnson's (1982) analysis of Japan in the

1950s and 1960s. See Amsden (1989), Wade (1990), Chang (1993), Evans (1995), Akyuz (1999), and Woo-Cumings (1999) for subsequent elaborations. World Bank (1993) and World Bank (1997) also grudgingly acknowledge the fundamental role of the state.

12 Alice Amsden (1991) first highlighted the potential danger to the Korean economic model of the rapid increase in the numbers and intellectual ascendancy of what she calls the ATKEs (American-educated Korean economists). In the annual listing of economics PhDs published between 1987 and 1995 in the *Journal of Economic Literature*, Korean names constitute approximately 9.7 per cent of all listed names (776 out of 8,040). This is an astonishing statistic, given that Korea accounts for about 0.75 per cent of the world's population (and that very few of these names represent Korean-Americans). An overwhelming proportion of these economists subsequently returned to Korea, steering university economics education increasingly in a neoliberal direction. In addition, many elite bureaucrats, increasingly educated along neoliberal lines in Korean universities, were sent to the US for advanced study; most eventually returned to their old jobs in the Korean government.

13 It is interesting to speculate on why the 'planning' ministry became the home of pro-market neoliberal thinking in the Korean bureaucracy. One possibility is that, not tied to particular 'clients' as were other economic ministries, the EPB had traditionally behaved more 'ideologically', whatever the ideology in favour. Another is that the EPB, as the top economic ministry, always recruited people with top scores in the economics section of the High Civil Service Examination; this meant that its bureaucrats were likely to do better in graduate studies in the US, and hence to earn more prestigious degrees.

14 By the mid-1990s Korea was one of the largest foreign investors in a number of developing and transition economies, not just in Asia but also in Europe (Indonesia, Vietnam, Poland, Uzbekistan). It was also one of the largest investors in the UK electronics industry.

15 Korea was accepted as a member of the OECD in 1996.

16 Of course, this is not to say that the Korean developmental model was without flaws. There were some obvious weaknesses, such as the excessive concentration of even high-tech export industries in commodity-type products (specialization in DRAM rather than custom chips), which made the country vulnerable to international demand cycles. However, it is not entirely clear how much of this was due to the Korean developmental state *per se*. The lopsided character of Korean industrialization, and the emphasis on scale economies (DRAM chips) over niche markets (custom chips), for example, are responses to the technological and organizational obstacles associated with breaking into the more sophisticated segments of export markets. In any event, the lopsided specialization of Korean industries only intensified with the state's abandonment of investment coordination across sectors and firms (see Chang *et al.* 1998).

17 On the importance of Weberian elite bureaucracy in economic development,

see Evans and Rauch (1999); Rauch and Evans (2000).

18 Prior to the crisis, elite bureaucrats would have moved to the private sector only later in their careers, after exhausting their career possibilities within the government, via a process known in Japan as *amakudari*.

19 Support for developmentalism may remain at the grassroots level as well. While many Koreans regard Park's developmentalism as the root cause of the current crisis, 20 years after his death Park consistently ranks in the top ten in various opinion poll rankings of individuals who are most influential in running today's Korea.

20 Economic development may increase the complexity of the task of coordination, but it also develops the society's administrative and coordination capabilities both within and outside the government. Therefore, it may, on the whole, make such an exercise easier, rather than more difficult (for a more detailed discussion on this issue, see Chang 1999).

21 For an interesting discussion of Zerzan's 'anarcho-primitivist' ideology, see the *Wall Street Journal*, 6 December 1999, A17.

22 Its only formal power is to legitimate the right of countries to engage in bilateral trade sanctions when their interests have been damaged by trade restrictions that violate WTO agreements.

23 In principle a similar logic applies to European trade unions, but for these unions the question of labour standards within the EU takes political precedence, leaving US labour unions as more salient actors on the issue.

24 In some cases (the Indian National Trade Union Congress, for example), the response has been consistently and strongly negative (Haworth and Hughes 1997). In other cases (for example, CUT in Brazil, COSATU in South Africa), the response has been ambivalent at best.

6

Banking and the Financing of Development: A Schumpeterian and Minskyian Perspective[1]

JAN KREGEL
AND
LEONARDO BURLAMAQUI

Schumpeterian creation and destruction occur in finance as well as in products and processes. The essential point of Schumpeter's view of money and banks is that new combinations in production and in products could not appear without being financed: finance and development are in a symbiotic relation. Restricting the Schumpeterian vision to technology or even industrial organization misses the integrated character of Schumpeter's vision.
– Hyman Minsky (1990)

■

Introduction

This chapter uses the theoretical traditions associated with Schumpeter, Penrose, and Minsky to examine the role of competition and capabilities in finance and in economic growth.[2] From that perspective, two aspects of the role of financial firms in economic growth and dynamics are important. One is the crucial role played by financial firms in providing manufacturing firms with the credit they require to engage in the competitive process of creative destruction. The second is the competitive behaviour of financial firms themselves, which transforms financial markets and, in turn, affects the ability of all firms to finance new innovations. The uncertainty and risk that underlie Minsky's financial fragility hypothesis are seen to result from Schumpeterian innovation, and spur further innovations. And knowledge-based innovation is a key strategic response to an environment of uncertainty and financial instability: financial innovations that facilitate the financing of innovation in business tend to decrease transparency concerning the risks being borne in the system, raising the possibility of ever-increasing financial risks and ever-decreasing understanding of the extent of these risks.

These considerations suggest that developing countries should be given the means to mould national financial structures which best facilitate the growth of knowledge-absorbing sectors (Christensen 1992; Nelson 1993), given their economic and social structures, their historical trajectories, and their institutional inheritances. But this does not mean that each nation will be able to identify a single financial model that facilitates growth and minimizes risks at every point in its development process. Growth requires financing, and both the process of growth and the process of financing growth are inherently volatile and unstable, as both Schumpeter and Minsky emphasized.

The next section briefly sketches out two approaches to the firm inspired by the ideas of Schumpeter and Penrose and Minsky. The two sections that follow then summarize Schumpeter's and Minsky's ideas about the role of finance in economic dynamics, in the light of these ideas about the firm. Competition and innovation in the financial sector are discussed, followed by attention to the impact of globalization, especially on developing nations. Two case studies of the provision of Schumpeterian finance are then considered, those of Germany and the US. A brief discussion of policy implications and a short summary conclude the chapter.

■

Schumpeter, Penrose, and Minsky on the Firm: Knowledge-based and Cash-flow Approaches

The knowledge-based approach to the firm

Schumpeter understood capitalism as an historical process whose defining feature is not equilibrium (as in the neoclassical canon), but change. Chandler (1990) validates Schumpeter's conception by providing historical chronicles that illustrate how firms compete in market settings. He shows that firms engage in ongoing struggles not simply to survive, but to achieve and hold dominant market positions. In these struggles, continuous change and unforeseen circumstances are the most significant threats to firms' survival.

A key element of the firm, emphasized by Penrose and Chandler, and by other theorists in different ways, is the creation and strategic management of knowledge-based resources. These resources include individual employees, teams, processes, and technologies. Some firm resources are acquired through arms-length purchases (as when new employees are hired); others are developed through processes internal to the firm. Firm managers' strategic management involves decisions about how to use existing firm capabilities, how to create new capabilities, and how to respond to uncertainty.[3]

Different authors exploring the knowledge-based theory of firm organization have emphasized different aspects of firm behaviour. Chandler views managerial organization itself as a production technique that confers 'first mover' advantages. Edith Penrose (1995) emphasizes that firms are not only more efficient in organizing factors, they are more efficient in developing new techniques that cope with changes in uncertain environments. They accomplish this by creating internal environments – 'pools of relative certainty' – capable of combining and coordinating responses to external volatility, and thereby generating endogenous innovations. These are just two ideas of many that have been proposed regarding how firms react to changing, uncertain environments. A fuller accounting of these responses would include adaptations in the existing management and organization of production, and changes in the organization itself (Best 1990 and 2001; Lazonick 1991; Chandler et al. 1997).

In any event, firms that survive invariably innovate – that is, they exploit opportunities for change by applying new ideas, methods, or combinations of resources.[4] Further, the innovation process is ceaseless. The very success of firms' reactions to competitive challenges acts to reinforce uncertainty and instability, calling forth new reactions and innovations and leading to self-perpetuating economic change. Firms thus compete continuously for market advantages, with asymmetric results: success for some, with strengthened technological and organizational capabilities, and above-average profits; failure for other firms, which either disappear or are reduced to marginal activities. Schumpeter, whose core ideas are elaborated by these theorists, put it as follows: 'to escape being undersold, *every* firm is compelled to follow suit, to invest, and to accumulate' (Schumpeter 1997: 32).

Competition is therefore the struggle for survival and growth in a structurally uncertain environment (Nelson and Winter 1982, parts 2 and 5). The profits that result from dominant market positions are always under threat from imitative strategies or other firms' innovative behaviours; they can only be maintained by continuous product differentiation and productivity enhancement. The continuous competition for profit provides the dynamic connection between innovations, market structures and business and organizational strategies.

The cash-flow approach to the firm

Minsky's analysis of the firm emphasizes the firm's cash flows and their sustainability in the light of the borrowing required to acquire assets. Minsky defines three balance sheet configurations: hedge, speculative and Ponzi. The asset side of a 'hedge' balance sheet produces expected cash inflows that always exceed their financing costs and operating expenses, including dividends, by a margin capable of absorbing any unforeseen changes in cash inflows and outflows. If the liquidity cushion covers, say, 2.33 standard deviations of the historical data on past gross operating returns, then the firm would be unable to meet its cash-flow commitments on average only one time in a hundred. A company that can meet its payments with 99 per cent probability is close to what a banker considers risk-free – a hedge unit.

As the cushion of safety declines, the probability of being unable to meet cash-flow commitments rises; at some point it will be 99 per cent probable that in some future periods the firm's cushion will not be sufficient to meet its payment commitments. Nonetheless, the cumulative cushion over the life of the loan should be sufficient to cover them; so the project has a positive expected net present value. The firm may need an additional extension of short-term credit on occasion to meet its cash payments, but by the end of the project the loan will have been fully serviced. This is what Minsky calls a 'speculative' financing position: both the banker and the borrower are speculating that by the end of the project there will be enough money to repay the loan, despite some shortfalls along the way. A bank loan officer with good expertise in credit assessment will accept such loans.[5]

Finally, when the cushion of safety is non-existent and there is a high probability of shortfalls in nearly every period, the firm may have to borrow additional funds just to meet current commitments. Minsky calls this 'Ponzi' financing, making reference to a well-known post-war pyramid investment scheme. These are companies that must increase their borrowing just to stay in business; according to standards of good credit assessment, bankers should not lend to such units under any circumstances (Kregel 1998c). For Ponzi units, profit expectations are based solely on the possibility of the resale of assets at higher prices.

Building on Keynes's and Schumpeter's analytical frameworks, Minsky argues that in a capitalist economy in which the future is subject to unforeseen changes, the value of hedge and speculative financing positions changes with variations in the overall macro behaviour of the economy. For example, a change in economic policy that produces a rise in interest rates affects firms' financing positions in two ways: it reduces the present values of the expected cash flows from operating projects; and it increases the cash-flow commitments for financing charges if interest rates are set on an adjustable or rollover basis.

■

A Schumpeterian *Capabilities* View of Finance, Innovation, and Growth

All the innovative competitive reactions discussed above, insofar as they require additional expenditures, can be undertaken only if they can be financed. This was a key link in Schumpeter's vision of the process of economic growth. Schumpeter considered finance as the motor force of industry; only with financing can firms appropriate the resources necessary to introduce innovations (Schumpeter 1997).

Enlarging Schumpeter's perspective involves identifying the characteristics of banks or of other financial firms that lead them to play this role in the innovation/growth process. This means accounting for the existence of banks and other financial firms within the economy. In the contemporary economic literature, many different rationales for the existence of banks have been established. One set of explanations attributes banks' existence to the advantages of large-scale operations *per se*. Banks may arise because they specialize in the investment of depositors' funds, and thus are more efficient than households in acquiring information about potential investment opportunities and hence in earning returns through the placement of savings. Banks' existence can also be explained by their scale advantages in monitoring the performance of borrowers. A more recent explanation attributes banks' existence to their involvement in financial engineering processes, especially the unbundling of large indivisible investments for sale to households.[6]

These approaches, while elaborating on banks' use of scale economies in achieving informational advantages, do not explain the unique role that Schumpeter attributed to the institutions financing the innovation process. The above explanations could also be used to explain the existence of money market mutual funds, which offer transactions and transfer facilities to their clients but make no loans (Mayer 1974), or the existence of collateral-based lenders. It might be more useful to begin with the two archetypal activities of the commercial bank: credit creation through lending to business firms in support of productive economic activity; and the proprietary purchase and sale of financial assets to benefit from pricing differentials that occur at a point in time or over time.[7] These two activity types are significant from a Schumpeterian perspective, since the former aims to increase total income and wealth, while the latter has no impact on the absolute level of income

Productive lending in the sense suggested by Schumpeter in his *Theory of Economic Development* (published in its first, German, edition in 1911) provides firms with access to the resources they require to undertake production. Lending of this type requires particular knowledge of the production process, costs, and future market conditions for the products produced by each firm to which credit is extended, and thus of its prospects for repayment. It facilitates the activities of the high-return, knowledge-absorbing sectors that produce dynamic industrial growth (in the same vein, see Minsky 1990: 60–5).

Management of the bank's proprietary investment portfolio, by contrast, requires information about the formation and evolution of prices in various securities markets; this process may have no relation at all to the information required to make decisions on lending to industrial borrowers. The motivation for such activity is, according to the theory of efficient markets, based on the idea that arbitrage in free competitive markets can eliminate any differences in the prices of identical titles to expected future income streams traded as financial assets. The impact of financial arbitrage is limited to the static efficiency of the competitive market process: it forces uniformity in market prices and helps allocate given resources to their optimal risk–return combinations. The successful arbitrageur profits from the elimination of such differences by being able to recognize them early; by contrast, the successful borrower profits from the organizational or managerial innovations that grant the firm a dominant market position.

Both types of knowledge-based activities are carried out by many commercial banks. When carried to extremes, they are reflected in the two basic organizational forms characteristic of financial institutions: relationship or house banking; and competitive market-based activity, sometimes known as 'transactional' banking. In the former, the knowledge advantage possessed by the bank involves its clients' production activities, and the potential profitability of these activities in producing the earnings needed to pay debt service and repay principal. This type of bank operation is usually associated with German Kreditbanks; US investment banks have historically played a similar role, although in a slightly different context and on a reduced scale (see Madeleine 1943; Robertson 1964; Hammond 1957). Indeed, German banks often employed engineers and scientists to help evaluate the technology and thus the long-term prospects of borrowers to fully exploit knowledge-based advantages.

One characteristic of relationship banking is that it does not permit free market competition among banks for business; no firm would willingly provide the proprietary information required for a banking relationship to a financial institution if it thought that institution might be working for a competitor in the near future. For full information sharing between bank and borrower, confidentiality in the treatment of information must be present; this implies the exclusivity of the services provided by the bank. Neither would a firm be willing to offer all the information necessary to allow a number of competing banks to make competitive bids for its business. By contrast, financial arbitrage – the basis of most of the transactional activities of banks – is based on knowledge of particular characteristics of the payment flows represented by financial assets, the prices of these assets that prevail in the market, and/or the prices that other market participants expect to prevail at future dates and places. One might say that the relationship bank is speculating on the nominal profitability of an innovative industrial process embodied in the firm that it is financing, while the transactional bank is speculating on its ability to identify anomalies in the efficient operation of the market mechanism and on the capacity of market competition to eliminate these anomalies.

In this regard it is important to remember that although financial institutions have certain peculiar characteristics and function in a special regulatory environment, they are nonetheless business firms and compete much like other firms. So just as the industrial structure is driven by competition, financial institutions seek to earn profits from the exploitation and protection of the various knowledge-based advantages they have acquired. That is, organizational and production advantages will produce dominant competitive positions that can only be challenged by firms capable of reproducing innovations, or of perfecting other techniques that are more attractive to the market and hence more profitable (Burlamaqui and Lagrota 1998, part 5).

As already mentioned, in financial systems where main banks or house banks provide relationship services, there is a tacit agreement, as well as a practical imperative, that banks do not compete for business. By contrast, market-based systems, wherein the required knowledge involves markets or instruments, but not information about clients, present the possibility of financial innovation via rapid reverse engineering. This permits the competitive emulation that provides for eminently contestable markets; financial institutions will compete for business by seeking to replicate the financial instruments and services that other institutions offer to their clients. Competition of this type can encompass either the direct confrontation of competitors or the expansion of activities into other sectors or areas of the production process. As the introduction of new information-processing technology increases organizational capacity, and enhances economies of both scale and scope, financial firms can integrate additional services into their activities.[8] The creation of financial firms capable of this activity requires the evolution and concentration of financial institutions and financial markets to a size that is sufficient to achieve similar economies of scale and scope.[9] Note that this growth in financial firms' capacity makes it possible for non-financial firms, too, to achieve greater economies of scale and scope.

■

A Minskyian View of Banks, Finance, and Liquidity

For Minsky, as well as for Schumpeter, debt financing is the core of the very logic of capitalist production. In exploring the link between finance and economic activity, Minsky shifts attention away from the problem of productive credit and focuses on the problems of liquidity and credit over-expansion. His work belongs to the post-Keynesian approach to economics, a perspective that takes money and finance (rather than technology or innovation *per se*) as the most important organizational features of capitalist systems. The post-Keynesian view emphasizes the crucial importance of uncertainty and liquidity preference in understanding the multiple rationalities for, and the volatility that guides, investment decisions; it also explores the implications of these elements for economic instability. Minsky emphasizes the need to fully incorporate *real world phenomena* – and specially finance – into the core of economic analysis, so as to grasp the *intrinsically unstable* nature of capitalist economies.

Minsky's 'Wall Street Paradigm' develops a theory of endogenous macroeconomic instability by connecting the dynamics of debt structures and interest rates. According to Minsky, modern capitalism could only be understood via this approach, which he explained as follows:

Looking at the economy from a Wall Street board room, we see a paper world – a world of commitments to pay cash today and in the future. These cash flows are a legacy of past contracts in which money today was exchanged for money in the future. In addition, we see deals being made in which commitments to pay cash in the future are exchanged for cash today. The viability of this paper world rests upon the cash flows (or gross profits after out-of-pocket costs and taxes) that business organizations, households, and governmental bodies receive as a result of the income-generating process. (Minsky 1982: 63)

In his vision, understanding money means understanding a vital process shaping a social evolution whose future course remains open-ended and contingent. In this sense, Minsky's theory should be taken as an essentially institutionalist one, in that he viewed the structure of the economic world – much as did his former teacher Schumpeter – not as immanent in some set of underlying data (such as endowments or technology) but rather as constituted by a set of key economic institutions. Money was the most important of these. His way of fleshing out that idea was to look at every economic unit – firm, household, government, and even country – as though it was a bank balancing cash inflow generated by a stock of assets against cash outflows required to maintain the liabilities created to acquire those assets. From that point of view, categories of activity such as production, consumption, trade and investment represent, first of all, exchanges of stocks of real and financial assets with particular monetary flow characteristics and attached conditions. To put it bluntly, money and finance are *the most real aspects of capitalism*, from which everything else springs.

In this approach, the most basic element of the economy is cash flow, and the most basic constraint on economic behaviour is the 'survival constraint', which requires that cash outflow not exceed cash inflow if existing stock positions are to be maintained (Minsky 1978: 157). Because the exact co-ordination of payments is impossible, even this simple constraint involves finance. From that perspective, finance and financial relationships are fundamental because they *oxygenate* economic units, allowing them to purchase without previous savings; and they make growth and structural transformation possible, by providing current purchasing power to those who would use it to expand the boundaries of the system.

However, in Minsky's thinking, finance has a double-edged quality. The other side of the 'positive' roles mentioned above is that finance allows economic units to become illiquid in the present (by way of cash commitments) in exchange for the *possibility* of recovering liquidity (plus profitability) in the future; specifically, it permits these units to acquire assets whose expected cash flows will exceed the cash commitments entered into to acquire them. Thus finance allows the undertaking of future commitments that may turn out to be impossible to fulfil. Failure to realize expectations then takes the form of liquidity crunches, or, in severe cases, insolvencies and bankruptcies.

The subjectivity and volatility of expectations thus make financial asset prices more volatile than other prices in the economy (Keynes 1936; Strange 1998). Second, given the inherent volatility of financial asset values, liquidity provides an important 'protective device' or 'defensive strategy' to manage uncertainty, for two reasons. First, since money is the unit of account its value is less volatile and more certain in terms of other goods than other financial assets; thus it represents a refuge from price volatility. Second, it provides assurance that future cash commitments can be met with certainty. Thus firms whose income flows are subject to fluctuation may want to hold cash cushions to make sure that they can meet recurrent cash commitments. This is the basis of Minsky's theory of financial fragility:

> The liquidity preference schema of Keynes transformed economics into a study of intertemporal relations: not only is the future now but the past is also now. After Keynes, there was no reason to do economic theory that was presumably relevant for a capitalist economy without examining the relations in production, consumption and finance that link yesterdays, today and tomorrows. (Minsky 1990: 6)

Commercial banks face a series of risks, the most important being liquidity or funding risks. To fund their lending, commercial banks borrow from the public by issuing sight deposits, which may be redeemed at any time. If the bank has lent these funds to a commercial borrower it will have to attract alternative lenders in order to avoid calling in loans. It may not always be able to do so; indeed, its liquidity or refunding risk arises because at times it may lack the liquidity to repay its liabilities and to renew this lending by finding other depositors. If the commercial bank is lending to business it also faces credit risk, for the firms that have borrowed from the bank may not be able to repay on a timely basis. The bank will have become what Minsky calls a speculative unit – that is, a unit whose required interest payments exceed its earnings – and it will find difficulties in attracting additional deposits. Finally, a bank that funds lending at interest by issuing liabilities on which it has made a commitment to pay interest must make sure that the positive differential (net interest margin) between the rate on its liabilities and the rate on its assets is maintained. If the term or the reset rate of the interest on the liabilities is shorter than that of the assets, the bank faces market or interest rate risk. Should the rate it has to pay to attract funds exceed the rate at which it has committed to lend, then a loan is subject to net present value reversal, and the bank will make losses and be unable to meet its commitments.

It is thus extremely important for a bank to present itself to its depositors as a hedge-financing unit that is able to make payments to its creditors on demand with perfect certainty. This would seem to imply holding a cash cushion against potential deposit withdrawals of 100 per cent of the deposits, and this would imply that the bank could do no lending. But commercial banks do make business loans, so the question is how it does this without incurring unmanageable risks. The term 'unmanageable' here means without running the risk of becoming a speculative unit and being unable to meet depositors' withdrawal requests. So, although banks will incur both liquidity and credit risks, they seek to make them manageable by fully hedging these risks (Kregel 1998d).

We may see how this might be done by considering an archetypal commercial bank that only makes short-term commercial and industrial loans of less than 90 days that are over-collateralized against goods in warehouse or contracts for sale of outputs. In this case, the value of the loan is some fraction of the anticipated realization value of the collateral. So if a borrower fails to repay, the bank takes possession of the goods and sells them for an amount equal to the value of the loan. Manageability here means making loans that are less than 100 per cent of the total value of the property pledged as collateral.

Bankers can calculate with reasonable certainty the amount of their total deposits that have to be repaid in the course of any given day. At the same time, banks can arrange their lending so that the total of loans repaid each day equals the cash turnover requirement. This minimizes the amount of cash that has to be available to meet cash outflows. Since these calculations are only statistical probabilities, they have a margin of error. Thus bankers maintain a cash cushion or liquidity reserve that can be used when net outflows of funds are positive, as frequently occurs. Usually this reserve against deposits has averaged much less than 10 per cent. When the value of collateral is less than loan value, the bank's owners can, if necessary, fall back on their capital to make payments to depositors. Thus for average daily operations a bank can 'safely' lend a relatively large multiple of its capital and of its deposits, with its risks fully hedged by the value of the collateral, its cash reserve cushion and the bank owner's capital. As a result, banks are usually very highly leveraged – with gearing and deposit multipliers well in excess of 10 to 1 – without being considered excessively risky. In this way a bank can maintain a hedged balance sheet that protects it from becoming a speculative unit (in Minsky's sense).

Hedging the risks of a highly leveraged balance sheet does have an opportunity cost, however, since one main source of bank earnings, given a positive lending differential, is the multiple by which the bank can create deposits by lending in excess of the deposits it has borrowed from the public. To increase this ratio beyond that associated with the hedging of risk means increasing the probability that the liquidity and capital cushion will be insufficient to meet repayment requests – and hence the probability that a liquidity crisis and a loss of confidence could produce insolvency due to demands for repayment in excess of reserves and capital resources. Thus banks also face a trade-off between risk and liquidity, which translates into a trade-off between profitability and liquidity.

Notice that the decision on how to hedge the various risks depends on the subjective perception of these different risks and the values of the collateral pledged against loans; the type and degree of hedging will thus be represen-tative of the bank's liquidity preference. A decision to expand credit lending through additional deposit creation, other things being equal, is thus a decision by the bank to reduce its liquidity cushion and either an explicit decision to increase risk, or a *subjective* revaluation of the bank's position that reduces the perceived risks faced by the bank or increases the collateral values pledged against loans. For example, a more optimistic evaluation of the resale value of collateral will allow a bank to increase its lending but not its perceived risk. In this case, the reliability of the new estimate of collateral value is crucial.

Consider the case of Japanese banks, which generally grant loans on the basis of collateral valuation. As the property market boomed after the Louvre Agreement in 1987 led the Japanese authorities to reduce interest rates, Japanese banks either lent to or created their own property companies, increasing their exposure *pari passu* with the rise in prices. These prices were being driven up by the increased demand for property, which was fuelled by purchases of the property companies. Since many of these companies were quoted on the stock exchange, this increased lending to property companies stimulated a rise in their stock market value and the creation of investment companies which qualified for bank lending because of the rise in the stock market value of the property companies. A vicious circle was thus created, in which the banks fuelled both a property and a stock market boom without increasing what appeared to be fully hedged and thus manageable risks. When interest rates were increased and the markets turned in 1989, the banks' exposure could not be reduced to restore collateral coverage to acceptable levels and the loans effectively became valueless.

■

Competition, Regulation, and Innovation in Banking

The two previous sections spell out some of the dynamics of banking behaviour, from two complementary theoretical perspectives. How then do banks compete? The first wisdom here is that banks compete differently depending on the state of their own balance sheets and the state of the economy as a whole. When financial institutions are competing aggressively they seek to maximize their market share; but when faced with difficulties they restrict their market expansion and compete for liquidity and/or solvency. As a result, competition in banking carries an inbuilt tendency to underestimate risks when the economy is expanding at a steady and seemingly predictable pace, and to overestimate them when the economy is in decline. It is the former that is more dangerous for the survival of the bank, and that constitutes the banking sector's contribution to the overall uncertainty and instability of the economy.

In the United States, this sort of process of banking competition culminated in the stock market crisis of 1929 and the banking crisis of 1933, when a majority of US banks became insolvent due to a liquidity crisis that turned into insolvency, as described in Minsky's theory. Regulations were then introduced, based on the 'real bills' doctrine, which attempted to institutionalize commercial banks and to limit their operations in financial markets to transactions services and short-term commercial lending (Kregel 1996).

To avoid such crises, most countries have introduced formal regulations, in the form of compulsory reserve ratios and minimum capital ratios, which impose bank hedging and thus create uniform standards for bank liquidity. Central banks in some countries have accepted the responsibility of acting as lender of last resort: that is, they stand ready to advance credits against a bank's doubtful assets in an emergency, thereby allowing banks to meet payment commitments even when they are in a speculative position and lack the liquidity to meet depositor withdrawals.

However, this governmental support has not protected commercial banks from competition with other providers of financial services. Indeed, in the past three decades, a competitive struggle has been waged between financial institutions facing different types of financial regulation. Banks have lost business to financial institutions that were not so highly regulated. The regulations covering commercial banks have limited their use of financial innovation to protect their deposit base and thus their net interest margin on normal lending activity. Thus, commercial banks have initiated primarily counter-regulatory innovations; and these have led banks to expand their activities in new directions.

This process began in the United States when a credit crunch and regulations on capital flows introduced during the 1960s balance of payments and dollar crises created incentives for US banks to shift some of their borrowing operations out of the United States to 'offshore' markets, primarily London. In addition to providing new sources of dollar funding for US banks, these markets provided an environment free of the segmentation imposed by US bank regulation. Commercial banks could thus operate internationally much like investment banks in the US, making many US banks global players, dealing in financial assets from around the globe.

Then, in the 1970s, savings and loan institutions started to compete with banks by offering to pay interest (and in some cases a free toaster or mink coat) on transactions deposits, while commercial banks remained restricted to zero interest deposit accounts. Since regulations apply to reserve ratios and interest rates payable on deposit funds, banks innovated by seeking new sources of funds not technically classified as deposits. This was the primary source of competitive innovation in the 1970s and early 1980s (Mayer 1974); competition within classes of depository instruments remains fierce today. Within each regulatory class, the competitive pressure is extreme: the products that a bank uses to decrease its required reserves or regulatory capital (and hence increase its earnings) are easily replicated through reverse engineering techniques that are widely known in the markets and sold publicly to clients.[10]

Further, by the late 1970s, a large share of banks' traditional lending to corporate borrowers passed to more efficient forms of organization, such as commercial paper and money market mutual funds. Banks responded by branching out into areas such as term lending, and they deepened their involvement in offshore lending and other activities. This led to a series of lending crises involving overseas loans, one consequence of which has been the establishment of minimal risk-weighted capital/asset ratios.

Overall, these shifts have caused banks' most important source of earnings, the net interest margin between borrowing and lending rates, to decline dramatically. To meet earnings shortfalls, commercial banks have been forced into other areas of activity, such as providing financial services to generate fee and commission income, and engaging in proprietary trading of financial assets (Kregel 1996 and 1998d). These shifts have fundamentally altered bank behaviour.

As noted above, proprietary trading by commercial banks requires a different type of information than does conventional lending. Earnings from financial arbitrage are based on the knowledge of prevailing market prices, and of the prices that other financial market participants expect to prevail. This shift toward fee-based income has altered the kind of information that banks collect, and the relative value of market-based and firm-based inform- ation within banking firms. Further, the introduction of risk-weighted capital– asset ratios led banks to create new types of assets that either have lower risk weightings or do not appear on bank balance sheets at all (hence requiring no capital). The result has been a rash of new product innovation in which banks act as market makers in derivatives products.

These new activities represent substantially different types of risk and different trade-offs between risks and returns, with a likely overall increase in risk. Proprietary trading, for example, carries large price risks which banks traditionally have not been accustomed to manage (Strange 1998). An average US commercial bank now generates roughly one third of earnings from lending on net interest margin, a third from its proprietary trading portfolio and a third from fee and commission income. The latter is especially important because it carries a zero capital charge and virtually no liquidity or credit risk.

Finally, much bank lending is now securitized into collateralized loan obligations, which banks sell to final investors so as to move loans off their balance sheets. This frees up bank capital; it also generates fee and com- mission income from booking the loans and from underwriting and selling the securitized packages. Lending to firms is being done increasingly through derivative packages arranged by banks and sold to bank clients, often with banks themselves taking the opposite side of the hedges or providing sub- sidiary guarantees (that also are off-balance-sheet). Thus, the new activities that banks are creating to protect earnings are transforming their package of risks and making it much more difficult to identify appropriate 'margins of safety'. Further, innovations involving derivative contracts frequently shift risks. It is usually argued that this process shifts risks to those who are most willing to bear them. But since identifying the true risks of derivative instru- ments is difficult, it cannot be assumed that those most able to bear these instruments' risks are bearing them. This generates yet another source of potential financial instability. Overall, it is readily seen that these innovative products, practices, and strategies in the banking system have not only reshaped, but also deepened, this system's tendency towards financial fragility.

In Schumpeterian terms, continuous product innovation is required for banks to create monopoly profits, conquer new clients, and improve competitive position against other banks. Financial product innovation diffusion occurs almost instantaneously, since patent protection is difficult to attain and information is rapidly diffused (by product imitation) among institutions. Thus, first-mover profits are ephemeral: once created, they almost instantaneously evaporate (Burlamaqui and Lagrota 1998; Burlamaqui 2000: 12–19). Consequently, much competitive innovation has taken the form of rapid bank consolidation: it is easier to buy competitors than to gain a dominant advantage over them, and the gain in size leads to hoped-for gains from economies of scale and scope. Since 1980, consolidation has occurred rapidly both within and across regulatory classes (Dymski 1999). In 1999, US banking legislation opened the way for consolidation across financial product lines, thus removing the regulatory classifications that have driven much of the competitive activity in the financial sector over the past thirty years.

■

Globalization, Financial Fragility, and Developing Countries

Exchange rate fluctuations and reinforced financial fragility

How is our analysis affected when we consider the increasingly important global context? To begin, for firms with a high proportion of imported inputs, export sales, or foreign borrowing, depreciation of the exchange rate will have the same effect on cash-flow commitments as an increase in interest rates. For countries operating in an open trading system these two exogenous changes usually occur together and reinforce one other, since higher interest rates are often used to stabilize a weak currency after devaluation.

Cash cushions or margins of safety thus are necessarily larger for firms operating in countries with open capital markets and uncontrolled capital flows (Kregel 1998a and 1998c). For some borrowers, safety cushions will not be large enough to cover exogenous changes in both interest rates and exchange rates; these units may be transformed immediately from hedge finance units to Ponzi finance units. Shifts that reduce borrowers' cushions of safety also increase lenders' credit risk on their outstanding bank loans. Firms' borrower's risk also increases as they find it more difficult to realize the cash flows they initially expected. Overall, the *fragility* of the domestic financial system increases with either a rise in interest rates, or a depreciation of the currency.

Obviously, this same reasoning can be applied to domestic banks that borrow or lend in international capital markets. They will require higher cushions of safety against possible changes in international interest rates or in exchange rates. A bank with international operations is also exposed because a rise in interest rates and depreciation of the exchange rate also reduces the present value of its cash flows from domestic assets (represented by the interest payments received from its outstanding domestic loans), increases the interest costs of its foreign funding, and reduces the credit quality of its domestic loans. Any one of these shifts reduces the bank's credit rating as a borrower, and forces it to pay higher credit spreads on its domestic and international funding. If the change in rates is sufficiently large, banks may also find themselves suddenly in the condition of a Ponzi unit; in this case, banks' net present values fall below zero and institutions in this position become technically insolvent.

Banks' response to such conditions – especially if their own funding sources refuse to roll over or extend credits – is to reduce lending to firms that are classified as hedge and speculative units, and call in loans to Ponzi financing units. If domestic banks are also unwilling or unable to lend, the domestic interbank market will also contract, and a generalized liquidity shortage will arise. As both firms and banks attempt to reduce their foreign currency exposure, a breakdown in the foreign exchange market may also occur. In this manner, cross-border financial linkages can readily transform a financially fragile system into a financially *unstable* system.

The consequences of these financial shifts can be dire. As noted, the special characteristics of speculative and Ponzi firms is that they need increased finance from the banks just to stay in business. In such conditions, Ponzi financing firms have no choice but to reduce their own cash outflows, delaying current payments to suppliers, cutting back on expenditures, and attempting to raise cash in any way possible – selling out inventories and any output they can produce at distress prices. If these measures are not sufficient to cover their cash-flow needs, they will be forced to suspend investment projects, sell other assets, and lay off or fire workers.[11]

Any number of factors, and not just shifts in exchange rates, can generate the scenario just outlined: among these are the tendency toward under-estimation of risks in periods of sustained economic stability, periods of epochal Schumpeterian technological changes that increase optimism regarding the profit potential of new technologies, and so on. Significant balance-sheet exposure to foreign markets – either through loans or goods – reduces the size of the external shock required to trigger financial stress. Further, a period of prolonged exchange rate stability may in itself lead to over-optimism regarding the stability of the domestic currency values of foreign commitments, tempting units to reduce the margins of safety they maintain on foreign commitments. This endogenous change in margins makes the passage from a fragile to an unstable system that much more rapid in the event of an exogenous shock.

However, every period of tranquillity and every technological revolution is interrupted; so expectations are eventually disappointed, challenging financial and non-financial units alike. Irving Fisher warned of a combination of events in which rising supplies and falling prices lead to a collapse in demand – a process he termed a 'debt deflation'. Minsky modified

Fisher's description, placing more importance on the rising credit risks on bank balance sheets; increased charge-offs and a general decline in asset quality result, placing some banks in difficulty as their capital cushion is overwhelmed by loan losses, and a full-fledged financial panic is threatened. In Minsky's model, this spread of fragility from the productive to the banking sector characterizes the passage from financial fragility to financial instability and crisis.

The special fragility of developing countries

Minsky's original analysis of the passage from financial fragility to financial instability focused on changes in domestic monetary policy or the persistence of stable domestic conditions. This analysis is easily extended to the open economy case of an exogenous exchange rate shock, which affects companies operating in open trading systems and banks borrowing and lending in international money and capital markets. With increasingly interdependent capital markets and increased capital flows, the analysis of changes in monetary policy should be extended to encompass changes in the monetary policy of the largest international lenders.

Changes in interest rates of the major international lenders, especially the US and Japan, have been especially important in creating financial instability in developing countries during the debt crises of the 1970s and 1980s; their impact on exchange rates has been a major factor in the 1997 Asian financial crisis. However, that crisis was exacerbated by an additional element: the conditionality imposed on the borrowers seeking support from the multi-lateral agencies (Kregel 1998a, 1998b and 1998c).

As noted above, the normal scenario for a developing country financial crisis involves domestic firms borrowing in foreign currency from foreign banks at interest rates that are reset at a short rollover period. Note that it makes little difference if the loans have a short or long maturity; the point is the change in interest costs on cash flows produced by the short reset interval for interest rates. Short reset periods mean that a rise in foreign interest rates is quickly transformed into an increased cash-flow commitment for the borrower, instantly reducing margins of safety. If the change in international interest rate differentials leads to a depreciation of the domestic currency relative to the borrowed foreign currency, then the cushion of safety is further eroded by the increase in the domestic currency value of the cash commitments and the principal to be repaid at maturity.

Developing-country governments sometimes respond to the weakness of the domestic currency in international markets by increasing domestic interest rates, with the aim of stemming currency speculation or increasing foreign demand for the currency; however, such policy steps adversely affect domestic demand, reduce domestic cash flows, and increase domestic financing costs. Firms may thus pass rapidly from hedge financing to Ponzi finance units as the result of a rise in foreign interest rates. Whether this increase in financial fragility turns to instability and crisis depends on the willingness of foreign banks to extend additional foreign currency lending to cover payment shortfalls on current commitments. If foreign banks follow the bankers' aphorism, they may be unwilling to do this.

As a result, firms may be forced to try to improve their foreign earnings by increasing foreign sales. But this usually leads to falling prices in international markets, compounding losses from depreciation of the exchange rate; any cutback in domestic operations simply makes domestic demand conditions worse. The knock-on or contagion effect thus hits both the domestic financial system and the foreign banks, which now have increasingly dubious loans on their books. If foreign and domestic banks' capital cushion is insufficient to absorb the losses, then fragility turns to global systemic instability. In any case, the initial shock and the recommended policies combine to increase fragility and thus make instability possible in any exchange rate crisis.

■

Perspectives on Financial Policies and Development: German and US Experiences

In Schumpeter's view, economic growth requires that the financial system provide a means for the most dynamic entrepreneurs to obtain resources from the dying, static parts of the economy, in a process he called 'creative destruction'. Schumpeter's student Minsky agreed that the financing of innovation is a core element in economic growth. This implies, as argued above, a banking system capable of identifying knowledge-based innovation and supporting it through credit- and capital-market outlays. At the same time, the framework has shown that the macrodynamics of open capitalist economies tend to endogenously generate financial fragility, and that banking competition has shifted the information that banks rely on to generate revenue away from detailed understanding of borrower firms' capacity and toward price movements in financial markets. In other words, the banking relations that Schumpeter viewed as crucial in supporting growth are threatened by current global trends.

This raises the question of whether a different kind of banking system must be created as a prerequisite to growth based on appropriately financed competitive innovation. What can be learned from the historical experience of Germany and the US?

The German experience

The institution that provided the model and historical reference point for Schumpeter's banks was the state-owned German Kreditbank or 'mixed bank'. In Germany joint-stock banks played an active role in financing the innovation that led to German industrialization in the second half of the nineteenth century, but their role remained limited until the unification of Germany in the 1870s. The Kreditbanks founded at the middle of the century were weakened by the difficulties of the 1857 crisis. During the disturbed financial conditions of the war years they committed substantial sums in an effort to support the price of the shares of the companies they owned, thus tying up a larger proportion of their capital in holdings of company stocks than their normal operations would have dictated. It was during this period that the banks sought to develop the current-account (*kontokorrent*) connections with firms that were eventually to dominate the banks' business activities and produce the idea of a *haus* bank. These banks reached the peak of their power at the turn of the century; it can be assumed that they exercised a great deal of influence on Schumpeter's thinking in the *Theory of Economic Development*.

Despite Schumpeter's optimistic view that the German Kreditbanks could support dynamic economic growth, there is some historical evidence that these industrial or 'mixed' banks are more unstable than banking systems in which banks are 'separated' or segregated as in the US after the 1930s depression. Examples are the difficulties faced by German industrial banks in the 1857 crisis, the Italian industrial banking collapse in the 1920s, and the difficulties of mixed banks throughout Europe in the 1930s as the value of their industrial holdings collapsed in the aftermath of the Credit Anstalt bankruptcy.

Nonetheless, mixed-bank systems, including that in Germany, survived this period of deep financial crisis in the inter-war period. How did these mixed banks manage to avoid the worst consequences of the price risks associated with financing their investments in long-term capital assets? Initially, German mixed banks took a bifurcated approach to financing the creation and subsequent activities of German firms, in response to German banking law (Kregel 1992, 1995) and to regulatory changes imposed on German banks after the 1930s crisis.

How did this bifurcated system work? It was closely linked to the existence of an active stock market. For start-up companies, mixed banks' activities were very similar to those of venture capitalists in a segregated system (such as the US after the 1920s), seeking good new prospects and taking an active interest in their management until they could be floated on the stock market in an initial public offering (IPO). Then, once these start-up companies had taken off, the mixed banks operated as 'traders' for these companies, playing much the same role as investment banks in the US.

Behind this approach was German law, which does not restrict the types of business in which banks can engage, but places constraints on the composition of bank balance sheets. The most basic of these is the *liquidity principle*, which limits long-term lending to the sum of a bank's long-term funding (defined as the bank's own equity plus sale of bank bonds), its long-term borrowing, 60 per cent of its savings deposits, 10 per cent of its current accounts, and its time deposits from non-financial entities. This means that German banks were required to match assets and liabilities within particular segments of the yield curve. Reduction in liquidity risk for banks holding long-term capital assets is achieved by imposing a rough matching of maturities in the long and short segments. So, instead of segregating the financial system, German legislation segregated the individual bank's balance sheet into short- and long-term activities, with maturity matching in each section. This produces the logical equivalent of the separation of commercial and investment banks by imposing asset separation within any mixed bank's balance sheet.

This approach did not survive. In the German system of today, fixed-interest term lending has replaced venture-capital-type lending as was done by nineteenth-century Kreditbanks; and these banks' reliance on the equity market has all but disappeared. Why did institutional behaviour change? One reason is that banks could never expand their equity fast enough to provide sufficient equity capital for even the emerging-firm portion of industrial-sector investment. To maintain the use of pure equity finance, German banks would have had to convert themselves into either massive mutual investment funds or market makers in securities, rather than long-term lenders. A second reason is that the First World War and the currency reform had the effect of virtually wiping out the existing supply of government and private securities, eliminating the secondary capital market. Subsequently, new investment was financed primarily through retained earnings and short-term bank borrowing.

This situation sharply changed the operations of the large banks. These banks could not launch new firms by financing and underwriting the issue of these firms' share capital because there was no capital market on which to float shares. So the Schumpeterian activity of German banks effectively came to an end with the 1930s recession; the subsequent war made it impossible for them to recover their initial activities.

In the strengthening recovery after the war, the banks accumulated demand and time deposits, and rolled over short-term loans to firms into medium and long-term loans. By 1954, the ratio of short to medium-long lending was evenly split. Banks were thus faced with an ever-increasing maturity mismatch. This method of financing reconstruction, in the absence of capital markets, renewed the threat of banking instability, by generating the threat of liquidity crisis. Deposits could be withdrawn at any time; so in the event that short rates had to be increased rapidly to retain deposits while long-term lending rates remained fixed, any change in yield differentials (such as might be caused by inflation) could lead to insolvency. There were a number of initiatives to revive the capital market, none of which had any impact.

Banks thus operated under risk of instability, due to the threat of inflation and of a deposit drain, which was especially significant for smaller banks. To meet the prudential regulations in this situation, banks issued long-term bonds, which were initially held within the financial sector. These fixed-interest liabilities matched the term lending of the banks to firms. Reliance on bond finance may thus be seen as a structural result of the way in which price risks are hedged in the German system, and as a substitute for the pre-war use of the equity market. The German mixed bank system is thus no less dependent on capital markets to reduce risk than are segmented bank systems; both require these markets as a means of providing a reduction in price risks. The difference is in the type of asset, bonds or equity, which dominates capital markets, and in whether the finance provided is direct or intermediated.

The US experience

The Schumpeterian banking function was accomplished very differently, in a bootstrap fashion, in the US. While the US Constitution forbade state governments the right to issue currency, they retained the authority to charter banks; many of them used this legal right to create banks that effectively functioned as state development agencies – or what would now be called venture capital funds – to raise finance for the development of state industry. 'State legislatures resorted to the practice of granting banking privileges to railroad and canal companies, to gas and water works, to turnpike and power companies, and other similar enterprises to enable them to secure the necessary funds by issuing paper money' (Madeleine 1943: 66–7). These banks could be private or publicly owned, as in Kentucky. They could also have specific purposes. For example, the Union Bank of Louisiana was chartered as a 'property bank' in April 1832; it sold bonds to residents of the Northern States and Europe. The proceeds were invested in real estate, which served as the security for the bonds. When state banks found it difficult to raise funds by selling their own liabilities they were aided by state governments, who issued their own bonds and then turned the funds over to the banks, or lent their bonds to the banks for resale. Thus, the states applied the Schumpeterian principle that they could finance their own development plans by creating banks playing the same role as Kreditbanks in Germany. These banks, too, experienced substantial instability over time, leading to an extended series of chartering reform efforts.

Since banks' spread position in a unified system can generate instability, a possible institutional reform suggests itself: limit commercial banks' operations to the short end of the yield curves for particular, low-risk assets, then leave the rest of the curve to investment banks, whose investors – not risk-averse depositors – can take on the additional risk.[12] Policy shifts would thus segregate the longer-term financing function of banks from their provision of safekeeping and transactions services, ensuring financial stability and the full financing of innovative competitive activity.

The only problem with this argument is that investment banks in the US have shown no revealed preference for risk and do not generally play the entire yield curve and spectrum of available assets. According to Morris (1999), US merchant banks such as J. P. Morgan, while important in financing railway development in the US and Germany, were far from the ideal of the Schumpeterian banker. Morris argues that Morgan was primarily interested in eliminating competition of all sorts, rather than financing innovation. He observes:

Rather than attempting to free entrepreneurs to pursue new applications of technological innovations, Morgan ... was attempting to *freeze* technology. None of the motley collection of tube, wire, bridge and other steel-product companies that he had merged into US Steel were technologically advanced, and all had been under threat from Carnegie. (Morris 1999: 60)

Over time, investment banks in the US have generally used their capital for short-term trading of new and existing capital assets in the longer segment of the yield curve forbidden to commercial banks. This experience and others suggests that investment banks in segregated systems have not assumed the Schumpeterian role of investment financing.[13]

What investment banks in segregated systems *have* done, however, is to make capital markets more liquid. In so doing, they reduce the liquidity risk of holding long-term assets, which in segregated systems is borne by the final holders, the general public; by taking very short-term positions in long-term assets they are also able to avoid most of the price and interest rate risk associated with such assets. Investment banks in a segregated system tend to be traders, rather than risk-taking long-term investors. Thus, instead of providing long-term finance, these banks have organized liquid capital markets by intermediating between the long-term holders of assets and long-term borrowers. While they commit their own capital, borrowing, usually from commercial banks, finances the majority of their transactions.

In practice, then, the 'separation' in such policy-segregated systems is not between risk-averse commercial banks making short-term business loans and risk-loving investment banks committing their own capital long-term, but between banks (both commercial banks as lenders to the investment banks and investment banks as dealers) acting as market makers, and households providing long-term investment finance and bearing price risk. The more efficient banks are in reducing liquidity risk, the more willing households are to accept price risks, and the more direct capital-market intermediation occurs through the financial markets. For the economy as a whole, overall risks are spread over a larger base, as there are more households than investment banks. Since households are generally limited to lower leverage in financing their asset holdings than financial institutions, they are less likely to experience insolvency as a result of price risk. This suggests that the important characterizing feature of a financial system is the distribution of risks across types of banks and households, rather than whether finance is accomplished via the market or bank intermediation. The policy conclusion, then, is that intervention to separate banks' activities is not the decisive step in ensuring or undermining the provision of Schumpeterian finance.

Policy implications

The comparison of German and US methods of imposing prudential segregation to achieve stability suggests that instead of referring generically to mixed (or universal) banks *versus* commercial banks, it would be more informative to refer to balance sheet segregation and functional segregation. The fact that neither investment banks nor mixed banks are willing or able to raise sufficient equity capital to provide equity finance for the industrial sector leads to long-term financing via public equity markets in the investment-banking case, and reliance on bond market finance in the mixed-bank case. So in terms of risk and instability, there seems to be little difference between the two forms of bank regulation.

This suggests that much policy discussion, contrasting the stability of segregated and mixed-bank regulatory structures, has been misplaced. From the point of view of Schumpeterian 'creative destruction' or Minskyian 'endogenous financial fragility' a certain amount of evolutionary instability is necessary to allow the competitive innovation that makes the system viable. When banks and other financial institutions provide the financial resources that lead to successful innovation by some firms, they will also be financing firms whose competitive strategies are unsuccessful. Perfectly safe and stable banks would mean stagnant economic development. It thus seems clear that the major objective of policy cannot be the elimination of change and instability, for this would eliminate economic development. Rather, policy should be directed towards ensuring financing of innovative capital projects. Our historical comparison suggests that policy should not focus on the contrast between market and bank-based financial systems, since even Schumpeter's 'ideal' German Kreditbank was in fact fully integrated into the equity markets (before the war) and capital markets (after it).

The role of policy is to prevent the endemic systemic instability that can cause reversals of capital flows and changes in financial prices (and lead to Minsky–Fisher debt deflations) by providing for appropriate integration of financial institutions and markets. This will involve several major areas. One is risk management. As seen above, the major activity of banks is risk management, not undertaking the risks of maturity mismatches. A second policy focus should be on monitoring the manner in which risks are shifted from financial institutions to other balance sheets, primarily those of the public. This puts emphasis on the provision of market liquidity. Households will be more willing to hold long-term assets if some of their price risk is offset by their ability to sell these assets at short notice in liquid markets. This liquidity, in turn, depends on the activity of financial institutions serving as market makers, either directly or indirectly. Their ability to make markets depends on their financing, in particular on their gearing or leverage ratios. In the near financial crash of August 1998, the excess leverage of a number of major financial institutions caused them to retrench, destroying market liquidity. This caused a collapse in asset prices bordering on a Minsky debt deflation, and caused the flow of new financing of competitive innovations by firms to dry up completely. In sum, policy must focus on risk management techniques of financial institutions, the manner in which this risk management shifts risks to balance sheets outside the financial sector, the provision of market liquidity, and the degree of leverage of balance sheets.

■

Summary

In Minsky's view, capitalist economies have an inherent tendency to increasing leverage and financial vulnerability that leads sophisticated financial systems to be biased towards financial fragility. The competitive behaviour of banks contributes to this momentum: banks tend to increase their lending to more highly leveraged companies linked to creative destruction and/or new technologies during periods of sustained economic expansion; but they drastically revise these companies' credit ratings, reducing lending and even calling in loans, as soon as they *suspect* that these debtors may face solvency problems.

From a dynamic Schumpeterian point of view, when banks are strategizing aggressively in a stable expansion they compete for market share by increasing the volume of their lending, especially to more aggressive innovators. This reinforces the process of endogenous change and inherent market instability, and increases lenders' exposure to risk. When banks strategize conservatively they compete for liquidity and/or solvency, which has the effect of worsening borrowers' balance sheet positions and increasing overall instability.

Both theorists thus describe how periods of sustained expansion and/or of the introduction of new technologies endogenously lead to the reduction of margins of safety and the generation of financial fragility – what Minsky (1986, introduction) described as *'destabilizing stability'*. Competition in banking markets, especially in light of globalization, also endangers banks' performance of their Schumpeterian function of financing innovation and growth. This leads to the question of whether one or another approach to organizing banking activities can best guarantee that the financial system both facilitates growth and avoids (to the extent possible) instability. A review of German and US experience suggests that there is not. Both Germany and the US used policy to reach broadly similar results – that is, a financial structure that provided financing for growth and innovation – very differently, adapting their financial regulations on the basis of their respective industrial and financial-market structures, and of their different historical trajectories.

These two examples make it clear that the question is not so much whether more market allocation or less is beneficial, but rather how to develop and support the financial system in a manner that ensures its participation in building up the knowledge-based activities that can assure greatest *per capita* income growth. Extending this example to developing nations, the lesson is that indigenous financial systems should be developed and defended in much the same way as nations have acted to develop and protect industrial competitive advantage. A good recent example is the German policy of Finanzplatz Deutschland (Kregel 1998d; Dore 2000). In an increasingly integrated and globalized economic environment, the challenges faced by countries seeking to better their lot will become ever more difficult and may require increased regional integration.

Bibliography

Arthur, B. (1994) *Increasing Returns and Path Dependence in the Economy*, Ann Arbor: University of Michigan Press.

Best, M. (1990) *The New Competition*, Cambridge, MA: Harvard University Press.

—— (2001) *The New Competitive Advantage*, Oxford: Oxford University Press.

Burlamaqui, L. (2000) 'Schumpeterian competition, financial innovation and financial fragility: an exercise in blending evolutionary economics with Minsky's macrofinance', paper given at the Eighth International J. A. Schumpeter Conference, Manchester, June.

Burlamaqui, L. and C. F. Lagrota, (1998) 'Evolutionary macrofinance', paper given at the workshop-conference on Production Capitalism vs. Financial Capitalism – Symbiosis and Parasitism: An Evolutionary Perspective, SUM/ Oslo, September.

Chandler, A. (1990) *Scale and Scope*, Cambridge, MA: The Belknap Press of Harvard University Press.

Chandler, A., Amatori, F. and T. Hikino (1997) *Big Business and the Wealth of Nations*, Cambridge: Cambridge University Press.

Christensen, J. L. (1992) 'The role of finance in national systems of innovation', in Lundvall, B.-A. (ed.), *National Systems of Innovation*, London: Pinter.

Coase, R.H. (1991) 'The nature of the firm', in Williamson O. and Winter, S. (eds), *The Nature of the Firm. Origins, Evolution and Development*, Oxford University Press.

David, P. (1985) 'Clio and the economics of QWERTY', *American Economic Review*, Vol. 75, No. 2, May.

Dore, R. (2000) *Stock Market Capitalism/Welfare Capitalism – Japan and Germany Versus the Anglo-Saxons*, Oxford: Oxford University Press.

Dymski, G. (1999) *The Bank Merger Wave: The Economic Causes and Social Consequences of Financial Consolidation*, Armonk, NY: M. E. Sharpe.

Freixas, X. and J.-C. Rochet (1997) *The Microeconomics of Banking*, Cambridge, MA: MIT Press.

Hammond, B. (1957) *Banks and Politics in America*, Princeton: Princeton University Press.

Keynes, J. M. (1936) *General Theory of Employment, Interest and Money*, London: Macmillan.

Kregel, J. A. (1992) 'Universal banking, US banking reform and financial competition in the EEC', *Banca Nazionale del Lavoro Quarterly Review*, Vol. 44, No. 182, September.

—— (1995) 'Market form and financial performance', *Economic Notes*, Vol. 24, No. 3, November.

—— (1996) *Origini e Sviluppo Dei Mercati Finanziari*, Arezzo: Banca Popolare dell'Etruria e del Lazio.

—— (1997) 'Margins of safety and weight of the argument in generating financial fragility', *Journal of Economic Issues*, Vol. 31, No. 2, June.

—— (1998a) '*Yes, "It" Did Happen Again – A Minsky Crisis Happened in Asia*', Jerome Levy Institute Working Paper, Annandale-on-Hudson, NY.

—— (1998b) 'East Asia is not Mexico: the difference between balance of payments crisis and debt deflations', in Jomo, K. S. (ed.), *Tigers in Trouble: Financial Governance, Liberalization and Crises in East Asia*, London: Zed Books.

—— (1998c) 'Derivatives and global capital flows: Applications to Asia', *Cambridge Journal of Economics*, Vol. 22, No. 6, August.

—— (1998d) 'The past and future of banks', in *Ente Per Gli Studi Monetari, Bancari e Finanziari Luigi Einaudi, Quaderni di Ricerche*, No. 21, Rome: Bank of Italy.

Lazonick, W. (1991) *Business Organization and the Myth of the Market Economy*, Cambridge: Cambridge University Press.

Litan, R. (1987) *What Should Banks Do?*, Washington, DC: Brookings Institution.

Madeleine, M. G. (1943) *Monetary and Banking Theories of Jacksonian Democracy*, Philadelphia: Dolphine Press.

Mayer, M. (1974) *The Bankers*, New York: Ballantine Books.

—— (1988) *Markets*, New York: Norton.

—— (1992) *Stealing the Market*, New York: Basic Books.

Minsky, H. (1978) 'The financial instability hypothesis: an interpretation of Keynes and an alternative to standard theory', in Minsky, H. (1982) *Can 'IT' Happen Again: Essays on Instability and Finance*, Armonk, NY: M. E. Sharpe.

—— (1982) *Can 'IT' Happen Again: Essays on Instability and Finance*, Armonk, NY: M. E. Sharpe.

—— (1986) *Stabilizing an Unstable Economy*, New Haven and London: Yale University Press.

—— (1990) 'Schumpeter: money and evolution', in Heertje, A. and M. Perlman (eds), *Evolving Technology and Market Structure – Studies in Schumpeterian Economics*, Ann Arbor: University of Michigan University Press.

Morris, C. R. (1999) *Money, Greed, and Risk: Why Financial Crises and Crashes Happen*, New York: Times Business Random House.

Nelson, R. (ed.) (1993) *National Systems of Innovation*, Oxford: Oxford University Press.

Nelson, R. and S. Winter (1982) *An Evolutionary Theory of Economic Change*, Cambridge, MA: Harvard University Press.

Penrose, E. (1995) *The Theory of the Growth of the Firm*, Oxford: Oxford University Press.

Pierce, James L. (1991) *The Future of Banking*, New Haven: Yale University Press.

Robertson, R. M. (1964) *History of the American Economy*, New York: Harcourt Brace.

Schumpeter, J. (1997) *The Theory of Economic Development*, New Brunswick, NJ: Transaction Publishers.

Strange, S. (1998) *Mad Money*, Manchester: Manchester University Press.

Notes

1 This chapter is based on a longer essay entitled 'Finance, competition, instability, and development: the microfoundations and financial scaffolding of the economy', which was funded by The Other Canon Foundation (Oslo). In this regard, we would like to deeply thank the foundation's chairman, Dr Erik Reinert, for his sharp advice, as well as for the Foundation's generosity. We would also like to thank Professors Gary Dymski and Silvana De Paula for their extremely consistent and competent help with this version of the text.

2 Minsky, while a noted post-Keynesian, often commented on the affinity of Schumpeter's and Keynes's views on finance; see Minsky (1986: 113) and Minsky (1990).

3 The longer version of this chapter (available from the authors) shows how this strategic management involves considering when and how to reduce the uncertainty that arises from relative price instability by shifting from the use of contracted services to the hiring of employees. These considerations, of course, build on the core insights of Coase (1937 [1991]).

4 This does not mean the application of 'best practices,' as Nelson and Winter (1982), Paul David (1985), and Brian Arthur (1994) have stressed. Indeed, in this context the idea of 'best practice' may be without analytical content.

5 In Minsky's terms, Schumpeterian entrepreneurs are always *speculative units*, and *true Schumpeterian entrepreneurs* are quasi-Ponzi units.

6 For a recent summary of this literature, see Freixas and Rochet (1997).

7 Such trading may be beneficial in that it provides liquidity in financial asset markets; however, the spillover benefits of such proprietary trading are greatest when markets are buoyant and do not lack liquidity, and least when markets are under pressure and traders are seeking liquidity.

8 For example, the process Chandler (1990: 28) describes – wherein producers that achieve sufficiently large scale expand to provide wholesale and retail distribution of their outputs, thus internalizing external markets and eliminating wholesale and retail distribution costs – has a counterpart in financial services.

9 Mayer (1988, 1992) shows the impact of these changes in the organization of financial firms on the operation of financial markets.

10 Two examples make this point. The negotiable certificate of deposit (CD), offered to business clients by First National City Bank was quickly offered by all commercial banks to their clients. The securitization of bank assets through special purpose vehicles was pioneered by Salomon in mortgage banking after the collapse of the savings and loans associations, but was soon extended to other assets.

11 Perverse macroeconomic consequences can readily follow: a generalized condition of excess supply in all markets, placing downward pressure on prices of both output and assets, accompanied by declining overall demand. In extreme cases, investment can decline due to tightening monetary policy, and consumption can fall because of declining household incomes and

increased unemployment. Ironically, these developments may place additional pressure on short-term money markets, and even push short rates upwards as credit conditions deteriorate, current payments are delayed, and more units seek temporary financing to keep operating.

12 This remedy recalls the 'real bills' doctrine, the Chicago proposals for 100 per cent reserve banking advanced by Simons, von Hayek, and Friedman, as well as recent proposals (Litan 1987; Pierce 1991) for 'core' banks limited to investing depositor funds in government securities.

13 For example, banks in the UK, though not subject to special regulations on their activities, behave as if they were subject to segregation, limiting their activity to short-term lending.

Rethinking the Microstructure of Development: Individuals and Communities in Global and Local Spaces

7

Consumer Society: What Opportunities for New Expressions of Citizenship and Control?

JOHN WILKINSON

■

Introduction

First in the Anglo-Saxon world and later, although unevenly, in almost all countries, developed and developing alike, deregulation and privatization transformed the basis of legitimacy of economic life. With strategic services (water, energy, health, education) and the 'commanding heights of the economy' firmly moving into private hands, the market increasingly became coterminous with society. At first, a minimalist approach to the regulation of potential market failures was combined with a generalized belief in both the self-sufficiency and the efficiency of market mechanisms. This pure neo-classical model, made flesh under Reagan and Thatcher, was reluctantly buried in the wake of Eastern European resistance to the workings of a market economy. Healthy institutions, it was now clear both to governments and international bodies as exalted as the World Bank, were a precondition for the generalized trust necessary for workable markets.

In the neoclassical market both technology and preferences are exogenous factors, but in the real world, where markets increasingly impinge on all aspects of social and cultural life, legitimacy demands that the consumer be actively drawn into both the economic game and the drawing up of its rules. In varying degrees, the shift to a more radically market society has been accompanied by efforts to interpolate and 'internalize' the consumer. This has occurred first of all in the production process itself. The consumer is no longer the exclusive object of the marketing department but is increasingly engaged in the elaboration and design stages of new products and services. The shift to an 'economy of quality' and the uncertainty involved in new product launches has led firms to anticipate user response through the resort to trials, focus groups, and the permanent mobilization of consumer feedback. The frontier between the later design stages and market launch has now become blurred. Computer design and intelligent software systems allow for a radical reintroduction of 'made-to-order' products in the context now of mass consumption. The parallel shift from products to services, in which the client replaces the purchaser, accentuates this tendency to incorporate the consumer within the production cycle. Although the involvement of the consumer may often represent little more than a strategy for externalizing costs, products and services are increasingly open to consumer inputs and scrutiny prior to purchase.

A sharp politicization of the consumer has also accompanied privatization and deregulation, giving rise to two basic tendencies. On the one hand, there has been an institutionalization of the consumer interest as a counterweight to that of business. On the other, consumer organizations themselves have extended their focus from the monitoring of individual products and services to a preoccupation with underlying processes and consequences – health, environment, social and ethical conditions of production, animal rights. In their turn, alternative trading networks have emerged, in developed and developing countries alike, to mobilize the productive potential and latent consumer demand of those excluded from the dominant circuits of consumer society.

In this chapter, we begin by exploring the novel features of consumer society, through a comparison of the highly influential but awesomely pessimistic vision of the new consumer presented by Z. Bauman (2001), a leading theorist of consumer society, with the more optimistic identification of the new consumer elaborated by R. Rochefort (1997), director of the French research institute specializing in consumer studies, CREDOC. Bauman, from a starkly critical and pessimistic perspective, argues that the construction of individual and collective identities in contemporary societies has been progressively reduced to that of compulsive consumerism. Rochefort, on the contrary, sees an increasingly virtuous interpenetration of consumption and production and the emergence of what he calls the 'consumer entrepreneur'.

As an alternative to these radically opposed perspectives, and as an antidote to their degree of conceptual generality, we will then explore different patterns of consumer involvement along the economic cycle in an attempt to identify the precise ways in which the consumer, individually or collectively, is redefining the content and direction of economic values and priorities both at micro and macro decision-making levels.

Within this framework, we distinguish different consumer practices: (1) at the point of purchase; (2) in post-purchase activities; (3) in the design stage of products and as inputs in the conception of products; (4) in the definition of the contours of product markets; and (5) in the construction of (alternative) exchange circuits. An analysis of the literature in the above light may pinpoint better the differential leverage that the new consumer is able to exert at different stages in the conception, regulation, production, and distribution of products and services. Consumer involvement and organization, at present still in their infancy (paralleling the initial situation of workers in the earlier production-based capitalism), can, in this way, be seen to comprise a necessary and strategic component of any shift to a more virtuous phase in the organization of consumer society.

■

Zygmund Bauman – Consuming Life

For over a decade, Bauman has refined his views on consumer society in a remarkable series of publications that have provided a new language to analyze the position of key social categories – intellectuals shifting from legislators to interpreters, citizens divided into consumers seduced by the market and the excluded who are repressed by their dependence on state services. In a recent contribution, 'Consuming life', the abstract to the article admirably captures the significance that Bauman (2001) attaches to consumption in contemporary society:

This article posits a 'mutual fit' between consumer culture and the task posed to individuals under conditions of modernity: to produce for themselves the continuity no longer provided by society. It therefore explores the new forms of consumption formed from a shift from the functionality of needs to the diffuse plasticity and volatility of desire, arguing that this principle of instability has become functional to a modernity that seems to conjure stability out of an entire lack of solidity. (Bauman 2001: 12)

In a breathtaking lope through Montaigne, Pascal, R. L. Stevenson, Kierkegaard and Max Scheler, Bauman discusses the pre-eminence of desire over satisfaction and of the hunt over the catching of the prey, which afford priority to the distraction of an eternal present, continuously shielding the individual from the fate of his common mortality. The originality of consumer society, he argues, is that it has transformed this 'distraction' into a way of life and the only widely accessible way of life. In pre-modern society, socially defined needs established upper and lower ethical boundaries on consumption, with 'conspicuous consumption' still being bewailed by Thorstein Veblen (1979) 'at the threshold of the consumer age'. Modern consumer society, on the other hand, is not defined so much by the increase in levels of consumption as by the latter's emancipation from needs and justificatory norms. 'In the consumer society, consumption is its own purpose and so is self-propelling.' Needs have been replaced by desire, 'a self-begotten and self-perpetuating motive that calls for no justification or apology either in terms of an objective or a cause' (Bauman 2001: 13). Even desires, however, have psychic limits and have now yielded to the liberation of wishful fantasies, which are not disciplined by any reality principle so that the act of purchasing becomes 'casual, unexpected and spontaneous'. Throughout modernity, rational systems of organization had kept the sphere of the pleasure principle at the margin. In a producer-oriented society, distraction represents a mortal threat but in a consumer society it can now become transformed into the engine of profit. Here, pleasure becomes 'miraculously transmogrified into the mainstay of reality and ... the search for pleasure ... becomes the major (and sufficient) instrument of pattern maintenance' (Bauman 2001: 16). Irrational human wishes now become the guardians of rational order, and volatile desires the foundation of routine.

According to Bauman, consumer society is not the result of policy, strategic management or media brainwashing, but should be seen as 'the unanticipated consequence of the more than two centuries-long history of modern capitalism' (Bauman 2001: 18). In the age of modernity, the durability of social structures permitted behaviour oriented to the future and provided 'a bridge into immortality' for 'transient individual life'. Today 'it is now each of us, individually, that is the longest living of all the bonds and institutions we have met: and the only one whose life-expectation is steadily rising rather than shrinking' (Bauman 2001: 21). Spouses, families, skills, jobs, and possessions have all become more transient than the individual. Society, once the guarantee of stability, has now become a mere player and a source of constant surprise, even danger. In such a situation, the future can only be grasped as a succession of nows and 'individual(s) must compensate for the irrationality of their Lebenswelt by resorting to their own wits and acumen' (Bauman 2001: 22). According to Bauman,

> there is a 'mutual fit', an 'elective affinity', between the inanities of the consumer market and the incongruities of the tasks which individuals are presumed to perform on their own, their duty to compose individually the continuity which society can no longer assure or even promise. (Bauman 2001: 24)

And Bauman concludes on the following tenebrous note:

> the powers and weakness, the glory and the blight of consumer society – a society in which consuming through the ... succession of dis-continuous consumer concerns ... are rooted in the same condition, the anxieties born of and perpetuated by institutional erosion coupled with enforced individualization. And they are shaped by the consumer market-led response to that condition: the strategy of rationalization of irrationality, standardization of difference, and achieving stability through the induced precariousness of the human condition. (Bauman: 2001: 28)

■

Rochefort and the Consumer Entrepreneur

For Bauman, 'To become a consumer ... means to forget or fail to learn the skills of coping with life challenges, except the skill of seeking (and hopefully finding) the right object, service or counsel among the marketed com- modities' (Bauman 2001: 25). Bauman's analysis focuses on the extension of the market into all spheres of exchange. Robert Rochefort in the second of his books on the consumer, *Le Consommateur Entrepreneur* (1997), approaching the subject from a consideration of transformations in industrial organization and the wage relation, arrives at a very different, and decidedly (although cautiously) more optimistic interpretation of the emerging 'new consumer'.

For Rochefort, the world of the wage relation, which had separated producer and consumer, is coming to an end. The new consumer is now a professional consumer, a producer consumer, or, as he finally describes him, an entrepreneur consumer, involved in 'co(nsumer)-production'. The three- stage process of education, qualification and life career now gives way to the need for the permanent development of new competences to adjust to continuously changing work and market situations. This has led to an explosion of knowledge services – courses, magazines, television programmes and channels, books to lower entry barriers to new knowledge (the '... for Dummies' series), confounding the distinction between leisure and a new style of permanent apprenticeship. In parallel fashion, the separation between domestic life and work is breaking down, and the home (and even the car) must now accommodate office-style facilities. The strict division between public and private, work and home will increasingly be seen as a specific historical interlude as the interpenetration of their respective times and spaces promotes a re-approximation with earlier rural and artisan modes of life.

New products reflect this dual or rather hybrid character of modern life. The computer can be used simultaneously for leisure, for work, for purchases or for communication. The cellphone allows parents at work to maintain contact with each other and their children no matter where they are, and has become the key support of 'office-less' entrepreneurs. Not only are con- sumption and production inextricably mixed, but in many cases consumption now becomes the precondition of work rather than its reward. The messenger must be already equipped with a scooter, the salesperson a cell- phone and computer, the deliverer a car. It is not simply, therefore, that the consumer has become more reflexive, but that the consumer, who is also a producer, has a more professional involvement in consumption.

Rochefort's account also provides a sharp contrast to Bauman's individualization thesis where the consumer is locked into the permanent recreation of a never-satisfying present: 'The enjoyment of an instant present as the most obvious characteristic of consumption without concern for the day after is now at an end, replaced by a focus on the search for a long-term equilibrium, assuming responsibility for one's human capital in terms of health and training' (1997: 22). Here again, the integration of changes in production and consumption provides a clearer vantage point for the analysis of tendencies. The effects of privatization are not restricted to the extension of market relations combined with social exclusion, nor to the stimulus this may provide towards a more politicized role for the consumer. They also impose on each the need to situate present needs and desires within the long term of the life cycle, both one's own and that of one's family, as regards healthcare, training, retirement insurance schemes and the strategic education of one's children. On this view, it was rather the welfare state and the expectation of a permanent career that reinforced an orientation to the present and endorsed a lack of preoccupation with the future.

While it was the anonymous 'individual' who was the privileged object of market segmentation and niche strategies, Rochefort considers that the consumer is now beginning to be seen as a 'person' with a history, a project, a concern with coherence and a body which is not simply a 'size'. The fine, aesthetic distinctions of hyper-segmentation, which catered for an exacerbated and competitive individualism, give way to 'made to measure' strategies that allow for the reintroduction of personal, more utilitarian criteria (shoes and clothes designed for *your* body, etcetera). At the same time, Rochefort's 'person' is also the antithesis of Bauman's individual in that the autonomy of the new consumer-producer is premised on interdependence and connectedness, captured in the centrality of such emblematic products and services as e-mail and the cellphone.

It should be added that Rochefort is not oblivious to the downside of the new consumer society, and he includes detailed sections on the perils of strategic 'one-to-one' marketing together with an analysis of the extent of social exclusion, provoked not only by high levels of unemployment, leading to the phenomenon of the 'assisted' (and what Bauman calls 'the repressed') consumer, but also by the new phenomenon of the 'working poor' consequent on the diffusion of precarious patterns of employment. Both of these issues will be considered in more detail below.

■

Consumers at the Point of Purchase

Broadly speaking, economics has focused on pre-purchase conditioning factors: structures of provision and income disposability, together with preestablished and hierarchically stable buying preference systems. Sociology and anthropology, for their part, have traditionally explored the indirect social and cultural influences on purchasing decisions, also tending to reinforce the notion of stable preference systems, though from a socially constructed rather than psychological perspective. Economic studies on the constraints imposed by different distribution systems provide, however, a welcome internal critique to the consumer sovereignty thesis of the neoclassical tradition (Fine and Leopold 1993). Systematic empirical studies, for their part, have shown the fragility of presuppositions of stable preferences, with declining relative prices impotent to sustain markets and rising relative prices coexisting with rapid market expansion (Herpin 2001; Verger 2000 apud Herpin and Verger 2002).

The gap between social science theories and the dynamics of actual purchasing decisions led to the emergence of a new interdisciplinary undertaking – marketing studies – dominated initially by highly pragmatic and behaviouralist psychological research methods. The key issue here was to understand purchasing decisions within substitutable alternatives which persist and are critical even in oligopoly markets and where price competition is chosen only as a last resort. While this area of freedom of choice may be insignificant from a sociological point of view, it is decisive for firm profitability; strategic marketing, combined with advertising, emerged to understand and influence this purchasing behaviour.

From the 1970s onward, the saturation of traditional Fordist markets and the systematic orientation to (often radical) product innovation, combined with important changes in demographic trends and the surge in prospective studies, led marketing to adopt more strategic approaches, moving to a broader social science perspective (Arnould, Price, and Zinkham 2002). So much is this the case that market researchers on US university campuses are now often referred to as 'anthropologists' (Kline 2000)! On the other hand, the enormous transformation in shopping practices – out of town hyper- or supermarkets replacing the 'mama and papa' or 'corner' shops, and the shopping centre or mall emptying the high street stores – has led sociologists and anthropologists to focus increasingly on the significance of the shopping experience itself, the arena *par excellence* of 'choice'.

Theorists of individual identity construction have focused on the mall, either reworking the figure of the *flaneur* (Baudelaire 1978; Benjamin 1986) or situating themselves within the reflexive sociology of Giddens (1991) and Beck (1992), where consumption becomes a key element in the elaboration of personal biographies. The mall itself has become an important object of research as it has been transformed from a functional agglomeration of purchasing sites into a locus of multiple thematic experiences, reinforcing the 'aestheticization of everyday life' theses. Historical research has shown that, in many respects, the postmodern mall harks back to the style of the grand department stores in Paris, London and New York in the nineteenth century, with the Fordist period appearing, in this light, as a prolonged, more functionalist interlude (Chaney, W. apud Featherstone 1991; Jacobs 2001).

The pathologies of individual consumer behaviour have also attracted the attention of social science analysis, with the downside of identity construction being revealed in the phenomenon of shopping addiction, humorously explored in the film 'Rosalyn goes Shopping' and in the less damaging condition of 'terminal materialism' exhibited by collector fanatics (Arnould, Price and Zinkham 2002).

Sociological analysis of supermarket shopping, on the other hand, has tended to focus on the habitual nature of much purchasing behaviour, which imposes barriers to impulse buying. In these routine purchases, it is the woman who assumes managerial responsibility for meeting the collective needs of the family members, who, for their parts, delegate many of their consumer decisions in food, clothing, and personal hygiene (Warde 1994). Miller, in his *A Theory of Shopping* (1998), reinterprets shopping as an act of love in which routine is replaced by considerations of devotion, care, and sacrifice in attending to the different needs and preferences of family members while, at the same time, placing a premium on 'saving' as one of the accomplishments or arts of shopping. Writers in the French anthro-pological tradition, renovated in the publications of the MAUSS group, develop a complementary approach in their analyses of the importance of gifts as a motive for purchasing behaviour. Although the gift relationship has been increasingly commoditized, it remains important to note that it is the 'social bond' (*lien social*) maintained by gift giving that fuels a great deal of commerce (Godbout 1992). Whether analyzed in terms of routine, family love, and responsibility or the persistence of the gift economy, the free play of consumer desire and fantasy, in Bauman's terms, is tempered by social constraints and cycles.

These considerations, however, should not suggest that the consumer, at the point of purchase, is immune to the intense strategic attention of business. In the first place, industry and retail mobilize all the resources of behavioural psychology in their tactics of shop lay-out, involving atmosphere creation, bargains, product positioning, size of trolleys, and the targeting of children (Lewis and Bridger 2001). Second, the extension of the fashion concept, first analyzed sociologically by Simmel (1971), from clothing to a wide range of other products and services, imposes obsolescence by aesthetics, independently of criteria of usefulness or durability, progressively diminishing the 'dead time' of purchasing intervals (Gronow 1997). Third, systematic data analysis on the basis of barcodes, bankcards and fidelity cards, now so complex that it is largely outsourced to the giants of informatics – Microsoft, IBM, Oracle – allows retail to develop more tailor-made logistical ('effective consumer response') and publicity strategies, where the 'effort to convince' is being replaced by the 'ability to respond', in the timely offer of goods and services according to revealed, increasingly indi-vidual, preferences (Green and Hy 2001; Martucelli 2002). A fourth strategy, identified most forcefully by Rifkin (2000), but also elaborated by Rochefort in the study referred to above, draws out the implications of a broader shift from the supply of goods to that of service provision. The aim here is to capture, in Rifkin's vivid expression, the 'lifetime value' (LTV) of the client. Instead of selling cars, personal and household goods or property, firms are shifting to the provision of services, in which the goods are continuously replaced in accordance with a customer's varying 'needs' and desires. Here the 'point of purchase' is dissolved into contingency contracts, and the shift from supply-side imposition to demand-driven adaptation is consolidated in the provision of long-term services, where, as Lewis and Bridger (2001) define it, ' the soul of the new consumer' is at stake and can be effectively 'seduced' by the generalization of flexible production and logistical systems.

The vulnerability of the individual consumer at the point of purchase in the urban industrial environment quickly led to the development of new forms of collective action and cooperative movements, spread through Europe and the United States in the second half of the nineteenth century. In many countries, these developed into alternative retail networks often as an extension of trade union organization. Consumer cooperativism remained effective well into the twentieth century, providing a competitive alternative for the provision of basic commodities, where bulk purchases and credit lowered prices and eased means of payment for the urban working class. It proved incapable, however, of offering an alternative to the post-war boom in consumer durables, with the concomitant expansion of a white-collar and professional middle class. As a result, consumer cooperativism became marginalized well before the crisis in the production-based trade union movement.

If the challenge to the early consumer was the lowering of prices through bulk purchases, the post-war consumers were faced with new complex goods and services produced by a powerful oligopolist industrial sector. Consumers in this context needed new sources of information to enable both effective comparison between products and guarantees as to the durability of the new consumer durables. Consumer associations provided the organizational response, first in the US and then across Europe, mobilizing around consumer rights and information asymmetry. The right to return products, minimum guarantees for product and part replacement, and the right to adequate information all became incorporated in legislation, and the notion of the consumer citizen became popularized. At the same time, consumer associations developed an independent source of information on product quality, performance, and prices. Whereas the consumer cooperatives were clearly anchored around the point of purchase, the new consumer associations, in addition to providing point of purchase services, rapidly evolved into political organizations in their own right, launching campaigns and lobbying for legislation (Daunton and Hilton 2001). We will, therefore, come back to a discussion of these associations in the section on consumers and market regulation below.

Collective action by consumers is as old as the bread riots in the Middle Ages, of which a more modern expression would be the shop lootings of excluded would-be consumers. It is the boycott of products and services, however, which is emerging as the consumers' typical instrument of collective action. Consumer boycotts were already a feature of consumer movements in the US in the 1920s and 1930s (Cohen 2001) and would emerge in the post-war period in Europe (Trumbull 2001), directed basically against high prices. As a potent instrument of pressure, however, the boycott can be associated with the emergence of brand products as a dominant competitive strategy, which makes industry extremely vulnerable to 'image destruction', especially when the brand is quantified as an asset in the balance sheets. The threat of consumer boycotts has become particularly acute as the Internet transforms this instrument into a powerful counter to the globalization of leading firms' brand products.

If the consumer entrepreneur provides a more positive alternative to Bauman's consumer at the micro level, the consumer boycott represents an instrument capable of harmonizing individualism with collective action. Unlike the strike or the demonstration, whose logic is collectivist, the effectiveness of boycott movements depends on the aggregate of reflexive individual decisions at the point of purchase (Drillech 1999). The consumer boycott has also become a major weapon in strengthening the political power of non-governmental organizations (NGOs), to the extent that it can be associated with media-intensive initiatives, captured best in the militant tactics of Greenpeace, and poses a threat of uncertain, but potentially drastic, dimensions to the immaterial assets of global players. In a similar fashion to the consumer associations, NGOs identified with consumer-citizen issues tend to be strategically oriented to the implementation of new legislation and/or regulation and will be considered in the section below, which deals with these questions.

■

The Dynamics of Post-purchase Use

Hirschman (1982) is a now classic reference for the importance of focusing on the post-purchase context. In his analysis of the historical oscillation between market and political involvement, he identifies the gap between purchasing expectations and the degree of user satisfaction over time, especially in the case of consumer durables, as an important factor in the pendulum swing back to political rather than market participation as the principal expression of citizenship. Sociologists and anthropologists, in their turn, have insisted on the need to see consumption not simply as a question of purchasing activities but as involving also their subsequent use. It is by examining their 'value-in-use' (Arnould et al. 2002) that the meanings attributed to products and services can be most effectively understood, and the varying degrees of autonomy between the market and social life best gauged.

In the first place, many authors draw attention to the ambivalence of equating purchasing activity with consumption, and purchasers with consumers. Feminist studies have argued that shopping should be seen as an aspect of 'family production', with the great majority of habitual purchases corresponding to inputs involved in subsequent housework. Hidden behind the female consumer figure, therefore, is the role of the housewife, and the supposition, in many analyses, that consumption closes the economic cycle and serves to mask the unpaid labour of household activity. At the same time, this focus on the 'post-purchase production phase' has exposed the partiality of appeals to 'labour-saving' as a stimulus for the purchase of consumer durables. While the unit of time for different household activities may have declined, their frequency has often increased markedly – as in the case of clothes washing. In addition, the time dedicated to shopping itself increased fourfold from the 1920s to the end of the century (Lury 1996). While most feminist analysis focuses on the continued subordination of women in patriarchal households, other authors (Rochefort 1997) have highlighted the notable expansion of 'do-it-yourself' (DIY) activities largely carried out by the male partner. These have often been camouflaged as 'hobbies', especially in the case of gardening, but in fact are to a great extent a response to the prohibitive costs of necessary domestic services. Here again purchases, officially characterized as consumption, correspond to inputs for subsequent production activities.

Beyond revealing key areas of economic life that have tended to remain under-analyzed, the attention to post-purchase use of commodities captures the creativity and autonomy of social life as it constantly adapts and reworks consumer products in the continuous renegotiation of social bonds. De Certeau (1990), in a large-scale research programme undertaken for the French government at the end of the 1970s, analyzed consumption as a form of hidden 'fabrication' in which consumers, while basing themselves on the dominant production system, express their social creativity in the ways in which they employ these products, whether they be television images, newspaper stories, urban space or supermarket products. In so doing, he provides a conscious and welcome qualification of Foucault's influential writings on the generalization of micromechanisms of surveillance and control.

Many studies in this vein have focused specifically on the construction of neo-tribal identities and the consolidation of subaltern group resistance. An emblematic case of the former would be the Harley Davidson motor-bike. Here power is no longer identified with speed, but with solidity and posture. For this purpose, the handlebars were repositioned and typical motor-bike market accessories (helmets and protective clothing) rejected. In cases such as Harley Davidson, user clubs often emerge which provide novel technical and aesthetic adaptations, subsequently fed back into the production of new models. Here the users become the critical input for the design stage of future innovations.

Black youth in the US, for their part, have systematically subverted traditional uses of music, art and clothes to contest dominant consumer culture from within, although on the periphery. In this way, dance music is 'de-labelled', caps are worn back-to-front, hugely baggy clothes mock 'tailor-made' standards, and car hi-fi systems playing at full volume reclaim urban acoustics. Fashion and the music industry, in their turn, have transformed these expressions of social creativity into new waves of product innovation (Lamont and Molnar 2001; Gilroy apud Lury 1996) In postmodern consumer culture, the 'trickle-down' effect, identified by Simmel and Veblen, has been complemented by 'trickle-up' and 'trickle-across' tendencies. The hooliganism of British football fans can, perhaps, be seen as a nihilistic version of contestatory consumption. Although with more pugilistic than soccer motivations, they nevertheless are consumers of the travel and sporting services involved. In this case, however, they provoke innovations designed for exclusion (prices, surveillance, etcetera).

A striking methodological approach to the question of the autonomy of social life in relation to consumption has been provided by Appadurai (1986), who proposes to invert normal procedures and track 'the social life of things'. Such heterodox longitudinal analysis is able to capture the way in which products acquire their own history, expressed through the varied forms of their social appropriation. The scooter is a particularly good example here because it has been analyzed both as a clear expression of the social autonomy or 'indeterminacy' of consumer practices (Hebdige 1988), and as the outcome of strategic marketing (Arvidsson 2001), which echoes the 'performative' analysis of science in relation to economic life, adopted by Callon (1998). This suggests that the 'social life of things' methodology may also be a way of overcoming the 'supply versus demand' dilemma. In Hebdige's account, the scooter began its life as the British by-product of the motor-bike but clashed with a sexist culture in which it was seen as 'effete' and unmanly: 'a form of transport which (even) women could handle' (Hebdige 1988: 104). The scooter then re-emerges in the 1950s as part of the Italian challenge to the British motor-cycle industry and the same features acquire now a new meaning, as the expression of Italian superiority in design and style. In England, the scooter is then reappropriated by the 'mods', the new, well-dressed, sophisticated, white-collar, 'working-cum-middle-class' youths in their rejection of traditional working-class and 'rocker' cultures. In Italy, on the other hand, the scooter becomes the symbol of the liberated young woman, able to escape the family and its controls and no longer dependent on the transport options of potential boyfriends.

Analysis of the subsequent use(s) of purchased products reveals a complex mix of market, domestic, second-hand, and informal exchange relations. Many domestic and personal consumer items gain new lives as products are redistributed among household members. Clothes are passed from one child to the next and the old television goes into the bedroom or the children's room to make way for a new model in the living room. This may also be the case for the car, although here a sophisticated second-hand market with appropriate guarantees to exclude the moral hazard of information asymmetry has been structured to adapt to and facilitate the emergence of short-life-cycle, fashion-based purchasing. For other products, charity, second-hand outlets, and informal exchange systems both refuel formal market purchases and permit greater access to consumer goods by the excluded or the only partially included. In England, it is estimated that one million people visit car-boot sales each weekend.

Economic sociology has drawn attention to the way in which any product, even money, can become 'earmarked', thereby transforming its conditions of exchange (Zelitzer 1989). An example here would be the mundane object that becomes transformed into a collector's item. These items give rise to clubs for the purpose of exchange and can subsequently be transformed into markets, with prices and catalogues. New products, however, permanently emerge with the status of collectors' items, organized at the margins of formal markets. This phenomenon has become increasingly incorporated into consumer culture, particularly in markets geared to children, and products are often organized in series with a view to mobilizing the collector urge to buy the whole range of any particular product. A parallel phenomenon is the promotion of previously mundane products to the status of art items, but in this case there is a concomitant qualitative shift in the product's monetary value and in the fortunes of its owner. This development is very much related to the passing of time, no longer in the sense of patina but time in relation to which products are revalued as artistic fashion, a process that could very appropriately be analyzed from the 'social life of things' perspective.

An increasingly important part of post-purchase use relates not so much to the product but to packaging and waste disposal. The shift to 'black box' technology, the recourse to a 'throw-away' ideology and the generalization of technological and aesthetic obsolescence sums up business's initial strategy for inducing consumers into new purchases when the original product still remained 'functional'. We have seen above some of the ways in which consumers have negotiated the economic and moral implications of replacing still-usable products. Resistance, however, has also been a permanent component of consumer responses, characterized in the UK Channel 4 series as 'the scrimpers' or 'the new frugals', identified in the US via *The Cheapskate Monthly*, in Japan through the bestseller *The Concept of Honest Poverty*, and receiving in France the designation of 'aconsumption' (Lury 1996; Dobré 2002). These movements, linked to strategies of recycling and re-use, have now become increasingly integrated into civil, regulatory, and public policy measures relating to the environmental implications of waste, and will be discussed below in these contexts. In varying degrees industry and retail are themselves adjusting, voluntarily or under the whip of regulation, to the needs of recycling, and Rifkin's radical vision of the shift to services would firmly place the responsibility of recycling back on these actors.

The ecological modernization literature has highlighted collective consumption initiatives for the alternative use of strategic resources – water, energy – that traditionally have been regarded as public goods, but in the recent period have also been subject to privatization or third-party access (TPA). The DOMUS project, financed by the European Commission, has documented what it calls 'environmental innovations' in relation to water, energy, and waste, carried out by grassroots organizations (Raman *et al.* 1998). Many such actions involve regulatory, planning, and policy issues, and will be discussed further below.

Traditionally, strategic marketing has also been interested not so much in post-purchase use as in the response of consumers to innovations, particularly focusing on rates and patterns of adoption and diffusion, which in its turn has led to a consideration of the influence of cultural and social factors (Arnould *et al.* 2002). In the examples we have discussed above, reciprocal feedback between marketing strategies and social practices, sometimes collaborative, often conflictive, captures the dynamic of consumer culture more accurately than supply-versus-demand scenarios. This is particularly the case given that 80–90 per cent of new product innovations are market failures, with the overwhelming majority of these being line extensions. In the case of 'discontinuous innovations', which involve ruptures in social practices, the uncertainties are more acute and different strategies of consumer involvement in the use and testing of these products have become common practice. It is to the role of consumers in the innovation process that we now turn.

■

Consumers as Actors in the Innovation Process

Recent sociological and anthropological literature has tended to highlight the autonomy and/or creativity of social actors in their use of consumer goods, and a lack of understanding by firms of the different social meanings attributed to products is now seen to be an important factor in their high innovation failure rates, as noted above. Much of the social science literature, however, has tended to focus on the capacity of social actors to redefine the attributed meanings of commodities in assertions of collective identity. The current period would seem to be characterized by a shift in firm strategy towards the prior engagement of consumers in pre-purchase phases, which would open up the possibility of having their meanings taken into account in the formulation of products.

Even for the most banal products, focus groups, tasting sessions and local launchings precede full commitment by firms to a new product or line extension. In certain markets, consumer acceptance of products may be more predictable, even though the rigours of testing may be extremely time-consuming and costly. The paradigmatic case here is pharmaceuticals, where the efficacy of drugs is first tested on animals, followed by volunteer testing on humans. On approval, diffusion is guaranteed by the medical expert system and is only checked over the long term by research based on monitoring users or eventually by the outbreak of scandals. With more complex products, which involve unpredictable factors of accommodation to existing social practices, thoroughgoing consumer experiments are increasingly adopted prior to launching. Functional foods would be a case in point here, with their success often depending on the establishment of a more interactive discursive relation with the consumer. Altus, the joint-venture between Quaker and Novartis (subsequently discontinued), claims to launch products only after focus groups and testing sessions have declared the product equal or superior to anything on the market (Wilkinson 2002). For these products, traditional mass media publicity has shown itself to be less effective than face-to-face sales and word-of-mouth diffusion, what Lewis and Bridger (2001) call the shift from 'high cost hype ... to grassroots buzz'. When Toyota introduced the Prius hybrid-electric car in the US, it selected five families in each of twelve cities out of more than 15,000 applicants for a free test period of one month. Applicants were a mix of early-adopter, environmentally friendly and general consumers selected in an effort to obtain reliable feedback, possibly involving significant modifications prior to large-scale investments, making this strategy a considerable advance on simple 'end-of-pipeline' testing (Arnould *et al.* 2002).

Neo-Schumpeterian innovation literature has captured this trend, particularly in the case of intermediary users rather than final consumers. The focus of early innovation analysis within this tradition was the firm (Nelson and Winter 1982) but as more macro-level discussion on innovation advanced, systemic factors received greater treatment. The notion of 'national systems of innovation' was developed by Lundvall (1992) and elaborated in broader OECD studies. Sectoral (Malerba 1993), cluster-based (Lash and Urry 1994; Piore and Sabel 1984; Porter 1990) and territorial (Storper 1997) analyses all called attention to the more interactive processes involved in innovation. Lundvall (1988) and researchers at Aalborg coined the notion of 'user–producer interaction' in their research into the development of new equipment, showing both the positive effects of such interaction and the negative consequences of its absence.

In addition to a more radical microconcept of innovation as 'process', Callon developed a network theory of innovation that extends the range of decisive actors to include strategic intermediary and end users. Here, however, we are no longer concerned with the simple veto power of final consumers but with their involvement in the conception and design of the products in question. His classic study of the strategies for the development of the electric car in France is exemplary in this sense, as also is his work on the promotion of computer mapping systems in urban vehicles (Callon 1986 and 1998). This line of analysis has been developed by researchers on the development of telecommunications systems (Walsh *et al.* 1998), who have demonstrated that in many high-technology areas the distinction between early adoption and final design is being eroded, as users are becoming endogenized in the innovation system.

A crucial difficulty here, however, is that of protecting the confidentiality of products at the pre-commercial stage, which may often lead to the option for 'surrogate' users and computer simulations, even at the risk of higher uncertainty at the moment of product launching. The diffused innovation process model (DIP) developed by the Centre for Research on Innovation and Competition (CRIC) group, Manchester, also involves a renewed reflection on the way consumption has become a component of innovation (Harvey *et al.* 2001).

The blurring of the line between early adoption and late design is one aspect of a more general blurring of the frontiers between products and services. At the simplest level, this involves the consumer taking on the onus (labour and also expenditure) of activities such as selecting and transporting supermarket goods, filling up the tank at the gas station, and acquiring information on automated telephone services. More substantively, it involves the expansion of computerized, tailor-made products where the buyer, in addition to furnishing exact measurements, decides the materials and the style of the product in question. Services, such as house design and a whole range of leisure activities are increasingly joint or 'co-production' activities where the idea of the 'consumer entrepreneur' is most in evidence.

Jeremy Rifkin, with his notion of the 'age of access', has developed perhaps the most radical view of the shift from products to services. In his view, emerging business strategy is now dominated less by the sale/purchase of products as discrete transactions and more by an effort to 'commodify relationships' between the firm and the client over the long term. The resultant shift from property exchange to leasing is seen to be related more to an increase in relative prices and the dramatic reduction in product life cycles, than to the involvement of the consumer in product creation. Nevertheless, this notion is tied to the idea of the banalization of production systems through flexibilization and computerized automation, allowing the consumer much greater freedom in defining the products and services required.

In the Fordist period in Europe, the exertion of influence over the production system was still seen primarily in terms of movements for the historic demands of 'workers' control' (Coates and Topham 1970), which was to have its apogee in the efforts to re-run the Lipp watchmaking factory in France in 1973 on the basis of priorities determined by local demand. Today we see a rather different movement, involving the partial endogenization of consumers in product and service determination. This would seem to be a dual tendency, motivated on the one hand by transformations in the profile of the new consumer, captured in Rochefort's characterization of the consumer entrepreneur, and on the other by business strategies compensating for the uncertainty of more complex and shorter-life-cycle products in a new technology paradigm that permits them to respond to consumer demands in real time.

■

The Consumer Citizen in the Regulation and Definition of Markets

Three phases in the politicization of consumption can be identified in the leading European nations, corresponding broadly to the reorganization of capitalism in the last quarter of the nineteenth century until the crisis of the Second World War, the post-war boom, and the period inaugurated by the rolling back of the interventionist, welfare state model in the 1970s and

1980s (Winward 1994). In the US, on the other hand, the unique period of the New Deal, prolonged into the war years (Cohen 2001), led to a distinct dynamic allowing four phases to be identified, which may also perhaps explain some of the current differences between consumer movements and politics in Europe and the US. While sharing common patterns, it should be clear that the differences in state, business and labour articulation in each country also affect also the way in which consumerism is transformed into a political issue. In addition to the differences mentioned above, consumerism became intertwined with issues of civil rights in the US, influenced by the corporatist business model in Germany, overshadowed by the massive predominance of trade unionism in England, and dominated by more grass-roots activism in France (Trumbull 2001).

The first phase in the politicization of consumerism was dominated, as we have mentioned earlier, by cooperativism in Europe and progressivism in the US, and was directed primarily towards intervention at the level of distribution to ensure measures of price control, with the complementary adoption of state legislation to establish controls over basic quality and adulteration. The focus was very much on 'necessary' products; it had strong ethical and religious overtones and was aimed at the organization of the working class. Consumerism, here, had little to do with modern shopping, which at this time was still the preserve of 'ladies' in the luxury malls (Zola 1980; Jacobs 2001).

In Europe, war, depression, and further war put a brake on consumer politics, whereas in the US, the New Deal recovery and continued, even accelerated, economic expansion during the Second World War was explicitly premised on a response to under-consumption and the adoption of Keynesian demand creation policies. In addition, consumer representation on the New Deal agencies created by the National Industrial Recovery Act was institutionalized, alongside business and labour, in the form of the Consumer Advisory Board, (Cohen 2001). With this state recognition, the 1930s and 1940s saw the consolidation of an impressive consumer movement, headed largely by women and involving nation-wide collective action, while at the same time African Americans adopted consumer boycotts as a weapon for the implementation of civil rights. The movement was further reinforced in the war years through the activities of the Office of Price Administration, which appealed to consumers and mobilized Consumer Interest Committees for price controls and savings policies.

In the US, therefore, after the war, when the 'citizen consumer' finally ceded ground to the 'customer consumer' (Cohen 2001), both the legitimacy of consumer rights and normative expectations of compatibility between product quality and availability (cheapness) were solidly anchored in US society. In England, by contrast, consumer issues were still considered as somewhat frivolous in parliamentary circles at the time of the creation of the Moloney Committee on Consumer Protection in the later 1950s and early 1960s; the notion of the consumer citizen would only emerge much later in the wake of privatization and deregulation.

In the post-war boom, consumer cooperativism and social movements gave way to consumer associations, based now on the middle class and with a fundamentally individualist orientation. The format of these associations was similar in most countries: non-profit organizations supported by subscriptions to a consumer information journal. The key demands now were qualified information to allow for comparison between the proliferation of different brands of consumer durables, together with the testing of products for their conformity to basic standards. Since reliable information was the issue, independence became the discriminating criterion, and those consumer associations which eschewed business or government involvement flourished the most – in Britain, the Consumers' Association and the magazine *Which?*, rather than the British Standards Institute and its *Shopper's Guide*; in the United States the Consumers' Union rather than Consumer Research. The journals, which carried no publicity, served as a counter to the advertising industry, which now replaced its early educative and instrumental orientation with more emotive and irrational appeals as standards became more uniform and the stimulus to purchase more challenging. Consumer organizations also lobbied for the implementation of specific legislation and participated in the elaboration of standards, while government enacted consumer protection legislation on issues of information (labelling) and the monitoring of competition. Paradoxically, consumer associations' line of defence was to promote the 'rational economic consumer', while the advertising industry, at the service of business, tried to loosen the hold of the reality principle in favour of caprice and pleasure *à la* Bauman.

Post-war consumer organizations were thus designed to equip consumers to negotiate a mass, standardized, production system; their persistence in a period when segmentation and differentiation have now become the norm, and when instrumental consumer concerns have been replaced by symbolic values and identity construction, would seem to be problematic. Nevertheless, consumer organizations still thrive, which would suggest that in most cases a precondition for new meanings is that products and services perform well in their 'primary' functions (Winward 1994).

While consumer organizations persist, however, two important changes have occurred. In the first place, there has been a sharp politicization of the consumer, particularly in Europe. In the earlier period, government action on consumer issues had been characterized by paternalist considerations of protection, with consumers being confused with 'the public at large', who could be represented variously by business, the trade unions, housewives, or 'representative' figures. Again, we must be careful here to discriminate between government measures in Europe and the much stronger legitimacy of consumer representation in the US. Now, in the wake of privatization and deregulation, the European Union is actively institutionalizing the consumer interest as a counter to business. Second, consumer organizations have extended their focus from the monitoring of individual products and services to a preoccupation with underlying processes and consequences – with health, the environment, social and ethical conditions of production, animal rights, and a general concern with origins (peasant, artisan, indigenous) characterizing much consumer mobilization. As a result of these two tendencies, there has been a proliferation of consumer associations and an increasing convergence with social and political movements and alternative trading networks.

Burgess, in a polemical article, has argued that different European governments and particularly the European Union have deliberately promoted the political status of consumers and have thereby institutionalized a culture of 'complaints' and 'mistrust', culminating in the adoption of the 'precautionary principle'. As a result, he argues: 'The terrain of governance is narrowed and options removed' (Burgess 2001: 43). In England, this tendency is identified with the Thatcher-era privatizations and the perceived need for countervailing systems of accountability. In France, the shift to absolute priority for consumer safety followed the collapse of the political elite's legitimacy in the wake of the 'HIV-infected blood affair of the '80s'. In Europe, 'in order to avoid the perception that the concept of European integration existed exclusively for the benefit of industry, EU consumer protection initiatives evolved as a corollary to the internal market programme which culminated in 1992' (EC 1998: 9, apud Burgess 2001). Within the EU, the strengthening of consumer representation is seen to be a constituent component of the shift from a welfare to a regulatory state, and the EU has provided financial assistance for the promotion of consumer associations in countries where these are weak, as in Southern Europe.

This 'political construction' of the consumer is contrasted with the bottom-up view of consumer activism that has emerged from the reflexive modernization literature, although it could well be seen as complementary (Beck, Giddens and Lash 1994). Here, a world dominated by 'manufactured risks', whose scale and level of uncertainty transform them into the dominant social and political issues of global society, is being countered by a new form of 'sub-politics', in which grassroots citizen movements, based on increasingly reflexive individual and collective behaviour, offer alternatives to the traditional political system (Guivant 2001). The adoption by the European Union of the precautionary principle, initially launched at the Rio 1992 Summit, would point to the strength of these movements, which have been most effective in the campaign against the commercialization of transgenic products in agriculture and food. Here, national policies have been accompanied by innovative forms of civil participation, involving consensus conferences, citizen conferences and popular juries. A similar politicization of the consumer has been noticeably absent in the US, where it has been widely argued (when, for example, comparing US and EU reactions to transgenics) that US consumers have more confidence in government and regulatory institutions. Although these differences may be exaggerated, there is clearly a historical basis for such claims, as our discussion of the New Deal and the Second World War period has indicated.

name for environmentally friendly products. This drift from consumer politics to trade has its parallel in the (as yet timid) social responsibility initiatives of established firms, and may prefigure the emergence of a more hybrid model combining business and social activities.

◼

Market Exclusion – What Future for Bauman's 'Flawed Consumer'?

Even the most optimistic commentators are acutely aware that a growing number of citizens in the industrialized countries and even the majority of the population in developing countries have only fragile access to most of the goods and services on offer, which does not mean, of course, that their aspirations are not increasingly moulded by the consumer values ever present in the visual enticements of billboards and television. Globally, two thirds of the world's population are classified as living in poverty: 'horrible living and housing conditions, illness, illiteracy, aggression, falling apart families, weakening of social bonds, lack of future and non-productiveness' (Kapuscinski 1997). In the industrialized countries, tolerated levels of unemployment are now in double figures: Italy, 12 per cent; Germany, 12 per cent; Spain, 20 per cent; France, 11 per cent; England, 8 per cent. Only the US has pushed its rate below 5 per cent and Japan has seen its historically low level of unemployment almost double during the 1990s (Rochefort 1997). In addition, for those in work the expectation of lifetime employment has been replaced by short-term contracts, which has tended to drive down wage levels and also reduce the number of those benefiting from holiday, sickness, maternity, and retirement benefits. Income distribution has worsened in Europe as the ravages of unemployment have been accompanied by reduced access to and levels of social benefits. In the US, 'in the last twenty years, the total income of the 20 per cent poorest American families fell by 21 per cent, while the total income of the 20 per cent richest rose by 22 per cent' (Bauman 1998: 92).

In Bauman's analysis, the 'unemployed' have now been redefined as the 'poor' and, rather than comprising a temporarily displaced fraction of the 'working class', a subaltern but legitimated social grouping, they have become the 'underclass', a heterogeneous grouping of abandoned old, single mothers, school drop-outs, drug users, ex-detainees, and those dependent on social welfare. Their plight is no longer related to the oscillations of the business cycle or to recession, but to problems of personal biography for which they are primarily responsible, thus justifying the decline in social provisions.

Rochefort, while recognizing the dark side of current transformations, situates this within a framework of transition, in which growth depends on the consolidation of the consumer entrepreneur, already apparent in the tendencies to longer schooling, continuous recycling and the increasing predominance of small and medium enterprises (SMEs) in employment creation. In the US, he argues, SMEs were responsible for 7.5 million jobs in 1990–4, of which half were in firms employing from one to four people. In France, very small firms of less than 10 employees make up one third of all employment, and of these half are one-person firms. Such small firms account for almost half of private sector urban employment in Italy, while in England small firms account for more than 40 per cent of non-government employment, with more than 50 per cent of these being one-person firms. In France, employment in very small firms grew 20 per cent in 1985–95, whereas the increase was 6 per cent for small firms, while there was a decline of 30 per cent in large firm employment. Rochefort's more optimistic analysis is congruent with the notion of the 'learning' or 'knowledge' rather than 'consumer' society, a notion developed by Lundvall and others whose work we referred to earlier.

Two broad scenarios emerge in the literature as providing long-term alternatives to the impasse of social exclusion identified with the consumer society. The first would combine a decoupling of income entitlement from income-generating capacity and a concomitant shift from a work to a life ethic. It is founded on the idea of ever-fewer people being directly involved in productive activity and has, as its corollary, some version of a distinction (albeit attenuated) between basic and luxury consumption. Converging with ecological preoccupations, it would advocate frugal *consumption* as the precondition of generalizing development (Gorz 1991; Offe 1996; Bauman 1998; Dobré 2002) The alternative would focus on the collapse of the antagonism between consumption and production through their fusion in the consumer entrepreneur and the consolidation of a learning economy, which permanently creates new products and services and therefore new needs and desires. Advances in science and technology in the direction of 'dematerialization', evident in tendencies towards miniaturization, and the productive adoption of more radical energy- and resource-saving solutions would ensure the viability of continued economic growth (Rifkin 2002; Spaargaren 1994 and 2000; Rochefort 1997).

■

Conclusions

In this analysis, after presenting an overview of recent contributions on the dynamics of consumption and considering in some detail the contrasting views of Bauman and Rochefort, we attempted to go beyond the more generalized notions of 'the new consumer' by looking at consumers and consumer activity during different phases of the economic cycle. In so doing, we have shown how consumers, both individually and collectively, are much more active in product creation and subsequent use than studies which focus on the consumer as purchaser would suggest.

Our characterization of different consumer practices throws light on the diffuse patterns of consumer influence over the economic cycle. At multiple points, varied and overlapping consumer initiatives engage with design, production, distribution, and subsequent use. The frontiers between firms and consumers become less precise and, at the same time, consumers look increasingly behind firms to the conditions of their suppliers and the origins of their inputs. Many firms, for their part, see the 'endogenization' of consumption as a key mechanism for reducing uncertainty and concentrate on long-term client relationships rather than the sale of individual products, in line with the shift from property to access identified by Rifkin (2000). Both firms and consumers and their organizations move easily between the economic, social, and political spheres, and the new consumer is becoming as much a politician as an entrepreneur, especially if we extend the political sphere to include Beck's notion of 'sub-politics'. Both Bauman and Rochefort build strong cases for their radically counterposed views of the consumer, but we would argue that the limits and possibilities of current consumer practices are better captured through an appreciation of varied consumer involvement in the different phases of the economic cycle, in the definition and regulation of markets, and in the expressions of social creativity that allow existing markets to be subverted and alternative networks to be created.

Bibliography

Allaire, G. and R. Boyer (1995) *La Grande Transformation*, Paris: INRA.

Appadurai, A. (1986) *The Social Life of Things: Commodities in Culturel Perspective*, Cambridge: Cambridge University Press.

Arnould, E. J., Price, L. L. and G. M. Zinkham (2002) *Consumers*, London (International Edition): McGraw Hill.

Arvidsson, A. (2001) 'From counterculture to consumer', *Journal of Consumer Culture*, Vol. 1, No. 1, March.

Baudelaire, C. (1978) *Oeuvres Complètes*, Paris: Bibliothèque de la Plêiade.

Bauman, Z. (1998) *Work, Consumerism, and the New Poor*, Maidenhead, England: Open University Press.

—— (2001) 'Consuming life', *Journal of Consumer Culture*, Vol. 1, No. 1, March.

Beck, U. (1992) *Risk Society*, London: Sage.

Beck, U., Giddens, A. and S. Lash (1994) *Reflexive Modernisation*, Cambridge: Polity Press.

Benjamin, W. (1986) *Paris Capitale du XIXe Siecle: Le Livre das Passages*, Paris: Editions du Cerf.

Burgess, A. (2001) 'Flattering consumption', *Journal of Consumer Culture*, Vol. 1, No. 1, March.

Callon, M. (1986) 'The sociology of an actor-network: The case of the electric vehicle', in Callon, M., Law, J. and A. Rip (eds), *Mapping the Dynamics of Science and Technology*, London: Macmillan.

—— (ed.) (1998) *The Laws of the Markets*, Oxford: Blackwell.

Coates, K. and T. Topham (1970) *Workers' Control – A Book of Readings*, London: Panther.

Cohen, L. (2001) 'Citizens and consumers in the United States in the century of mass consumption', in Daunton, M. and M. Hilton (eds), *The Politics of Consumption*, New York: Berg Publishers.

Daunton, M. and M. Hilton (eds) (2001) *The Politics of Consumption*, New York: Berg Publishers.

De Certeau, M. (1990) *L'Invention du Quotidien*, Paris: Gallimard.

Dobré, M. (2002) *L'Écologie au Quotidien*, Paris: Harmattan.

Drillech, M. (1999) *Le Boycott*, Paris: LPM.

Featherstone, M. (1991) *Consumer Culture and Postmodernism*, London: Sage.

Fine, B. and E. Leopold (1993) *The World of Consumption*, London: Routledge.

Friedman, H. (1993) 'After Midas' feast', in Allan, P. (ed.), *Food for the Future*, New York: John Wiley.

Giddens, A. (1991) *Modernity and Self-Identity*, Cambridge: Polity Press.

Godbout, J. T. (1992) *L'Esprit du Don*, Paris: La Decouverte.

Gorz, A. (1991) *Capitalisme, Socialisme, Ecologie*, Paris: Galilée.

Granovetter, M. and P. McGuire (1998) 'The making of an industry: electricity in the United States', in Callon, M. (ed.), *The Laws of the Markets*, Oxford: Blackwell.

Green, R. and M. Hy (2001) *Technologies de l'Information et Evolutions Organisationnelles Dans la Distribution Alimentaire*, Paris: INRA.

Gronow, J. (1997) *The Sociology of Taste*, London: Routledge.

Guivant, J. S. (2001) 'Global food risks: environment and health concerns in Brazil', in Hogan, D. J. and M. T. Tolmasquim (eds), *Human Dimensions of Global Environmental Change, Brazilian Perspectives*, Rio de Janeiro: Brazilian Academy of Science.

Harvey, M., McMeekin, A., Randles, S., Southerton, D., Tether, B. and A. Warde (2001) 'Between Demand and Consumption', Discussion Paper No. 40, mimeo, Centre for Research on Innovation and Competition (CRIC), University of Manchester.

Hebdige, D. (1988) *Hiding in the Light: On Images and Things*, London: Routledge.

Herpin, N. (2001) *Sociologie de la Consommation*, Paris: La Découverte.

Herpin, N. and D. Verger (2002) *La Consommation des Français*, Paris: La Decouverte.

Hilton, M. (2001) 'Consumer politics in post-war Britain', in Daunton, M. and M. Hilton (eds), *The Politics of Consumption*, New York: Berg Publishers.

Hirschman, A. (1982) *Shifting Involvements: Private Interest and Public Action*, Princeton: Princeton University Press.

Jacobs, M. (2001) 'The politics of plenty: consumerism in the twentieth-century United States', in Daunton, M. and M. Hilton (eds), *The Politics of Consumption*, New York: Berg Publishers.

Kapuscinski, R. (1997) *Lapidarium 111*, Warsaw: Czytelnik.

Keat, R., Abercrombie, N. and N. Whitely (eds) (1994) *The Authority of the Consumer*, London: Routledge.

Kline, N. (2000) *No Logo*, London: Flamingo.

Lamont, M. and V. Molnar (2001) 'How blacks use consumption to shape their collective identity', *Journal of Consumer Culture*, Vol. 1, No. 1, March.

Lash, S. and J. Urry (1994) *The Economy of Signs and Space*, London: Sage.

Lewis, D. and D. Bridger (2001) *The Soul of the New Consumer*, London: Nicholas Brearley.

Lundvall, B.-A. (1988) 'Innovation as an interactive process: from user–producer interaction to the national system of innovation', in Dosi, G. (ed.), *Technical Change and Economic Theory*, London: Pinter.

—— (ed.) (1992) *National Systems of Innovation: Towards a Theory of Innovation and Interactive Learning*, London: Pinter.

Lury, C. (1996) *Consumer Culture*, Cambridge: Polity Press.

Malerba, F. (1993) 'The organisation of the innovation process', in Rosenberg, N., Landau, R. and D. Mowery (eds), *National Innovations Systems: A Comparative Analysis*, New York: Oxford University Press.

Martuccelli, D. (2001) *Dominations Ordinaires*, Paris: Belland.

—— (2002) *Grammaires de l'Individu*, Paris: Gallimard.

Miller, D. (1995) *Acknowledging Consumption*, London: Routledge.

—— (1998) *A Theory of Shopping*, Cambridge: Polity Press.

Offe, C. (1996) *Modernity and the State*, Cambridge: Polity Press.

Piore, M. J. and C. F. Sabel (1984) *The Second Industrial Divide: Possibilities for Prosperity*, New York: Basic Books.

Porter, M. E. (1990) *The Competitive Advantage of Nations*, New York: New York Free Press.

Raman, S., Chappells, H., Klintman, M. and B. van Vliet (1998) 'Inventory of environmental innovations in domestic utilities: the Netherlands, Britain and Sweden', mimeo, Wageningen University, Holland.

Raynolds, L. T. (2002) 'Consumer–producer links in fair trade coffee networks', *Sociologia Ruralis*, Vol. 42, No. 4, November.

Rifkin, J. (2000) *The Age of Access*, London: Penguin.

—— (2002) *The Hydrogen Economy*, New York: Tarcher Putnam.

Ritzer, G. (1998) *The McDonaldization Thesis*, London: Sage.

Rochefort, R. (1997) *Le Consommateur Entrepreneur*, Paris: Editions Odile Jacob.

Simmel, G. (1971) 'Fashion', in Levine, D. (ed.), *On Individuality and Social Forms*, Chicago: University of Chicago Press.

Simmons, P. (1994) 'Construction of the green consumer: rhetoric, agency and organisation', unpublished paper, Manchester.

Slater, D. (1997) *Consumer Culture and Modernity*, Cambridge: Polity Press.

Spaargaren, G. (1994) 'Environment and consumption', mimeo, University of Wageningen.

—— (2000) 'The ecological modernisation of domestic consumption', mimeo, Lancaster University.

Storper, M. (1997) *The Regional World: Territorial Development in a Global Economy*, New York: Guilford Press.

Trumbull, G. (2001) 'Strategies of consumer-group mobilisation: France and Germany in the 1970s', in Daunton, M. and M. Hilton (eds), *The Politics of Consumption*, Oxford: Berg.

Veblen, T. (1979) *The Theory of the Leisure Class*, London: Penguin.

Walsh, V., Cohen, C., and A. Richards (1998) *The Incorporation of User Needs in* the Design of Technologically Sophisticated Products, Manchester: Manchester University Press.

Warde, A. (1994) 'Consumers, identity and belonging – reflections on some theses of Zygmund Bauman', in Keat, R., N. Whitely and N. Abercrombie (eds), The Authority of the Consumer, London: Routledge.

Wilkinson, J. (2002) 'The final foods industry and the changing face of the global agrofood system: up against a new technology paradigm and a new demand profile', Sociologia Ruralis, Vol. 42, No. 4, October.

Winward, J. (1994) 'The organised consumer and consumer information co-operatives', in Keat, R., N. Whitely and N. Abercrombie (eds), The Authority of the Consumer, London: Routledge.

Zelitzer, V. (1989) 'The social meaning of money: "special monies"', American Journal of Sociology, Vol. 95, No. 2, September.

Zola, É. (1980) Au Bonheur des Dames, Paris: Gallimard.

8

Society, Community, and Economic Development[1]

MICHAEL STORPER

■

Society or Community?

California's Silicon Valley, the heart of the world's microelectronics and Internet industries, is described by some analysts as a tightly woven community, whose economic performance depends on informal networks of entrepreneurs and techno-nerds (Saxenian 1994). But by others it is described as a set of overlapping markets, with research universities, government financing, venture capitalists, law firms, stock options, high labour mobility, brutal competition, and 'accountability' (reputation) rather than trust underlying its business networks (Cohen and Fields 1999). In the latter version, Silicon Valley takes American commercial culture to its limits; in the former, it is a high-technology version of the networked entrepreneurialism and high levels of social capital commonly associated with European small-firm clusters (Piore and Sabel 1984). Is it society that leads to success, or is it community?

Failure stories in the economic development literature share this ambivalence. We frequently hear criticisms (in the Western press, at least) of 'crony capitalism' in Asia. Family-based production networks – certainly a form of cronyism – work well in Taiwan, and are often cited as one aspect of the 'good' communitarian structures found in the Third Italy, but they are deplored when they become clannish, as in the Mezzogiorno (Gambetta 1988; Leonardi 1995). In the garment, toy, and jewellery industries in Los Angeles, by contrast, ethnic and family community networks of small firms seem not to lead to long-term development, but rather to lock in to a vicious circle of cheap products, very low wages, and Third World competition (Scott and Soja 1996). France has been viewed by some economic historians as owing her successes in economic modernization to a strong state that had the strength to destroy strongly localist, family-oriented capitalism: society triumphed over community (Rosenvallon 1990 and 1993). But others complain that this same state has left an institutional void, with weak spontaneous associational capacities – weak communities, that is – making it impossible for France to have a vibrant entrepreneurial economy (Reynolds *et al.* 2001; Levy 1999).

Underlying these debates is the classical sociological question of society and community as different types of social order – rule-bound and anonymous exchanges between groups and individuals versus social bonds within groups – via which social life gets organized. In place of this pitched debate between partisans of society or community as key to development, we shall argue that both societal and communitarian bonds between economic agents shape long-term economic development, and that it is the specific nature of their interrelations that matters.

To consider the importance of societal and communitarian forces to economic development is to think about institutions – referring not only to the formal private and public sector organizations and rules that influence how agents interact, but also to the relatively stable collective routines, habits, or conventions that can be observed in any economy. Institutionalist approaches to economic development are concerned not only with whether and how much development takes place in the medium and long terms, but also with the different types of institutional arrangements prevailing within capitalism. Institutions have many functions, including the redistribution of wealth, definition of property rights, governance of firms and labour relations, the rule of law, and resolution of disputes. These kinds of institutions vary greatly among countries and have significant impacts on economic performance and socio-economic structures. Comparative institutionalism shares with institutional economics 'the recognition that the pure competitive model is not a useful way to think about capitalist economies, and that political and economic institutions crucially shape performance' (Schleifer 2002: 12). In contrast to institutional economics, which stresses the universal and common institutional foundations of modern economies, however, comparative approaches emphasize institutional diversity.[2] Comparative institutionalism shares with public choice theory an interest in political processes, but, unlike the latter, admits that a wide variety of political and social factors will affect the choice of institutions and their efficiency.

The argument of this chapter is that relations between societal and communitarian forces shape key incentives to economic action. They do this by shaping the conventional forms by which individuals can participate in the economy, and hence the institutional forms by which incentives are constructed. It then argues that these patterns of participation and their associated incentives are critical to determining the amount of long-term economic development which takes place, as well as the evolutionary self-selection of economies into particular mixtures of strengths and weaknesses.

■

What Do We Mean by Society and Community?

Sociologists invented the analytical distinction between community and society as a way of considering different forms of social integration. A century later, most theories of the 'social foundations of development' still rely on the fundamental concepts of sociology – *gemeinschaft* (community), and *gesellschaft* (society) – derived from the classical formulations of Weber and Tönnies, or from Durkheim's cognate notion that there are two different kinds of bond between people, *solidarité mécanique* and *solidarité organique* (Durkheim 1984 [1893]). These distinctions have largely been retained, with 'community' conventionally used to refer to forms of collective life in which people are tied together through tradition, interpersonal contacts, informal relationships, and particularistic affinities, interests or similarities, while 'society' generally refers to collectivities held together through anonymous, rule-bound, more transparent, formal, and universalistic principles.

From the late nineteenth to the mid-twentieth century, sociologists for the most part fell into line with the other social sciences in seeing community largely as an obstacle to modernization. Community was seen by many social theorists, starting with Max Weber, as inimical to the expansion of formal, distanced, rule-bound, transparent social linkages, held to be key to the achievement of successful market economy and industrial society. This idea is strongly compatible with formal notions in contemporary economics and political science that most communities are groups that, given the opportunity, will engage in rent seeking and develop pervasive principal–agent problems for their members, and hence reduce both freedom and efficiency (Weber 1968 [1921]).

From Durkheim onward, there have also been fears that too much society and too little community could be problematic to individuals, if not for societal development itself. More recently, this latter idea has gained credence and there is a vibrant debate today about the role of community as a potentially necessary underpinning of a well-functioning society and economy. The precursor of such change was the work of K. Polanyi in *The Great Transformation* (1957), and that of M. Polanyi (1966) on personal knowledge and tacit knowledge as essential elements of any modern social order. From the 1940s to the 1960s there were regular scattered warnings to social science about the importance of community, and not merely emphasis on its dysfunctional progress-blocking nature. Daniel Bell (1976) warned about alienation and excessive anonymity, rekindling old Durkheimian themes.

Thus, calling attention to the importance of community is no longer necessarily considered to be evidence of 'irrational' anxiety associated uniquely with temporary crises of modernization. There is today a debate as to whether large-scale, rational, bureaucratic principles – along with the individualization, ephemerality, and mobility they seem to call forth – have not gone too far, weakening forms of community necessary to social order (Putnam 2000; Sandel 1996; Etzioni 1996; Levy 1999; Bellah *et al.* 1995). Among the many concepts deployed in this debate are 'social capital' (Putnam 2000; Coleman 1990); 'civil society' (Douglass and Friedmann 1997); 'hypermodernity' (Giddens 1990), and a wide variety of reflections on the recrudescence of religious, spiritual, and identity politics in the advanced countries (Fogel 2000).

This type of reasoning has also become centrally involved with questions of economic development. In one of the most explicit efforts along these lines, Fukuyama (1995) argues that low-trust, highly communitarian societies are less likely to generate successful large enterprises than are high-trust societies, and low-trust societies typically have lower long-term rates of growth than do high-trust ones. Intriguingly, Fukuyama holds that capacities for direct, spontaneous, or informal association of persons facilitate the establishment of large-scale, transparent, and bureaucratic forms of economic life, such as the large corporation. Rather than the two forms of association being mutually incompatible, the one is precondition for the other.

Giddens (1990) and other sociologists extend the field of potential positive effects of community in the modern economy. They start from a general point that contemporary modernization cannot be merely bureaucratic, whether statist or corporate, because this tends to downplay individual auto-nomy and responsibility. Giddens comes to the conclusion that in order to avoid the pitfalls of a rigid, administered society and economy, on the one hand, and a chaotic 'jungle' on the other, intermediate levels of association are critical. Giddens and others specifically refer to communities as means to improve the functioning of labour markets, generate entrepreneurship, and organize the provision of the public goods that alleviate both private and state burdens in creating prosperity and social integration. Along these lines, success in small-firm-based industrial clusters or districts, ranging from the most famous cases of Italy to examples drawn from Taiwan, Denmark, Mexico, or Germany, are also said to depend critically on the existence of com-munities that regulate complex inter-firm and firm–worker relationships through shared norms, reputation effects, and mutually aligned expectations.[3]

Subsequently, Putnam (2000) has claimed that 'social capital' – which he defines specifically to mean levels of voluntary participation and civic engagement – is good for economic development and social integration. Social capital creates positive externalities for the members of the societies that have high levels of it, so that even those who do not actively create it benefit from its existence. They concern such things as limiting moral hazards (less cheating in the economy, less crime in neighbourhoods, for example) and encouraging unpaid efforts (which then create benefits that spill over to others).

A closer look at Putnam's theoretical argument allows us to see some of its limits, but also how it may be adapted to a richer analysis of the institu-tional foundations of economic development. Putnam argues that there are two components of social capital: 'bonding' among similar types of persons (class, ethnicity, background, interests) and 'bridging' between different such groups or what he terms 'people unlike ourselves'. Bonding, in other words, operationalizes the classical notion of community, and bridging that of society. Moreover, Putnam argues that bonding is a lot easier to come by than bridging, and that where many different groups are present, it is much more difficult to achieve high levels of social capital than in more homogeneous societies. This suggests that bonding and bridging spring from different sources, and that they have complex relationships to one another.

Putnam's concept of bonding bears obvious similarity to the standard notion of *gemeinschaft*. In his study of the Third Italy (Putnam, Leonardi, and Nanetti 1993), the definition of social capital is strongly linked to the particular case at hand, where groups are based on local, family networks and civic associationalism has long historical roots. Actors trust each other because of their common cultural background, shared values, and strong reputation effects due to dense interpersonal networks. This notion can also be found in many other empirical studies of regional economic development (Becattini and Sforzi 2002). But it is clear that groups can exist in many other forms. Professional associations are based on shared norms of professional performance, not on shared history or interpersonal trust, for example. Along these lines, Aydogan (2002) has shown that even in the presence of shallow corporate cultures in Silicon Valley, due to a high level of labour turnover, professional culture makes possible a high level of industry- and region-specific social capital. There is considerable bonding in Silicon Valley, but its networks of venture capitalists, technologists, and others have little to do with the trust- and tradition-based communities of the Third Italy. The bonds between members of a community can be modern as well as traditional, based on ascriptive or acquired traits, each activated through different signalling and screening mechanisms. It follows that communities should not be equated to the classical notion of mechanical solidarity or *gemeinschaft*. In the same vein, the notions proposed by Fukuyama (trust), or the 'civil society' theorists may well be valid as empirical statements about the cases at hand, but they probably cannot be seen as general foundations of all community-type bonding. In addition, groups or communities do not necessarily express themselves as organizations or deliberate associations, or through Tocquevillian civic engagement. Along these lines, Coleman (1990) distinguishes 'primordial' from organized social capital, considering the former to be more powerful than the latter.[4] Primordial social bonding, in our view, should not be considered merely as synonymous with ascriptive traits; there is no persuasive reason to believe that an acquired professional identity, for example, cannot be as primordial as, say, a regional or ethnic identity, with neither having to assume the form of organized civic associationalism or group membership. Thus, though the classical sociological distinction between community and society is just as relevant as it ever was, the classical definitions of these terms have now become more confusing

	SOCIETY: INSTITUTIONAL FORMS OF BRIDGING			
	Group-oriented (groups are recognized as principal societal unit in legal system and in social policy)		Individualist (groups have secondary status in legal system, social policy, constitutional framework)	
	Non-comprehensive or decentralized group order: uneven corporatism or clannism	Comprehensive, centralized or organized group order: corporatism	Weak or incomplete liberalism and contractualism: tendency to distrust, fragile and limited circles	Strong and widespread liberalism and contractualism
COMMUNITY: LEVELS OF CIVIC ASSOCIATION				
Strongly associational	Third Italy Hong Kong Taiwan Jalisco, Mexico	Japan Germany Denmark Sweden		USA Netherlands
Weakly associational or hierarchically associational	Italy Mezzogiorno Most of Mexico SE Brazil	France Singapore		United Kingdom Canada Australia New Zealand

Figure 8.1: Institutional Forms and Levels of Civic Association

than useful. Therefore, 'community' will henceforth refer here to a wide range of reasons and ways of grouping together with others with whom we share some part of our identity, expectations, and interests.

Social life is not just about the groups to which we belong, of course. Bridging is the core concern of all the social sciences interested in collective action and coordination: how can diverse agents reconcile their interests? In the presence of strong, or primordial groups of agents, how do such groups relate to each other? Most scholars of associationalism have been concerned with issues of social integration rather than economics. However, there is longstanding concern with the role of voluntary association in social and economic development, with Fukuyama and Putnam the latest major entrants. Tocqueville (1986 [1830]) thought that the Americans' capacity for association was not only one reason for their vibrant democracy, but also contributed to the strength of American entrepreneurship. The empirical indicator of these studies has always been the intensity of associational life, though there is considerable controversy over which empirical measures should be used and how to interpret them (Norris 2002). Nonetheless, the literature is largely inconclusive about the relationship between associational life and economic development. For one thing, there are many cases of weakly associational societies that have done well as developers, including France, Singapore, the UK, Canada, and Australia. This is probably because associationalism can assume many different institutional forms, which determine its ultimate effects on economic development. Figure 8.1 illustrates some of the many possible combinations of these institutional forms, albeit in a highly schematic and simplified way.[5] Some readers might quibble with the characterization of individual cases, but the illustration strongly suggests that there is no definite relationship between associationalism and developmental success or failure, because there are so many different ways to bridge.

This analysis echoes a broader point made forcefully by Granovetter (2001) and Lin (2001). It is not just the density of ties that matters, but the structure of such ties (that is, bridges). The structure of ties is closely related to the mixture of power, compliance, sanctions, sharing, and cooperation on the part of the actors that are tied together. This is important because it suggests, again, that bonding and bridging are not additive components of a single index of social capital, but rather independent and mutually shaping social forces.

In this light, it can legitimately be asked whether there are certain kinds of bonds that are more suited to certain kinds of bridges, and vice versa. If this were the case, there would be a kind of functionalist law of institutional structure and the forms of action it shapes. But most sociologists have long ago abandoned the idea of a single, unified social order, and few empirical students of institutions would subscribe to this notion today (along these lines, see Boltanski and Thevenot 1987; Giddens 1984; Fligstein 2001; DiMaggio 1994). Thus, rather than some kind of fixed functional compatibility ('certain kinds of communities are compatible with certain kinds of society', etcetera), the institutional landscape of society and community is better thought of as being shaped by a tense, dynamic, uncertain relationship between bonds and bridges.

Institutional context and the incentives to development

This leads to a problem hitherto insufficiently dealt with in theories of economic development. Economics has done very well in the 'sophisticated analysis of how individuals pursue incentives in well-defined social spaces' (Granovetter 2001). The problem is, of course, that more complex institutional contexts of real development tend to drop out of that 'well-defined' picture. The social sciences are particularly divided and confused about how to deal with the effects of more complex institutional contexts on action. Economics tends simply to send this question of context back to the meta-principle of the importance of societal forces – transparent and anonymous market-style relations between economic agents that sustain the whip of competition – and institutional context drops out of the picture once again. Other disciplines (and certain outliers in economics) tend to admit more of a potentially constructive role for communities, which are not seen exclusively as sources of sclerosis and rent seeking, but also as efficient ways of bonding people and giving them the basis to act together in a positive fashion. As we shall now see, it is possible to retain economics' valid focus on incentives, but to resituate it in a richer, more realistic and less-controlled context, that of the interaction of bonding and bridging in shaping incentives and giving them concrete institutional forms. Bonding and bridging are the conventional types of participation[6] in the economy, which give rise to bargaining situations that define the type and institutional forms of incentives faced by individuals. This is also a fruitful way into a truly comparative institutionalist approach to economic development.

■

The Economic Contributions of Society and Community

There is a rich vein of theory and evidence on society, community, and development. At the same time, most literatures strain too hard for a single thing that makes economies institutionally successful or unsuccessful (more/less society; more/less community; more-embedded states, more autonomous states; more association, less association; etcetera), and maintain the notion that society and community have opposed effects on development. In so doing, these literatures actually tend to ignore some of the most important lessons from recent theories of economic growth and comparative political economy.

One of the principal lessons that can be drawn from recent theories of growth is that a number of the principal incentives to agents to pursue growth-creating courses of action depend on the existence of communities as well as societies. Moreover, all development depends, in the medium-to-long run, on successful policy choices and, especially, on the ability to adjust the rules and governance to the changes and shocks that are the inevitable by-products of successful development. Achieving such problem solving is fundamentally a result of society–community relations. Each of these themes can now be seen in more detail.

Successful markets require communities
Against what is frequently held by the contemporary theoretical consensus in economics and political science, I shall argue here that both society and community have positive and necessary contributions to make to development: both minimize moral hazards, reduce transactions costs and generate certain kinds of positive externalities and increasing returns effects. There is considerable reason to doubt that societal and communitarian forms of institutions and collective action necessarily promote opposing microeconomic behaviours.

Some of the founding figures of modern economics – such as Alfred Marshall (1919) (inspired by the Smithian moral philosophy origins of the discipline) – intimated that community was sometimes indispensable to superior economic performance. Marshall's writings about the textile districts of Lancashire, which he so admired, are shot through with ambivalence. In some passages, he describes them as fully competitive systems; in others, he observes that 'the secrets of industry are in the air' – that is, they are the collective resources of the community of producers. Twentieth-century economists, however, progressively came to the view that perfect markets depend on the existence of *gesellschaft*, seeing *gemeinschaft* as a barrier to their full realization. Contemporary economics, especially in its public choice versions, is essentially sceptical about the utility of institutions for economic development.

There is yet another critique of the role of groups in the economy, which goes under the rubric of the 'positive theory of institutions'. Solid micro-foundations have been provided for the point of view that communitarian forms of order often lead to rent-seeking, non-transparent behaviour, and are prone to overwhelming principal–agent problems that frustrate the members of groups and give small groups with passionately held views undue influence over large, less passionate majorities. These properties are then argued by economic historians and political economists to lead to sclerosis and lower levels of economic growth than can be had with clear dominance by societal (market) institutions (North 1981; Olson 1965; Moe 1987).

This is a powerful critique of group life, and it has considerable empirical support; these are indeed fundamental tendencies in group behaviour and widespread impacts on the economy. It leads to a dominant perspective that the only institutions we should have are those – such as property rights and the rule of law – that enforce the roles of competition and exit, and hence limit the role of bonding or communities.

It does not follow theoretically or empirically, however, that the economy would be better off entirely without communities. One can certainly question the veracity of this scepticism about communities on empirical grounds alone. As we have already noted, the continuing tendency to define groups or communities using the nineteenth-century sociological distinction is an ongoing source of confusion. Margaret Thatcher attracted attention by her provocative declaration that 'society doesn't exist, only individuals exist'. From a social science standpoint, of course, she mangled the standard notion, according to which it is precisely society (*gesellschaft*) that is an aggregation of individuals organized according to transparent, modern principles; she probably meant to criticize communities as the source of hide-bound tradition and corporatism. Nonetheless, economics is also at fault when it sees all traditional, primordial groups as anti-competitive and rent-seeking; there is a huge case study literature on economic networks that shows the contrary (for example, Grabher 1993; Lorenz 1984; Lin 2001). Moreover, as noted previously, groups or communities are not necessarily held together through tradition, interpersonal relations, and non-rational bonds between people. This is indeed sometimes the case, but it is not true as a matter of theoretical necessity. The case of Silicon Valley is exemplary in this regard.

The response to this mainstream view of institutions creating excessive transactions costs, moral hazards, and rent seeking is not only empirical, however. Transactions costs economics, as developed by Williamson (1985) and others, points to the necessary emergence of certain kinds of non-market-based coordination; for example, under some circumstances, relational contracting is more efficient than spot markets in perfect competition. The efficiency of such contracting is enhanced by inter-firm networks of actors. Nonetheless, in economics there remains a great deal of ambiguity about this point. Much of the 'new institutional economics' strains to find the perfectly rational character of participation in networks and governance, denying that these could be – even partially – dependent on group membership, or that the participants could be socially 'embedded' in ways important to the functioning of these groups. Many students of such networks hold that relations are not enforced merely by the threat of sanctions, but by some kind of bonding, whether primordial or acquired (Lorenz 1992). These may be combined with the 'societal' pressures of sanctions, but even sanctions may be more efficient in some communitarian contexts.

A second challenge within economics to the society-only view of economic coordination is even more fundamental. The new economics of information shows that information-based market failures are general to modern capitalism, and other kinds of organization than markets must fill the breach. Greenwald and Stiglitz (1984 and 1986) note that when information is not complete, and it is almost never complete, markets are incomplete. The resulting market failures are not the same as the classical market failures of welfare economics, because the new ones are pervasive and difficult to identify and isolate. In turn, Stiglitz (1994) suggests that communities are one of the ways that these market failures can be efficiently overcome, and that they are often superior to bureaucracies. No precise definition of community is given, but it is clearly intimated that groups have a necessary role in achieving optimal coordination of a well-functioning modern economy.

This critique takes on both the positive theory of institutions and trans-actions costs economics on their own grounds, for it suggests that there is no way for markets always to be the route to optimal reduction of transactions costs, moral hazards, and other incentive problems. In other words, it gives theoretical support to the notion that emerges from much empirical work – that communities are actually quite good, under some circumstances, at all these tasks.

But this is not all. Contemporary growth theory has shown that accumu-lation of human capital is the central element in growth, and that there is often a rather tight human capital/technology capital complementarity. Lucas (1988) argues that human capital accumulates when the rate of return to additional increments of human capital is higher than the discount rate.

Acquiring such human capital, however, is a social process and not just the result of individual education or effort. The reason, of course, is that the application of acquired knowledge is inevitably socially interdependent. Sometimes, the application of human or technological capital requires the bond of 'matching' with those who have similar skills or capital – in other words, scale effects are necessary. Sometimes it requires linking up with those who have complementary skills or technologies, without which our capital cannot be used in isolation. Only when these matches or complements are present can the central mechanism of growth – increasing returns – be sustained. Thus human or technological capital are not applied as a merely individual process, or as a simple aggregation of individual actions; they are collective action processes. When collective action of this type is realized, through bonding, there are increasing returns and hence growth can be sustained indefinitely (Easterly 2001).

The bonds that permit achievement of such matching and complementarity are underpinned by confidence in what others are doing, something which is inherently problematic because of the uncertainty that reigns in any dynamic process of change. This is why so many empirical studies have shown that intra-group solidarity facilitates acquisition of human capital and deployment of new technologies, and inter-group conflicts and rivalries slow down or even impede growth from occurring (Amsden 2001; Easterly 2001). Moreover, even though pay-offs to individual effort and skill acquisition are important incentives to bond, in the context of matching and spill-over effects, distributional arrangements become important. This is because they encourage participation and discourage resignation – whether between or within groups. One way in which they do this is by providing incentives for those who are not the greatest beneficiaries of new technologies to support (or at least not block) innovations, generally most strongly pushed by those who stand to benefit the most from them (Mokyr 1990). They are just as important, according to some analysts, as individually aligned, skill-differentiated incentives, and there is a balance to be achieved between individual and group incentives in order to minimize moral hazards but maximize complementarity effects. All in all, then, there are secure economic reasons to believe that communities – as we have defined them – are essential underpinnings of the incentives to rational maximization. They exist not as replacements for individual incentives or societal forces that discourage rent seeking and moral hazards, but as complements.

Bridging: the politics of development

Though much economics claims that sclerosis is the almost inevitable outcome of institutionalization of inter-group relations, even such theory does not deny that there are better and worse ways to weave particular groups together. Much recent research on economic development has demonstrated that political coalition formation is essential to the process. The principal explanations supplied for why coalitions are so important are that they provide a context in which good ideas and policies can be implemented; they allow problem solving and conflict resolution. Much recent analytical effort has gone into theorizing how much democratic political competition, institutional checks and balances, or administrative isolation are necessary to counteract the tendency for special interest politics to extract rents and drag down efficiency, the latter being the favourite theme of such political economy classics as Schattschneider (1935), Buchanan and Tullock (1962) and Olson (1965).

As we shall now see, however, almost all of the research on coalitions is about inter-group relations, with relatively little attention given to underlying social forces, especially bonding, and hence to the possible interaction of bonding and bridging in encouraging coalition formation and in shaping the ways that coalitions actually function. Two main versions of this argument will now be examined.

Democracy as a developmentalist community

Development economists have long speculated on a possible relationship between the long-term potential for economic development and the existence of democratic institutions, where democracy is, in the terms of the present argument, a form of society. Democracy permits the market system to function correctly, in this view, because democratic institutions presuppose the individual rights that underlie factor mobility and individual initiative, while democratic political processes encourage inter-group competition, which holds rent-earning behaviour in check and which also encourages compromise and moderation (Lipset 1963).

In the recent context of globalization, this argument has been refocused around the relationship between integration, democracy, and development.[7] One such theory is an extension of the classical *doux commerce* thesis (Hirschman 1997). Most cases of backwardness are attributed to an excess of community – clannism, rigidity, and closure – and a deficiency of societal structures capable of creating efficient markets to offset or defeat these communitarian forces. Trade brings about economic interdependency. Places then must develop institutional configurations that support such integration, in the form of markets and a commitment to transparency and property rights. This in turn necessitates certain kinds of democratic institutions, because they are the only ones truly compatible with high degrees of factor mobility, competition (instead of rent seeking), and entrepreneurship. Commerce thus brings these latter into existence and eliminates the excesses of community.

However, all of these arguments do rather poorly in empirical terms. Thus, Przeworski *et al.* (2000), in the most extensive statistical analysis of the relationship between democracy and development to date, show that there is nothing that can demonstrate whether democracy is the outcome of development or its precursor; there are also many examples of spectacular reversals of democracies in the face of rapidly rising trade, and of booms during authoritarian periods.

Another contemporary argument reverses the causality of the *doux commerce* thesis. Rodrik (1999) shows that there are strong relationships between the ability of a society to manage distributional conflicts when faced with shocks to the economy, and its ability to implement policies capable of maintaining growth. Shocks bring out latent conflicts and present strong dangers that wrong policies will be adopted, which reflect the interests of the most powerful (rent-seeking) agents and are likely to generate ongoing conflict. The successful resolution of such potential conflicts, goes the argument, is strongly linked to the existence of democratic institutions and processes, because these provide a forum for expression and consensus building, or at least for cooperation and acceptance of sacrifice in the name of the commonwealth. It is held that formal democracy depends on clear and transparent social interaction, very similar in form and flavour to the kinds of transactions that underpin a market economy, even if the rights and consti-tuencies associated with each are different. Thus, the culture that underpins these two kinds of processes is a common and mutually reinforcing one, with democracy necessary to reap the full benefits of commerce.

Even if the latter argument is still somewhat simplistic in its definition of the qualities of 'democracy', it does better empirically than the standard version of the *doux commerce* thesis. As Rodrik (1999: 101) notes, the 'voluminous empirical literature on the long-run consequences of political democracy for economic growth has generally yielded ambiguous results ... however, more recent studies show that democracies produce a better balance between risk and reward: that is, the level of aggregate economic instability tends to be much lower under democracies'. Hence, economies in formally democratic countries perform systematically better when confronted with external shocks, and have higher long-term growth rates.

There is further, albeit indirect, empirical support for this point of view. Below a certain income level, some forms of dictatorship may do as well as democracy because they can centralize and control corruption and rent seeking. Democracies, however, never collapse once a certain level of development has been achieved (the threshold is set at US$6,055 *per capita* today). This appears to be the case because wealthier democracies and dictatorships grow differently: the former are more technology-intensive and less labour-intensive in the way national wealth is increased. Ultimately, this translates into higher wages in democracies, because people respond by lowering fertility, which they also do because the rule of law typical of wealthy democracies makes them more confident in a predictable future, less dependent on arbitrary power (Alesina, Ozler, Roubini, and Swagel 1996). This also explains why there are no authoritarian regimes at extremely high income levels. It is a short extension from this to the notion that wealthy, internally heterogeneous democracies are more flexible and efficacious at solving problems in a way that is compatible with economic efficiency.

However, the arguments of both Rodrik and the standard *doux commerce* notion are fundamentally unclear about whether the success of democratic processes is due to societal rules or to social forces that amount to a democratic community. The evidence amassed by Przeworski *et al.* (2000) can be interpreted as indicating that the existence of democracy is evidence of an achieved national political community based around shared conventions of free association, due process, and respect for individual and property rights. Democracy, underpinned by shared expectations about the relationship of individual to authority, is a community because it presupposes a certain degree of formal equality and mutual respect. Its institutional forms are able to cope with ongoing conflicts without disrupting economic progress because of the existence of this underlying community. In his seminal history of the American constitutional democracy, Bailyn (1967) holds that its durability has to do less with the formal institutional processes created by the constitution, and more with the sharing of norms of democracy among Americans (that is, community). This does not imply that democracy is unrelated to bridging. There is abundant evidence that religious, ethnic and regional fractionalization are strongly associated with more frequent regime change for both authoritarian and democratic regimes, and with a propensity to authoritarianism. Negotiating the bridges generally occurs when democratic principles are widely accepted, and, when this occurs, the resulting democracies are longer-lasting and more stable than authoritarian or corporatist marriages of different groups, with better effects on long-term growth (Easterly 2001; Przeworski *et al.* 2000).

In this light, it seems likely that the existence and survival of democratic institutions is due to both bonding and bridging. Appealing to the mere existence of formally democratic institutions in more developed economies largely begs the question of how – politically – a society's communities are brought into an economically successful relationship with each other. Even if commerce has a role in this process, it is certainly not anything like the automatic 'calling forth' of the institutions and social practices, cited above, that are seen to be functionally necessary to markets. Indeed, much of the causality must run the other way around, with patterns of bonding and bridging likely to determine the extent to which both economic development and democracy can flourish, because they define the capacity of specific institutions for solving economic problems.

Developmental coalitions as bridges between communities

Political scientists and sociologists who are more interested in the classical questions of politics and interests, rather than the microfoundations of institutions, have tried to identify the political and institutional processes that encourage development, most especially the politics and strategies of successful developmental coalitions, and the institutional forms of successful developmental states. Of course, public choice theory has its answer to this situation: the notion that aggregation of interests can be generated spontaneously, so that both who bonds and how they bridge with other groups emerge from rational action under a condition of full information transparency and low-to-nil transactions costs. Such 'Coasian' bargains,[8] as we have argued above, assume away precisely the conditions that are necessary and pervasive features of the modern economy and that create necessary and efficiency-enhancing roles for groups. More promisingly, in our view, political economists observe that certain political opportunity structures allow for the creation of developmentally effective political coalitions and the containment of rent-seeking, non-competitive behaviour. Sociologists deal with this issue by emphasizing relations between institutions (especially states) and their societies, in determining whether states have the societal backing to organize good development strategies.

Along these lines, a wide body of detailed, close-to-the-ground research has shown that the long-term upward spirals of the East Asian, Irish, Israeli (until recently) and even Mauritian economies – to name just a few – have been made possible by intelligent developmental strategies (Wade 1990; Evans 1995; Amsden 1992 and 2001; O'Malley 1998). These strategies have been implemented by well-trained and honest bureaucrats[9] with significant long-term public policy involvement; they depend on successful regulation of capital markets and channelling of foreign investment; and they rely on institutionally nurtured, long-term entrepreneurship as a principal source of efficiency and competitiveness.

The question then is: why have these places been able to develop the institutional wherewithal to succeed, aside from large doses of good timing, good luck, and good training of their bureaucrats? The economic practices favourable to development[10] emerge when they can be made to prevail in domestic politics, through formation of coalitions that back these practices (Amsden 2001; Evans 1995). Where do such coalitions come from? One response is to claim that success has come from the establishment of political coalitions whose interests, fortuitously, corresponded to 'good economics', while less successful places are dominated by coalitions whose interests correspond to bad economics (Haggard 1990). However, even Haggard admits that all such coalitions cannot simply be based on a fortuitous coalescence of the interests of each member. This is because many involve distributional trade-offs, and short-term sacrifices from certain members.

This modifies the question about interests to ask how such coalitions can emerge on the basis of short- to medium-term sacrifices of interests, and development of a common vision of common long-term interests. Haggard claims that, in part, this has to do with the insulation of political elites from certain kinds of interest-based pressures, so that they can formulate policies, and then for these elites to have access to good ideas and to sell them to the people; that is, there is substantial mediation of political choices by institutions and ideas, not just by interests (or, at least, that ideas transform the time horizons used in defining interests). Political opportunity structures in these cases are characterized by political incentives for the policy-formulating elites that insulate them from certain kinds of short-term pressures (such as the electoral cycle), and enable them to implement ideas with high long-run pay-offs. If this is the case, however, then successful development would simply require the right political opportunity structures – appropriate formal institutions that respect the independence of technocrats (see, for contrasting positions, Amsden 2001; and Grossman and Helpman 2001). The two principal doubts about this argument are, on the one hand, that countries with similar political opportunity structures do very differently with their experts; in some, the isolation seems to work, while in others it does not. On the other hand, even isolated technocrats often make catastrophic mistakes. Isolation does not hold up as a universal panacea for intelligent economic decision making, any more than does total immersion in the 'will of the people'.[11] Moreover, there is still the problem of where different degrees of isolation come from, in both formal institutional architecture and in the actual functioning of institutions. For these questions, no purely institutional explanation of public policy will do: some deeper set of constraints conditions the genesis of political decision-making structures.

In this vein, Aghion *et al.* (2002) propose an endogenous theory of institutions, in which the degree of underlying social polarization or fragmentation[12] is positively associated with the insulation of decision making from day-to-day politics.[13] Hence, potentially conflictual societies 'choose' insulation, while more unified ones choose more 'democratic' systems. Yet this view has a difficult time accounting for the high level of insulation in Japan and Korea (relatively homogeneous societies), the low level in the USA (another homogeneous country according to their definition), and the evident fact that developmental success can be had in low-insulation political structures like those of the USA or Canada, as well as in high-insulation situations such as Korea or Japan.

Still, many authors confirm that primordial bonding patterns set the basic parameters for the problem of societal bridging. These include the degree of racial, ethnic, language, economic, and geographical homogeneity or diversity of the society in question. Easterly (2001) shows that the more ethnic or racial divisions there are in a society, the more tendency there is for rent-seeking behaviour to undermine developmentalist policy and efficient use of foreign aid. Amsden (2001) shows that societies with less income inequality tend to have done better in implementing developmentalist strategies for becoming major manufacturing powers. This is because equality between individuals cuts across groups and makes it more difficult to disenfranchise other groups and/or subject them to rent-earning behaviour by the dominant groups. It also, as Aghion (1998) points out, eliminates the disincentive to effort that extreme inequality can generate, a point echoed by Amartya Sen (1999). Both racial and ethnic homogeneity often, but not always, correspond to lower levels of income inequality and hence have synergies in promoting bridging, and hence the formation of consensus around developmental objectives. Amsden (2001) claims specifically that such consensus manifests itself in the capacity to establish 'control systems', consisting of mutual obligations between states and firms, that are respected and hence lead to the

	HIGH EQUALITY	HIGH INEQUALITY
HETEROGENEITY/ DIVERSITY	• Corporatist democracy? • Paralysed corporatism? • Beneficial political competition? • Special interest paralysis?	• Authoritarian, plundering elite? • Insider/outsider developmental regime?
HOMOGENEITY	• Developmentalist dictatorship? • Scandinavian democracy?	• Plundering elite? • Developmental elite?

Figure 8.2 Societal Unity and Development Regimes

success of development policy. Alesina and Rodrik (1994) argue that lower inequality reduces the need for redistributive policies, which sap growth-producing investment. In another vein, sociologists such as Pizzorno (1980) have emphasized that societies become 'middle-class' both as a result of the acquiring of common values – echoing the point made in the previous section about democracy as a form of community – and because the habits of the middle class are bridges between people with different primordial bonds, a set of practices they share, a common language.[14] Nonetheless, the contemporary field of political economy shows that there can be no direct passage from these underlying parameters of diversity and equality to developmental outcomes, as is suggested by Figure 8.2.

Political economists point out that there are political opportunity structures in between these structural features of the society and the type of regime which is established. But then we are simply back to the issue raised by Aghion and the school of comparative institutions – how underlying configurations of social forces give rise to institutions (political opportunity structures and economic governance regimes). To get around this risk of infinite regress in the analysis, then, the question must be reframed, in three ways. One is to lower the level of aggregation or abstraction, and to analyze bonding and bridging in relationship to specific domains of economic behaviour, such as those identified in the previous section in relationship to growth and the incentives it requires. Another is to see bonding and bridging as interactive, mutually transformative processes, rather than determined by fixed functional parameters, at one extreme, or totally malleable according to Coasian bargains, at the other extreme. A third is to hold that bonding and bridging have causes that are, at least partially, independent of formal institutional architecture and political opportunity structures, that they drive the different economic performances of institutions and governance regimes and also affect the 'choice' of such regimes.

■

How Society and Community Frame Incentives

As we have seen, markets and development pathways require both bonding and bridging. In markets, transactions costs and moral hazards may be reduced by communities and by societal rules and practices. Spill-overs, which are at the heart of achieving the increasing returns central to the growth process, can only be achieved in the presence of certain kinds of bonds between people, but rigid bonds or too much social hierarchy may also

INCENTIVES NECESSARY TO LONG-TERM DEVELOPMENT	PRINCIPAL MICRO-ECONOMIC EFFECTS OF EACH INCENTIVE	OPERATIONAL INSTITUTIONS: BEHAVIOUR, ROUTINES, REGULARITIES
Generalized confidence: incentives and coordination	• Reduces transactions costs (coordination) • Reduces moral hazards (incentives) • Raises expectations and efforts: discount rate (incentives)	• Encourages Schumpeterian entrepreneurship • Improves coordination of firm–firm transactions • Raises investment levels
Effective and acceptable distributional arrangements: incentives	• Precedent encourages ongoing 'sacrifices' in face of shocks (incentives) • Overcomes disincentive to participate and make effort: limits to exploitative rent seeking (incentives) • Overcomes disincentive to invest and create employment: limits to revanchist rent seeking • Improves willingness to pay taxes (incentives)	• Raises investments in skills • Raises work and entrepreneurial participation rates • Raises public investment levels, some of which lower business costs
Ongoing conflict resolution and problem solving: Adjustments of incentives and coordination, prevent sclerosis	• Participation of groups enhanced (incentives, coordination) • Minimization of rent seeking from corporatism (incentives, coordination)	• Better adjustment of rules governing entrepreneurship and labour markets. • Intelligent ideas more likely to receive support as public policy • Coalitions can form, avoiding chaotic instability

Figure 8.3 The Foundations of Development

inhibit them from coming about. Developmental pathways require bridging between people, without which the coalitions that make it possible to deal with problems and governance are impossible, but bridging is ultimately strongly shaped by the underlying patterns of bonding or communities, and the one does not dictate the other.

Communitarian and societal forces interact, necessarily, in shaping the complex institutional contexts that actors face. What do they do when they interact? They shape the basic ways that individuals can participate in the economy, creating incentives for them to do some things and not do others. This is why considering society and community in interaction allows us to embed the consideration of incentives, which are at the heart of economic action, in institutional conditions that are *not* 'well controlled', where society and community are in a sort of delicate interaction with each other, sometimes propitious to development and sometimes not, and introducing a wide variety of strengths and weaknesses in the development process, within and between places.

What are these incentives? As shown in the first column of Figure 8.3, successful economies are characterized by generalized confidence in the economic process and especially in the transactional relationships upon which it depends; effective and acceptable distributional trade-offs between groups; and means for successful problem solving and conflict resolution. In the second column, the principal microeconomic effects of each of these features are indicated.

To take the first such feature, any set of forces that systematically reduces transactions costs and moral hazards comes across to individual actors as the possibility of having confidence in the economic process and better estimating future rewards. This reduction constitutes a positive incentive, which is manifested through discount rates, risk perceptions[15] and the estimation of long-term wealth accumulation prospects, leading to higher expectations and effort levels. These in turn have many beneficial effects on long-term economic performance by encouraging actors to participate in routines that are favourable to the economy, which are shown in the third column. They include encouraging innovative (Schumpeterian) entrepreneurship; improving the coordination of inter-firm transactions, both lowering costs and raising the willingness of firms to try to construct them, hence improving the growth-inducing effects of the economy-wide division of labour (Young 1928; Stigler 1951); and raising investment levels through the above-mentioned effects on discount rates and risk perceptions.

Confidence is directly related to the central mechanisms of contemporary growth theory. In the latter, knowledge accumulation and application are central to the achievement of long-term growth. Knowledge is different from many other factors of production, in that it can have increasing returns, in part because it can be re-used at no additional cost, and can be applied in many different ways and can be recombined into different uses; this permits it to escape the law of diminishing returns. But how is this realized as a concrete process? Knowledgeable (skilled) agents need to match up with other skilled agents, so that their knowledge is not wasted; they tend therefore to function via selective affinities, within selected economic communities. If these affinities do not exist at all (either because knowledgeable people are extremely rare, and so can match up with nobody, or because they are extremely distrustful), knowledge is likely to be wasted and have little positive developmental effect. At the same time, if knowledge stays too much inside such communities, then development cannot spread: there need to be ways of bridging between knowledgeable and less knowledgeable agents – in other words, ways of providing the former with the confidence that their knowledge will be well used and the latter with the confidence that they will realize a pay-off from trying to get and apply new knowledge through necessary cooperation with those who know how to use it. Mutual confidence through both bonding and bridging is essential, then, to creating a process of growth. In addition, confidence encourages governments to be less myopic in their policies, and myopic governmental policies are harmful for growth (Persson and Tabellini 2002).

The second feature is effective distributional arrangements – not to be confused with the absence of distributional conflict. When there are social forces that generate acceptable distributional arrangements, such arrangements will encourage necessary sacrifices to be made when economies undergo the inevitable shocks and setbacks of any development process (Rodrik 1999). Thus, it also has a positive incentive effect. Aghion (1998) has argued that excessive inequality is just as bad as excessive income levelling, because too much inequality simply leads to withdrawal of effort by potentially productive actors; formally, it amounts to a capital market imperfection.[16] Alesina and Rodrik (1994) and Persson and Tabellini (2002) show that less inequality has a positive relationship to growth. And this is consistent with the empirical evidence, which shows that the Highly Performing Asian Economies (HPAEs) have all been characterized by limited inequality, in contradistinction to the poorly performing Latin American economies. These features arguably improve investments (internal or external) in skill creation, raise the incentives to participate fully in the formal economy and to become an entrepreneur (hence, participation rates and levels), and improve the willingness to pay taxes and to invest. Effective distributional arrangements are central to achieving the spill-overs identified above as essential to long-term growth.

Veblen and other precursors of evolutionary thinking in economics (Hodgson 2002) gave us the basic notion that an economy's institutions would allow it (if successful) to self-select in an ongoing way into the things it could do well, and hence to develop. Behind this is the notion that no institutional arrangements resolve all problems for good. Ongoing adjustment of the rules governing investment, entrepreneurship and the regulation of labour markets are necessary as an economy undergoes structural change in the course of development (what are good institutional forms at one stage are

INCENTIVES NECESSARY TO LONG-TERM DEVELOPMENT	PRINCIPAL MICRO-ECONOMIC EFFECTS OF EACH INCENTIVE	OPERATIONAL INSTITUTIONS: BEHAVIOUR, ROUTINES, REGULARITIES	ROLE OF COM-MUNITARIAN 'BONDING' IN BRINGING ABOUT EACH INCENTIVE	ROLE OF SOCIETAL 'BRIDGING' IN BRINGING ABOUT EACH INCENTIVE
Generalized confidence ↓	Reduces transactions costs Reduces moral hazards Raises expecta-tions and efforts ↓	Encourages Schumpeterian entrepreneur Improves coordination of firm–firm transactions Raises investment levels ↓ →	Reputation effects, shared conventions, identities (these depend on process of group formation) overcome certain information problems in low-cost way (but can encourage rent seeking) →	Overarching rules promote transparency and limit rent seeking, help to complete markets ←
Effective and acceptable distributional trade-offs ↓↓	• Precedent encourages ongoing 'sacrifices' in face of shocks (Rodrik) • Overcomes disincentive to participate and make effort (Aghion) ↓↓	• Raises investments in skills • Raises work and entrepreneurial participation rates • Improves willingness to pay taxes (investment) ↓↓ →	• Voice and loyalty • Being in the same boat enhances acceptability • Membership may involve real forms of intra-group redistribution →	• Counteracts corporatism and distributional hold-ups • Standards of fairness and efficiency constrain group demands • Inter-group mobility (exit), disciplines groups ←
Successful ongoing conflict resolution	Participation of groups is enhanced Minimizes rent seeking from corporatism	Better adjustment of rules governing entrepreneurship and labour markets Intelligent ideas more likely to receive support as public policy Coalitions can form, avoiding chaotic instability →	Secure groups encourage coalition formation Voice that gets heard (but risk of principal–agent problems) →	Limits to group power encourage compromise Exit options, defection, make other coalitions possible, hence dynamically limit principal–agent problems ←

Note: →↓ cumulative and/or one-way causal effect   →← two-way interactions and feedbacks

Figure 8.4: Society–Community Interactions and Incentives

no longer appropriate at others) and as external circumstances change (Bremer and Kasarda 2002). These three broad features and their associated economic behaviours characterize a wide variety of successful long-term economic development experiences. By contrast, cases of stagnation or long-term developmental regress manifest failure to achieve these features and to enjoy the microeconomic efficiencies and aggregate effects described in Figure 8.3.

Figure 8.4 now shows how each of these types of incentive is shaped and given concrete institutional form by society–community interactions (horizontal), and in turn on their mutual interactions (vertical). The crux of our argument is shown in the fourth and fifth columns.

Generalized confidence emerges when the pervasive information problems, attendant moral hazards, and market failures of all modern economies are attenuated, especially in their most creative and innovative activities and sectors. Communities are low-cost ways of resolving these problems, by creating trust, reputation effects, and shared conventions. No fully 'societal' system – whether markets or administered, centralized bureaucracies – has ever succeeded in doing everything that communities can do in this regard. But, as is well known, communities can be prejudicial to economic development if they lead to rent seeking; hence, they must be in a delicate and dynamic relationship with the forces that promote transparency, entry, and exit, and limit rent seeking, helping to complete markets where communities might stifle them. Generalized confidence, in other words, requires both society and community.

The same is true of the achievement of effective and acceptable distributional trade-offs. These cannot be administered by a societal overseer; neither will they emerge from the spontaneous interaction of different communities with each other (and certainly they will not come about from the spontaneous interaction of individual agents). Communities are based on loyalty, and they can give voice to agents whose claims would otherwise go unheard by markets. Moreover, group membership has the virtue of diffusing a sense of 'being in the same boat', and those who are in the boat can contribute to a mutual sense that fairness has been achieved (as well as injustice and anger). In the former case, the acceptability of any distributional trade-off is enhanced. Finally, communities – even in the most modern of economies – often have concrete effects on distributional matters. Families in some economies carry out income redistribution and smoothing, mobilize savings at low interest rates, and share work. But society is necessary as well, if undesirable forms of cronyism or enduring hierarchy are to be avoided. Competition and political interaction between groups counteract corporatism and distributional hold-ups; generalized standards of efficiency and fairness can constrain certain group demands and privileges; and inter-group mobility (the possibility of exit) can have disciplining effects on what groups do to obtain their piece of the pie. Once again, effective distributional trade-offs are achieved through community and society in interaction.

Though such interactions may also produce catastrophe, it is difficult to imagine that for effective distributional outcomes all that is needed is society (and a minimalist version of it, at that).

Ongoing conflict resolution is, in many ways, the overall dynamic outcome of these other features of development. Resolving such conflicts involves, at the very least, adjustment of rules governing the vital centre of the development process: entrepreneurship, labour markets, and investment. Effective problem solving and institutional adaptation come about when it is difficult for groups to practise excessive corporatism and rent seeking and when problem-solving bridges are built between the relevant groups. On the one hand, the community-based social bonds referred to above provide groups with a certain degree of security, allowing them to be 'at the table' so that their voices can be heard, whether formally or in a more diffused manner. The societal forces described create limits to group power, parameters for their actions, so that the position of groups is not so secure that other coalitions are impossible. Participation of many different groups prevents them from practising negative forms of exit (resignation or winner-takes-all) from the problem-solving process. This helps avoid the twin dangers of 'bad' stability in the form of interest-based but non-developmentalist (rent-seeking) coalitions, on the one hand, and extreme instability on the other (Alesina, Ozler, Roubini and Swagel 1996). Hence, there is less danger that intelligent ideas will be blocked, because the principal interest groups have less ability and incentive to bind themselves to rigid, exclusively self-serving positions. This makes institutional learning more probable (Haggard 1990) and may even allow ongoing revision of the most basic institutional infrastructure, such as legal principles, the system of political power sharing, and other factors that influence political opportunity structures and hence the possibility for competing ideas to be heard (Aghion *et al.* 2002; Evans 1995).

What exactly is this relationship between bonding and bridging, however? Community and society are essentially the fundamental units and principles of participation that individuals can follow when they take part in the collective economic process. These forms are conventional, in the sense that each individual incorporates them into her expectations in deciding what actions are rational to undertake. They are like stabilized patterns of collective interaction, and the expectations accompanying them, that each actor uses in her strategic approach to individual interaction under uncertainty.[17]

Notice that in each area, the ideal-type outcomes described above are based on a sort of bargain, where a favourable balance of society and community allows the positive effects of each to emerge, while each also acts as a check and balance on the potentially negative effects of the other, taken alone. Thus, together society and community permit actors to reduce transactions costs, limit moral hazards, and reduce rent seeking, while also reducing the exercise of absolute power by any group and hence promoting competition and innovation. All are critical to the definition of the expectations of agents and hence how they identify and project their interests into the collective sphere.[18] A favourable balance comes about when the right mix of forms of participation exists.

Thus, society and community shape each other, but paradoxically they do so because of their independence from one another; each consists of different kinds of social practices and interactions, constituted at different spatial-temporal scales. Hence, for the purposes of a theory of the institutional bases of economic development, Putnam's categories, rather than being added together into a single index of social capital, may be better kept separate, as their effects are offsetting or corrective. This is also why the tendency for the social sciences to become partisans of either society or community as the source of development is very likely wrong and why we have argued for a reformulation of the problem of the social foundations of economic developmental institutions.

This approach is useful in two principal areas, which can now be made explicit. First, it should help explain degrees of success in long-term economic development. Roughly speaking, we expect that bonding without bridging or bridging without bonding lead to the undesirable outcomes described in the NW and SE cases in Figure 8.4. Some kind of interaction between the two is most favourable to creating the incentives to long-term economic development.

■

Conclusion: Social Forces, Politics, and Economics

The central proposition of this chapter requires much more analytical precision and theoretical elaboration than I am able to give it here. While it is likely never to be as analytically parsimonious as certain other theories of the institutional foundations of development, it does respond to the need to reintroduce a realistic view of social forces into the theory of comparative economics, relaxing the over-restrictive assumptions commonly used in political economy and institutional economics in the theorization of economic development. It is nonetheless still relatively parsimonious because it locates sources of variety in the interaction of two basic forms of social organization, community and society.

This approach can be used for both of the main purposes of comparative economics: to shed light on the degree of success in long-term economic development, and on the variety of institutional forms both success and failure can assume. Society and community can interact in many efficient ways (not necessarily pareto-efficient[19]), such that the concrete institutional forms of confidence, distributional arrangements, and coalitional behaviour that lead to development are many and sundry, and lead to complex evolutionary selection dynamics of economies into what they do best. But economies also fail: a workable balance between society and community – and thus the creation of solid incentives to development – is often not

COMMUNITY SOCIETY	LOW	HIGH
HIGH	Insufficient public goods Lower confidence, higher transactions costs Long-term, unacceptable distributional trade-offs Costly conflict resolution, confrontational society	Facilitates confidence Facilitates sustainable distributional trade-offs Facilitates conflict resolution Strong society modernizes community Strong community reduces costs associated with anonymity
LOW	Chaos Law of the Jungle	Prevalence of 'primitive' forms of community Hierarchical relations between groups Rent-seeking groups Low-trust, lack of confidence Unacceptable distributional effects due to rents and hierarchy Permanent conflicts

Figure 8.5: The Many Possibilities

achieved, and this framework can be used to illuminate such failure. At the same time, and on a more positive note, there are also many concrete real-world ways to achieve workable interactions – and hence the many surprising figures of developmental success, often well beyond the explanatory capacity of conventional theories or even imaginings. Some of these different possibilities are suggested, in a highly schematic way, in Figure 8.5.

Moreover, if the argument made in previous sections is correct, then there is no simple mapping of associational patterns or institutional forms onto success and failure, but rather the question of how institutions substantively resolve society–community relations. The task of our theory is not to search for consistent institutional forms – a putative isomorphism of institutions to development – but rather to find context-sensitive 'razor's edge' interactions between bonding and bridging that achieve the substantive outcomes identified in economic theory and evidence.

Current debates over development theory and policy, however, show just how far away we are from any such sense of the problem. Market fundamentalists and institutionalists debate each other but seldom use a common language, with the former claiming the high ground of incentives but losing sight of how they are really constructed, while the latter tend to emphasize control and authority over the development process and needlessly concede incentives and microefficiency to the context-less analyses of market fundamentalists.

The task proposed is complicated by the fact that the starting points for each society are different, while the ending points, in terms of the precise articulations between society and community that are achievable and correspond to the desires of each society, also show considerable variation. This in no way calls for complete relativism, nor is it a parsimonious approach to the issue of institutional reform. It does help place the lessons from certain valuable parsimonious economic theories into a more grounded and realistic sociological framework.

Bibliography

Aghion, P. (1998) 'Inequality and economic growth', in Aghion, P. and J. Williamson (eds), *Growth, Inequality and Globalization*, Cambridge: Cambridge University Press.

Aghion, P., Alesina, A., and F. Trebbi (2002) 'Endogenous political institutions', NBER Working Paper 9006, Cambridge, MA.

Alesina, A. and D. Rodrik (1994) 'Distributive politics and economic growth', *Quarterly Journal of Economics*, Vol. 109, No. 2, May.

Alesina, A., Ozler, S., Roubini, N., and P. Swagel (1996) 'Political instability and economic growth', *Journal of Economic Growth*, Vol. 1, No. 2, June.

Amsden, A. H. (1992) *Asia's Next Giant: South Korea and Late Industrialization*, Oxford: Oxford University Press.

—— (2001) *The Rise of the 'Rest': Challenges to the West From Late-Industrializing Economies*, Oxford: Oxford University Press.

Aydogan, N. (2002) 'Notes on the Merger Strategy of High versus Low-tech Industries: Complementarities and Moral Hazard', *Economics Bulletin*, Vol. 12, pp. 1–12.

Bailyn, B. (1967) *The Ideological Origins of the American Revolution*, Cambridge, MA: Harvard University Press.

Becattini, G. and F. Sforzi (eds) (2002) *Lezioni Sullo Sviluppo Locale*, Turin: Rosenberg and Sellier.

Becker, G. S. and K. Murphy (2000) *Social Economics – Market Behavior in a Social Environment*, Cambridge, MA: Harvard/Belknap.

Bell, D. (1976) *The Cultural Contradictions of Capitalism*, New York: Basic Books.

Bellah, R.N., *et al.* (1995) *Habits of the Heart: Individualism and Commitment in*

American Life, Berkeley: University of California Press.

Boltanski, L. and L. Thèvenot (1987) *Les Economies de la Grandeur*, Paris: Gallimard.

Bremer, J. and J. Kasarda (2002) 'The origins of terror: implications for US foreign policy', *The Milken Institute Review*, Fourth Quarter, December.

Buchanan, J. and G. Tullock (1962) *The Calculus of Consent*, Ann Arbor: University of Michigan Press.

Casson, M. (1995) *Entrepreneurship and Business Culture*, Aldershot, Hants, UK: Edward Elgar.

Cohen, S. and G. Fields (1999) 'Social capital and capital gains in Silicon Valley', *California Management Review*, Vol. 41, No. 2, Winter.

Coleman, J. S. (1990) *Foundations of Social Theory*, Cambridge: Harvard University Press.

DiMaggio, P. (1994) *Structures of Capital: The Social Organization of the Economy*, New York: Cambridge University Press.

Douglass, M. and J. Friedmann (eds) (1997) *Cities for Citizens*, Chichester: John Wiley and Sons.

Durkheim, E. (1984) *The Division of Labor in Society*, translated by W. D. Halls, New York: The Free Press.

Easterly, W. (2001) *The Elusive Quest for Growth*, Cambridge, MA: MIT Press.

Etzioni, A. (1996) *The New Golden Rule: Community and Morality in a Democratic Society*, New York: Basic Books.

Evans, P. (1995) *Embedded Autonomy: States and Industrial Transformation*, Princeton: Princeton University Press.

Fligstein, N. (2001) *The Architecture of Markets: An Economic Sociology of Twenty-first Century Capitalism and Society*, Princeton, NJ: Princeton University Press.

Fogel, R. W. (2000) *The Fourth Great Awakening and the Future of Egalitarianism*, Chicago: University of Chicago Press.

Fukuyama, F. (1995) *Trust: The Social Virtues and the Creation of Prosperity*, New York: Simon and Schuster.

Gambetta, D. (ed.) (1988) *Trust: Making and Breaking Cooperative Relations*, Oxford: Oxford University Press.

Giddens, A. (1984) *The Constitution of Society*, Cambridge: Polity Press.

—— (1990) *The Consequences of Modernity*, Palo Alto: Stanford University Press.

Grabher, G. (ed.) (1993) *The Embedded Firm: On the Socioeconomics of Industrial Networks*, London: Routledge.

Granovetter, M. (1986) 'The sociological and economic approaches to labor market analysis: a social structural view', in Farkas, G. and P. England (eds), *Industries, Firms and Jobs*, New York: Plenum.

—— (2001) 'A theoretical agenda for economic sociology', in Guillen, M., Collins, R., England, P., and M. Meyer (eds), *Economic Sociology at the Millennium*, New York: Russell Sage Foundation.

Greenwald, B. and J. E. Stiglitz (1984) 'Informational imperfections in capital markets and macro-economic fluctuations', *American Economic Review*, Vol. 74, No. 2, May.

—— (1986) 'Externalities in economies with imperfect information and incomplete markets', *Quarterly Journal of Economics*, Vol. 101, No. 2, May.

Grossman, G. M. and E. Helpman (2001) *Special Interest Politics*, Cambridge, MA: MIT Press.

Haggard, S. (1990) *Pathways from the Periphery*, Ithaca, NY: Cornell University Press.

Hirschman, A. (1997) *The Passions and the Interests*, Princeton, NJ: Princeton University Press.

Hodgson, G. (2002) 'Reconstructing institutional economics: evolution, agency and structure in American institutionalism', book manuscript, University of Hertfordshire.

Kirzner, I. (1973) *Competition and Entrepreneurship*, Chicago: University of Chicago Press.

Knight, F. (1921) *Risk, Uncertainty and Profit*, New York: AH Kelly.

Lavinas, L., Garcia, E., and F. Barros (2000) *'Salários e Volume de Emprego Industrial no Nordeste'*, paper prepared for our research project, Rio de Janeiro.

Lavinas, L. and M. Storper (1999) 'Trajetórias Para a Economia do Aprendizado: Os Novos Mundos de Produção no Nordeste', research report to the Banco do Nordeste, prepared at IPEA, Rio de Janeiro.

Leonardi, R. (1995) 'Regional development in Italy, social capital, and the Mezzogiorno', *Oxford Review of Economic Policy*, Vol. 11, No. 2, Summer.

Levy, J. (1999) *Tocqueville's Revenge: State, Society and Community in Contemporary France*, Cambridge, MA: Harvard University Press.

Lin, N. (2001) *Social Capital: A Theory of Social Structure and Action*, Cambridge, UK and New York: Cambridge University Press.

Lipset, S. M. (1963) *Political Man*, Garden City, NY: Doubleday Anchor.

Lorenz, E. (1984) 'Neither friends nor strangers: informal networks and subcontracting relations in French industry', in Gambetta, D. (ed.), *Trust*, New York: Oxford University Press.

—— (1992) 'Trust and the theory of industrial districts', in Storper, M. and A. J. Scott (eds), *Pathways to Industrialization and Regional Development*, London: Routledge.

Lucas, R. E. (1988) 'The mechanics of economic development', *Journal of Monetary Economics*, Vol. 22, No. 1, July.

Marshall, A. (1919) *Industry and Trade*, London: Macmillan.

Moe, T. (1987) 'Interests, institutions and positive theory: The politics of the NLRB', in Orren, K. and S. Showronek (eds), *Studies in American Political Development*, Vol. 2, New Haven: Yale University Press.

Mokyr, J. (1990) *The Lever of Riches: Technological Creativity and Economic Progress*, New York: Oxford University Press.

Norris, P. (2002) *Democratic Phoenix: Reinventing Political Activism*, Cambridge: Cambridge University Press.

North, D. (1981) *Structure and Change in Economic History*, New York: Norton.

Olson, M. (1965) *The Logic of Collective Action*, Cambridge, MA: Harvard University Press.

O'Malley, E. (1998) 'Industrial policy in Ireland and the problem of late development', in Storper, M., Thomadakis, S. and L. Tsipouri (eds), *Latecomers in the Global Economy*, London: Routledge.

Persson, T. and G. Tabellini (2002) *Political Economics: Explaining Economic Policy*, Cambridge, MA: MIT Press.

Piore, M. and C. Sabel (1984) *The Second Industrial Divide*, New York: Basic Books.

Pizzorno, A. (1980) *I Soggetti del Pluralismo: Classi, Partiti, Sindicati*, Bologna: Il Mulino.

Polanyi, K. (1957) *The Great Transformation*, Boston: Beacon Press.

Polanyi, M. (1966) *The Tacit Dimension*, New York: Doubleday.

Przeworski, A., Alvarez, M., Cheibub, J. A. and F. Limongi (2000) *Democracy and Development: Political Institutions and Well-being in the World, 1950-1990*. Cambridge: Cambridge University Press.

Putnam, R. (2000) *Bowling Alone: The Collapse and Revival of American Community*, New York: Simon and Schuster.

Putnam, R., Leonardi, R., and R. Y. Nanetti (1993) *Making Democracy Work*, Princeton, NJ: Princeton University Press.

Reynolds, P. D., Camp, S. M., Bygrave, W. D., Autio, E., and M. Hay (2001) *Global Entrepreneurship Monitor; 2001 Executive Report*, Kansas City, MO: Kauffman Center for Entrepreneurial Leadership at the Ewing Marion Kauffman Foundation.

Rodriguez-Pose, A. (1999) 'Instituciones y desarollo económico', *Ciudad y Territorio: Estudios Territoriales*, Vol. 31, No. 122, April–June.

Rodrik, D. (1999) *The New Global Economy and Developing Countries: Making Openness Work*, Washington, DC: Overseas Development Council.

Rosenvallon, P. (1990) *L'Etat en France de 1789 à Nos Jours*, Paris: Le Seuil.

—— (1993) *Le Sacre du Citoyen*, Paris: Gallimard.

Sandel, M. (1996) *Democracy's Discontent: America in Search of a Public Philosophy*, Cambridge, MA: Harvard/Belknap.

Saxenian, A. (1994) *Regional Advantage*, Cambridge, MA: Harvard University Press.

Schattschneider, E. E. (1935) *Politics, Pressures and the Tariff*, Englewood Cliffs, NJ: Prentice Hall.

Schleifer, A. (2002) 'The new comparative economics', *NBER Reporter*, Fall, September 22.

Schumpeter, J. A. (1991) *The Economics and Sociology of Capitalism*, Princeton, NJ: Princeton University Press.

Scott, A. J. and E. W. Soja (eds) (1996) *The City: Los Angeles and Urban Theory at the End of the Twentieth Century*, Berkeley: University of California Press.

Sen, A. (1999) *Development as Freedom*, New York: Knopf.

Stigler, G. J. (1951) 'The division of labor is limited by the extent of the market', *Journal of Political Economy*, Vol. 59, No. 3, June.

Stiglitz, J. E. (1994) *Whither Socialism?*, Cambridge, MA: MIT Press.

Storper, M. (1997) *The Regional World: Territorial Development in a Global Economy*, New York: Guilford Press.

Storper, M. and R. Salais (1997) *Worlds of Production: the Action Frameworks of the Economy,* Cambridge, MA: Harvard University Press.

Tocqueville, A. (1986) *De la Démocratie en Amérique,* Paris: Gallimard.

Wade, R. (1990) *Governing the Market: Economic Theory and the Role of Government in East Asian Industrialization,* Princeton, NJ: Princeton University Press.

Weber, M. (1968) *Economy and Society,* translated by G. Roth and C. Wittich, New York: Bedminster Press.

Williamson, O. E. (1985) *The Economic Institutions of Capitalism: Markets, Firms, Relational Contracting,* New York: Free Press.

Young, A. (1928) 'Increasing returns and economic progress', *The Economic Journal,* Vol. 38, No. 152, December.

Notes

1   Earlier versions of this chapter were presented to the Third International Seminar of the University of São Paulo, Faculties of Economics and Sociology, October 2002, to the SPURS Geography of Innovation Seminar at MIT, February 2003, to the NOLD Doctoral School in Tromsø, Norway, April 2003, and to the Hettner Lectures in Heidelberg, June 2003. The field research which stimulated this chapter was carried out jointly with Lena Lavinas (Federal University of Rio de Janeiro), in a project financed principally by the Banco do Nordeste Brasileiro (BNB). Thanks also go to the Brasilian Econometrics Society for administration of the funds. Additional financial support came from the William and Flora Hewlett Foundation and the UCLA Centre for Latin American Studies. Logistical support was provided by UCLA, the Instituto de Pesquisa Econômica Aplicada (IPEA), Rio de Janeiro, and the Center for Research on Territories, Technologies and Society (LATTS) at the École Nationale des Ponts et Chaussées, France. The views expressed in this chapter are exclusively those of the author. Special thanks are due to Eduardo Garcia, chief research assistant to Lena Lavinas, for his extraordinary intellectual and logistical contributions to the research. Additional research assistance was provided by Yun-chung Chen, PhD candidate at UCLA. I also thank my LSE colleague Andrés Rodriguez-Pose for his insightful comments, and especially for Figure 8.5.

2   Institutionalist economics, in this sense, refers principally to transaction-cost economics, which are centrally interested in whether the conditions for Coasian bargains exist; if they do not, how to secure them; and, when they do, what kinds of optimal institutional arrangements exist for a given problem.

3   There is a vast literature on this subject. For extensive reviews, see, *inter alia,* my own writings: Storper, 1997; Storper and Salais 1997, as well as the chapters in Becattini and Sforzi 2002.

4   Thanks to Arnaldo Bagnasco for calling my attention to this point.

5   Jalisco, Mexico is specifically listed in Figure 8.1 because it is a site of fieldwork conducted by Lena Lavinas and I.

6   On the notion of a 'convention of participation,' see Storper and Salais (1997).

7   Whether of less-developed regions into their respective national economies or integration of national economies with different levels of development – as in the EU or NAFTA, or integration generally into the world economy.

8   This term 'Coasian' bargain is rooted in Ronald Coase's notion that a firm can be understood as a nexus of contracts, and any externalities generated by firm behaviour (for example, pollution of the surrounding environment) are best handled by 'bargains' between firms and those whose welfare is affected (and not by governmental intervention).

9   The New Comparative Economics emphasizes, in this regard, the very long run of 'law and order' and the 'rule of law,' defined respectively as the extent to which a rule-bound state is in place, and the extent to which actors are obliged to follow the rules that are established (Schleifer 2002).

10 Amsden (2001) calls them 'control systems', consisting of good mutual obligations and the respect of these obligations.

11 Along these lines, the coalitions brought into being by such political opportunity structures must in any case have means of surviving. One could argue, simply, that they either survive in the successful cases because of their success with development, while in the other cases, they survive by providing rents to the powerful. But all development processes generate ongoing potential for conflict, and require internal adjustments. Are these adjustments achievable simply through the inertia of political opportunity structures (intelligent insulated elites in the successful cases, or powerful rent-seeking coalitions in the others)? This seems more plausible for developmental blockage than success. Successful coalitions must ultimately be good at resolving the real conflicts engendered by development, by drawing on the real communities of interest in existence and maintaining them in some viable societal relationship to one another. In other words, successful political coalitions depend for their formation not only on fortuitous institutional set-ups and good ideas; they also respond to ongoing interactions of communities which make up the society in question. This brings us full circle to the existence of law and order and the rule of law, but these do not exist as abstract societal forces; they exist as concrete practices that different communities use to bridge their interactions with other communities.

12 The sources of such fragmentation might be ethnic, regional or class-based.

13 But this relationship weakens as countries become richer, because the need for large reforms becomes smaller and losses can be compensated at costs which represent small proportions of total societal wealth. Hence, there is a generally lower need for political insulation.

14 This also echoes Lipset's (1963) notion of cross-cutting diversified alliances as generating a kind of moderation, generalized bridging.

15 I am reminded here of the fundamental distinction between risk and uncertainty, introduced by Frank Knight (1921). When confidence is weak or absent, the problem is that risks can no longer be estimated and hence

    minimized, and actors must face true uncertainty, with strongly negative effects on many of the foundations of long-term growth.

16 This has an indirect link to Sen's (1999) notion that extreme inequality expresses the lack of, but also impedes the construction of, the social bonds which are crucial to development, because it discourages provision of certain necessary social goods and deprives the poorest of the preconditions (basic resources) which would enable them to contribute to their own, and society's, development.

17 For extensive discussion of the notion of 'conventions of participation' in the economy, see Storper and Salais (1997).

18 The principal–agent problem and impossibility theorem show us that even within a group, such tensions can exist. However, there is a major difference in degree of tension and hence in the intensity of relationships within groups and between groups. If this were not the case, bridges between groups would be transformed into bonds within groups as different groups of principals merged and decided to have unified agents working for them.

19 In economic theory, an allocation of goods and resources is termed pareto-efficient when no agent can be made better off without making at least one other agent worse off.

9

Poverty and Social Discrimination: A Spatial Keynesian Approach

GARY A. DYMSKI

■

Introduction

This chapter develops a spatial Keynesian approach to the problems of poverty and social discrimination. This approach shows that the spatial distribution of households and businesses is a key factor in shaping the character and extent of poverty in any society. Poverty involves not simply the circumstances of households who are poor, but structural characteristics of the bordered spaces within which most lower-income people live. These structural characteristics are deeply impacted by spatially specific social and economic dynamics. These dynamics involve economic clustering combined with social separation, and create distinct areas with very uneven cross-border patterns of goods and financial flows. These cross-border patterns tend to systematically encourage accumulation in some spaces and decumulation in others. Some areas become locations for the long-term cultivation of asset growth, while others become sites for finding prey to exploit for short-term returns. Similarly, the impact of social discrimination depends not just on the depth and pattern of personal animus, but on the degree to which those who are targets of this discrimination are segregated into distinct spatial communities, and on whether these communities are sites of production and wealth building.

This spatial wealth/income perspective shows first that the disadvantages associated with social discrimination invariably have a spatial and community dimension. Further, when mobility between spatial communities is constrained (by social custom or by wealth variations), social discrimination and poverty cannot be attacked meaningfully at the individual level. Policies aimed at reducing poverty and social discrimination must be informed by the spatial configuration of economic and social resources. Third, any attack on social discrimination should not focus solely on the personal level, but instead should encompass the structural inequality that personal discrimination invariably creates. In addition, this analysis shows the relevance of core elements of the Keynesian approach for understanding and intervening in situations of poverty and discrimination. Finally, this chapter makes the point that anti-poverty policies are inherently development policies, and development policies cannot avoid being anti-poverty policies. In particular, the larger the percentage of a nation's population that experiences poverty and social discrimination, the more will policies for reducing poverty and social discrimination overlap with overall national economic policies. In sum, this chapter argues that an attack on poverty, inequality, and social discrimination must be a component of any sustainable development strategy.

■

Defining Poverty and Discrimination: Agent-based versus Structural Approaches

While our interest is primarily in spatial aspects of poverty and discrimination, this section sets out aspatial definitions of poverty and discrimination. The next section brings out the often implicit spatial dimension of these concepts.

Poverty

All definitions of poverty aim at establishing objectively how many people are in need in a given place. Some definitions of poverty identify an absolute standard for the minimal levels of income and resources necessary for survival or, in Sen's (1995) definition, for achieving essential human capabilities. Other definitions use a societally relative approach – for example, the poor might be defined as those with less than 50 per cent of the median income level. For any nation, relative definitions of poverty focus attention on the relationship between the national standard of living and the national distribution of income and wealth.

Another choice in defining poverty is whether to focus on individual characteristics of the poor or on the social structures that generate and reproduce poverty. The personal characteristics approach quickly leads to distinctions between the 'deserving' and 'undeserving' poor. Those who are subject to some form of physical disability may not be responsible for their inability to earn a living, and hence are 'deserving'. Those without such disabilities or preconditions can be defined as 'undeserving'.[1] The notion of a 'culture of poverty' (Lewis 1961) follows from using an individualistic approach to understanding why people remain in the latter category over sustained periods of time.

Alternatively, poverty can be understood as a condition that follows from systematic differences in the flows of resources and opportunities to different kinds of agents – that is, as a structural phenomenon at root, not a behavioural one. The dividing lines between people are invariably linked to histories of exploitation and exclusion – the domination of women, of aboriginal peoples, of the descendants of African slaves, and so on.

Discrimination

Generally, social discrimination occurs when agents who are members of different social categories (men/women, whites/blacks, citizens/non-citizens, etcetera) have different levels of access to resources and/or goods, due in some way to the impact of this social distinction. Either market processes or governmental allocation mechanisms can bring about this differential access to resources and/or goods. The impact of social discrimination is to widen differences in access to or control of economic resources for members of the groups subject to discrimination.

Discrimination comes to life in economic processes when those who discriminate also control a disproportionate amount of resources. Indeed, we might speculate that those who are discriminated against may very well harbour personal dislike of the class of agents containing discriminators. For example, a person of colour may be suspicious of all whites as a consequence of the fact that some whites dislike people of colour and deny them fair and full access to economic resources. If those suffering discrimination do not control resource flows on which those doing the discriminating depend, this dislike has no impact on economic processes or outcomes.

The distinction between agent-based and structural approaches also helps in understanding social discrimination. Three types of discriminatory market processes can be identified: (1) personal discrimination (bigotry): differential outcomes that result from personal preferences regarding a membership distinction (whites/blacks, for example); (2) rational discrimination: differential outcomes which arise when agents use a membership distinction to make valid statistical inferences about the distinct market prospects of the members of different groups; (3) structural discrimination: differential outcomes that arise because of identifiable differences in the resources controlled by (or available to) the members of the groups in question.

Category (2) refers to outcomes based on anticipated disparities, category (3) to those based on existing disparities. An example based on gender discrimination will clarify the difference. Suppose men and women are members of a loan pool for a limited number of loans; and suppose credit will be allocated on the basis of their current levels of wealth and their prospective levels of earned income. Women are subject to structural discrimination if they have lower average wealth levels than men and are chosen less often for loans on this basis; if female and male wealth levels are the same, women are subject to rational discrimination if loans are based on prospective income and females' average prospective incomes are lower than males'.

The personal and structural approaches to poverty are paralleled by discrimination categories (1) and (3). Category (1), however, shifts the spotlight from the poor to victims of discrimination. To see the difference, consider a middle-class household that attempts to refinance its home in a neighbourhood with many nearby residents who are in poverty. This household may be subject to discrimination because of lenders' unwillingness to finance homes in areas with large proportions of poor households. This sort of practice is termed 'redlining'. Redlining, a form of rational discrimination, occurs when the location of a household or business is used as the criterion for making low-cost 'rational' decisions. Banks that seldom or never make loans in areas with large numbers of black or poor residents are redlining.[2]

Social discrimination cannot be traced exclusively to personal hostility (personal discrimination) by those controlling resources: the second and third categories of discrimination can arise even with neutral racial preferences. Indeed, the battleground of much litigation and controversy over racial discrimination in the US is the middle category. 'Rational' discrimination can arise for several reasons, and can take the form of either discrimination against individuals or redlining. Rational discrimination against individuals may arise if a strong correlation exists between the members of a given social group and some characteristics that systematically affect group members' desirability in a given market transaction. For example, if blacks are 'last hired and first fired' in the labour market, then blacks will be less creditworthy in the loan market, all else equal, owing to their being more likely than whites to have reduced income flows (and hence to default). A lender would then use rational discrimination if blacks were systematically denied credit *because they were black*.

So there can be racial bias without racial intent – there can be, so to speak, 'benign' perpetrators of discrimination, motivated not by blind hatred but by profit. This middle category of discrimination is insidious because it can affect the judgement of those who discriminate very subtly. For example, a person controlling wealth may regret that those discriminated against are less creditworthy than others, without investigating his own biases.

Poverty and discrimination

Clearly there are overlaps between the categories of discrimination and poverty. In effect, poverty is a condition, a situation, and discrimination denotes social processes that can generate or deepen this condition. Investigations of discrimination have generally been undertaken far more frequently in higher-income nations than lower-income nations. We might speculate that the problem of fair access to resources arises to a greater extent when there are more resources to be accessed. This doesn't mean that latent or even overt processes of social discrimination are not at work in nations with high population proportions in poverty. Social discrimination, in these cases, may take an overtly political form, or may spring to life as material circumstances improve.

Policies aimed at reducing poverty and discrimination also intertwine. When those in poverty include populations that are subject to discrimination, policies aimed at encouraging initiative by individuals in poverty can work hand-in-hand with anti-discriminatory legislation. Ensuring fair access to resources allocated through the market will in this case increase the numbers of those escaping poverty by their own initiative. Turning to the structural view of poverty, reducing the extent of poverty depends on decreasing some of the structural inequalities with which they contend. If most or all of those who are poor are members of a class that is subject to discrimination, then reducing the extent of discrimination will have the effect of reducing poverty. Indeed, in many societies poverty reduction can be a powerful justification for overturning discriminatory practices.

■

A Spatial Approach to Development, Poverty, and Discrimination

This section and the next consider poverty and discrimination in the context of two distinctive approaches to social and economic dynamics. This section explores the implications of spatiality, and the next major section (p. 240) develops some Keynesian perspectives. This is followed (p. 246) by a section that explores a spatialized Keynesian approach to poverty, discrimination, and development.

Spatial separation is a fundamental component of human existence. After childbirth, no two people can occupy the same space at the same time. This means that all transactions between people, whether economic or otherwise, occur across space. Despite this omnipresent reality of spatiality, spatiality *per se* is often only implicit – even when clearly present – in discussions of poverty, discrimination, and development.[3]

The notion of the inherently spatial character of social life is associated with the fields of economic and social geography. This is not to say that spatiality has been treated in a consistent way. In recent years, some geo-graphers (notably Lefebvre 1991 and Soja 1996) have insisted that the spatial dimension of social reality has an independent impact on the charac-ter of social processes, which cannot be subsumed in any other dimensions of reality (such as social class, race, and so on). On the other hand, other geographers have argued that the spread of information technology together with the globalization of economic flows have led to the obliteration of geography. This latter view is too strong – it ignores the continuing significance of borders and of spatial separation.

Indeed, we might argue that the very fact that space–time separation has been reduced or even virtually eliminated for some – the global citizens of the new world order – only deepens the significance of spatial separation and of borders for those without the means to communicate or send resources instantaneously across borders. At the same time, it is impossible to write about space without acknowledging that it is virtualized – that the centre of decisions disappears, even while action can occur at an ever-amplifying distance. A decision taken in Tokyo can affect Rio as if it were in the same neighbourhood. This cannot but affect development plans. Then there is the impact of what is decided. There we cannot get away from the traditional sense of space.

This section first reviews three sets of ideas that provide insights into the implications of space for understanding discrimination, poverty, and development – racial/poverty proximity models, urban agglomeration models, and city-as-small-open-economy models. The last two spatial approaches have been developed to explain phenomena other than poverty and discrimination; however, they are introduced because they constitute key links in understanding the spatial dynamics of social discrimination and poverty.

Spatial aspects of social discrimination

Some scholars interested in the problem of racial inequality in the US have explored the role of space in the dynamics of social discrimination.[4] Schelling (1971) created a framework that shows how racial animus can lead to racial segregation. Specifically, every agent occupies a square within a checkerboard grid; some agents are type B, and some type W, and some squares are empty. Each agent decides in turn whether to stay still or move. The W agents move when too high a share of their neighbours are B, if a square with a lower B-neighbour share is available. B agents never move due to the proportions of B and W agents nearby. It is readily shown that racial segregation occurs. This model then depicts a kind of tragedy, in that racial hostility colours outcomes even when only a significant minority of one racial group has racial animus.

Massey and Denton (1993) developed a more complex checkerboard model. These authors were not focused on white flight, but on the related hypothesis that minorities had been left behind in the inner-core areas due to cultural deficiencies of the sort that Lewis (1961) identified. Whites' shifts away from the urban inner core may thus be due to their desire to avoid contact with the urban underclass, not inherent racial bias. This proposition provided cover for the federal government's shift from policy activism to 'benign neglect' of the inner city (in Daniel P. Moynihan's phrase) in the 1970s and 1980s. Wilson (1987) mounted an energetic counter-attack by arguing that class dynamics and not cultural dysfunctionality explain the emergence of the minority underclass in American cities.

Massey and Denton link Wilson's argument to the residential mobility process. They posit that concrete social and economic characteristics of urban residents affect the social viability and stability of the various locations of the urban grid they occupy. Suppose, as does Schelling, that every agent occupies a cell in a matrix. Then if an agent lives in a cell surrounded by residents whose probability of employment is lower than elsewhere, her welfare is affected because she lives in a high-unemployment area. If this agent also lives in a neighbourhood whose residents have low levels of educational attainment and high crime rates, then this agent's chances for success may be systematically affected by these environmental character-istics.

These two frameworks suggest two key implications of the spatial dimen-sion in social relations. First, agent preferences can encompass the spatial distribution of other agents. There are spill-over effects rooted in preferences that can generate agent mobility for reasons that would be invisible if space were ruled out. Second, spill-overs across space can carry dense socio-economic content, and deeply affect behaviour. These two frameworks have a common limitation – neither incorporates any attention to economic processes. As it turns out, two economic frameworks are available that explicitly incorporate spatial considerations. We elucidate these economic approaches and then consider their implications for these two social models.

Increasing returns to scale and agglomeration

In recent years, due to the impulse provided by Paul Krugman, theorists and practitioners have increasingly recognized the importance in urban develop-ment of industrial (and other types of) agglomeration due to increasing returns to scale, spill-over effects, and externalities.[5] Indeed, Krugman has argued that industrial agglomeration is the outstanding 'stylized fact' in the field of economic geography (Krugman 1991a: 7).

Krugman's work on spatial questions was initiated by his May 1989 paper 'History vs expectations' (published as 1991b). Krugman observes that 'positive external economies in production' can be seen as 'a way to formulate rigorously a number of heterodox challenges to standard economic doctrine' – among them, the idea of the uneven pace of development of rich and poor nations.[6]

Krugman then developed an increasing-returns spatial model, which he refined over a period of years (see, in particular, Krugman 1991a). In this model, households are spread evenly across the spatial landscape; they engage in agriculture, which provides their subsistence and also income they use to buy products manufactured by the industrial sector. Meanwhile, every producer makes and sets the price of a unique good. Industrial monopolies arise naturally because every firm's average costs fall as its output expands.[7] But firms do not earn excessive profits, for, if they did, new firms would enter, produce close substitutes for existing goods, and drive profits to zero.[8]

This framework shows how competitive, high-productivity industrial clusters can emerge. The question is why. Marshall, 80 years earlier, under-stood that spill-overs – externalities – of some kind must be involved. Marshall suggested two kinds of spill-overs: the benefits from pooling the supply of labour and the demand for specialized non-tradable inputs; and the spill-overs from concentrated technology and training expenditures. The second set of factors have been emphasized in models of 'endogenous growth' (Romer 1990). Krugman suggests another sort of externality: if the industrial sector itself constitutes a principal source of demand for industrial products, and if transportation costs increase with distance, then firms will cluster because they produce under increasing returns. In formulating this model, Krugman inverts two assumptions of standard trade theory: in the received wisdom, tradable goods can be costlessly transported, but factors of production are immobile; in his model, factors of production are costlessly mobile but the transportation of tradable goods is costly. Thus, whereas comparative advantage results from 'natural' advantages, in this agglomeration model it may be socially constructed, and trade flows may be what they are due to historical accident, not necessity. Increasing returns of the technological and market spill-over type, together with transportation costs, can generate both core–periphery patterns within a country and the surprising localization of some economic activities (Krugman (1991a) uses the example of musical instruments in Elkhart, Indiana).

Other theorists have supplemented Krugman's work on industrial agglomeration by examining other path-dependent processes driven by increasing returns and spill-overs. Benabou (1993 and 1994) has shown how education and skill spill-overs can affect neighbourhood growth.

The spatial microeconomy as an open macroeconomy

The previous spatial concepts all pertain to market and social dynamics that can be observed within a given spatial unit at any scale – a region, a city, a neighbourhood. But one key aspect of space is, as noted, separation. Any region contains cities as sub-units; any city contains neighbourhoods; any neighbourhood, blocks. And between any separated sub-areas at any level are borders.

Borders are considered explicitly in macroeconomic models – trade flows and financial flows across them are commonly measured. Actually, the relationship of flows across the borders of any two distinct and enclosed spatial areas can be examined. Consider Figure 9.1 overleaf; there are two distinct spatial areas, the 'inner core' and the 'suburban ring'. The suburban ring has a goods-and-services 'surplus' or 'deficit' with the inner core over any period of time (such as a quarter). The situation is exactly analogous to the case of trade across national borders. The consequences of unbalanced trade flows are well known. The trade balance of a given nation equals its exports (X) minus its imports (M). Countries with a trade surplus (such that the trade balance, X − M, is positive) can export capital to the rest of the world, and vice versa. In general, the dollars that nation A uses to buy imports must be generated either by other nations' (financial or direct) dollar investments in nation A, or by nation A's previously accumulated stock of dollars. The financial balance for nation A can be written as follows:

(Change in A's dollar reserves) + (Foreigners' savings in A)

= (Nation A trade balance) + (Net income transfers to A)   (1)

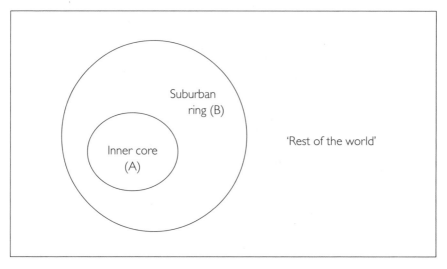

Figure 9.1 A Metropolitan Area: 'Inner Core' versus 'Suburban Ring'

Equation (1) is sometimes understood as 'trade-driven', such that trade deficits (surpluses) net of transfer flows are understood to dictate movements in foreign savings. But it is important to see that equation (1) can just as readily be 'finance-driven', with capital inflows dictating the resources available for disposal within an area, in the form of either trade deficits or through the build-up of wealth stocks. In any event, (1) *must* balance.

Stock-flow imbalances normally occur across borders; hence disequilibria occur frequently, and adjustment processes are continually at work. In the case of the United States, for example, a negative trade balance is offset by positive foreigners' savings. Recent experience in Latin America and Asia illustrates that severe macroeconomic disruptions can occur when large-scale inflows to borrower nations slow or reverse, especially when these nations' reserves are exhausted. Indeed, the financing of investment positions across national borders creates an additional source of Minskyian financial instability (Dymski 1998b). To repeat, then, there will be equilibrium in the value of goods, services, and financial flows across spatial borders only by an unplanned coincidence. The *general case* is one of disequilibria across borders. This means that *adjustment* is an ongoing process.

For the intra-metropolitan border between inner core and suburb in Figure 9.1, equation (1) becomes:

(Change in inner-core financial wealth) + (Inner-core investment outside the inner core) – (External investment in inner-core)

= (Inner-core trade balance) + (Income transfers)　　　　　(2)

Equation (2) shows that the inner core must finance its expenditures on imported goods and services either by selling goods or labour 'abroad' (in the suburbs or outside the city), by accepting income transfers, by attracting 'foreign' savings, or by spending down accumulated wealth. This equation emphasizes that the 'inner core' area of an urban area can be viewed as a developing country. This dichotomization can be used at multiple levels – for example, within Brazil, the capital and current account of the *favelas* in Rio with the formalized portions of that city could (in principle) be computed. Within the formalized areas of Rio, in turn, a current account–capital account balance could in principle be computed for every square block, and in turn for every apartment house in any given block.

As in the case of national development, the location of production and consumption, the volume of cross-border trade – both with foreign buyers and with buyers in other domestic locations – and cross-border capital and credit flows provide the architecture of cash flows against which successful or abortive local development plays out. And as in the case of developing nations, urban cross-border balances can be finance-driven, not trade-driven. Consider the case of the creation of new suburban developments (such as those currently being constructed in Corona in Southern California, or in Barra de Tijuca, in Rio). This construction takes the form of initial invest-ment flows into an undeveloped region (the construction site) with a trade deficit (imported bricks and wood, 'guest workers,' and so on). This perspec-tive makes clear that all physical development in urban areas involves financial speculation in the sense of an inflow of moneys in advance of any promise of a return flow of revenues.

Implications for discrimination and poverty

What are the implications of these two spatial economic approaches for discrimination and poverty – especially given that discrimination and poverty already have spatial social dimensions? These frameworks show that the spatial distribution of businesses will affect (and be affected by) the revenues and profits of individual firms; and consequently, firms tend to cluster to capture spill-overs of various kinds. Consequently, the location of firms and businesses across urban space will tend to be 'lumpy', not smooth. Further, agents and firms invariably exist within spaces that are bordered, the flows across which alter the wealth/goods balances in individual neighbourhoods, regions, and nations. Wealth thus either builds up or is subtracted over time, in spaces in which households and businesses capture positive and/or negative spill-overs.

To link these economic processes to the social spatial dynamics that Schelling and Massey and Denton explored, note first that occupying any formal-sector spatial location in a capitalist economy (especially urban locations) requires substantial wealth, income, or both. This holds *a fortiori* for moves from one formal-sector location to another. So these social models are both unrealistic in that households cannot locate where they wish – they cannot hop like chequers among open 'squares.' Instead, economic units must have resources, usually substantial resources, if they are to move. And if income flows are too low, as in the case of dire poverty, it may be impossible even to maintain occupancy of a given space.

Thus, implementing a strategy of moving from one 'square' to another in an urban setting, in search of 'squares' surrounded by fewer non-white units, requires resources. Conversely, a unit may be located in a neighbourhood with negative spill-over affects, which adversely affects its socio-economic opportunity set; but this doesn't mean that it can do anything about it. The poverty 'trap' involves, in part, a spatial fix.

These ideas about spatialized social and economic processes – discrimination as a mobility dynamic, poverty as a spill-over effect, agglomeration effects in industrial location, and cross-border balances – together suggest a coherent story of the relationship between spatialization, discrimination, and poverty. The work of Massey and Denton suggests that (1) proximity to neighbours that are lower-income has a palpable social cost, which carries a market value; (2) so those who have the ability to move away from cost-generating neighbours, do so when they can; (3) leading to concentrations of lower-income residents in some places, and of upper- and middle-income residents in other places. Schelling's work on racial preferences indicates that widespread racial preferences could have the same effect. So either 'real, if barely measurable' spill-overs or 'irrational racial preferences', or both, could generate a separating dynamic in the population of residents.

Because of this separating dynamic, social discrimination motives and sensitivity to socio-economic spill-overs will reinforce one another. Layered on top of this are economic processes of business and regional development. Businesses, especially successful ones, tend to group together to capture spill-overs of various kinds. So business firms will be over-represented in some spatial areas, but under-represented in others. Consequently, some areas will have strong cross-border balances, permitting the build-up of wealth and/or the purchase of many goods and services from external areas. Other areas will have current-account deficits and low levels of good/service exchange. The poor will be disproportionately in areas of the latter type. These lower-income/wealth areas will also tend to have over-representations of households that are subject to social discrimination. In sum, poverty and discrimination have implications for community development because of the spatial specificity of social processes of exclusion; further, there are community or social dimensions of the economic or social exclusion experienced by households whose members are poor and/or subject to social discrimination.

■

Some Keynesian Ideas about Economic Development and Poverty

Writing on Keynesian approaches to economics fills entire libraries.[9] Here, we bring in some ideas from Keynes and the Keynesian tradition which are pertinent to our discussion of poverty and discrimination: uncertainty; aggregate demand; financial fragility; and financial structure. This section presents these ideas largely without emphasizing the implications of spatialization *per se*; that is done in the following major section.

Uncertainty, development, and poverty

Our selective intervention begins with the recognition that, in any Keynesian approach, the notion that processes with stochastic outcomes can be uniformly treated as if they confront situations of probabilistically defined risk is set aside as an impossibility. One of Keynes's deepest methodological commitments is to the idea that the future is fundamentally unknowable. At the same time, all economic units are engaged in 'real time' processes: processes wherein irreversible decisions are made at one point of time, and realizations are had only later. The degree of unease that this causes to economic units depends on how uncertain is any project they might consider, how much time will pass between initial commitment and final outcome, and the size of commitment required. Everyday tasks normally can be regarded as governed by probabilistic risk without much harm; non-repetitive tasks with large consequences entail uncertainty. For many urban investment projects, uncertainty arises at least in part because irreversible investments must be sunk into spatial areas whose longer-term prospects are not clear. Faced with uncertainty about outcomes, those undertaking time-using projects can mitigate their fear and improve their odds of success by pre-coordinating their activities, looking for new ways to get involved, etcetera.

Uncertainty and economic development are linked in that the gradual construction of infrastructure and capacity in a given location creates more predictability, more confidence for those who might risk long-term commitments. Poverty is linked with uncertainty in that economic units who are poor have much more uncertainty about their life circumstances than upper-income units. They control less of their environment, have a more constrained choice set, and have less protection against downside loss.

Aggregate demand, macroeconomic balance, and development

A second key aspect of Keynesian theory is its recognition of the importance of aggregate cash flows in determining levels of economic activity. In macroeconomic theory, these aggregate cash flows generally involve the level of aggregate demand. The aggregate demand consists of expenditures on currently produced goods and services. The focus on goods produced in the current period means that this concept implicitly measures employment and capacity utilization. In Keynesian theory, this demand for goods and services determines the level of output the economy can absorb. This notion is embodied in the Keynesian multiplier – the notion that expenditures on goods in a given economy that are independent of that economy's level of economic activity will lead to further rounds of expenditure. Demand leads supply in the sense that demand independently validates supply commitments.[10]

In urban economics, the Keynesian multiplier concept is transformed into the base-multiplier model. In this model, the level of expenditure in a given area (a metropolitan area, usually) depends on two factors: first, the goods or services that this area's firms sell to other areas; second, the multiplier effects of the production of these goods and services. This latter depends in the case of an urban area on the extent of supply-side inter-linkages internal to this area. Because many interlinkages are incomplete, and in effect many intermediate goods are imported into any given urban area, urban multipliers are normally considerably smaller than those for national economies.

In sum, aggregate demand is viewed in Keynesian theory as providing the financial scaffolding for supply–demand relations in any set of micromarkets. It will be useful here to set out a simple formal representation of aggregate demand and supply. Aggregate demand (AD) can be written as follows:

Output demanded: $AD = C + I + G + X$ (3)

where C = consumption, I = investment, G = government spending, X = exports. Consumption is defined here as the act of buying and consuming domestically produced goods and services for everyday use. Investment refers to the purchase of goods and/or services so as to expand the level of a unit's assets.[11] G and X represent the government sector's and foreigners' purchases of locally produced goods and services. These are the dollars chasing currently produced goods and services, and thus determining how much of what is produced is taken. Now consider a depiction of aggregate supply, AS:

Output earned: $AS = C + S + T + M$ (4)

where S = domestic savings, T = taxes, M = imports. Equation (4) represents the idea that the production of goods and services in any time period gives rise to income claims of several types, and these incomes can be used in one of the four ways shown here: to buy locally made goods and services (C), or foreign-made goods and services (M), to pay taxes (T), and to save (S). Saving, the act of not-spending income, can involve either building up idle monetary stocks or purchasing financial assets (bank deposits, bonds, securities, etcetera).

To determine an equilibrium find the level of output at which aggregate demand equals aggregate supply (AD = AS, using (3) = (4)):

$I + (G\text{-}T) = S - (X - M)$ (5)

This macroeconomic balance specifies that investment spending plus net government spending must be supported by domestic savings net of export earnings. This is a key equation in understanding the determinants of any area's economic growth. A useful way to think of this balance is as follows. Macroeconomic policy stimulus in the Americas and Western Europe in the 'Golden Age' period from the Second World War to the early 1970s focused on the manipulation of investment spending (via monetary policy) and of government spending as means of maintaining stable growth. When applied to developing nations, investment is especially privileged, because investment expenditures build up assets and hence socially and economically productive capacity. More investment now means not only enhanced demand for goods and services in this period, but an expanded capacity to generate goods and services in future periods. Investment is financed by savings – by some units' withholding of income from consumption. This pool of savings may also be required to support government deficit spending (which occurs when $G > T$). From a Keynesian perspective, the key to development is then private and public investment expenditure, prominently featured on the left-hand side of equation (5).

An important alternative view is the neoclassical approach, a more market-oriented perspective held by many economists at the International Monetary Fund. The neoclassical approach asserts that export earnings (the other term on the right-hand side of equation (5)) and fiscal discipline are crucial for successful sustained development. One component of this view is the 'financial deepening' hypothesis, originated by MacKinnon and Shaw in the early 1970s, which prioritizes the right-hand side of equation (5). In this hypothesis, the key to development is the creation of a market-driven structure of financial intermediaries that can encourage saving behaviour and channel available saving to the highest-return activities available.[12]

One implication of the neoclassical approach is the Kuznets hypothesis: that is, at the 'take-off' stage, the development process entails increasing income and wealth inequality; as a developing society achieves economic maturity, its inequality levels will be reduced. The Kuznets hypothesis is premised on the financial deepening model: the increasing inequality it anticipates is required to permit the creation of the savings pools required to support rapid accumulation. Insofar as the development process often entails the creation of new urban spaces, this means that economic development will go hand-in-hand with the creation of more urban impoverishment.

The relative merits of development strategies built, respectively, on the left-hand and right-hand sides of equation (5) have been the subject of sharp disagreement and controversy among policy makers and economists. The rapid growth of many East Asian nations in the 1970s and 1980s provided evidence that financial liberalization and higher interest rates were not required to generate high saving levels. These nations also followed a path led by government guidance and planning, not a market-led path; they were able largely to avoid the creation of impoverished urban areas, and in fact enjoyed a more egalitarian distribution of income and wealth than the US and most European nations. The late-1990s crisis of East Asia, more than a decade after the government-led economies of Latin America were plunged into the 1980s Latin American debt crisis, provided fuel for sceptics of market-led growth, even while illustrating the dangerous volatility of a post-financial-liberalization world.

Financial fragility and poverty

As a micro perspective, a key theme in Keynesian theory is the financial fragility of economic units and the financial instability of the economy. Hyman Minsky developed the notion of financial fragility to describe the impact of uncertainty on economic units that must take illiquid asset positions in real time to build up their wealth and resources. An economic unit is financially fragile to the extent that the interest obligations it has to meet to support its asset position may exceed its net operating revenue. Minsky (1975) argues that financial fragility rises over the economic cycle, because economic units tend to take on more debt and become more leveraged in 'good' times; eventually, however, some overextended economic units cannot meet their obligations, triggering a period of financial instability characterized by asset-price devaluations, bankruptcies, and debt deflation. Subsequent work on Minsky's framework has shown that in an open-economy setting, rapid and unanticipated downward revisions in currency value are sufficient to generate financial instability (Dymski 1998b).

The details of Minsky's theory need not be pursued here. Instead, the links between Minsky's financial-fragility framework and poverty might be highlighted. The key point is that those who are poor and who are subject to discrimination are especially vulnerable to financial fragility and instability. Living in poverty means surviving with an inadequate and unstable cash flow. Being a target of social discrimination means being subject to unfair treatment in market transactions, and sometimes being denied access to financial and non-financial assets for arbitrary reasons. These circumstances result in precarious cash flows, enhance the extent of financial fragility and instability, and thus make financial crisis more likely. Just as small businesses are far more likely to enter bankruptcy than are larger ones, poor households are far more likely to experience financial turmoil than are middle-income and rich households. And breakdowns in cash flow and overwhelming debt obligations bring locational and vocational shifts, as new sources of income are sought in new places, and as new household members enter the labour force or migrate elsewhere. If successive generations of a family are poor, they are unlikely to be poor in the same way and in the same place.

Financial structure and local investment and savings

The three elements of Keynesian theory identified thus far are well established. A fourth, only tangentially related to Keynes's work, should also be mentioned because of its relevance for the theme of this chapter. That is, the financial structure of any neighbourhood or city is an important determinant of economic outcomes therein.[13] Financial structure here means the population of formal- and informal-sector firms and offices that are engaged in the payments mechanism, the collecting and disposition of financial savings, the assessment of creditworthiness and financial investment options, and the provision of credit and capital. Commercial banks are uniquely important because they engage in all three activities of credit provision, deposit collection, and payments services. However, many institutions in a given community may provide one or more of these services. Further, there may be some specialization in financial services, depending on the income and wealth levels of households and businesses.

There are several impacts of a robust financial structure on economic outcomes in any local community. First, financial service providers have some of the characteristics of public goods – a community with conveniently located and plentiful financial firms will have low transactions costs for merchants and households, plentiful financial savings options, and numerous professionals specializing in localized credit provision. Second, a robust structure of credit-granting institutions that compete among themselves and with lenders in other areas will generate a substantial volume of information about individual borrowers and about the area as a whole. This will overcome informational barriers to lending that may arise due to asymmetric and incomplete information regarding potential borrowers. Third, a substantial volume of credit commitments in a given area will signal other prospective lenders regarding the viability of this area as a credit risk. Given the path dependence of credit-market outcomes, this will lead to a fourth impact: the community will be on a trajectory to receive more credit and capital, creating opportunities for more wealth accumulation – especially on fixed geographic assets such as homes and local businesses – than in areas that are less well-served. In effect, the financial structure in any locality provides the physical embodiment of the investment–savings mechanism that is at the heart of the entire macroeconomic process (see equation (5)).

In communities without adequate financial infrastructures – that is to say, in lower-income communities, and in communities of residents who are subject to social discrimination – a very different scenario unfolds. Transactions are insecure and costly; merchants must operate with low levels of cash, and take special provisions to protect their premises. It will be difficult for residents to find outlets for financial savings – indeed, there may be none. At the same time, residents and local business owners may regard the economic circumstances of this area as too uncertain to merit investments in local fixed geographic assets (except those that enhance personal security). The area will be regarded as a poor credit risk based on second-hand information; indeed, the theory of rational discrimination suggests that if prospective lenders anticipate very few loans in this area, it will not be cost-effective to replace this second-hand data with the first-hand information that might overturn this impression. So informational barriers to lending will be high. Few or no other lenders will be attracted to this area, except for bottom-feeder lenders interested in earning some fast money by exploiting the absence of mainstream credit and savings mechanisms. Rather than building up financial wealth and fixed real assets, local residents and businesses will gradually spend down their balances and liquidate their assets; the local financial structure facilitates decumulation, not accumulation.

■

A Spatial Keynesian Approach to Development, Poverty, and Discrimination

Earlier, I emphasized that spatial social and economic dynamics are always present, even if not given explicit theoretical recognition. For our purpose, explicit attention to spatial boundaries is crucial because of the physical divides and different structural circumstances that separate communities on the basis of poverty and social discrimination. This section, then, explores spatial aspects of the Keynesian ideas introduced above, concerning macroeconomic balance, uncertainty reduction, financial fragility and instability, and financial structure. We begin with the Keynesian aggregate demand/supply framework. This can be spatialized in two different ways: first, by emphasizing cross-border goods flows; second, by emphasizing cross-border financial flows and the investment/savings nexus.

A spatialized Keynesian multiplier approach

When applied to a region or city, as noted above, the Keynesian multiplier is transformed into the base-multiplier model, a framework that regards all economic activity within this spatial area as activated by external demand for tradable goods and services.[14]

One version of this model is of special interest – the two-region case, which involves a region or city with two spatially distinct zones, that in turn trades with the rest of the world. Let us suppose, as we did above, that the poor and those who are subject to social discrimination are segregated spatially from the remainder of the population – in the area we denoted region A. For simplicity, the area in question produces just two goods that are exported to the outside world: inner-city region A produces X_1, and suburban region B produces X_2. These two goods are both 'basics' – that is, X_1 is required for the production of X_2 and vice versa. Suppose also that the workers and capitalists making X_1 live in A, and those making X_2 live in B. A sustainable equilibrium for this two-region economy entails balance in production levels, in monetary value, and in intra-regional 'trade'. Equilibrium in production requires that:

(X_1 produced) = (X_1 used in making X_1 and X_2) + (External demand for X_1)

(X_2 produced) = (X_2 used in making X_1 and X_2) + (External demand for X_2) (6)

It is easy to solve this equation to find the overall amounts of X_1 and X_2 that should be produced given the level of external demand. 'One-region' urban multiplier models stop there. But two-region models have extra conditions, which make sustainable equilibria between regions A and B unlikely. For one thing, long-run equilibrium requires two monetary inter-sectoral balances between A and B (which is to say, between industries 1 and 2).[15] These are unlikely to prevail, since the variables involved are determined nationally, not locally. Further, for a self-sustaining equilibrium: flows of value between regions A and B must equate.[16] If workers live and work in their 'home' regions, this balance is:

(Value of X_1 used in producing X_2) + (Value of X_1 consumed and invested in region B) = (Value of X_2 used in producing X_1) + (Value of X_2 consumed and invested in region A)   (7)

Equation (7) entails an intra-regional restriction on the relative prices of X_1 and X_2 which does not arise in aspatial input–output models. Urban or other contiguous areas are likely to systematically violate this equation, as no direct mechanism for bringing about a spatial equilibrium exists. Equation (7) is a zero probability event. If so, then, it implies arbitrary transfers of value from A to B or vice versa. These transfers are aligned with the distribution of the production of goods and services in these areas. In the US, the spatial distribution of production has evolved considerably over time. Initially, production facilities were located in inner-core areas such as A, while workers and managers increasingly moved to suburban areas such as B. Then came a period in which some production facilities moved to suburban areas, generating intensive if uneven exchanges between A and B areas as described above. The next phase was one of the isolated urban core, wherein no production facilities remain active in the inner core. In this situation, the inner core runs a trade deficit with the suburbs (and with the rest of the world); it can subsist only through wealth reductions or payments transfers (as when inner-core residents work in the suburbs).

In other nations, production and residential spaces have very different relationships. In most cities outside the US, marginalized areas have historic-ally been suburban; the inner core has been, and often remained, a locus of elite commercial activity and residences. In Brazil, *favelas* are the equivalent of the US's segregated inner-core 'slum' communities. But most *favelas* have never been focal points for the production of tradable goods and services: they have always relied, in effect, on earnings brought back by residents working in formalized communities beyond the *favela* borders. This is not to say that no economic activity takes place in *favelas* or other marginal communities in Latin America, Africa, Asia, and Europe; to the contrary. However, most of the economic activity of these marginal communities involves the redistribution of cash earned outside and brought back – not production integrated into the broader matrix of tradables and basic goods.

A spatialized investment-saving nexus

To explore the implications of shifting industrial locations further, we now turn to a spatialization of the investment/savings approach. This involves re-imagining the aggregate-demand/supply framework as a subnational construct and considering explicitly the interlinkages between cross-border conditions and aggregate demand/supply equilibria.

Equation (2) showed how equation (1) for national cross-border constraints could be reinterpreted for subnational closed economic spaces. We can similarly reinterpret equation (5) by again recontextualizing equation (1). To see this, note first that equation (1) and equation (5) both share a term – the trade balance, X – M. We can substitute for (X – M) in equation (5) using the 'Nation A trade balance' term in equation (1), giving us this expression for aggregate demand and supply in a given nation (or in a given subnational area):

$$I + (G - T) + dW = S + S^F + Y^F \qquad (8), \text{ or, in words,}$$

(Investment expenditures) + (Government expenditures net of taxes collected) + (Changes in financial wealth held internally)

= (Domestic saving) + (Foreigners' savings) + (Net income transfers to this area) (8').

That is, investment and net-government expenditures can be financed by domestic savings, foreigners' savings, and earnings and transfer payments to residents (including residents who work outside the community). If these transfers and savings flows are significant, then financial wealth levels will build up; but when income transfers and savings flows fall, domestic wealth stocks may erode. For example, when new suburban areas such as B are developed, investment expenditures there rise, supported by 'foreign savings' committed by developers, prospective residents, and financial institutions. An inner-core area subject to 'disinvestment' – the closure of production facilities being relocated elsewhere – has negative investment, paralleled by negative foreign savings.

Spatial aspects of uncertainty, financial instability, and financial structure
One of the foremost Keynesians, Paul Davidson (1994), has emphasized the uncertainty-reduction role of government stabilization and regulation policies: establishing fixed or predictable exchange rates and cash flows, with low and stable interest rates, permits economic agents to develop longer-range plans than they otherwise would. We might add that when agents make the illiquid investments that implement their longer-run plans, these commitments build up real asset structures in the spatial communities that house their facilities. As noted, these sorts of investments are unevenly distributed across space – hence, some areas become more secure sites for investment, while others lag. Similarly, prospective homeowners look for homes in areas with secure values and active resale markets; prices and resale prospects elsewhere are far more uncertain.[17] In effect, just as overall uncertainty about investment prospects can be increased or dampened by macro-level policies, this same sort of uncertainty varies across space within cities and

regions. Insofar as market dynamics involve path dependence and spill-over effects (that is, increasing returns), then if left alone market forces will tend to widen the uncertainty gap between neighbourhoods.

Financial fragility and instability can also vary systematically across spatial communities. At least two of the key elements affecting the degree of financial fragility – asset values and cash flows from economic activities – are more unstable for those living in lower-income communities and/or in communities whose residents are subject to social discrimination. So whatever the degree of financial fragility in an economy as a whole, the degree of fragility will be exaggerated in some areas. Any given economic unit will thus be affected not only by its own balance-sheet stress, but by that of the residential and business units surrounding it. We have already noted that the character of the financial structure in a given spatial community can encourage or discourage savings, long-term investment, and the acquisition of geographically fixed assets.

Aggregate Keynesian dynamics, poverty, and discrimination

These structural Keynesian dynamics, as they play out over the spatial terrains of urban areas the world over all, have remarkable implications for the problems of poverty and discrimination. For one thing, they create an encompassing macro situation that no small business can avoid. Micro market equilibria are overwhelmed by these macro dynamics.

To the extent that the poor are spatially isolated from the broader society, and that those subject to social discrimination are segregated as well, distinct spatial communities of the poor and of discriminatees will arise and persist. Poverty and social discrimination then take on a spatial and community dimension just as real as individuals' material and capability deprivation. Communities of the poor, insofar as they are isolated from the broader economy's production nexus, are sustained by repatriated earnings, income transfers, and the decumulation of wealth.[18] The earnings and transfers received in these communities are just sufficient to meet subsistence needs, ruling out saving or wealth building on a systematic basis.

This perspective makes it clear that anti-poverty or anti-discrimination initiatives that address one dimension of the community's structural deficit, especially on an individual basis, may be insufficient to reverse the community's fix. For example, a homeownership initiative aimed at encouraging neighbourhood revitalization will not succeed if cash flows from residents' jobs are not systematically strengthened as well. This is not to say that such an initiative is useless: to the contrary, the formula for successful upper-income suburbs is precisely a combination of repatriated earnings and transfer payments combined with community-specific investment. A *favela* or inner-core area in which a significant share of residents have good jobs for a sustained period can be an investment locus. The transformation required is profound, however: the common wisdom that only a fool would keep her money anything but liquid must be replaced by a belief that investment in neighbourhood-specific assets will pay off. It is not only macroeconomic circumstances that are crucial in imagining this kind of shift; the presence and behaviour of mainstream financial institutions are also crucial.

■

Conclusion

Everywhere in the world, policy makers, activists, and government officials find areas whose residents have substantial levels of poverty, however that is defined – inner-city neighbourhoods in the US, *favelas* in Brazil, townships in South Africa, and so on. How can we explain the poverty we see? There are many different views, most focusing on whether the people in such communities are responsible for their conditions, or whether they have lacked access to the resources required for self-improvement. This chapter has asserted that the very spatial separation of these communities itself has important economic consequences, which are very well illuminated by ideas associated with Keynesian economics, suitably adapted to subnational areas. The Keynesian bottom line regarding successful management of national economies is that this requires attention to the sufficiency of aggregate demand, to the level of uncertainty, to the consequences of financial fragility, and to the character of financial structure. Maintaining growth and avoiding the social damage associated with unemployed labour, idle factories, and shuttered shops requires attention to the structural integrity of the economy, at both macro and micro levels. This chapter has developed a framework showing that these same points hold for spatial sub-areas within national economies.

This chapter has explored the overlooked spatial dynamics of economic development, poverty and discrimination. Poverty involves, in part, systematic differences in the resources available to people in different spatial communities. Social discrimination also often involves resource differentials linked to residential segregation and other forms of social exclusion. These spatial dimensions of poverty and discrimination arise because economic clustering, driven by increasing returns and uncertainty-reduction motivations, goes hand-in-hand with social separation. The structural aspects of poverty and discrimination thus have spatial and community-level dimensions as well as household dimensions. This emphasis on the structural is not meant to deny the relevance of cultural and behavioural elements for understanding poverty and discrimination: the point of this discussion is instead that any cultural and behavioural elements are always shaped by macrostructural forces, forces that operate unevenly at regional, urban, and neighbourhood levels.

This chapter has introduced three impacts of spatiality on economic and social relations: first, the spatial distribution of households will affect the socio-economic opportunity sets of individual units via spill-overs, since each agent is spatially embedded (and it is costly to change locations); second, the spatial distribution of businesses will affect (and be affected by) the revenues and profits of individual firms; third, agents and firms invariably exist within spaces that are bordered, the flows across which alter the wealth/goods balances in individual neighbourhoods, regions, and nations. Wealth thus either builds up or is subtracted over time, in spaces in which households and businesses capture positive and/or negative spill-overs.

An impoverished area, then, is likely to have the following characteristics: (1) low-level and unstable income flows, especially in terms of earnings from the rest of the world; (2) the absence or shortage of institutional mechanisms for securely saving, leading most area residents to be unable to accumulate financial savings; (3) problems in achieving capital accumulation either through the construction of new real assets or the appreciation of the prices of existing ones; (4) dependence for capital on capital inflows from the rest of the world; (5) the presence of a disproportionate number of residents who are subject to social discrimination.

It follows that efforts to attack poverty should involve a developmental strategy for impoverished areas. Residents' opportunities for income earning in the broader economy must be strengthened, business capacity enhanced, and financial structure built up. If the economy as a whole enjoys a period of sustained prosperity, and if the geographic extent of the impoverished area is relatively small, it is conceivable that the impoverished area will gradually be transformed into a place in which real wealth can be accumulated and the path-dependent downward trajectories leading toward ever-more economic exclusion and isolation can be reversed. Conceivably – because this sort of experiment has perhaps never had a chance to play out over time: either the broader macroeconomy turns sour or long-term residents are elbowed aside by new residents engaging in gentrification.

Anti-poverty policy versus development policy versus anti-discrimination policy?

The policy implications of this analysis might be summarized as follows. First, market dynamics interacting with processes of social discrimination will tend to produce spatial separations between the poor and non-poor, and between those who are subject to social discrimination and those who are not. Second, development strategy, anti-poverty policies, and efforts to reduce the impact of social discrimination are invariably interrelated. Third, poverty and discrimination never operate solely at the level of individual units – they almost invariably involve structural differences reflected in and amplified by spatial separation on the basis of poverty and social discrimination.

The idea that anti-poverty and anti-discrimination policies cannot be separated from development policies creates different challenges for nations with higher *per capita* incomes and with lower *per capita* incomes. In nations with high *per capita* incomes, anti-poverty policy is controversial because people hold different preconceptions regarding the root causes of poverty. At one extreme is a view of poverty as a timeless condition reflecting the cultural deficits and social isolation of the poor (for example, Murray 1984). This view attributes poverty primarily, if not solely, to individual characteristics, and asserts that policy interventions must aim to alter the behaviour of the poor – either by carrots (low-income tax credits) or by sticks (sunset provisions for family welfare benefits). At root, 'heal thyself' is the diagnosis. At the other extreme is the notion of poverty as a structural problem, remediable through intelligent social intervention underwritten by political will. Well-crafted governmental programmes can cover poor peoples' asset and income deficits and reduce poverty.

Views on social discrimination also range between two extremes. One view is that government need take no action regarding discrimination against, say, women or blacks, because market forces will punish perpetrators.[19] At the other extreme is the view that all instances of discrimination should be targeted for aggressive litigation so that discriminators will modify their behaviour; furthermore, compensation for disadvantages due to the historical legacy of discrimination should be considered. As with poverty, there is nothing or everything to be done.

As might be expected, there is a high correlation among the proponents on the two sides of these divides regarding poverty and social discrimination. The idea of poverty as a characteristic of individuals, albeit rooted in cultural characteristics, is readily combined with the idea that discrimination will disappear because it is economically costly. Government policy thus should simply let market processes work, as these will reward the deserving and leave the undeserving behind. The structural views of poverty and of discrimination both lead to advocacy of a redistribution of income flows and a levelling of economic opportunity. Controversy then ensues in that those holding the former view(s) regard as unnecessary and even socially wasteful what those holding the latter view regard as essential.

In nations with lower *per capita* incomes, as noted above, the problem of discrimination receives little attention. The proper approach to poverty, however, remains controversial. One view is that the very presence of widespread poverty makes its eradication a priority of the first order. A contrary view (associated with the Kuznets curve) is that continuing and even deepening levels of inequality and hence poverty are a necessary accompaniment of development policy. Development policy is thus emphatically *not* anti-poverty policy: elites and the formal institutions that will be at the commanding heights of the economy must be encouraged, not democratized. Some justification for this view is found in the emergence of informal marketplaces, of start-up businesses, and of lending circles in *favelas* and inner-core areas. Authors such as De Soto (1989) have achieved wide currency because their views resonate both with this approach to development policy and with those in high-income nations who believe that the poor can and should heal themselves.

This chapter constitutes a warning against this view. The greater-inequality portion of the Kuznets curve is not an abstract area that a population of representative agents enters on the way to a brighter future. Greater inequality and more poverty mean the differentiation of people across space;

and categories of social discrimination are converted very readily into divisions in income and wealth. As growth proceeds, social discrimination can be a criterion for deciding who should be first in line for access to scarce resources. Once these divisions are made, overturning them requires redistribution, and not just more growth. And redistribution based on categories of social discrimination forces societal confrontations with historical legacies that are normally tangled and disputatious. Awareness of the potential economic consequences of social discrimination and social separation alone is not sufficient to avoid drinking repeatedly from the bitter cup of history's legacy; but it is the first step toward a different future.

Bibliography

Becker, G. S. (1971) *The Economics of Discrimination*, Chicago: University of Chicago Press.

Benabou, R. (1993) 'Workings of a city: Location, education, and production', *Quarterly Journal of Economics*, Vol. 108, No. 3, August.

—— (1994) 'Human capital, inequality, and growth: a local perspective', *European Economic Review*, Vol. 38, Nos 3–4, April.

Davidson, P. (1994) *Post Keynesian Macroeconomic Theory: A Foundation for Successful Economic Policies for the Twenty-First Century*, Brookfield, VT: Elgar.

De Soto, H. (1989) *The Other Path: The Invisible Revolution in the Third World*, New York: Harper Row.

Dymski, G. A. (1995) 'The theory of credit-market redlining and discrimination: an exploration', *Review of Black Political Economy*, Vol. 23, No. 3, Winter.

—— (1996) 'On Krugman's model of economic geography', *Geoforum*, Vol. 27, No. 4, November.

—— (1998a) 'Banking in the new financial world: from segmentation to separation?', *Arte, Special Issue on Macroeconomics*, Rio de Janeiro: Cândido Mendes University.

—— (1998b) 'Asset bubbles in the Korean and Japanese crisis: a spatialized Minsky approach', *Journal of Regional Studies*, Korea, May.

—— (2001) 'Can entrepreneurial incentives revitalize the urban inner core? A spatial input–output approach', *Journal of Economic Issues*, Vol. 35, No. 2, June.

Dymski, G. A. and L. Mohanty (1999) 'Credit and banking structure: insights from Asian and African-American experience in Los Angeles', *American Economic Review Papers and Proceedings*, Vol. 89, No. 2, May.

Dymski, G. A. and J. M. Veitch (1992) 'Race and the financial dynamics of urban growth: LA as Fay Wray', in Riposa, G. and C. Dersch (eds), *City of Angels*, Los Angeles: Kendall/Hunt Press.

—— (1996) 'Financial transformation and the metropolis: Booms, busts, and banking in Los Angeles', *Environment and Planning A.*, Vol. 28, No. 7, July.

Katz, M. B. (1989) *The Undeserving Poor: From the War on Poverty to the War on Welfare*, New York: Pantheon.

Keynes, J. M. (1936) *The General Theory of Prices, Employment, and Interest,*

London: Macmillan.

Krugman, P. (1991a) *Geography and Trade*, Cambridge, MA: MIT Press.

—— (1991b) 'History versus expectations', *Quarterly Journal of Economics*, Vol. 106, No. 2, May.

—— (1995) *Development, Geography, and Economic Theory*, Cambridge, MA: MIT Press.

Lefebvre, H. (1991) *The Production of Space*, translated by D. Nicholson-Smith, New York: Basil Blackwell.

Lewis, O. (1961) *The Children of Sanchez: Autobiography of a Mexican Family*, New York: Random House.

Martin, R. and P. Sunley (1996) 'Paul Krugman's geographical economics and its implications for regional development theory: a critical assessment', *Economic Geography*, Vol. 72, No. 3, June.

Massey, D. S. and N. A. Denton (1993) *American Apartheid: Segregation and the Making of the Underclass*, Cambridge, MA: Harvard University Press.

Minsky, H. (1975) *John Maynard Keynes*, New York: Columbia University Press.

Murray, C. A. (1984) *Losing Ground*, New York: Basic Books.

Nijkamp, P., Rietveld, P., and F. Snickars (1986) 'Regional and Multiregional Economic Models: A Survey', in Nijkamp, P. (ed.), *Handbook of Regional and Urban Economics*, Volume I, Amsterdam: Elsevier Science Publishers, 1986.

Omi, M. and H. Winant (1994) *Racial Formation in the United States: From the 1960s to the 1990s*, New York: Routledge.

Papageorgiou, G. J. (1979) 'Agglomeration', *Regional Science and Urban Economics*, Vol. 9, No. 1, February.

Porter, M. E. (1995) 'The competitive advantage of the inner city', *Harvard Business Review*, May–June.

Romer, P. (1990) 'Endogenous Technological Change', *Journal of Political Economy* 98, October, pp. S71–S102.

Rosser, J. B. (1999) 'On the complexities of complex economic systems', in *Journal of Economic Perspectives*, mimeo, Department of Economics, James Madison University.

Schelling, T. (1971) 'Dynamic models of segregation', *Journal of Mathematical Sociology*, Vol. 1.

Sen, A. (1995) *Development as Freedom*, Cambridge, MA: Harvard University Press.

Shackle, G. L. S. (1974) *Keynesian Kaleidics: The Evolution of a General Political Economy*, Chicago: Aldine Publishing.

Soja, E. W. (1996) *Thirdspace: Journeys to Los Angeles and Other Real-and-Imagined Places*, Cambridge, MA: Blackwell.

ten Raa, T. (1994) 'On the methodology of input-output analysis', *Regional Science and Urban Economics*, Vol. 24, No. 1, January.

ten Raa, T. and Mohnen, P. (1994). 'Neoclassical input-output analysis', *Regional Science and Urban Economics*, Vol. 24, pp. 135–58.

Wilson, W. J. (1987) *The Truly Disadvantaged: The Inner City, the Underclass, and Public Policy*, Chicago: University of Chicago Press.

Notes

1 As Katz (1989) points out, much anti-poverty policy in the US is aimed at those selected as the 'deserving' poor – a designation that requires deciding whether or not any segment of the impoverished (such as the disabled, or Vietnam veterans) are responsible for their circumstances. The 1996 welfare-reform legislation in the US essentially accomplished a significant contraction in those who are presumptively eligible for public support, as most families with dependent children were shifted from the former into the latter category.

2 Redlining on the basis of neighbourhood racial composition has been an object of social struggle in the US for three decades. Banks have altered their behaviour in the wake of continued criticisms – often in ways that accommodate community protests of unfair practices. One recent credit-market phenomenon that has drawn renewed criticism is the emergence of predatory loan practices. The term predatory loan refers to credit contracts that have significantly worse terms and conditions (and hence are more onerous for borrowers) than loans for similar purposes elsewhere in the same market area.

3 For example, Omi and Winant (1994); Katz (1989).

4 If these authors had described discrimination in another nation, they might have used income inequality rather than racial difference as the basis of social animus. This section emphasizes racial discrimination because this form of discrimination has dominated social-scientific investigations in the US. Note that some forms of discrimination – such as gender discrimination – are not easily assimilable in spatial terms. For discrimination to have a spatial dimension, there must be the possibility of systematic separation between discriminators and discriminatees. This is clearly feasible in the case of racial difference and income inequality; it is less clearly feasible for other types of discrimination.

5 Increasing returns *per se* have attracted a disproportionate amount of attention. However, increasing returns are sufficient for agglomeration in urban development, they are not necessary (Papageorgiou 1979). Externalities and spill-overs can also introduce nonlinearities in urban spatial interactions and lead to activity clustering, path dependence, and uneven development. To a significant extent, the concepts of increasing returns, externalities, and spill-overs represent different ways of framing the same core concepts (Rosser 1999).

6 An externality arises when market transactions give rise to benefits or costs to agents other than those directly engaged in these transactions. Increasing returns occur when increasing the level of output reduces the per-unit cost of producing it. Increasing returns occur frequently in formal models. For example, suppose there is a fixed cost X associated with starting up a given firm; then as output Y expands, the fixed cost per unit of Y, X/Y, falls. So even if marginal production costs, dx, remain constant, the per-unit return increases as output rises. The evolution of Krugman's ideas on increasing

returns are discussed in Dymski (1996); also see Martin and Sunley (1996).

7 With increasing returns, one firm can meet market demand more efficiently than multiple firms. Prices cannot be set competitively because one firm supplies the whole market.

8 This construct shows how firms that each have an absolute productivity advantage can set prices which allow no one firm to earn excess profits.

9 For scholarship of and on Keynes, there is no better place to start than Keynes's *General Theory* (1936). Also see Shackle (1974) and Davidson (1994).

10 If demand were not at least partially independent of supply, then 'supply could generate its own demand', a macroeconomic proposition known as Say's Law of Markets. Say's Law implies that the stimulation of supply is the core macroeconomic problem: for if producers can be induced to make additional goods, the incomes they generate will be used to purchase these goods. Keynesian theory disputes this conclusion. Certainly, creating additional output simultaneously generates new income claims equal in value to that output – and hence capable in principle of buying it. But those accruing this additional income are not compelled to spend it; indeed, they can withhold it from expenditures, storing it as savings in some form. Non-Keynesian macroeconomic theory is confident that market equilibration will lead *someone* to borrow these savings so as to purchase the untaken stock of produced goods and services. Keynesian theory objects that this may not occur if agents instead desire liquidity; hence, agents' expenditure decisions are more fundamental determinants of realized output in any period.

11 This definition of investment differs completely from the financial-market use of this term; there, 'investment' means the purchase or exchange of financial assets.

12 The rapid growth of many East Asian nations in the 1970s and 1980s provided evidence that financial liberalization and higher interest rates were not required to generate high saving levels. These nations also followed a path led by government guidance and planning, and thus were following an alternative path to that laid out in the neoclassical view.

13 The ideas presented in this subsection are based on several publications, especially Dymski and Veitch (1992 and 1996); Dymski and Mohanty (1999); Dymski (1996, 1998a and 2001).

14 This model is actually an application of the Sraffian/Leontief input–output framework. See Nijkamp, Rietveld, and Snickars (1986) and especially ten Raa, T. and Mohnen. P. (1994). Implementing this model requires many arbitrary assumptions, which are discussed in these sources and in Dymski (2001).

15 These conditions are as follows: (Revenues earned on X_1) = (Cost of X_1 and X_2 used in making X_1) + (wages paid to labour employed in making X_1) + (Profits of owners of means of production for X_1); and (Revenues earned on X_2) = (Cost of X_1 and X_2 used in making X_2) + (wages paid to labour employed in making X_2) + (Profits of owners of means of production for X_2).

16 This constraint also exists in the interregional urban model; but in that

model, different regions produce different basic goods by definition (which are exchanged across regional borders). Our inner-core/suburban model defines regions solely on the basis of geography.

17 Of course, such uncertainty gaps might be capitalized into asset prices in these various neighbourhoods. If increasing-returns processes are at work, however, this sort of capitalization will always lag events.

18 Wealth decumulation processes sometimes involve sales of wealth assets, a service associated with the many pawnbrokers that arise in many inner-core neighbourhoods. However, these processes can be passive – notably, they can involve the failure to perform timely maintenance and upkeep. Of course, small savings from deferring maintenance in the short run can hasten asset devaluation in the longer run.

19 Becker (1971) argues that those who discriminate will pay some cost for restrictively refusing to transact with a significant share of the market. Dymski (1995), among others, shows that the opposite scenario – wherein victims of discrimination pay costs such as higher prices and worse employment prospects – may also occur.

Rethinking the Participatory Process: Local and Global Connections

10

The World Social Forum: A Space for the Translation of Diversity in Social Mobilization

NELSON GIORDANO DELGADO
AND
JORGE O. ROMANO

This chapter argues that the World Social Forum (WSF) can be considered to be a space for the translation of the diversity of struggles and social movements against neoliberal globalization. The WSF has created the opportunity for a political effort that comprehends different kinds of collective struggles, and has also led to the construction of a dialogue between distinct actors with diverse visions, characteristics, and purposes – without the imposition of a single 'tongue'. This effort at translating diversity so as to achieve a better understanding of the divergences and possibilities for sharing is not exclusively an intellectual exercise – its explicit objective is mobilization and social action.

The chapter is divided into five parts. We first describe the WSF as a process and a social fact, and contextualize it in the field of 'new' social movements. We then present an overview of the WSF of Porto Alegre, held since 2001: its principles, its administrative organization, and the trajectory of its activities over time. We also discuss the systematization process which was initiated in 2003. The third part 'enters' the Forum of Porto Alegre, systematically presenting its structure and thematic areas, and explaining the activities and programmes that have constituted the three Forums held to date. Next, we use the 2003 systematization effort to compare the 2002 and 2003 WSF panels on the WTO and international trade, external debt, and the solidarity economy. Our objective is to show how the substantial complexity and multiplicity of participants' approaches to these subjects was accompanied, at the same time, by substantial agreement on many points. Our chapter concludes with our evaluation of these events.[1]

■

The World Social Forum in the Context of the New Social Movements

In 2003, the city of Porto Alegre hosted the World Social Forum for the third consecutive year. Approximately 100,000 people were present, according to the media, of whom more than 20,000 were delegates from the networks, non-governmental organizations (NGOs), and social movements of all continents. Approximately 1,600 activities were held over the five days of the 2003 mega-event. The numbers of participants and of activities have increased significantly in each year of the WSF. Paralleling this growth has been a significant rise in the number of organizations, movements, and participants adhering to its motto that 'another world is possible'. Recognition of the WSF by the international media, by government and multilateral leaders, and by the general public has also been growing.

In this context of the increased recognition of the WSF, it is important to look at its social and political meaning as an event and as a process in the field of social movements. Following Denning, we ask what are the connections of insurrectional events – such as revolts, strikes, occupations, pacifist marches, mobilizations like Seattle, and the WSF itself – with the social movement as a whole. In other words, how can the WSF – and the social movements it brings together – change from an event (an insurrection) to a movement (since insurrections are always enigmatic, residing in some nebulous place between hidden resistance and the revolutions that overturn established order and regimes)? Insurrections are 'unexpected interruptions, the arrival of something new, which manage to open up a social text for parallel interpretations: insurrections are social dreams, an exaggerated demonstration of some buried content, whether it is of a movement or a moment' (Denning 2002: 63).[2]

These mobilizations can be interpreted in several different ways. Some writers (especially those engaged in sociological studies) emphasize access to resources (MacAdam 1997); others consider mobilizations to be narratives told not by the insurgents but by the defenders of order (Guha 1999); while others – rejecting the reduction of these mobilizations to their organizations – see them as true moments of insurrection, the expression of conjunctural crises (Piven and Cloward 1977).

In our view, the social and political meaning of the WSF, both as an event and as a process, is best understood through the perspective developed by Thompson (1987) and Denning (2002). Adopting a historical perspective, these authors consider mobilizations as signs of movements and cultures of resistance that have existed over a long time, if frequently almost unnoticeably. Sometimes underground, the libertarian tradition of popular radicalism has survived both violent repressions and the indifference of the *status quo*.

To what extent, therefore, are events and processes such as the WSF and recent demonstrations contesting the contradictions of hegemonic globalization (such as the 'battle of Seattle') the heirs of the tradition of popular libertarian radicalism – whose high point in the last half of the twentieth century occurred in 1968? Are these contemporary events and processes simply renewing the legacy of 1968 or are they expressing something new?

In debates among social scientists, 1968 is considered to be a notable moment of social and political revolt, a real landmark in the growth of the new social movements. Autonomy and distinction are fundamental aspects of these new movements, making it difficult to identify a common denominator among them. Some authors believe the new movements should be viewed as versions of populism, given their constant 'we the people' rhetorical assertions. Others, such as Manuel Castells (1999), emphasize that the new movements are constructed around tranches of specific identities. Finally, authors such as Michael Denning (2002) consider the common element in the new social movements to be their emphasis on 'liberation'.

Liberation has been a keyword for the gay, black and women's movements. Liberation movements have corresponded to the historical moment in which the world was regarded as divided into three worlds – the first capitalist, the second communist, and the third decolonized. Even though there were impressive parallels – and in some cases, links – between the liberation movements of the three worlds, the real division of the world system prevented the strengthening of connections among movements in the different worlds. This three-world division was diluted by the fall of the Berlin Wall in 1989. Indeed, this momentous event, along with the growth of the 'global factory', suggests the pertinence of Denning's remark: the only non-polemical definition of globalization is that we are all in a single world (Denning 2002: 69). We would amend his comment by emphasizing that we are nonetheless in very different positions and situations in this single world.

The intellectuals of the social movements of 1968 brought the state back into social thought. At the same time, these authors questioned two of the fundamental hypotheses of the 'old left' social movements: first, that the objective of social struggle should be the capture of the state, through either parliamentary or insurrectional means; second, that the party – either of the masses or vanguard – was the main instrument of this struggle (Denning 2002: 70).

As Wallerstein has highlighted, the central part of this 'old left' strategy was the idea of two stages: first, state power was to be won; and afterwards, the world would be transformed. The strategy failed. If the first stage was won, the new regimes showed themselves to be impotent when it came to achieving the second. Wallerstein suggests that this 'old left' strategy contained elements which contributed to this failure and even today make construction of a new strategy difficult. The first element was the belief that homogeneity is better than heterogeneity. This led to the views that diversity is a threat and has to be eliminated, and that centralization is superior to decentralization. The supposition was that equality signified identity. A second element was an emphasis on the role of the state as a mechanism for the defence of collective interests within the world system. Statism was thus reinforced, based on the (false) belief that any state, within the modern system, could serve collective interests instead of the interests of privileged groups. Finally, the left rejected the priority that liberalism gave to 'liberty' (defined in political terms) over 'equality' (defined in economic terms and seen as a threat to this liberty). In other words, (economic) equality had to take priority over (political) liberty. This inversion led to the tragic mistake of separating liberty from equality. But as Wallerstein goes on to observe, these cannot be separated: no one can be free to choose when their choices are limited by an unequal position, nor can anyone be equal if they do not have the same degree of liberty. The failure of the 'old left' strategy is connected, then, at root, to the impossibility of constructing an alternative path in the ambit of a capitalist world system that was basically stable (Wallerstein 2002: 27–30).

According to Wallerstein, 1968 marked a new world revolution. Throughout the world, social movements had the state regimes as their privileged focus: whether the social democrats with their trade union-based parties in the first world, the communist governments with the *nomenklaturas* in the second world, or the post-colonial states with their nationalist elites in the third world. The struggle was over the democratization of these states; at the same time, this struggle questioned the old left's theory of inevitable progress and its emphasis on anti-systemic historical movements. A quandary emerged: the state structures that were delegitimized by the 'old left' (and by the increasingly mobilized populations of these societies) were at the same time the fundamental mechanisms for progressive change. The popular sectors turned against the neoliberal apologists for the capitalist system and the state structures that had been put in place to defend and advance it.

Subsequently, however, as economic globalization and deregulation proceeded, all state structures – not just those formerly behind the Wall – lost legitimacy. Consequently, anti-statism did not reinforce the political stability of the world system; instead, it further weakened it. So at the beginning of the new millennium, after 500 years of existence, the capitalist world system faces a systemic crisis. This puts us in a period of transition. There are real prospects for change, even if the result is fundamentally uncertain, and even if this result may or may not be progressive. The strategy of the forces of the left as anti-systemic movements, developed since the nineteenth century, has been shattered; consequently they are acting with a high degree of uncertainty in a context of generalized depression (Wallerstein 2002: 18–19).

Despite this, the world battle for the construction of a new historical system has already begun (Wallerstein 2002: 30). A new type of anti-systemic action has begun to emerge among the forces of the left, even if diffuse, lacking any consensus over its name, and without a clearly acknowledged chronology.[3] This action is the expression of an anti-globalization movement, heir of the libertarian tradition. According to Denning (2002: 72–6), this movement has been manifest in a series of mobilizations that have taken place at different times since 1968. The first wave corresponded to the 'revolts against the IMF' that began at the end of the 1970s with urban food demonstrations in Peru, Poland, Egypt, and Jamaica, and led to protests in 40 countries against IMF fiscal austerity packages. Despite achieving little success in reversing proposed structural adjustments, these protests played an important role in the social movements of that time – including those that led to revolution in Iran and to the rise of Solidarity in Poland.

A second moment in this incipient anti-globalization movement occurred in the late 1980s and early 1990s. The regimes created after the collapse of Eastern European communism, after the fall of South Africa's apartheid regime, and after the transition to democracy in Latin America did not succeed in building lasting new social contracts. This weakened the recently installed political democracies. At the same time, revolts against new structural adjustments imposed by international financial organizations continued in other countries, such as Venezuela (1989), Morocco (1990) and India (1991 and 1992).

A third moment was triggered by the revolt of the Zapatistas in Chiapas in 1994: a rural revolt in defence of communal lands; asking for aid from a new civil society and defining neoliberalism as its ultimate enemy, this movement reformulated the discourse of the left. A fourth moment, since the end of the 1990s until now, has involved revolts against the IMF and protests against the WTO in the G7 countries. The 'battle of Seattle', the protests in Quebec and in Genoa are manifestations of this fourth moment, but so too are the mobilizations in 2000 against structural adjustment programmes in Southern countries such as Argentina, Uruguay, Nigeria, India, South Korea, South Africa and Venezuela (Denning 2002: 76). From our perspective, the three World Social Forums in Porto Alegre and the associated thematic, regional and national Forums can be considered part of this fourth moment, since they represent the new policy of real and virtual networks in the struggle against market-based globalization.

While there are common elements to the anti-globalization movement, the wide variety of mobilizations and events it encompasses suggest that this movement necessarily involves diverse analyses and strategies. From the third moment (the mid-1990s) onwards, four tendencies have been present: first, a debate about whether to 'fix it or nix it', concerning whether to impose alternative rules on the world economy through a struggle with multilateral organizations; second, the emergence of global trade unionism, related to the sharp increase in 'proletarianization' throughout the world, and to the effects of the new trade unionism on countries such as Brazil, South Africa and South Korea; third, a reformulation of the theory of recolonization, opening the way for new connections among the countries of the South (the case of Chávez in Venezuela provides a good example of this rhetoric); fourth, a new way of imagining public goods, with the fight against the commercialization and privatization of social life, such as the struggle against the commercialization of genetic material and information (Denning 2002: 76–7).

The politics of most people are rooted in their social identities and positions. And because the social components that potentially constitute the forces of the left across the globe face very different immediate problems and arise out of diverse cultural systems, a strategy of democratic centralism cannot work. This limitation has been recognized in various ways in recent years – one example is the 'rainbow coalition', which began in the United States and then spread to other countries. Another example is the 'plural left', based in France and also widely diffused: this approach defers less to identities and emphasizes instead the multiplicity of priorities and political traditions (Wallerstein 2002: 32).

These slogans point to a new style of the left-wing coalitions that are gaining so many new adherents. The challenge facing these coalitions is to strengthen contact with one another, with the aim of consolidating their different movements, even while engaging in debates and collective analyses based on the presupposition that alternatives exist to the primacy of a single way of thinking. It is in this context that the new slogan spreading from the South, 'another world is possible' – promoted and put into practice by the process of the World Social Forum of Porto Alegre – has to be understood. Adherents of the anti-globalization movement are now, in effect, bound by more than their common questioning of the end of history and of the imperial dominance of the capitalist world system, of which market-centred globalization is a primary manifestation; these coalitions are now engaged, via the 'another world is possible' vision of the WSF, in explorations of the possibility of a global rethinking of politics and democratic institutions. The WSF is currently a live laboratory of world citizenship, in which 'a *social perspective* on everything' is practised and diffused. The Social Forum vision of the world contrasts with the business vision of the world, embodied in the Economic Forum held in Davos, that governs neoliberal globalization (Grzybowski 2003: 4–6).

The tasks for the new coalitions that Wallerstein highlights can be used for the WSF process. This process should aim at the creation and reinforcement of a culture of collective political action in opposition to the traditional hierarchies that have so dominated both the capitalist elites and the 'old left'. At the same time, the systematic unmasking of the liberal rhetoric of neoliberalism needs to be carried out – in particular, the way in which this rhetoric limits the freedom of choice of the majority of people (Wallerstein 2002: 32).

Through the WSF (and the many meetings of coalitions and networks that occur as part of the WSF process), it is possible to advance the discussion of multiple inequalities. The capitalist world system has, in its neoliberal phase, generated the greatest polarization between wealth and poverty that the world has known. The international left is now learning to approach seriously the biggest problem for almost everyone: the daily reality of multiple in-equalities (such as region, nation, class, race, ethnicity, gender, generation), (Wallerstein 2002: 33–5). Adapting a phrase of Santos (2000: 27), we can say that the WSF can represent a *space for translation* for the political effort of comprehending the different collective struggles now under way, permitting the collective actors to 'converse' 'about the oppression they are resisting and the aspirations which animate them'.[4]

■

The Forum as a Social Fact[5]

The World Social Forum considers itself as an open international meeting space for civil society organizations and movements that are opposed to neo-liberalism and concerned with the construction of a planetary society centred on the primacy of the human being. This meeting space encompasses many kinds of interaction – the deepening of reflections, the democratic debating of ideas, the formulation of proposals, the free exchange of experiences, and the organizing and articulation needed to carry out actions efficiently. The WSF proposes to debate alternative ways to construct a 'solidarity' globalization centred on the defence and implementation of human rights, supported by democratic international systems and institutions in the service of social justice, equality and the sovereignty of peoples.

The WSF annually organizes a large international meeting. The first three World Social Forums (2001, 2002 and 2003) were held in Brazil, in the city of Porto Alegre, Rio Grande do Sul, on the same dates as the World Economic Forum in Davos. The 2004 meeting was held in Mumbai, India, and the 2005 meeting again in Porto Allegre. The WSF also holds regional, national and thematic Social Forums. The organizing committees of these diverse forums have organizational and facilitating tasks, and are linked to the Inter-national Committee. All the Forums must always comply with the WSF's Statement of Principles, the 'centrepiece of the engineering policy of WSF' (Grzybowski 2003: 6). This Statement is reproduced here as Figure 10.1.

All organizations, movements and entities from civil society that declare their agreement with the WSF's Statement of Principles can participate in the WSF's annual international meetings, sending delegates and proposing activities. Other activists or interested parties who do not belong to any organization can participate as observers in open meetings.

Since the WSF is a meeting space for organizations, networks and move-ments from civil society, the participation as delegates of organizations or individuals linked to governments or political parties is not allowed. Nonetheless, governments that host WSF events can be partners in organi-zing these events. Leaders and parliamentarians who agree with the Statement of Principles can be invited to participate in a personal capacity. Since the WSF proposes the construction of another world without the use of violence, it does not allow the participation of armed or military organizations.

Figure 10.1: Statement of Principles of the World Social Forum

The Committee of Brazilian organizations which conceived and organised the first World Social Forum, held in Porto Alegre from 25 to 30 January 2001, consider it necessary and legitimate, after having evaluated the results of the Forum and the expectations which led to its creation, to set out a Statement of Principles to guide the continuation of this initiative. The principles outlined in the Statements, which shall be respected by all those who wish to participate in this process and organize further World Social Forums, consolidate the decisions which led to the holding of the Forum of Porto Alegre and ensured its success, and have broadened its scope, defining guidelines which result from the logic of these decisions.

1. The World Social Forum is an open meeting space for the deepening of reflection, the democratic debating of ideas, the formulation of proposals, the free exchange of experiences, and the articulation of efficient actions, on the part of organizations and movements from civil society which are opposed to neoliberalism and which are concerned with the construction of a planetary society aimed at a fertile relationship between human beings, and between humans and the Earth.

2. The World Social Forum of Porto Alegre was an event located in time and space. From now on, in the certainty proclaimed in Porto Alegre that 'another world is possible', it will be a permanent process searching for and constructing alternatives, which will not be reduced to the events with which it supports itself.

3. The World Social Forum is a process with an international nature. All the meetings which are held as part of this process have an international dimension.

4. The alternatives proposed by the World Social Forum are opposed to a globalization process led by the large multinational corporations and by the governments and international institutions at the service of their interests, with the complicity of national governments. They aim to lead to, in a new stage in world history, a 'solidarity' globalization which will respect universal human rights, as well as those of all citizens in all nations and the environment, based on democratic international systems and institutions at the service of social justice, equality and the sovereignty of peoples.

5. The World Social Forum brings together and articulates entities and movements from civil society from all the countries in the world, but it does not intend to be a representative institution of international civil society.

6. The meetings of the World Social Forum do not have a deliberative nature as the World Social Forum. Therefore, no one is authorized to express in the name of the Forum, in any of its years, positions which intend to be on behalf of all of its participants. Participants shall not be called on to make decisions, by vote or acclamation, as a group of the participants of the Forum, about any declarations or proposals for action in which all, or the majority, are engaged, and which intend to lead to the adoption of positions by the Forum as the Forum. It is, therefore, not created to be a sphere of power, to be disputed by participants in its meetings, nor does it intend to be the only alternative for the articulation and action of the organizations and movements which participate in it.

7. Therefore, for the organizations which participate in the meetings of the Forum must be ensured the freedom, during these meetings, to deliberate on declarations and actions which they decide to undertake, either in isolation or in a joint manner with other participants. The World Social Forum is committed to widely diffusing these decisions, through the means within its reach, without any directives, hierarchies, censorship or restrictions, but only as the deliberations of the organizations, or groups of organizations which have assumed them.

8. The World Social Forum is a plural and diversified, non-confessional, non-governmental and non-partisan space, which brings together in a decentralized manner in a network, the organizations and movements engaged in concrete actions, at a local and an international level, aimed at the construction of another world.

9. The World Social Forum will always be a space open to pluralism and to the diversity of engagements and actions of the organizations and movements which decide to take part in it, as well as the diversity of gender, ethnicities, cultures, generations and physical capacities, once this Statement of Principles is respected. Neither representatives of political parties nor military organizations may take part in the Forum. Leaders and parliamentarians may be invited to participate, on a personal basis, once they commit themselves to this Statement.

10. The World Social Forum is opposed to all totalitarian and reductionist visions of the economy, development, and the history and use of violence as a means of social control by the state. It teaches respect for human rights, for the practice of a real participatory democracy, for equal and peaceful relations, based on solidarity, between individuals, ethnicities, genders, and peoples, condemning all forms of domination, as well as the subjection of any human being by any other.

11. The World Social Forum, as a space for debates, is a movement of ideas which stimulate reflection, and the transparent dissemination of the results of this reflection, about the mechanisms and instruments of the domination of capital, about the means and actions of resistance and the overcoming of this domination, about the alternatives proposed to resolve the problems of exclusion and social inequality that the process of capitalist globalization, with its racist, sexist and environmentally destructive dimensions, is creating both internationally and within countries.

12. The World Social Forum, as the space for the exchange of experiences, will stimulate the mutual knowledge and acknowledgement of the organizations and movements which participate in it, valorizing their exchange, especially that which society is constructing to centre economic activity and political action on meeting the needs of human beings and respect for nature, in present and future generations.

13. The World Social Forum, as a space for articulation, will try to strengthen and create new national and international connection between social organizations and movements, which will increase, in the both public and private life, the capacity for non-violent social resistance to the process of the dehumanization which the World is undergoing and the violence used by the state, and to reinforce the humanizing initiatives being put into action by these movements and organizations.

14. The World Social Forum is a process which stimulates the organizations and movements which participate in it to situate their actions, at a local and national level and to seek an active participation in international forums, with questions of planetary citizenship, introducing to the new global agenda the transformative practices which they have experiencing in the construction of a new world based on solidarity.

Approved and adopted in São Paulo, on the 9 April 2001, by the organizations which make up the Organising Committee of the World Social Forum, approved with modifications by the International Council of the World Social Forum on 10 June 2001.

Source: www.forumsocialmundial.org.br

According to the resolutions printed in the Statement, it is not the task of WSF, as such, to carry out campaigns or actions, nor does it produce declarations or final documents in its events. No one is authorized to express positions whose intention is to represent all the participants in the name of the Forum. Nevertheless, the WSF allows participants to propose concrete actions or to produce documents which express particular positions.

To further the aim of strengthening the international coalition of various social movements and organizations committed to the fight against neoliberal globalization, the WSF has begun to internationalize its scope. In addition to the annual meeting of the World Social Forum, regional and thematic social forums have been organized. Thus, after 2002 the Thematic Forum on the Crisis of Neoliberalism in Argentina, the European Regional Forum, the Thematic Forum on Palestine, the Asian Regional Forum, the African Regional Forum and the Pan-Amazon Forum were organized successively. In addition, national and local forums have multiplied beyond any expectations. This multiplication expresses the objective of internationalizing the WSF process by incorporating a wide variety of situations and issues, while mobilizing sectors of civil society in a wide range of countries.

The organizational structure of the WSF

The organizational structure of the Forum is composed of an Executive Secretariat and an International Council. WSF activities are directed by the Executive Secretariat, which is based in the head office of ABONG (see below) in São Paulo, Brazil. General political questions and discussions about the directions of the WSF and the methodologies of the annual events are debated and decided by the WSF's International Council.

The Secretariat of the WSF (previously the Organizational Committee) is responsible for the implementation and internationalization of the Forum. It is composed of eight Brazilian organizations who initiated the first WSF: ABONG – Associação Brasileira de Organizações Não Governamentais (Brazilian Association of Non-Governmental Organizations); ATTAC – Ação pela Tributação das Transações Financeiras em Apoio aos Cidadãos (Action for the Taxation of Financial Transactions in Support of Citizens); CBJP – Comissão Brasileira Justiça e Paz da CNBB (Comissão Nacional dos Bispos do Brasil), (Brazilian Commission for Justice and Peace of the CNBB – the National Conference of Bishops of Brazil); Cives – Associação Brasileira de Empresários pela Cidadania (Brazilian Association of Employers for Citizenship); CUT – Central Única dos Trabalhadores (Single Congress of Workers); IBASE – Instituto Brasileiro de Análises Social and Econômicas, (Brazilian Institute of Social and Economic Analyses); MST – Movement dos Trabalhadores Rurais Sem Terra (Movement of Landless Rural Workers); and Rede Social de Justiça e Direitos Humanos (Network of Social Justice and Human Rights).

The creation of the International Council (IC) in 2001 can be seen as an expression of the conception of the WSF as a long-term permanent process aimed at constructing an international movement that brings together the alternatives to neoliberalism in all their multiplicity and diversity. The International Council is currently composed of 112 thematic networks or organizations that have accumulated sufficient knowledge and experience to legitimately direct the debate about alternatives to hegemonic globalization. The IC has become a political and operational sphere that contributes both to the strategic direction of the WSF and to WSF activities. Among the specific responsibilities of the IC are: participating in the formulation of WSF strategies; maintaining articulation with movements, campaigns, struggles, and international events; making the WSF known in the IC members' own countries and regions; promoting broad participation and the debating of questions and proposals identified by the WSF; promoting and supporting regional Forums and the WSF itself; ensuring political, thematic, and operational coordination between the WSFs; supporting the creation of national mobilization committees in different countries; working with the organizing committees of the WSFs to structure the agenda, methodology, and format of the WSFs, and also to identify speakers and raise financial resources.

The composition of the IC is based on the following criteria: adhesion to the Statement of Principles; regional/geographical equilibrium and diversity; participation of trade union, social movement, NGO, and other sectors; participation of heads of global and regional networks; and commitment to the continuity of the WSF and the responsibilities indicated above. A predetermined number of members has not been established. There are two forms of participating in the IC (both with voting rights): permanent members, and occasional invitees and observers (whose participation may be considered important in the light of global events or the organizational dynamics of the WSF).

Despite its commitment to regional balance, the IC has since its creation had important regional imbalances – including a low participation rate from Africa, Asia, and the Arab world – and sectoral imbalances (for example, youth and blacks are under-represented). The IC is working to overcome these imbalances and absences through a process of consultation in the different regions. The IC's fundraising is aimed in part at assisting networks whose lack of resources might otherwise preclude their participation.

The trajectory of events in Porto Alegre

The importance and recognition of the three Porto Alegre meetings of the World Social Forum have increased significantly from the first WSF in summer 2001 to the third WSF in January 2003, as measured by the number of participating organizations, activities held, and media coverage. The WSF in 2001 encompassed approximately 20,000 people, including 4,702 delegates from 117 countries. There were 2,000 participants in the Youth Camp, and 700 participants in the Indigenous Nations Camp. Personal invitations were extended to 165 people, of whom 77 were Brazilian and 88 foreigners. There were 1,870 accredited representatives of the press, 1,484 national and 386 international. Organizational and administrative support was provided by a team of 1,074 people. Some 104 conference speakers gave talks in four thematic areas, and more than 420 workshops were held.

The next Porto Alegre WSF was preceded by the Social Forum of Genoa and the African Social Forum, held in Bamako, Mali. In the 2002 WSF itself, the number of delegates grew to 12,274, representing 4,909 organizations and 123 countries. Some 3,356 journalists from 1,066 media outlets attended, 1,866 Brazilian and 1,490 foreigners. Total participants numbered more than 50,000, exceeding all forecasts. Some 27 conferences, 96 seminars and 622 workshops were held. Several parallel events were held during the WSF: the Forum of Local Authorities, the World Parliamentary Forum, the World Forum of Judges, the Preparatory Meeting for Rio+10, the Intercontinental Youth Camp and the Youth World Social Forum.

The 2003 Forum WSF brought together approximately 100,000 people, including 20,763 delegates representing 5,717 organizations from 156 countries. The Youth Camp housed 25,000 people, of whom more than 19,000 were accredited as representatives of approximately 700 groups. Some 4,094 journalists from 1,423 media outlets and 51 countries were accredited. Some 1,286 workshops were held and the administrative support for the Forum counted on the work of around 650 volunteers. The 2003 Forum had total direct costs of US$3.5 million, along with significant indirect costs for personnel and speakers' lodging; the city government of Porto Alegre contributed much of the latter.

■

The World Social Forum 'from the Inside': Thematic Areas and Consensual and Planned Activities

For each of the 2001–3 Forums, the International Council has defined thematic areas, understood as the important issues challenging the movements and organizations of international civil society. The thematic areas have been regarded as the catalysts for 'concerns, proposals, and strategies, which are developed by the organizations participating in the World Social Forum process'.[6] As a space for collective strategic reflection, then, the WSF organizes itself around these thematic areas.[7]

In each thematic area the International Council creates consensual and planned activities, which bring together important organized social actors associated with the WSF. These activities allow participating organizations and movements from international civil society to share ideas and initiate debate around specific sub-themes, with the aim of both constructing consensus and identifying divergences in visions, diagnoses, proposals, and strategies. The main consensual activities were called conferences in the first and second WSFs and panels in the third.[8]

Briefly speaking, the conferences of the WSFs of 2001 and 2002 and the panels of the 2003 WSF had the following general characteristics:

- They are previously planned consensual activities, resulting from agreement at the level of the International Council. As such, they contrast with the 'free' activities that have been proposed directly by delegates, without any interference from the IC.

- They represent the 'public face of the WSF', the space through which the visions, diagnoses, proposals, and strategies of the various networks, campaigns, coalitions, organizations, and movements from international civil society are publicly expressed on previously agreed themes and questions. The participants are there as social actors to represent the positions of their institutions concerning the previously chosen sub-themes, with the aim of obtaining consensus concerning proposals for action and strategies to implement these proposals.

- The preparation of these activities is coordinated by international and national (Brazilian) representatives, nominated by the IC and by the Secretariat of the WSF.[9]

The 2001 World Social Forum

As Figure 10.2 shows, four thematic areas were defined in the 2001 WSF: (1) the production of wealth and its relationship to the conditions that guarantee social reproduction; (2) access to wealth and its relationship to the conditions that allow human life and the planet's environment to be sustained; (3) the affirmation of civil society and the recognition of its indispensable association with the opening of public spaces; and (4) the junction between public power and ethics as the basis for conceiving a new society. Production of wealth/social reproduction; access to wealth/sustainability; civil society/ public spaces; public power/ethics: these provide the conceptual and 'propositional' pairs around which areas of reflection and collective strategic proposals were organized in the economic, human and environmental development, citizenship and cultural identity, and power spheres.

In the first World Social Forum four conferences in each thematic area were organized on sub-themes considered by consensus to be relevant, from the point of view of both reflection and action, for clarifying the agreed-on basic themes. In *Area 1*, the conferences dealt with world trade, the international financial system, the functions of land, and the construction of an egalitarian system of goods and services. The first three sub-areas were readily specified, reflecting the considerable experience of participating organizations in addressing these questions. The conference on international trade emphasized questions and proposals related to the WTO and commercial negotiations, fair trade (especially terms of exchange between countries from North and South), and social and environmental clauses. The conference on the international financial system examined internal and external debt; financing for development and taxation systems and national credit; the regulation of the financial system and the Tobin tax;[10] monetary

	AREA 1: THE PRODUCTION OF WEALTH AND SOCIAL REPRO-DUCTION	AREA 2: ACCESS TO WEALTH AND SUSTAINABILITY	AREA 3: THE AFFIRMATION OF CIVIL SOCIETY AND PUBLIC SPACES	AREA 4: POLITICAL POWER AND ETHICS IN SOCIETY
Conference 1	How to construct a system for the production of goods and services for all?	How to translate scientific development into human development?	How to strengthen the capacity for action of civil society and the construction of a public space?	What are the basis of democracy and a new power?
Conference 2	What international trade do we want?	How to guarantee the public character of goods common to humanity, their de-commercialization and social control over the environment?	How to ensure the right to information and the democratization of the means of communication?	How to democratize world power?
Conference 3	What financial system is necessary for equality and development?	How to promote the universaliza-tion of human rights and ensure the distribution of wealth?	What are the limits and possibilities of planetary citizenship?	What is the future of nation states?
Conference 4	How to guarantee the multiple functions of the land?	How to construct sustainable cities?	How to guarantee cultural identities and protect artistic creation from com-mercialization?	How to mediate conflicts and construct peace?

Figure 10.2 Thematic Areas and Conferences of the First World Social Forum in Porto Alegre, 2001

Source: World Social Forum, Memorandum of the WSF 2001, Conferences (*www.forumsocialmundial.org.br*)

systems; fiscal paradises; pension funds; the social control and democratiza-tion of social insurance; and the new international financial architecture. The conference on the multiple functions of land discussed issues such as agrarian reform, the production of food and raw materials, family agriculture and gender, regional production, land and environment, land and the preservation of the landscape, and land and tourism.

In comparison with the other three areas, the conference on the construction of a system for the production of goods and services for all involved a more exploratory and complex range of themes and questions. The aim was to discuss four principal thematic components, which would then be developed further in the 2002 WSF:

- Economy and rights: the question of who produces, how, and for whom; the economy considered from the perspective of political, economic, social, and cultural rights.

- Labour and employment: employment and the perspectives for salaried labour; the alienation of work; the organization of labour, the sexual and unpaid labour of women; child, slave, and prison labour; the international regulation of labour.

- Labour and technological innovation: technological innovation, productive restructuring, and the increased flexibility of labour and its impact on the life of workers, especially women.

- Solidarity economy: micro, small and medium-sized enterprises, and the social responsibility of enterprises.

The first conference in *Area 2* discussed the question of access to scientific development and the way in which this development might contribute to (instead of hindering) human development. The issues considered included: the paths for scientific and technological research; the democratization of scientific knowledge; bio-ethics; genetic engineering and genetic modification; and the privatization of science and scientific development. The second conference dealt with access to public goods and goods common to humanity, with explorations of three interrelated issues:

- Access to goods common to humanity: genome and new reproductive technologies and complementary techniques; biodiversity; hydro resources; and energy sources.

- Private and mercantile appropriation of common goods: intellectual property and the privatization of knowledge.

- Social control of the environment: wastage of natural resources; deforestation; global warming of the planet; destruction of the ozone layer; pollution; chemical and atomic waste; biological war.

The third conference in *Area 2* approached the question of access from the perspective of the universalization of fundamental human rights: (1) the right to work; (2) the right to the income necessary for a dignified life – presupposing the combating of poverty and the eradication of misery, on one hand, and the redistribution of wealth and income, on the other; (3) the right (universal access) to health, education, habitation, sanitation, and so on; and (4) consumer rights. The fourth conference explored the question of access in urban life, especially the need to construct sustainable cities, from the social, economic, and political point of view. The objective of the conference – a better understanding of how to construct sustainable cities – was approached by treating sub-themes such as urban reform; peripheries and types of exclusion; access to habitation, health, sanitation, education; social equipment; protection of the environment; the public safety of citizens; and mass transport.

In *Area 3*, the first conference dealt with civil society's capacity for action and the construction of a democratic public space. This issue was approached through three sub-themes: (1) cultural policy and citizenship, and the social and alternative sources of power; (2) religion and solidarity; and (3) social, ethnic/racial, women, gay and lesbian, and youth movements. This area's other conferences focused on specific aspects related to this more general problem.

The objective in the second conference was to discuss the actions necessary to ensure the rights to information and the democratization of the means of communication. Presentations focused on the democratization of the already existing media; the monopoly of information; public space in mass communication; the Internet; access to television; community radios; and alternative agencies for the generation and exchange of information.

The third conference dealt with the limits and possibilities of planetary citizenship, emphasizing the importance of the connections between global actions, national identity, and local initiatives, with special attention to the role of civil networks and coalitions. The final conference dealt with this question: faced with neoliberal globalization, how is it possible to guarantee multiple cultural identities and protect artistic creation from commercialization? Three sub-themes were emphasized: globalization and cultural standardization; language as an expression of identity; and music, cinema, theatre, and handicrafts as forms of expressing and constructing cultural identities, and the subjection of artistic creations to commercialization.

The theme of the relationship between political power and ethics in the new society, which made up *Area 4*, was also divided into four conferences, which encompassed (1) the basis of democracy and power, (2) the possibilities for the democratization of world power, (3) the future of nation states, and (4) the mediation of conflicts and the construction of peace. The first conference focused first on key concepts such as cultural policy and ethical values, and then moved on to contemplate notions of direct democracy and participatory management, the various dimensions of power (local power, power and law, women and power, and power in the service of equity) (through the handling of the triad of equality, difference, and inclusion), and the problems of corruption and transparency.

The second conference dealt with the democratization of world power, taking into account three spaces/actors for the manifestation/expression of world government: (1) international multilateral institutions, such as the United Nations and international financial institutions, (2) power and regional blocs, and (3) multinational enterprises. The third conference about nation states emphasized three questions: independence, sovereignty, and the national question; privatization and national power; and the regulation of the power of enterprises. The final conference in the area, aimed at the mediation of conflicts and the construction of peace, in various spheres and at various levels of human experience, focused on the different levels at which conflict is manifest, and thus on which mediation(s) to consider as necessary for the construction of peace:

- the armed forces, the armaments industry, the arms trade, smuggling, the International Court of Justice;

- the criminalization of poverty and social movements; violence in the countryside; domestic and sexual violence; ethnic conflicts;

- the safety of citizens and the mediation of conflicts.

This very detailed presentation of the thematic areas and the conferences of the 2001 World Social Forum in Porto Alegre gives the reader a panoramic view of the organizational structure of these activities, and the way in which these substantial questions are dealt with. The discussion of the 2002 and 2003 WSFs will not repeat this level of detail, but instead will focus on structural modifications in form and content in the next two Forums.

The 2002 World Social Forum

Figure 10.3 shows the thematic areas and conferences programmed for the 2002 World Social Forum. The title and number of thematic areas remained unchanged, although the conferences were increased to seven in the first three areas and to six in the fourth. Further, one of the three new conferences introduced in each area is called a special conference and aimed at a specific (and distinct) sub-theme.

In *Area 1* (The production of wealth and social reproduction), the conference on world trade was kept as before, while that on the international financial system was split into two: 'the control of financial capital' and 'foreign debt', reflecting the importance of the question of foreign debt for a large number of the organizations participating in the WSF. The first Forum's conference on the 'construction of a system for the production of goods and services' was also transformed into two: one on work and the other on the solidarity economy. This change probably also reflected the increase in the importance of the collective actors operating in these areas in the second Forum. Two additional conferences were added in this area, one on multinational corporations and the other, a special conference, on Africa/Brazil. The conference on the question of land that had appeared in the first Forum disappeared from the area on the production of wealth and social reproduction.

	AREA 1: THE PRODUCTION OF WEALTH AND SOCIAL REPRODUCTION	AREA 2: ACCESS TO WEALTH AND SUSTAINABILITY	AREA 3: THE AFFIRMATION OF CIVIL SOCIETY AND PUBLIC SPACES	AREA 4: POLITICAL POWER AND ETHICS IN SOCIETY
Conference 1	World trade	Knowledge, reproduction rights, and patents	The fight against discrimination and intolerance	International organizations and the world architecture of power
Conference 2	Multinational corporations	Medicine, health, AIDS	The democratization of communications and the media	Participatory democracy
Conference 3	Control of financial capital	Environmental sustainability	Cultural production, diversity, and identity	Sovereignty, nation, state
Conference 4	Foreign debt	Water – a common good	Prospects for the global movement of civil society	Globalization and militarism
Conference 5	Work	Indigenous peoples	The culture of violence, domestic violence	Principles and values
Conference 6	Solidarity economy	Cities, urban populations	Migration, trafficking of persons (women, children, refugees)	Human rights (economic, social and cultural rights)
Conference 7	Special Conference: Africa/ Brazil	Special Conference: Food sovereignty	Special Conference: Education	—

Figure 10.3 Thematic Areas and Conferences of the Second World Social Forum in Porto Alegre, 2002

Source: World Social Forum website (www.forumsocialmundial.org.br)

In *Area 2* (Access to wealth and sustainability), only one sub-theme from the first WSF remained as a specific conference in the second WSF – that of cities. This signalled the expanded role of organizations active in cities. Regarding the other conferences, the first Forum's general sub-themes were replaced by more specific sub-themes linked to human groups and populations: there were conferences about knowledge, reproduction rights, and patents; medicine, health, and AIDS; environmental sustainability; water

– a common good; and indigenous people. Finally, Area 2 housed a special conference on food sovereignty. This was the only conference in which rural and land questions explicitly appeared; so these questions were dealt with in the second Forum from the perspective of food sovereignty alone. As in the case of the cities sub-theme, this shift reflected the expanding space of participant organizations such as Via Campesina, which supported this approach.

In *Area 3* (The affirmation of civil society and public spaces), the same pattern of greater specificity and more concrete themes for conferences was repeated. The 2001 WSF sub-themes 'democratizing communications and the media', and 'cultural production, diversity, and identity' were maintained (conferences 2 and 4 in Figure 10.3). The conference on 'the prospects for the global movement of civil society' brought together the sub-themes of conferences 1 and 4 from Area 3 in the previous year. Other sub-themes were defined with greater clarity and made into conferences: the 'fight against discrimination and intolerance', the 'culture of violence and domestic violence', and 'migrations and the traffic of people' all gained in prominence relative to the first WSF. Finally, education was the theme of the special conference held in the area.

In relation to *Area 4* (Political power and ethics in society), the two sub-themes 'international organization and the architecture of world power' and 'sovereignty, nation, state' were preserved as conferences. The other conferences featured new sub-themes: 'participatory democracy'; 'globalization and militarism'; 'principles and values'; and 'human rights (economic, social and cultural)'. All of these sub-themes had received some attention in the first WSF, but now were brought into sharp focus.

Overall, the thematic organization of the second WSF was better explained and sharper analytically, compared with the first WSF; as noted, this resulted in part from the political force of the networks, campaigns, and coalitions organized around certain themes. Those themes that figured explicitly as conferences both in the first and in the second WSF in Porto Alegre can be regarded as consensus priorities. These are: world trade; the international financial system and the control of financial capital; foreign debt; cities; the democratization of communications and the media; cultural production, diversity and identity; perspectives of the global movement of civil society; international organizations and the architecture of world power; and sovereignty, nation and state.

The 2003 World Social Forum

In the third World Social Forum in Porto Alegre five thematic areas were defined and six panels were organized per area, with the exception of Area 1, which included seven panels (see Figure 10.4).

Figure 10.4 demonstrates, first of all, that thematic areas were reorganized and renamed, but without altering in any significant way the substance of the general themes guiding the consensual activities of the Forum. There

Figure 10.4: Thematic Areas and Conferences of the Third World Social Forum in Porto Alegre, 2003

	Area 1: Democratic and sustainable development	Area 2: Principles and values, human rights, diversity and equality	Area 3: Media, culture and alternatives to commercialization and homogenization	Area 4: Political power, civil society and democracy	Area 5: Democratic world order; the fight against militarism and the promotion of peace
Panel 1	Restoring economic sovereignty through the cancellation of debts and the control of capital	The struggle for equality, men and women: how to implement real change?	Globalization, information and communication	Democratizing democracy, starting with the construction of new paradigms	Empire, war and multilateralism
Panel 2	The solidarity economy	For the complete implementation of rights	How can we guarantee cultural and linguistic diversity	New and old social movements: current spaces of confluence and tension between multiple global and local actors	Resistance to militarism
Panel 3	WTO: the road to Cancun	The struggle against intolerance and respect for diversity; solidarity as a transforming force in the struggle against the single thought	Strategies against the democratization of the media	Insurgent citizenship against the established order	Global economic governance and international institutions
Panel 4	Full employment and re-regulation of labour	Beyond national frontiers: migrants and refugees	New technologies and strategies for the digital inclusion and social transformation	New dimensions of the democratic state	The world order: sovereignty and the role of governments and the UN
Panel 5	For the rights of cities	For full access to water, food and land	Culture and political practice	Strategies of control	Democratic strategies for resolving international conflicts
Panel 6	For another economy; subsidiarity, localization, devolution and reproduction	For full access to education, health, habitation and social security rights	Symbolic production and the identity of peoples	Future prospects of the movements: new conceptions, and paths in the organization of social movements	Democratic cooperation, integration, multilateralism and peace
Panel 7	Beyond Johannesburg: property, control and the management of bio-diversity, water and energy	—	—	—	—

were changes in the structure of the main themes, but these alterations were primarily aimed at moving the thematic tradition of the WSF of Porto Alegre in the direction of the recognition of the consolidation of actors and themes during the process of the Forum; concern with guaranteeing space for the development of new actors and themes; accommodation of existing conflicts; and adaptation to the changes and the priorities of the international scenario and the agendas of social movements.

The thematic areas of production of wealth/social reproduction and access to wealth/sustainability (areas 1 and 2 in previous Forums) were replaced by a single area, 'Democratic and sustainable development' (*Area 1*). This new thematic area covers the same ground as the previous Area 1, with the economy as its central sphere, but adds some new sub-themes, primarily those originally covered under Area 2. This reframing signals that development must be approached as concerned with more than production and access to wealth; instead the qualifiers 'democratic' and 'sustainable' are benchmarks holding any discussion of development to a high standard (one not satisfied by attention to income levels alone). Panels 1, 3 and 5 reaffirm the importance of the questions of external debt, the control of capital, world trade, and cities. Panels 2 and 4 consolidate the themes of work and employment and the solidarity economy. Panel 6, 'For another economy: subsidiarity, localization, devolution and reproduction', represents an emerging theme. In the third Forum, then, with the suppression of the former Area 2, the themes of reproduction and patent rights, medicine, health and AIDS, and environmental sustainability lost visibility as consensual activities. Panel 7, 'Beyond Johannesburg', did focus attention on biodiversity, water and energy.

The themes formerly covered in areas 3 (The affirmation of civil society and public spaces) and 4 (Political power and ethics in society) of the 2001 and 2002 Forums were expanded in the 2003 Forum into four large thematic areas (2 to 5, for the 2003 Forum): human rights, diversity, and equality; media and culture; political power, civil society and democracy; and the world order, militarism and the promotion of peace.

For Area 2, the question of human rights – previously only a conference topic – was chosen as the dominant theme, and thus gained greater importance and visibility. It was examined in detail in panels focusing on equality, men, and women; the full implementation of rights, through the efficient globalization of the struggle for rights; full access of rights to water, food and land; and full access to rights to education, health, habitation, and social security. These panels were complemented by the inclusion of two other subthemes, both of which emphasized the role of solidarity in the struggle for human rights: the fight against intolerance and the respect for diversity as instruments for social transformation; and the question of the rights of migrants, refugees, and other social groups who are situated beyond national frontiers. Note that rural, agricultural, and land issues were again discussed from a different angle – in the third WSF, this was the perspective of full access to human rights, in particular to water, food, and land.

In Area 3, the topic of media and culture was examined from the perspectives of the political struggle against commodification and homogenization, as well as the affirmation of diversity and democratization. Panel 1 raised questions about globalization, the power of the media, the right to communication and to information, and the rights to intellectual property. Panel 2, in turn, debated what would guarantee cultural and linguistic diversity, in the context of the threats posed by World Trade Organization guidelines regarding trade in services. Panel 3 discussed strategies for democratizing the media, while Panel 4 took on an emerging sub-theme, strategies for democratization related to new technologies, digital inclusion, and social transformations. Panels 5 and 6 discussed the relationship of political practice (resistance to imperial domination, identity, inclusion, and social emancipation) to culture, symbolic production, and the identity of peoples (especially of the excluded: race, gender, and youth).

The central theme of Area 4 can be summarized as the radicalization of democracy. Panel 1 focused on new conceptions and paradigms of the political that might lead to the democratization of democracy; Panel 4 discussed new dimensions, roles, limits, and types of states, especially in the light of alternative projects for society; Panel 5 centred on the role of citizenship in the construction of a new society and the control of the market, including such approaches as social self-management, citizen vigilance, and consumer action.

The remaining panels (2, 3, and 6) considered what social actors and forms of action are necessary to radicalize democracy. Among the question raised were: (1) the relationship between the 'new' and 'old' social movements, and the conditions for broad democratic alliances confronting racist, sexist, and 'generational' hegemonies both in the movements and in society at large; (2) how new actors and spaces for struggles expand the limits of citizenship and create new political cultures, even while the scope of exclusion expands; (3) the impacts of globalization on people's subjective, emotional, and democratic horizons.

Finally, the theme of Area 5 was 'the construction of a democratic world order, the struggle against militarism, and the promotion of peace', considerably expanding the discussion space for this theme relative to previous Forums. Panel 1 analyzed the significance of the American imperial system. Panel 2 discussed the situation of the international civil movements against militarism and war. Panel 3 reflected on the concept of global economic government aimed at the sustainable development of all countries and possible alternatives to the WTO, the World Bank, and the IMF. Panel 4 explored the outlines of a democratic world order, including the prospective roles of popular sovereignty, states, and organizations from civil society, and also the future of the United Nations. Panels 5 and 6 examined strategies for: peaceful solutions to international conflicts; regional integration; alternatives to the ideology of the free market; and establishing democratic multilateralism and world peace via negotiation, cooperation, and solidarity.

In sum, the World Social Forum in Porto Alegre has over the past three years moved towards five thematic areas, around which the Forums' collective strategic and conceptual reflections and propositions have been organized: (1) the construction of development that is democratic and sustainable; (2) the global implementation of human rights, in a broad process that affirms diversity and seeks equality; (3) the democratization of the media and the preservation of cultural diversity, and resistance to commercialization and homogenization; (4) the radicalization of democracy; and (5) the construction of a democratic world order, capable of promoting peace and confronting militarism.

■

Advancing through the 'Inside' of the World Social Forum: An Illustration of its Thematic and Purposeful Multiplicity/Complexity

Let us now advance further in our attempt to 'enter the WSF' and understand the structure and content of its activities. To do this, we'll work with three sub-themes from the 2003 Forum's Area 1 ('Democratic and sustainable development'): 'WTO and world trade', 'Foreign debt', and 'Solidarity economy'. These sub-themes were also included as individual conferences in Area 1 of the 2002 WSF.[11]

Discussing these panels in detail also provides an opportunity to mention a key new dimension of the 2003 Porto Alegre Forum. For the 2003 WSF, the Executive Secretariat requested IBASE (one of the original sponsors of the 2001 WSF) to create a systematization team to accompany all the official panels and a sample of the free activities. The task of this team was systematically to record the decisions made and also the flow of discussion within these panels. In this way, the process of the Forum is recorded in even more depth than were the 2001 and 2002 Forums, permitting more of the gains from dialogue and exchange to be recorded as a basis for future Forums. The two authors of this paper were part of this team.[12] The information used here was obtained from Panel summaries prepared in the context of the systematization team's work.

Our objective in this section is to illustrate the richness of the attempted systematization of this path, and also the complexity and multiplicity inherent in advancing the WSF process. For each of these panels, we present the country and organizations of the participants; the principal questions, proposals, and strategies about which there was convergence and consensus; and the perceived divergences among speakers and the public in attendance. We will compare the 2002 WSF conferences and 2003 WSF panels in these thematic areas.

The World Trade Organization and world trade
The WTO and world trade are themes that the social actors participating in the 2002 Forum conferences and 2003 Forum panels believed to be

politically decisive in shaping the possibilities for global democratic and sustainable development.[13] The conference on world trade in the 2002 WSF consisted of a French convener (from ATTAC) and six panelists, from Malaysia (Third World Network), South Africa (Africa Trade Network), Belgium (European Trade Union Confederation), Spain (Via Campesina), Mexico (Alianza Social Continental), and the United States (Public Citizen). Participants reached a broad consensus on two central questions: first, 'free trade is not a guarantee of wealth or development for nations or for peoples'; and second, 'the WTO favours the rich states and has accumulated too many powers in sectors which should not be negotiated within this organization'.

The key consensual proposals and strategies on which these panelists agreed were:

- the need for the articulation of a global movement which reaches beyond countries, NGOs, trade unions, or particular sectors of society, and which confronts questions related to the WTO and world trade;

- the prohibition of agricultural dumping;

- the demand for food sovereignty as a new universal right;

- obtaining of the right to use productive resources (water, land, seeds);

- the malign effects of the actions of the IMF, the World Bank, and the WTO;

- the need to advise and, where necessary, pressure governments to change WTO policies;

- the need to question each new WTO agreement.

In the 2003 WSF Panel 'WTO: the road to Cancun', a Brazilian facilitator again convened six speakers, from Malaysia (Third World Network), Senegal (Oxfam International), the United States (AFL–CIO, Public Citizen), Spain (Via Campesina), and Mexico (Mobilization Committee Towards Cancun). The members of this Panel achieved consensus on these points:

- The WTO is not a really global organization, but is controlled by a small number of rich countries;

- the WTO is not just a commercial organization: it intends to extend its competence and its scope to all spheres of life throughout the world;

- the three new agreements being considered in the context of the WTO's Cancun Round – that is, the measures on foreign investment, on competition policy, and on governmental purchases – are of decisive importance for countries and their populations;

- the WTO decisively restricts the capacity for the formulation and implementation of domestic public policies in the countries of the South;

- the FTAA and the WTO are two sides of the same coin: they should not be considered independently of each other, but rather should be combated jointly;

- Brazil, under Lula's government, is a key to resisting the FTAA and the expansion of the WTO.

The convergent proposals that emerged from this panel included these points: interrupting the expansion of the WTO; preventing the signing of agreements on foreign investment, competition, and governmental purchases; altering the TRIPS agreement; ending agricultural dumping by the United States, and eliminating rich countries' subsidies; rejecting the FTAA. The convergent strategies chosen to implement these consensual proposals include:

- uniting the proposals of the social, trade union, and popular movements, in common campaigns;

- urgently advancing world campaigns to prevent the expansion of the WTO;

- creating the political necessity for governments to say no to the WTO, and to represent the interests of the population and not of corporations;

- supporting the Lula government's leadership in the struggle against WTO expansion;

- unifying the struggles against war and against the WTO and the FTAA.

Comparing the events from the two Forums regarding the WTO, there was an obvious consensus that the WTO is dominated by the rich countries, which benefit from its actions, and that the WTO has already gained too much power (which it seeks to expand even further), especially in sectors that should not be the subject of WTO negotiations.[14] There were virtually no differences among the participants on the main questions, proposals, and strategies formulated in the 2002 and 2003 events. For this panel, half the participants and organizations in the 2002 conference also appeared on the 2003 panel.

The 2003 panel differed in two ways from the previous year's session on this topic. One key difference was the importance attributed to the Lula government's leadership in the fight against the expansion of the WTO. Second, there was increasing appreciation of the need for the articulation of the various social movements, both 'new' and 'old', in the fight against the the WTO's expansion and for a world trade more consistent with democratic and sustainable development, especially in the poor countries of the South. In the 2003 panel, the most dissonant questions were raised by the attending public. Delegates complained about the lack of attention to the question 'WTO and gender', insisted on the importance of organizations in attempting to transform the 'no' posture into something more positive, and called attention to the possibility that, in the coming months, social movements would have to unify the fight against the agenda of the WTO's Cancun Round with the fight against war.

Foreign debt

In the 2002 WSF, the conference on foreign debt was moderated by a representative from International Cooperation for Development and Solidarity, with two conveners (from Jubilee South and the Committee for Third World Debt Cancellation (CADTM)), and debaters from Peru (Deuda y Desarrollo), Cameroon (Caritas Cameroun), Argentina, and Germany (Suedwind). The convergent questions to which these participants agreed include these points:

- Foreign debt constitutes one of the greatest obstacles to development in the countries of the South, owing to the enormous transfer of resources to the North that results;

- For this reason, foreign debt represents the main factor in the increase of global inequality;

- The actual system for the treatment of foreign debt is extremely unfair, since it does not recognize the co-responsibility of the creditor and the debtor in the accumulation of this debt;

- Some part (how much was contentious) of the foreign debt of poor countries is illegitimate;

- Foreign debt is an instrument of coercion used by the countries of the North over the countries of the South, for example when imposing structural adjustment policies.

The proposals and strategies that emerged as consensual in this conference included:

- The countries of the South have to break away from the spiral of foreign debt;

- The failure of creditor countries' plans for reducing foreign debt, especially in the case of African countries, reinforces the position that the cancellation of all or a part of the public foreign debt of the poor countries is a solution;

- In the context of this point, an independent audit of the foreign debt of the countries of the South should be conducted, and mechanisms that might accompany the cancellation of debt should be developed (with the involvement of civil society);

- The countries of the South should develop financial alternatives to international financial markets and conditional multilateral loans – and this means making domestic financing mechanisms viable;

- To support this process, a range of alternatives – creating development funds through a Tobin tax, increasing public aid for development, and an extraordinary global tax on large fortunes – were recommended;

- Funds misdirected by governing elites in the nations of the South, and invested in the North, should be returned to these nations and reinvested for development;

- The colonial, social and ecological debts accumulated by the North in centuries of political and economic domination over the South should be repaid;

- Structural adjustment programmes imposed by international financial organizations should be ended;

- International mechanisms for fair, transparent, and impartial judicial regulation should be created, to correct the structural asymmetry between creditors and debtors in the treatment of the debts of countries in the South.

As discussed above, the 2003 WSF combined the question of foreign debt with that of the control of financial capital. The idea was to confront the more general political and economic question of recovering the economic sovereignty of the countries of the South. In practice, however, the 2003 panel concentrated primarily on foreign debt and the difficulties that it creates for economic sovereignty in the nations of the South. This panel had a facilitator from SOFA (Solidarite Famn Aytian) of Haiti, and speakers from Argentina (Dialogue 2000), Brazil (ATTAC), Indonesia (the Anti-Utang Coalition), Senegal (Jubilee South), and Belgium (CADTM).

The 2003 Panel established a broad consensus on some questions:

- Financial foreign debt is illegitimate and illegal.

- Countries from the South are not debtors; they are creditors to whom the historical debt of colonialism is owing.

- Foreign debt is an obstacle to democracy and the implementation of human rights.

- The payment of foreign debt represents a massive liquid transfer of resources from the South to the North. A popular government cannot support necessary economic and social changes if it maintains its commitment to make payments on its public foreign debt; a crisis of disorientation and the demobilization of popular movements will result.

- Foreign debt maintains military dictatorships in many countries, stimulates the destruction of natural resources, and opens the way for privatization in many countries of the South.

- The non-payment of foreign debt is fundamental. A central question is how to change the correlation of existing forces and movements, in order to make non-payment viable. The first step for this is cultural: become aware that we are all creditors, and we should all be making demands.

The convergent proposals of the panel were as follows: repudiate foreign debt and suspend payment; hold a citizen audit of the foreign debt; demand that governments recognize the illegitimacy of foreign debt; demand reparations for foreign debt, especially for African countries. The following were accepted as convergent strategies:

- mobilization of citizen movements in the South and in the North;

- articulation of social movements and popular governments;

- preparation of an agenda for a world campaign against the payment of debt, respecting regional specificities;

- the pressuring of governments to repudiate foreign debt;

- the connection of debt repudiation with the need for internal savings to finance economic, social, and domestic investment.

As with the panel on world trade, divergences did not arise among participating speakers, but instead did arise in some of the public interventions. Among the divergent points and questions raised from the floor were these: the responsibility of the national governments of indebted countries for the creation of debt and the opening of their economies; the use of debt by some governments to support militarization; the need for concrete proposals about how countries from the South might avoid having to resort to the World Bank and the IMF; the absence of grassroots movements against the debt in Africa.

Another parallel with the trade panel is that no significant divergences occurred between the 2002 conference and the 2003 panel. There appear to be three principal consensual proposals concerning foreign debt: repudiation and suspension of payment; citizen audit of the debt; and reparations of the accumulated debt, especially for African countries. The minor divergences among the participating social actors in the 2002 conference, concerning what amount of foreign debt can be considered illegitimate and proposed for cancellation, disappeared in the 2003 panel.

This all indicates that the theme of foreign debt in the WSF faces an important political impasse. The monolithic character of these proposals makes them very difficult to operationalize in the daily political struggle; that is, it is difficult to break these proposals down into specific components so as to allow for differentiated strategies and give people ways to perceive the malign effects of foreign debt on their living conditions.[15] This quandary is reflected, for example, in the gap observed in the 2003 panel, between the more 'generalized' proposals of the speakers and the more 'concrete' doubts and perplexities of the public.[16]

One aspect of the 2003 panel deserves further mention: the focus on defining strategies that jointly mobilize citizen movements in the South and in the North, and articulate social movements and popular governments. This concern with articulation of different types of movements, both among themselves and with popular governments, was the area of political unease that was most pronounced in the consensual activities of the 2003 World Social Forum.

Solidarity economy

As we have shown, the theme of the solidarity economy gradually gained space with each of the three WSFs in Porto Alegre, eventually articulating a vast set of networks and organizations from all over the world. By the 2003 Forum, the solidarity economy was the central theme of eight seminars and 120 workshops, in addition to the 2003 panel discussed here.[17]

In the 2002 WSF, the conference on the solidarity economy included a Brazilian moderator and representatives of PACS (Instituto Políticas Alternativas para o Cone Sul, Institute of Alternative Policies for the Southern Cone) and RBSES (Rede Brasileira de Socioeconomia Solidária, Brazilian Network for the Social and Solidarity Economy). The speakers came from Spain (Alternative and Solidarity Economy Networks), France (Centre for Research and Information on Democracy and Autonomy), Argentina (National University of General Sarmiento), and Peru (Latin American Network of Women Transforming the Economy).

Among the questions this conference considered in 2002, we highlight four here:

- Is the solidarity economy, in its different forms, just a set of micro-economic practices, or is it a project that can have an impact on sustainable development and wealth-building goals? Does it propose an economy parallel to other economic systems (notably capitalism), or is it just complementary to other economic forms? What types of conflict and contradictions are characteristic of the solidarity economy?

- How can the designations social economy, solidarity economy, popular economy (and so on) be articulated, especially in view of regional and cultural diversity, and the peculiarities of the South–North and East–West axes?

- The networks of the solidarity economy include both the excluded, those who can no longer survive in the dominant system, and those who do not wish to do so. The compatibility between the perspectives of these two sets of participants, especially in view of the importance of democratic voice, is a key challenge for the solidarity economy movement.

- The solidarity economy is not just an economic project, but also social and political: it requires the democratization of the state and some support within civil society.

The proposals and strategies that emerged from the 2002 conference included many interesting points and areas of convergence. For one thing, the importance of the integration and articulation of networks of the solidarity economy, and of alliances with other organizations and networks (at the local, national, continental, and international levels) was recognized. For another, participants suggested the need to create new forms and methods of education and new curricula that introduce cooperative and solidarity practices.

Further, public policies favouring the growth and consolidation of the solidarity economy are necessary to that growth, as is the consolidation of successful practices for exchanges of goods and services at the local and international levels. Participants also acknowledged that it is crucial to create consistent base-line information and studies of the solidarity economy (especially via alliances with universities). The interaction of solidarity economy organizations with political forces and public sectors deserves considerable attention; so does the potential created by solidarity economy initiatives for the transformation of South–South, South–North, consumer–producer, and worker–employer relations – in other words, what is the paradigm for the solidarity economy? As with the other themes in the 2002 conference, no divergences were registered among the conference participants; however, those participating found some questions to be nebulous and polemical (for example, the scope of the solidarity economy, and its relationship to the capitalist system).

The panel on the solidarity economy of the 2003 WSF was convened by a Brazilian facilitator; it contained speakers from Mexico (Rural Coalition Mexico/USA, and Global Network), Peru (Plades), Senegal (Forum of African Women for a Solidarity Economy and the Intercontinental Network for a Social and Solidarity Economy /Africa), the Philippines (Fraternity of Asian Workers/CMT), and France (Pôle Socio-Économie Solidaire). The starting point for these speakers was the recognition of the enormous growth, in recent years, of different associative economic practices, as responses to social crises throughout the world (due to the selective and exclusionary character of hegemonic globalization).[18] One of the consequences of this process was increased articulation between networks and organizations linked to the solidarity economy movement, and the strengthening of these groups' presence at the third WSF in Porto Alegre.

Some of the convergent proposals in the 2003 Panel are the following: building an international work agenda for solidarity economy networks and organizations (focused on facilitating mutual knowledge and identifying areas of convergence); making the state open to public policies that promote the solidarity economy; understanding the implications of the singular role of women in the solidarity economy; combining the local dynamics of the solidarity economy with the national and international macroeconomic context; creating new judicial structures and institutions adapted to the solidarity economy.

Some convergent strategies were agreed for advancing the solidarity economy movement and implementing these proposals:

- The mapping (identification of actors, databases, etcetera) of the organizations and networks that operate in this field;

- coordination with and intervention in an ongoing series of international conferences on the solidarity economy;

- the preparation of socio-economic and environmental indicators suitable to the practices of the solidarity economy;

- the identification of possible strategic alliances with trade unions, social and cultural movements, religious institutions, and political and other actors;

- an integration of North and South agendas, with the aim of developing political alliances reinforcing the respective social struggles of solidarity economy organizations.

Participants agreed that the movement should concentrate its activism on two fronts: first, resistance to (and ultimately transformation of) the relations and institutions of global capitalism through campaigns such as Jubilee South for a Millennium without Debt, the Global Citizens' Initiative for Equitable International Trade, ATTAC, the Continental Campaign against the FTAA, and others; second, generating innovations and socio-economic transformations that can create an economy based on diversity, cooperation and solidarity.

As in the 2002 conference, important divergences were registered concerning the meaning and the scope of the concept of the solidarity economy: does it represent a way of organizing the economy and an alternative to capitalist development, or is it complementary to the so-called formal economy within capitalism, whose recent growth is fundamentally due to the exclusionary character of neoliberal globalization? The recurrent attention to this question is no surprise. In general, discussion of this theme goes beyond the literature about the theory and the practice of the solidarity economy, appearing as a tricky ideological trap without any analytical solution.[19]

■

Final Comments

At the beginning of this chapter we raised the question of whether the World Social Forum can be viewed as a 'mobilization' in the domain of social movements. We defined mobilizations as an expression of movements and cultures of resistance representing the continuation of a long and persistent libertarian tradition of popular radicalism. The material presented here provides an answer to this question: the three World Social Forums in Porto Alegre – as well as the thematic, regional and national Forums associated with them as part of the same process – are expressions of this culture of libertarian resistance, which has recovered the legacy of 1968.

However, in addition to continuing a long secular tradition, the social process of the WSF has also emerged as an exemplar of the new politics of real and virtual networks in the struggle against market-led globalization. As a type of anti-systemic action (Wallerstein 2002), the social process of the WSF represents a new approach to assembling left-wing coalitions that can confront the enormous challenges of both building new understandings and simultaneously overcoming the multiple inequalities (region, nation, class, race, ethnicity, gender, generation, among others) that characterize the current world reality. Through its own proposal for internationalization – specifically, the promotion of regional, national, and thematic Social Forums – the WSF has helped create a political strategy for a multi-polar world. This strategy, in the phrase of Carlés Riera, aims to construct another multiple polarity based not on military dominance, but on social creativity (Grzybowski, Riera *et al.* 2003).

The WSF presents itself as a very flexible set of coalitions, campaigns and networks of transnational, national, and local movements, with multiple priorities, united in their criticism of the neoliberal order. In the force of this arrangement can also be found its potential weaknesses. For example, the lack of centralization can make it difficult to coordinate tactics for 'the tougher battles to come' (Wallerstein 2002); the congregation of diversity can be threatened by a possible exhaustion of tolerance, given all the distinct interests and priorities that live together in the World Social Forum.

A large part of the Forum's impact is due to its open-space method, its capacity to transform diversity into a force. Even though it embodies a radical commitment to transformative action, the WSF is not a world assembly of organizations from civil society (Grzybowski 2003). Consequently, it does not aim at defining a hegemonic political orientation for them, nor at creating levels of political power to direct them. In this context, it is decisive to defend the conditions that reduce power disputes in this space: the absence of declarations imposing exclusive commitments; the stimulation of the multiplication of contacts between every type of organization, and the interaction of debates and agendas; the structuring of the process of the WSF through organizations and movements from civil society, which maintains its independence from political parties, national governments, and international governmental institutions. Even so, we must acknowledge the risk that the WSF could become the object of political disputes, with divisions and splits imposing themselves on the principle of expansion and respect for diversity.

As a broad citizenship movement, the World Social Forum can be characterized as a translation space that stimulates the coming together of global social movements whose principal common trait is their militancy against neoliberal globalization. The existence of this translation space is fundamental because the comings-together the WSF promotes involve movements that differ profoundly in their objectives and forms of organization, and also in the social groups they represent. Further, the dialogue these groups tend to favour does not presuppose – to the contrary, it vigorously refuses – the creation of a homogenization process with other movements and organizations. The crucial relevance of translation arises out of this: the recognition and the search for understanding do not require the abandonment of the various 'languages' spoken by different participants.

On the other hand, the translation space provided by the WSF is not constructed with the objective of the advancement of knowledge in different areas, but rather with the objective of mobilization and social action – literally, the construction of the reality that 'another world is possible'. Therefore, the WSF is not a university, nor is it circumscribed by the challenge of thinking without limits, keeping utopias and secular anxieties alive and creating new ones. The translation it provides has the purpose of furthering social action in the political struggle for the overcoming of neo-liberal globalization.

This condition of being open to multiple voices and energies for differentiated and autonomous social action, attentive to existing convergences and divergences, suggests the enormous complexity of the translation space that must be built into the configuration of the World Social Forum. In this light, the Statement of Principles of the WSF can be viewed as a set of norms establishing the rules of the game that have to be respected for the translation space to become viable.

In turn, the Forum's programme, in distinguishing 'consensual' and 'free' activities, recognizes that translation must be available not just in presentations and moments of contact, when the 'public face' of the Forum predominates via its principal actors, but also in places during the Forum when participants meet in a more individualized and free manner.

Although the number of free activities has grown spontaneously in the three WSFs held in Porto Alegre, there is still an enormous separation (and lack of contact) between these activities and the consensual ones, although both come under the umbrella of the thematic areas. The construction of channels of dialogue and interaction between these two types of activity is one of the challenges of the coming Forums. Here there is the possibility of exposing the 'public face' of the Forum to the anarchic and creative dynamism of its more individualized face. Allowing this contact will permit us to observe whether the themes, questions, and proposals 'officialized' by the large networks, coalitions, and campaigns can be open to the questions, themes, and proposals predominant in the free activities. Constructing mechanisms of interaction between these activities, without having activities on either side lose their identity and purposes, is one of the additional challenges of the WSF as a translation space.

The systematization of WSF activities

The two final parts of this chapter sought to exemplify the importance of the systematization (as of 2003) of the activities of the WSF. This systematization can be regarded as a method for recovering the history of the World Social Forum. The relevance of so doing is supported by at least three types of arguments.

First, this history is essential for the process of the translation of diversity into action, as previously discussed. It is fundamental both as a component of this process and as a mechanism through which learning about translation – so uncertain and challenging in the field of social movements – is fed and pushed forward. Furthermore, the recovery of this history can be seen as a strategy for the construction of the WSF's translation space. The institutional complexity, the simultaneity of events (so that it is impossible to participate in all) and the tendency for a multiplicity of thematic, regional, and national Forums to emerge in the future – all these factors emphasize that systematization as history can enhance the repertoire of the WSF's actions as a social process.

Second, systematization is also important for grasping the WSF as a social fact and a social movement. The results of this systematization can allow the wealth of exchange and advance that occur during the WSF – perceived almost unanimously by all who have participated in it – to be more broadly and more coherently socialized throughout the world. In effect, this systematization can play a key role in constructing a social history of the movement against neoliberal globalization.

Finally, the systematization effort enriches the self-evaluation capacity of the WSF – the possible impasses that can be anticipated, and the different perspectives likely to emerge in the future. As the discussion of the WTO/ world trade and other panels has shown, systematization of Forum activities creates a photograph of what the actors consider to be the principal questions, proposals, and strategies on the agenda; this snapshot also reveals the convergences and divergences within the approaches of the world networks that have participated in these activities. At best, systematization can document the state of the proposed alternatives to neoliberal globalization, permitting activists and organizations in every nation to reflect on their uses, limits, and possibilities.

Bibliography

Castells, M. (1999) *O Poder Da Identidade*, Rio de Janeiro: Paz e Terra.

Denning, M. (2002) 'Esquerda global? Os movimentos sociais na era dos Três Mundos', in Loureiro, I., Corrêa Leite, J. and M. E. Cevasco (eds), *O Espírito de Porto Alegre*, São Paulo: Paz e Terra.

Grzybowski, C. (2003) 'Por que pensar o fórum social mundial?', *Democracia Viva*, No. 14, Rio de Janeiro: IBASE.

Grzybowski, C., Riera, C., *et al.* (2003) 'Mesa redonda: uma nova agenda para a sociedade civil organizada', *Democracia Viva*, No. 14, Rio de Janeiro: IBASE.

Guha, R. (1999) *Elementary Aspects of Peasant Insurgency in Colonial India*, Durham: Duke University Press.

Klein, N. (1999) *No Logo*, New York: Picador.

MacAdam, D. (1997) *Political Process and the Development of Black Insurgency*, New York: New Press.

Piven F. and R. Cloward (1977) *Poor People's Movements and Why They Fail*, New York: Pantheon Books.

Quijano, A. (2002) 'Sistemas alternativos de produção?', in Santos, B. de S. (ed.), *Produzir Para Viver: Os Caminhos Da Produção Não Capitalista*, Rio de Janeiro: Civilização Brasileira.

Santos, B. de S. (2000) *A Crítica da Razão Indolente: Contra o Desperdício da Experiência*, São Paulo: Cortez Editora.

Santos, B. de S. and C. Rodríguez (2002) 'Introdução: para ampliar o cânone da produção', in Santos, B. de S. (ed.), *Produzir Para Viver: Os Caminhos Da Produção Não Capitalista*, Rio de Janeiro: Civilização Brasileira.

Thompson, E. P. (1987) *A Formação Da Classe Trabalhadora Inglesa*, Rio de Janeiro: Paz e Terra.

Wallerstein, I. (2002) 'Uma política de esquerda para o século XXI? Ou teoria e práxis novamente?', in Loureiro, I., Corrêa Leite, J. and M. E. Cevasco (eds), *O Espírito de Porto Alegre*, São Paulo: Paz e Terra.

Notes

1 This chapter was completed before the fourth World Social Forum was held in India in 2004, and the fifth in Porto Allegre in 2005.

2 Bearing in mind the Brazilian debate on social movements, we prefer the term mobilization to insurrection, though otherwise maintaining Denning's interpretation.

3 Naomi Klein, for example, suggests that, until a few years ago, the new axis of political contestation was centred on questions of discrimination and identity – in other words, on issues such as race, gender, sexuality – in the war of the politically correct. Recently, however, horizons are expanding; the agenda being contested includes questions such as the power of corporations and the rights of workers, thus allowing a critical analysis of labour in the global economy (Klein 1999: XIX).

4 Santos's original observation is as follows: 'In the absence of a single principle, it is not possible to unite all resistance and agencies under the scope of a common grand theory. More than a common theory, what we need is a *theory of translation* which will make the different struggles mutually intelligible and will allow the collective actors "to converse" about the oppression which they are resisting and the aspirations which animate them' (emphasis in the original).

5 This discussion draws heavily on information from the WSF website: www.forumsocialmundial.org.br. Note that at a website with an almost identical name – www.forumsocialmundial.org – all the activities of the WSF are systematically criticized. It is an 'anti-site', whose existence reflects both the ideological battle being fought in the virtual world and the importance given to the WSF by its enemies.

6 According to the methodology section of the 2003 WSF, which appears on the Forum's website. Note that much of the material presented here, including specific aspects of programmes and themes, is drawn from the WSF websites. Our narrative makes specific references to these websites only when we excerpt material taken directly from them.

7 The authors are fully aware that the discussion in this section focuses on programmed activities, and does not capture Forum events as a process. The next section goes further in that direction; however, limitations of space make it impossible to reproduce dialogues in WSF sessions.

8 The methodology section of the 2002 WSF website notes that WSF conferences 'have the objective of showing the proposals, platforms and alternatives that are being discussed by networks, movements and organizations from civil society who are fighting against a neo-liberal globalization. Each conference is a space for debates, the construction of consensus and the diversity of proposals. It is an opportunity for analysis and reflection in relation to the thematic areas.' In the third WSF the more appropriate term 'panel' was used to denote these activities. The methodology section of the 2003 website specifies that the panels, 'structured by the thematic areas, are, *par excellence*, the map of the actions and the public face of the WSF as the forum of world civil society. They involve the discussion of important questions, proposals and strategies, with their diversity of insertions and visions, and their action for the change of neoliberal globalization and for the emergence of "other possible worlds"'.

9 In the 2002 WSF, the selected representatives were divided into participants, who were asked to prepare proposals; debaters, who evaluated these proposals; and chairs, who organized the work. In the 2003 WSF the differentiation between selected participants and debaters was eliminated; instead a facilitator was selected for each panel, with the responsibility of outlining the proposals of each participant social actor, stimulating debate between panel members, and systematizing convergence and divergences.

10 Named after economist and Nobel laureate James Tobin, the Tobin tax proposes a small per-transaction fee on financial contracts, with the aim of reducing the amount of speculative financial transactions.

11 In 2003, foreign debt was treated jointly with capital controls in the panel 'Restoring economic sovereignty through the cancellation of debts and the control of capital'. In the event, this conference focused almost exclusively on the question of foreign debt.

12 Silvana De Paula, co-editor of this volume, was also a member of the systematization team. For the 2002 WSF sessions, we make use of the summaries submitted by the leaders of each conference, which are available on the Forum website.

13 It is worth remembering that while many speakers' presentations covered theoretical fundamentals, the treatment of these (and other) themes in the WSF is not academic. Forum participants tend to be pragmatically interested in theory, focusing on conceptual frameworks insofar as they deepen the knowledge necessary for mobilization and transformative action.

14 For example, Via Campesina's representatives in both Forums argued that agriculture and food should be withdrawn from inclusion in the WTO.

15 This problem does not arise regarding the theme of the WTO and world trade. The consensual proposals for the halting the expansion of the WTO and impeding the signing of agreements on investment, competition and governmental purchases, for example, can be applied to specific objectives that will permit their operationalization and their visualization relative to concrete targets.

16 Some speakers did suggest ways out of this apparent impasse. The CADTM representative argued that debt repudiation be linked to the social control of capital movements, and to the creation of conditions making it feasible to finance investment domestically. The representative from Jubilee South Africa insisted on linking foreign debt with the construction of other development paradigms, especially those which (as in Africa) had been destroyed politically.

17 In one of the sessions of the panel on the solidarity economy, the Lula government's Minister of Labour attended and announced the creation of a new national secretary of the solidarity economy linked to this ministry. The new secretary, Paul Singer, was also present.

18 The document 'Summary of Events' prepared by the solidarity economy movement defines the solidarity economy as designating 'all the activities of production, distribution and consumption which contribute to the democ-ratization of the economy based on the commitments of citizens, both at a local level and a global ... it is a dynamic of reciprocity and solidarity that links individual interests to the collective interest ... it is not a sector of the economy, but is a transversal approach which includes initiatives from all sectors of the economy' (p. 1). This statement goes on to align this move-ment with 'alternatives to neoliberal economic development ... for ... survival and ... collective political empowerment'. (p. 2)

19 For further discussion of this question, see Santos and Rodríguez (2002) and Quijano (2002).

Notes on
the Contributors

Ana Maria Bianchi is Professor of Economics at the University of São Paulo, Brazil. She teaches and conducts research on economic methodology and the history of economic thought. She has authored numerous articles and several books on these topics, including *The Pre-History of Economics – From Machiavelli to Adam Smith*, published in Portuguese. Ana Maria is a member of the editorial boards of *Energeia – International Journal of Philosophy and Methodology of Economics* and the Brazilian periodical *Revista de Economia*. She is currently conducting research on Albert Hirschman's contributions to development economics.

Leonardo Burlamaqui is Professor of Economics and Business at Candido Mendes University, where he is Director of Research of the Competition and Regulation Study Area in the Graduate Law Programme, and Adjunct Professor of Political Economy in the Economics Department of the State University of Rio de Janeiro. Leonardo is a member of the board of directors of the International Schumpeter Society and the Other Canon Foundation. He has been a visiting research scholar at the Institute for Development Studies in Tokyo, and in the Centre of Development and the Environment in Oslo. He has written extensively on evolutionary economics, innovation and competition, economic sociology, comparative capitalism, and development. His books include *Organized Capitalism in Japan* (IPEA/CEPAL, co-authored with Maria da Conceição Tavares and Ernani Torres) and *Institutions and the Role of State*, co-edited with Ana Célia Castro and Ha-Joon Chang.

Ha-Joon Chang is Assistant Director of Development Studies in the Faculty of Economics and Politics at Cambridge University. He is the author of *Reclaiming Development: An Alternative Policy Manual* (with Ilene Grabel, published in 2004 by Zed Books), *Globalisation, Economic Development, and the Role of the State* (2003), *Restructuring Korea Inc: Financial Crisis, Corporate Reform, and Institutional Transition* (with Jang-Sup Shin, 2003), *Kicking Away the Ladder: Development Strategy in Historical Perspective* (2002), and *The Political Economy of Industrial Policy* (1994, 1996). His edited works include *Brazil and South Korea: Economic Crisis and Restructuring* (with Edmund Amann, 2003), *Rethinking Development Economics* (2003), *The Rebel Within: Joseph Stiglitz at the World Bank* (2001), *Financial Liberalisation and the Asian Crisis* (2001, with Gabriel Palma and D. Hugh Whittaker), and *The Role of the State in Economic Change* (1995, with Robert Rowthorn).

Silvana De Paula is Associate Professor in the Graduate Programme on Development, Agriculture and Society (CPDA) of the Federal Rural University of Rio de Janeiro in Brazil. Her degrees include a Maîtrise en Socio-linguistique, a Master's in Development, Agriculture and Society, and a PhD in Sociology. In 1996–7 she used a Brazilian scholarship to pursue her research in the Department of Anthropology at Rice University. As a member of the CPDA faculty, she has taught and advised master's and doctoral students since 1978, as well as coordinating research projects and Lato Sensu Graduate Courses. Silvana's teaching, research and publications have focused on several topics: culture in the contemporary context, particularly in Brazil; cross-cultural processes; relations between countryside and city; Brazilian social thought; and civil society organization and movements. Silvana is a permanent member of the editorial board of the Editora Bom Texto in Rio de Janeiro. She has undertaken several projects with the Brazilian Institute for Social and Economic Analyses (IBASE), including studies on the World Social Forum events of 2003 (Brazil) and 2004 (India), and research on Brazilian civil society since the Rio Conference of 1992.

Nelson Giordano Delgado is full Professor at the Graduate Programme on Development, Agriculture and Society (CPDA) of the Federal Rural University of Rio de Janeiro in Brazil. He received his Master's in Economics from New York University, and his PhD in Development, Agriculture and Society from the Rural Federal University of Rio de Janeiro. He has published articles and essays about agriculture and macroeconomic policies, public policies for rural development, international trade regimens, Mercosur and regional integration, the World Social Forum, and democracy and public spaces for participation. He has been a consultant for several public agencies in Brazil, and has worked with numerous international agencies, NGOs and grassroots movements.

Gary Dymski taught at the University of Southern California before joining the faculty at the University of California, Riverside, where he is now Professor of Economics. Gary is currently serving as founding Director of the University of California Center, Sacramento. His publications include *The

Bank Merger Wave (1999), several edited books, and more than 100 articles and chapters on banking, financial fragility, urban development and poverty, credit-market redlining and discrimination, the Latin American and Asian financial crises, exploitation, and housing finance. He was a Research Fellow in Economic Studies at the Brookings Institution, and has been a visiting scholar at Tokyo University, the Bangladesh Institute for Development Studies, the Federal University of Rio de Janeiro, and the University of São Paulo. He is a Research Associate of the Economic Policy Institute and a member of several editorial boards.

Peter Evans teaches in the Sociology Department at the University of California, Berkeley, where he holds the Marjorie Meyer Eliaser Chair of International Studies. His past research has been on the role of the state in industrial development, an interest reflected in his book *Embedded Autonomy: States and Industrial Transformation* (Princeton, NJ: Princeton University Press, 1995). He has also worked on urban environmental issues, producing an edited volume, *Livable Cities: Urban Struggles for Livelihood and Sustainability* (University of California Press, 2002) and is currently working on labour as a global social movement.

Geoffrey M. Hodgson is a Research Professor in Business Studies at the University of Hertfordshire in England. He was formerly a Reader in Economics at the University of Cambridge. His eleven book monographs include *The Evolution of Institutional Economics* (Routledge 2004) and *How Economics Forgot History* (Routledge 2001). He has published over 80 articles in academic journals and is Editor-in-Chief of the newly established *Journal of Institutional Economics*.

Jan A. Kregel is Chief of the Policy Analysis and Development Branch of the United Nations (UN) Financing for Development Office. He formerly served as High Level Expert in International Finance and Macroeconomics at the United Nations Conference on Trade and Development. Before joining the UN, he was Professor of Economics in the Università degli Studi di Bologna as well as Professor of International Economics in the Johns Hopkins University Paul Nitze School of Advanced International Studies. Jan is a Life Fellow of the Royal Economic Society (UK), a member of the Società Italiana degli Economisti, and a Miembro Distinguido of the Association of Cuban Economists. His books include *Rate of Profit, Distribution and Growth: Two Views* (1971), *Theory of Growth* (1972), *The Reconstruction of Political Economy* (1973), *Theory of Capital* (1976), and *Origini e sviluppo dei mercati finanzieri* (1996). He has also published over 150 chapters and academic articles.

Erik S. Reinert holds an MBA from Harvard University and a PhD in Economics from Cornell University. Following a career as an industrial entrepreneur and manager, Erik has published extensively on evolutionary and production-based theories of uneven economic development. He is currently

Professor of Technology Governance at Tallinn Technical University in Estonia. He formerly worked with the Centre for Development and the Environment (SUM) at the University of Oslo. Many of his publications focus on the history of economic policy, especially the German and Continental European traditions. Reinert is an economic adviser to the Saami reindeer herders in Norway, the last aboriginal tribe in Europe. He edited the 2004 volume *Globalization, Economic Development and Inequality: An Alternative Perspective*. As President of the Other Canon Foundation, Norway, Erik organises courses in alternative development economics in the Third World.

Jorge O. Romano has been a professor in the Graduate Programme on Development, Agriculture and Society (CPDA) of the Federal Rural University of Rio de Janeiro for the past 20 years. He has published several books and papers about social movements, rural development and public policy making. During this period, he has also been an adviser to many non-governmental organizations, social movements and international cooperation agencies. Currently, he is Country Director of ActionAid Brasil, an international non-governmental organization which has the aim of fighting poverty worldwide.

Michael Storper is an economic geographer who shares his time between three institutions: the School of Public Affairs at UCLA, the Department of Geography at the London School of Economics, and the Centre de Sociologie des Organisations at the Institute of Political Studies ('Sciences Po') in Paris. He gained his PhD in Economic Geography at the University of California at Berkeley. His research concentrates on industrial location and regional economic development and policy. Recent research has focused on the role of face-to-face contact in the contemporary economy; on the relationship between trade and regional economic specialization; and on the geography of innovation and technology.

John Wilkinson is a senior lecturer in the Graduate Programme on Development, Agriculture and Society (CPDA) of the Federal Rural University of Rio de Janeiro. His research and teaching focus on transformations in the industrial organization of the agrofood system, including the family farm sector, and on the field of economic sociology and convention theory. He has worked on the biotechnology prospective studies of the FAST Programme of the European Commission, and been a consultant for the OECD, FAO and ECLA on the impact of new technologies in the agrofood system. In the early 1990s he was research fellow at INRA/Paris. His recent research includes the impact of the Mercosul on the reorganization of the agrofood system of the Southern Cone countries, biotechnology and agrofood in the context of the FTAA, the implications of a consumer-oriented food system, and the influence of social movements on markets. He has authored, co-authored, and edited more than 40 articles and 10 books, including *From Farming to Biotechnology*.

Index